Chronology
of Latin Americans
in Baseball, 1871–2015

Chronology
of Latin Americans
in Baseball, 1871–2015

LOU HERNÁNDEZ

McFarland & Company, Inc., Publishers
Jefferson, North Carolina

Library of Congress Cataloguing-in-Publication Data

Names: Hernández, Lou, 1958– author.
Title: Chronology of Latin Americans in baseball, 1871–2015 / Lou Hernández.
Description: Jefferson, North Carolina : McFarland & Company, Inc., Publishers, 2016. | Includes bibliographical references and index.
Identifiers: LCCN 2016021274 | ISBN 9781476662275 (softcover : acid free paper) ∞
Subjects: LCSH: Hispanic American baseball players—Biography—Chronology. | Baseball—United States—History—Chronology.
Classification: LCC GV863.A1 H474 2016 | DDC 796.357092/368073—dc23
LC record available at https://lccn.loc.gov/2016021274

ISBN (print) 978-1-4766-6227-5
ISBN (ebook) 978-1-4766-2236-1

British Library cataloguing data are available

Front cover: baseball player sliding to a base
© Moodboard/Thinkstock

Printed in the United States of America

McFarland & Company, Inc., Publishers
Box 611, Jefferson, North Carolina 28640
www.mcfarlandpub.com

For my aunt Verónica
a kind and loving woman

Acknowledgments

The Fielding Independent Pitching summations were procured from Bryan Grasnick, sabrnation.org, and MLB Network's *Clubhouse Confidential.*

I cited baseballreference.com for all WAR (Wins Above Replacement), OPS+ (On-base Plus Slugging Plus) and ERA+ (Adjusted Earn Run Average) metrics. The sole Extra Bases Taken (XBT) annotation was directly provided by the *Clubhouse Confidential* program. I also gleaned paraphrased explanations for all of these analytic measures from the same program.

The explanations for how WAR is derived, which I used in various entries, come from SABR member Jacob Pomrenke, from an article he wrote for the Hall of Fame's *Memories and Dreams* magazine, Spring 2014.

As always, retrosheet.org and baseballreference.com were valuable sources, especially for cross-checking information.

To all the great reference and record books out there—this project sprang primarily from their informative platforms. The ones I most relied on are listed in the bibliography.

Table of Contents

Preface

Most people are intrigued, if not fascinated, by first accomplishments. Especially grand-scale initial achievements, such as first to fly across the Atlantic, first to break the sound barrier, and first man on the moon.

Athletics by no means take a back seat regarding "fabulous firsts." We all know who was the first man to hit 60 home runs in a season, to run under a four-minute mile, and to score 100 points on the hard court.

This reference book, which is arranged chronologically, focuses on ethnic Hispanic first achievements—often great ones—that have occurred within the far-reaching influence of North American organized baseball. The historical content is presented in a self-explanatory, calendar date entry format. There are two corresponding appendices at the end for reference purposes. One appendix is divided into hitting, pitching and miscellaneous categories, and the other is presented in a straight, chapter-by-chapter collation of events. Not every single event or happening is catalogued in the back. A few entries qualified simply on intrinsic importance. For example, there are some Hall of Fame induction entries, noteworthy births, and deaths that are not indexed.

The historically significant big league inroads and accomplishments of the native sons of all the baseball-enamored countries of Latin American are chronicled on the following pages. From Esteban Bellán's 1871 pioneering debut in the National Association, to Zoilo Versalles as U.S. baseball's first Hispanic MVP in 1965. From Luis Castro as the majors' first Colombian player in 1902 to Édgar Rentería's World Series–winning hit in 1997. From Héctor López clouting Panama's first big league home run in 1955 to Mariano Rivera distinguishing himself as baseball's all-time saves leader in 2011.

The reader has at his or her fingertips a first of a kind reference book on Latin Americans at the highest levels of organized baseball. The operative term is *Latin American*; I draw a distinction between Latin American players and those such as Manhattan-born Alex Rodríguez and Californian Jesse Orosco, whose major league merits have earned them mention in big league record books but only indirect reference in this one. The reader will be able to find out who hit the first home run by a Venezuelan player in the major leagues. And who recorded the first big league win by a Venezuelan pitcher. (Hint: It is one and the same person and the deeds occurred in 1939.) He or she will discover who hit the first major league home by a Puerto Rican or Dominican player. Turning these pages, one can unearth who was the first Hispanic major league player to hit for the cycle. Or clout a grand slam home run in the League Championship Series and World Series. All Latin American nationalities are represented in similar pitching and hitting methodology.

The grand accomplishments of the people listed in this work are purposely kept within the context of the game itself. While ethnically self-congratulatory, at times, the players are not lauded over other similar lofty exploits by non–Hispanic players. In a larger sense, their praiseworthy achievements depict the history of a formerly homogenized sport in mainstream America evolving, over the decades, into the international conglomerate U.S. baseball has now become in the 21st century.

Though the book is weighted on major league performances, for obvious reasons, the scope of the project is broadened with numerous historic logs related to Hispanic Negro and Winter League players, and to the Negro League World Series and Caribbean Series. These spotlighted players and significant listings incorporate themselves well within the central theme of the book.

Being the "first" does not always guarantee being the "best," but it does ensure lasting impressions in one historic form or another.

I hope that, after finishing this book, readers will take with them some lasting impressions about the marvelous exploits of the ballplayers mentioned herein. And, for the most part, be able to say that they read about it here *first*.

Introduction

Not long after baseball established itself in the United States, it moved beyond the national borders, first into Canada and then Cuba, the island nation that served as a springboard for the game as it spread throughout the Caribbean and parts of Central and South America.

Cuba adopted and cultivated baseball during the latter part of the 19th century and sent the lion's share of early Latin American players into the top-rated North American professional leagues. Havana native Esteban Bellán played for the 1871 Troy Haym, in the first season of the first major league, called the National Association. In 1902, Colombia-born Luis Castro debuted for the Philadelphia Athletics as the major leagues' first Hispanic ballplayer of the 20th century. Castro's career lasted a total of 42 games.

One of the earliest and most recognized Hispanic players to appear in North American newsprint was José Méndez. The Cuban hurler gained U.S. sports page notice as a result of numerous impressive pitching efforts against major league teams that barnstormed through Havana, starting in 1908. In the initial series, Méndez pitched a 1–0, one-hit shutout over the Cincinnati Reds, and he threw 25 consecutive scoreless innings in three encounters against the club.

Nicknamed *"El Diamante Negro"* ("The Black Diamond"), Méndez's skin color denied him access into the major leagues. Méndez, therefore, became an outstanding pitcher in the Negro leagues of the 1910s and 1920s.

In 1924, as player-manager, he guided the Kansas City Monarchs to the Negro National League pennant with a record of 60–27. In the Negro League World Series, Méndez pitched the deciding game of the scheduled nine-game series against the Eastern Colored League champion Hilldale Daisies. The veteran right-hander shut out Hilldale on three hits, 5–0, to capture the ultimate championship for his team.

Méndez's career spanned 1908 to 1926. His exceptional pitching efforts have lived long after him. In 2006, José de la Caridad Méndez gained enshrinement into the National Hall of Fame through a vote by the Special Committee on the Negro Leagues. His Hall of Fame biography lists him as the author of a ten-inning perfect game in 1909 as a member of the Cuban Stars.

In the 1910s, Cuban players such as Armando Marsans and Mike González began making their own ground-breaking inroads into the big leagues. Marsans was a speedy outfielder with apparently a great deal of gumption on and off the field. In 1914, he challenged—with impunity—his contract's reserve clause and made a mid-season jump from the Cincinnati Reds to the St. Louis Terriers of the Federal League. González, much more reservedly, caught behind the plate for 17 Senior Circuit seasons and, in 1938, became the first Hispanic to manage a major league team.

The 20th century's second decade also witnessed the arrival of the first foreign pitcher to gain notoriety throughout North America. His name was Adolfo Luque. The Havana product started pitching abroad for the minor league Long Branch Cubans in 1913 and managed a long major league career, starting full-time in 1918. Luque shined in the National League for the better part of two decades, all while maintaining an annually glorious winter league showing in his home country.

Luque's big league career concluded in 1935, and four years later the first pitcher from the South American continent arrived in the major leagues. Venezuelan Alejandro Carrasquel also represented his country as its first big leaguer. Spending the bulk of his time as a relief pitcher, Carrasquel compiled a 50–39 record, toiling mostly for the Washington Senators in an eight-season career. He completed 30 of 64 games started. In 1938, St. Louis Browns outfielder Mel Almada, the initial Mexican player to don a major league uniform, hit in a remarkable 47 out of 48 consecutive games.

Puerto Rico and Mexico delivered their first major league pitchers in the 1940s. The hurlers, Hiram Bithorn of Santurce and Jesse Flores of Guadalajara, debuted a day apart in 1942 with the Chicago Cubs. Bithorn beat his Hispanic mound associate to the big league hill by one day, on April 15.

In 1943, Bithorn won 18 games for the fifth-place Cubs and tossed a league-leading seven shutouts. The right-hander's four-year big league career was cut short by military service and a later arm injury; his record was 34–31, with a fine 3.16 ERA.

Flores, mainly a starter, pitched for three teams in seven seasons, five with the horribly bad Philadelphia Athletics. The right-hander posted a losing 44–59 record, but with a striking 3.18 ERA in nearly 1,000 innings.

The 1950s saw several Cuban pitchers make singular pitching marks at the big league level—Conrado Marrero with the Washington Senators, Mike Fornieles with the Senators and later the Boston Red Sox, and Sandalio Consuegra with the Chicago White Sox. Consuegra won 16 games in 1954, pitching as a starter and reliever for the Pale Hose. Fornieles' major league debut with Washington in 1952 produced a one-hit shutout. He became only the second big league pitcher (Addie Joss, 1902) to start his career in such spectacular fashion. In 1951, Marrero became the first Hispanic pitcher to start an American League season opener.

But none of those 1950s hurlers compared to Camilo Pascual. The first Hispanic pitcher to win 20 games twice, Pascual emerged as the premier pitcher in the American League on more than one occasion in the late 1950s and early 1960s. He led the league in shutouts, complete games and strikeouts three times each. To date, no other Hispanic major league pitcher has equaled that feat. (Incorporating innovative analytical data with established pitching statistics, noted baseball sabermetrician Bill James crowned the former Senators and Twins hurler as the best pitcher in baseball in both 1959 and 1962.)

Baseball's "Golden Era" decade also witnessed the most dynamic player from Latin America to burst onto the big league scene. Orestes "Minnie" Miñoso, playing for the Cleveland Indians and Chicago White Sox, established himself as one of the best all-around players in the American League. Miñoso was the first black Hispanic star and paved the way for other dark-skinned Latin American ballplayers to follow his ascendant trajectory.

Two such players, both from Puerto Rico, Roberto Clemente and Orlando Cepeda, showcased their enormous talents in the National League for many years, commencing in the 1950s. The idolized Clemente became the first Hispanic player to collect 3,000 hits in his career. Cepeda, as a member of the San Francisco Giants, became the first Hispanic player to lead a major league in home runs and RBI.

In the 1960s and 1970s, three Hispanic pitchers collectively stood out yearly as elite major league moundsmen: Juan Marichal, Luis Tiant and Mike Cuéllar. Marichal and Tiant established Hispanic major league records that will probably never be exceeded, and Cuéllar earned for himself the title of best Latin American left-hander to toe the major league rubber in the 20th century.

During the 1960s and 1970s, Panamanian Rod Carew displayed exceptional hitting prowess on an annual basis. He captured seven batting titles on his way to reaping over 3,000 hits.

As Juan Marichal made special progress for the Dominican Republic as its first major league pitcher, so too did Dennis Martínez claim notable and treasured rewards for Nicaragua as his country's initial emissary to the big leagues. In a long career spanning parts of three decades (the 1970s, 80s and 90s), Martínez accumulated the most wins by any Hispanic pitcher in major league history.

In 1981, a few years after Dennis Martínez reached the major league scene, Fernando Valenzuela monopolized the big league limelight the way few first-year pitchers ever have. With his dazzling pitching the Mexican southpaw endeared himself not only to his own country's adoring *fanáticos,* but also to an entire cross-section of baseball fans in the United States.

While Valenzuela especially thrilled fans of the Los Angeles Dodgers, another Dominican pitcher tracked impressive mound marks in the Midwest. Joaquín Andujar posted back-to-back 20-win seasons with the St. Louis Cardinals in 1984 and 1985.

In the late 1980s, José Canseco joined the founding class of Hispanic sluggers such as Cepeda, Tony Pérez and Tony Armas, with an added offensive wrinkle—speed. The Oakland A's outfielder became the first player to hit 40 home runs and steal 40 bases in one major league season. Canseco's Cuban compatriot, Rafael Palmeiro, who also debuted in the 1980s, steadily accumulated career offensive numbers achieved by few players in the game's history.

In the early 1990s, two Dominican pitchers, Ramón Martínez and José Rijo, prominently distinguished themselves in the major league ranks. Rijo earned the first World Series MVP trophy by a Hispanic pitcher in 1990, as he helped pitch the Cincinnati Reds to a stunning upset victory over Canseco's Oakland A's. A winner of over 100 games by the age of 30, Rijo's career was, sadly, all but ended by an elbow injury in 1995.

Also in 1990, Ramón Martínez became the youngest Hispanic pitcher to win 20 games. He was a 22-year-old conscript with the Los Angeles Dodgers when he achieved the feat. Rotator cuff issues eventually brought Martínez's 14-year career to an end. His record was an impressive 135–88.

As the 1990s were coming to a close, Ramón Martínez' younger brother, Pedro, began thrilling baseball with his superlative pitching triumphs. The Quisqueyan pitcher's annual body of work inscribed his name at or near the top of many columns of new age statistics, including, at the time of his retirement, the best career ERA− for a starting pitcher (154).

Another Dominican, Sammy Sosa, electrified fans in Chicago with his titanic home run swings. The former Chicago Cub bowed out of the game, in 2007, as the all-time Latin American leader in home runs with 609.

Leading up to the new century, the Dominican Republic had, for decades, established itself as the greatest supplier of foreign talent to the major leagues. What originally began as a trickle of players in the late 1950s and early 1960s swelled into a cascade of prominent athletes who not only helped change the face—and voice—of major league baseball, but also helped enriched the game immeasurably.

Keeping with his country's tradition of excellence, Albert Pujols established himself as the majors' best player of the 2000s. The Santo Domingo product racked up historic offensive production during his initial ten National League seasons.

The 21st century's best Hispanic pitchers have been Venezuelans Johan Santana and Félix Hernández. For Santana, the continuance of his earlier brilliant career was placed in jeopardy by arm injuries and multiple surgeries. King Félix may not have peaked yet, which has to be a scary thought for American League batters who will have to face him for the foreseeable future.

No more fears, however, will persist for those same AL hitters in crucial late-game situations when playing the New York Yankees. The game's greatest closer, Mariano Rivera, brought the curtain down on his unprecedented 19-year big league tenure in 2013. No such relief is in store any time soon for American League pitchers, who must regularly square off against baseball's best hitter for the past several seasons, Maracay-bred Miguel Cabrera.

THE CHRONOLOGY

For 'tis your thoughts that now must deck our kings,
Carry them here and there, jumping o'er times,
Turning th' accomplishment of many years
Into an hour glass.—*King Henry V*

1871

MAY 9. In what is generally acknowledged as the first major league, the pitcher stood 45 feet from home base, there were nine teams, and no team played more than 30 games.

The first game for the Troy Haymakers of the newly formed National Association of Professional Base Ball Players—the antecedent of the National League—was hereby conducted. As he would in all of his club's 29 games on the season, infielder Esteban Bellán, 21-year-old son of the queen isle of the Antilles, participated. In doing so, Bellán accepted appointment as North America's first Hispanic player for posterity. With that appointment, an honorarium of categorical "offensive firsts" would soon follow. Bellán became the first Hispanic major leaguer to: record a hit, double, triple, score a run, drive in a run, and steal a base.

The Haymakers were defeated by the Boston Red Stockings, 9–5, at Haymakers Grounds, Troy, New York. Bellán went 1-for-4 with a run scored.

Exactly one week later, Boston hosted its first professional baseball game in a rematch between the clubs. The Haymakers gained their revenge and trounced the Red Stockings, 29–14. Bellán, playing third base, was credited with three hits in seven at-bats.

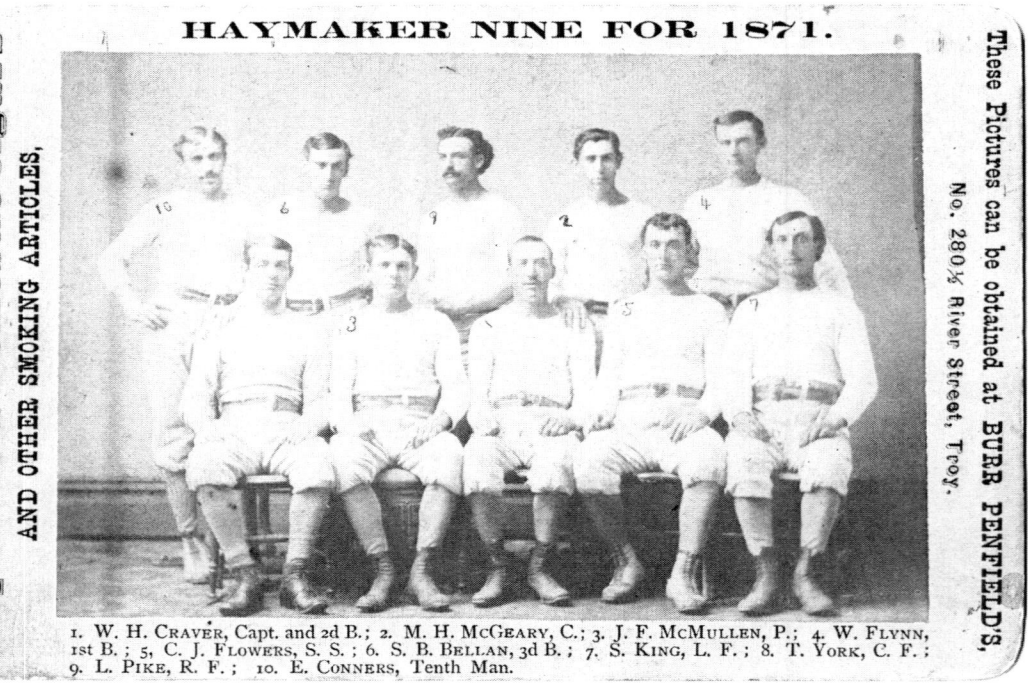

The 1871 Troy Haymakers of the National Association. Third baseman Estebán Bellán (#6) was the first Hispanic major league player (courtesy National Baseball Hall of Fame Library, Cooperstown, New York).

1874

DECEMBER 27. The first organized and widely recorded baseball game played outside the United States occurred between Club Habana and Club Matanzas, at *Palmar del Junco* ball field, in Matanzas, Cuba. The Habana team trounced Matanzas, 51–9 (seven innings, darkness). Esteban Bellán, the majors leagues' first Hispanic player, drilled three home runs for the winners.

Although evidence now exists of earlier games played in Cuba, the culturally rich city of Matanzas, approximately 55 miles east of Havana, lends itself as the Latin American equivalent of Elysian Fields in Hoboken, New Jersey, site of some of the earliest recorded baseball games in North America.

1876

NOVEMBER 25. Luis Castro was born in Medellín, Colombia. Long before soccer became king sport in his country, Castro broke ethnic barriers in the United States' most popular athletic pastime. Castro also became the first South American player to reach the major leagues and the first Hispanic manager in Organized Baseball

1878

DECEMBER 29. Club Habana outlasted Almendares, 21–20, in the first game of the *Liga Profesional Cubana*, trumpeting the commencement of the first professional baseball league outside of the United States. Through the rest of the 19th century and the better part of the next, the Cuban Winter League evolved into the second-oldest professional baseball league in the world.

1887

MARCH 19. José de la Caridad Méndez was born in Cárdenas, Matanzas, Cuba. As the best-known international pitcher of the 1910s, Méndez will establish himself as the Cuban Winter League's most difficult pitcher to beat. The successful right-hander achieved the all-time best winning percentage in the circuit.

1890

AUGUST 4. Adolfo Luque was born in Havana, Cuba. A rough and tumble, all- out competitor, Luque set pitching standards matched by few of his ethnic peers to this day.

SEPTEMBER 24. Miguel Angel González was born in Havana, Cuba. The major leagues' first Hispanic catcher and first manager, "Mike" broke into the big leagues with the Boston Braves in 1912. He first managed the St. Louis Cardinals on an interim basis in 1938. In his home country's winter league, González rose to become a most respected manager and influential franchise owner.

1893

NOVEMBER 16. Cristóbal Torriente was born in Cienfuegos, Cuba. Torriente developed into a left-handed slugger who hit for high average. He starred in his home country's circuit with Habana and Almendares, as well as with several teams in the Negro leagues.

1902

APRIL 23. In the tenth season since the relocation of the pitcher's mound to 60 feet, six inches from home plate, Colombian Luis Castro was brevetted as the 20th century's first Hispanic major leaguer. As a ninth-inning substitute for Napoleon Lajoie, Castro, a second baseman, played in the first of 42 games for Connie Mack's Philadelphia Athletics. Castro's debut, in which he recorded an assist, occurred on Opening Day; the Mackmen beat the Baltimore Orioles, 8–1, at Oriole Park.

Interestingly, Lajoie played his only game for the 1902 Athletics that day. The future Hall of Famer had made a cross-town jump from the National League Phillies to the Athletics of the start-up American League in 1901. The move by Lajoie elicited a legal challenge from the Phillies, which, after a year, came to fruition this same day with a Pennsylvania Supreme Court ruling in the team's favor. The decision prohibiting Lajoie from playing with the Athletics was handed down during the game and wired to manager Mack in the dugout. Mack was forced to remove Lajoie for the final inning, inserting Castro in his stead.

All ended well for Lajoie, who sat out a month before he signed with another American League team, the Cleveland Blues, for a princely sum of $7,000.

The American League was legitimized by the star player staying within its ranks. As a competitive complement to the established National League, the rival league soon gained stature and would promote the ultimate championship concept of a "world's series" between the two circuits, beginning the following year.

For Luis "Judge" Castro, 1902 was his only season of major league play. And it would take another 72 years for another Colombian player to reach the major leagues (Orlando Ramírez).

MAY 14. In his first starting assignment, Luis Castro recorded the first hit by a Hispanic major league player in the 20th century. The Philadelphia Athletics second baseman, who had seen action only as a defensive replacement in two games so far in the young campaign, singled in the seventh inning and later came around to score one of his two runs in the game.

The Athletics defeated the visiting Boston Americans, 5–1, at Columbia Park.

MAY 29. Luis Castro was a leader on offense and defense in the Athletics' 6–4 home win over the Detroit Tigers. Castro flawlessly accepted eight chances and made two gold star-worthy plays in the field. At the plate, Castro, with four singles, collected the initial four-hit game by a modern-era Hispanic major leaguer.[1]

MAY 30. Fifty-three years from now, *The Sporting News* announced plans for the military president of Colombia, Gustavo Rojas Pinilla, to throw out the season-opening first pitch of the Colombian Winter League, ceremonially marking the "fiftieth anniversary of the introduction of baseball into Colombia."[2]

Three years before baseball "officially" arrived in that South American country, the first Hispanic home run hit in the major leagues was stroked by Medellin's Luis Castro. Philadelphia's Columbia Park was the site of the Colombia-born player's most historic hit—a bases-empty four-bagger. It was surrendered by Jack Powell of the St. Louis Browns, in the second game of a morning-afternoon doubleheader between St. Louis and the A's.

The 25-year-old Castro also doubled in the 11–4 Athletics win, helping to erase the home team's memory of a first-game loss, 11–7.

Luis Castro hit the first home run by a Hispanic player in the major leagues. As a Philadelphia Athletics second baseman, he played in 42 games for Connie Mack's first American League pennant-winning team in 1902. Castro later became the first Hispanic manager in organized baseball.

1905

JANUARY 31. Pedro Cepeda was born in Cataño, Puerto Rico. The father of a future major league Hall of Famer, Cepeda would distinguish himself as the Puerto Rican Winter League's best hitter in the inaugural years of the circuit. Cepeda won the loop's first batting championship in 1938–1939 with a .465 average (79-for-170). He would capture top batting laurels again the following season with a .383 mark (82-for-214), and then hit .421 (75-for-178) in the 1940–1941 campaign.

1906

APRIL 11. Juan Esteban Vargas was born in Santo Domingo, Dominican Republic. In a more than 30-year playing career, beginning in 1923, Vargas excelled in international leagues throughout the Western Hemisphere, from Canada to Venezuela, and from Cuba to Puerto Rico.

MAY 25, 1906. Martín Dihigo was born in Matanzas, Cuba. Exhibiting multifaceted skills in national leagues throughout the Americas, Dihigo was destined to become Latin America's most legendary pre-integration period baseball figure.

1907

MARCH 10. The world champion Chicago White Sox became the first major league team to play in Latin America when they crossed the Rio Grande for an eight-day spring training visit to Mexico. After a four-day train trip from Chicago, the team reached Mexico City and played a split-squad exhibition game.

In the intrasquad game, the team captained by Fielder Jones defeated the team led by Nick Altrock, 8–2, in front of roughly 1,000 fans. The crowd was held down because of the uncertainty of the players' arrival, which ended up being 27 hours behind schedule. Because of the late arrival, the players were forced to dress on board the train and were taken by automobile to the ballpark. Mexican Vice President Ramón Corral met the White Sox club at the train depot.

The reigning "Hitless Wonder" champions played four games with teams from the capital city and three other "split squad" games during their eight-day stay.

APRIL 29. Jorge Pasquel was born in Veracruz, Mexico. A wealthy magnate who put Mexico on the North American baseball map right after World War II, Pasquel soon ran afoul of Organized Baseball—and some Mexican League officials—over his intrusive and free-spending ways as Mexican League president.

1908

NOVEMBER 15. The Cincinnati Reds became the first major league team to journey to Cuba. The club engaged in a series of ten exhibition games against representative teams of the Cuban Winter League. Today, pitching for Almendares, José Méndez took a no-hitter into the ninth inning against the visiting North Americans. He allowed a hit to the Reds' Miller Huggins before completing a 1–0 victory, with nine strikeouts and two walks, at Havana's Almendares Park.

The shutout was the first of two the 21-year-old Méndez threw against the Reds, initiating a string of 25 consecutive scoreless innings pitched in the series, two starts and one relief appearance of seven innings.

The Reds split the ten-game engagement, winning four out of five from Habana and only one from Almendares in five outings.

Pitching against other visiting major league teams in the years that followed, Méndez compiled a record of 8–7–1 against illustrious clubs such as the Detroit Tigers, Philadelphia Athletics and New York Giants.

1909

JANUARY 29. Francisco Coimbre was born in Coamo, Puerto Rico. Perhaps the most definitive thing said about the future player came from Roberto Clemente, who called Coímbre a better hitter than himself. Like many of the black players of his time, Coimbre became a multi-country performer. He spread the gospel of baseball within the circuit-ministries of Canada, Mexico, Colombia, Venezuela, the Dominican Republic, and the United States.

MAY 11. Ramón Bragaña was born in Havana, Cuba. Though he would not be welcomed into Organized Baseball because of his dark skin, Bragaña developed into one of the most prolific and well-regarded Latin American pitchers of the first half of the 20th century.

NOVEMBER 18. In the seventh contest of a 12-game exhibition series between the Detroit Tigers and two of Cuba's most prominent teams, Eustaquio "Bombín" Pedroso became the first Latin American pitcher to pitch a no-hit game against a major league team.

At Almendares Park, pitching for the park's namesake team, Pedroso held the Detroit Tigers without a safety for 11 innings before prevailing, 2–1. The winning run was "squeezed" home by second baseman Armando Cabañas, whose earlier throwing error had led to the Tigers' only score and the extension of the game. A "passing of the hat" occurred immediately after contest and netted $300 dollars for the right-handed Pedroso. Contributions came from the President of Cuba, José Miguel Gómez, and his son, and even Tigers players Charles O'Leary and George Mullin.

The Tigers won only four of 12 games against Cuban teams. Stars Ty Cobb and Sam Crawford did not accompany the American League champions on the trip.

1911

JULY 4. Rafael Almeida and Armando Marsans made a United States Independence Day debut with the Cincinnati Reds and became the majors' first Cuban players of the 20th century.

With their team trailing the Chicago Cubs, 8–1, in the first game of a morning-afternoon doubleheader at West Side Grounds in Chicago, Almeida and Marsans entered the game as late-inning substitutes. Almeida was the first to bat, in the top of the seventh inning, and struck out. He stayed in the game at third base. Marsans, a same-inning defensive replacement in right field, came up in the next frame and singled. The players batted again in the ninth and reversed their fortunes from their initial at-bats; both finished 1-for-2 on the day. The Reds were defeated by the Cubs, 8–3. Marsans' initial success earned him posterity laurels as the first Hispanic player to record a hit in his first major league at-bat. Mordecai "Three Finger" Brown retired Marsans as the last out of the game in the ninth inning with the bases loaded.

The afternoon affair ended in a 2–2 tie after ten innings, with the players conceding the outcome in favor of meeting their railroad travel schedules.

1912

JULY 24. Alejandro Carrasquel was born in Caracas, Venezuela. Carrasquel joined the Washington Senators in 1939 as the first athlete from Venezuela to play in the major leagues. As a member of the Senators, "Alex" reeled in a number of ethnic "first achievements" in the major leagues for his nation.

AUGUST 1. Cincinnati Reds outfielder Armando Marsans hit the first home run by a Cuban player in the major leagues and the first by a Hispanic player at the Polo Grounds. The blow was belted at the rebuilt Coogan's Bluff venue, whose wooden grandstand had been consumed by fire in April 1911.

The eighth-inning fence-topper, in the first game of a doubleheader, came with a man on base and put the Reds ahead, 4–3. But the first-place New York Giants rallied to win, 5–4, scoring twice in the bottom of the ninth inning, getting off the hook Hooks Wiltse, who had surrendered the home run to Marsans.

The McGrawmen also won the afterpiece, 7–5, as they steamrolled toward a World Series rendezvous with the Boston Red Sox.

SEPTEMBER 28. Mike González of the Boston Braves played in his initial big league game and became the first Hispanic player to don the "tools of ignorance" in the major leagues. Also the first Hispanic player in Boston Braves franchise history, González debuted in the second game of a doubleheader at the Polo Grounds. Winding down play in its first full rebuilt-year, the double-decked, horseshoe-shaped structure was still years away from the bleacher, clubhouse, and scoreboard additions that accentuated its unique configuration and made it a fixture of National League baseball in New York for decades.

This day, Giants baserunners challenged the green catcher on the base paths, stealing successfully four times. Although "caught stealing" was not yet kept as an official statistic, it is safe to assume González, with four assists recorded, was able to hold his own throwing behind the plate. The contest was called because of darkness after seven innings and ended in a 6–6 tie. The cellar-dwelling Braves (on their way to finishing 52 games behind the first-place New Yorkers) managed a 2–1 victory in the first engagement.

1913

FEBRUARY 7. Baldomero Melo Almada was born in Huatabampo, Sonora, Mexico. Reared in Los Angeles, Almada first starred in the Pacific Coast League before being purchased by the Boston Red Sox in 1933. In 1938, he accrued the longest hitting streak by a Hispanic major league player in the first half of the 20th century, 29 games.

MAY 16. Over the next decades, individuals hailing from all over Europe would reach the major leagues. Today, Alfredo Cabrera, born in the Spanish archipelago of the Canary Islands, made a simultaneous ethnic mark as the first player from that country to play big league ball and the first Hispanic player for the St. Louis Cardinals.

At brand new Ebbets Field (opened the prior month), the *guanche*, as natives of the Canary Islands are called, participated in his only major league game. The 32-year-old Cuban émigré posted two fruitless at-bats in the contest.

Cabrera's teammates fared better, but the team fell to the Superbas of Brooklyn, 6–5.

JUNE 5. Youth is served at National Park. Hispanic youth.

The number of Hispanic players having reached the big leagues could currently be counted on two hands. Two of those players set age records this day that will stand the test of time. At 18 years, 359 days old, outfielder Jack Calvo of the Washington Senators redirected a pitch from Roy Mitchell of the St. Louis Browns far enough away from any outfielder for him to circle the bases and become the youngest Hispanic player to hit a home run in the major leagues. Calvo debuted for the Senators on May 9 as the first in a long line of players from Cuba to play for the Washington team over the next half-century. The Havana native also became the first Latin American player to crack a home run at the later renamed Griffith Stadium.

In the same game, at only 17 years, 17 days old, teammate Merito Acosta pinch-hit, christening him as the youngest Hispanic player to appear in a major league game. Acosta batted for 36-year-old Nick Altrock, who, in 1931, became the first big league player to play in five decades—a deed which was matched nearly one-half century later by Acosta's countryman, Minnie Miñoso.

The Cuban players had little effect on the game's outcome, as the Browns beat the Senators, 12–3. But more than 100 years and many, many more Hispanic players later, Jacinto Calvo (a two-season major leaguer) and Baldomero Pedro Acosta (a five-year big leaguer) remained unsurpassed in their youthful ethnic accomplishments.[3]

SEPTEMBER 6. Seventeen-year-old Senators "prodigy" Merito Acosta batted for pitcher Joe Engel and produced a bunt single at Griffith Stadium. The eighth-inning safety bestowed upon Acosta, 17 years, 110 days old, the title of youngest Hispanic player to record a major league hit. Acosta came around to score, pushed along by one of nine errors the New York Yankees committed, contributing to their 9–1 road defeat.

In all, the juvenile outfielder batted 20 times in 12 games for the Senators on the season and obtained six hits. By age 23, Acosta's time in the majors had ended, but his Hispanic tender-age records for playing and hitting safety will long endure.

1914

MAY 20. In his mound debut for the 4–17 Boston Braves, Adolfo Luque threw the first pitch by a Latin American pitcher in the major leagues (to leadoff hitter Jim Viox). The historic delivery came against the Pittsburgh Pirates at Forbes Field. The 23-year-old Cuban was defeated, 4–1, as the Braves committed five errors behind him. Four of the fielding miscues were by shortstop Rabbit Maranville, five-time fielding leader in the league and future Cooperstown inductee.

Luque pitched just once more (in relief) with Boston before being released to Jersey City, an International League team. As a result, Luque was not part of the "Miracle Braves" stunning drive to baseball's pinnacle team achievement. Following the Luque defeat, Boston won an incredible 90 of its next 131 games. The team soared from last place in mid-July to first in early September. The Braves eventually won the pennant by 10½ games and then swept the Philadelphia Athletics in the World Series.

It took another 89 years before another team rebounded from a deficit of at least ten games under .500 in May to capture the World Series.

MAY 31. In the first game of a doubleheader at Redland Field, Cincinnati Reds outfielder Armando Marsans was called out for oversliding second base on a steal attempt. Disputing too strenuously the decision by umpire Al Orth, Marsans was ejected from the game. The Reds won the contest, 2–1, against the visiting Pittsburgh Pirates. The teams then played to a 5–5 tie in the nightcap, called because of darkness.

Marsans was later called to task by Reds manager Buck Herzog, and some 14 teammates, for getting himself run from the close game on the play. The criticism elicited petulant behavior from the Cuban player and led to a club suspension several days later.

The first ejection of a Latin American player in the major leagues turned out to have significant ramifications. Following his suspension on June 3, Marsans, who had been unhappy with his current pay scale with the Reds, brazenly advised the team, in writing, that he was not prepared to continue with the club past a ten-day notice period—unless the team was prepared to resign him for what he thought were more equitable wages.

JUNE 14. The standard baseball contract can be terminated by a ball club with a ten-day written notice to the player. In a bold, table-turning move, Armando Marsans, Cincinnati Reds outfielder, provided his ball club the same amount of advance time in announcing his intention of leaving the Reds, if the team did not provide him with a more satisfactory compensation deal. The Reds did not.

After the allotted time, Marsans simply left the Reds and signed with another team, the St. Louis Terriers of a new rival circuit called the Federal League. Marsans debuted with the Terriers on this day, as the team's first Hispanic player. The St. Louis club suffered an 9–2 setback, at home, to the Buffalo Blues.

Playing shortstop, Marsans went hitless in four trips and committed two errors for the losing squad.

JUNE 16. "I'll stand at the Battery, and for every dollar the major leagues wants to toss into the North River, I'll toss in another. And I won't be the first to run out of dollars."[4] A third major league had been formed, and one of its wealthier owners, Harry Sinclair of the Indianapolis Hoosiers, proposed, with that quote, to outspend the established National and American Leagues for quality players. The Federal League, by this time, had lured away several American and National League players with higher salaries.

The start-up circuit would pose a serious threat to the minor league channel of players into the big leagues with its soon-to-be-brought lawsuit against Organized Baseball. The lawsuit alleged that Organized Baseball's shackling player contracts were illegal.

One of the big league players who opted to play in the newly founded circuit was Armando Marsans, who thumbed his nose at the Cincinnati Reds and the "reserve clause" of his contract—*mid-season*. Two days earlier, Marsans had become the St. Louis Terriers' and the Federal League's first Hispanic player.

Today at Federal League Park, playing for St. Louis, Marsans stroked five hits in seven tries, and scored the winning run in the home half of the 12th inning, in a simply astonishing game that set the major league record for most runs scored in an extra inning (15). Amazingly, the Terriers rallied from a seven-run deficit (12–5) and plated eight runs in the bottom of the 12th frame to utterly demoralize the Brooklyn Tip-Tops, 13–12. Marsans became the first Hispanic major leaguer to record five hits in a modern-era game.[5]

Reliever "Three Finger" Brown, who gave up seven runs in the top of the inning, was the winning pitcher for the Terriers. Tip-Tops starter and loser Tom Seaton was charged with all of the home team's runs in 11⅓ innings. Two bullpen pitchers could not prevent the inherited winning runs from crossing the plate.

The Federal League lasted two years, folding with the acceptance of a large remuneration package from Organized Baseball. The deal allowed two rival Federal League owners to gain control of two major league clubs. The St. Louis Browns were purchased by the owner of Marsans' defunct team, and in the National League, Chicago Whales owner Charles H. Weeghman bought the Cubs and placed them in the park he had built especially for the Whales. Weeghman later sold his interests in the team and the park to a chewing gum chieftain named Wrigley.

AUGUST 20. Angel Aragón's first game as a New York Yankee produced a pinch-hit highlight. Batting for pitcher Ray Fisher in the second inning, the 24-year-old Aragón singled and drove in two runs. Purchased from the Long Branch Cubans of the Atlantic League, Aragón became the first Hispanic to play for the team that will become the most recognized franchise in all of North American sports.

On this day, the second-division Yankees lost to the Cleveland Naps, 11–8, at the Polo Grounds.

1915

SEPTEMBER 21. Twenty-year-old Emilio Palmero delivered a rocky debut as the New York Giants' first Hispanic player. The starting pitcher in the second game of a doubleheader at West Side Grounds, Palmero lasted but two-thirds of an inning. The Cuban allowed three runs to the home-team Cubs, the result of two hits, three walks and a hit batsman. Losers in the first game to the Giants, 5–4, Chicago prevailed, 5–3, in the nightcap, with Palmero absorbing the loss.

In his second start for John McGraw's last-place Giants, on October 6, Palmero hurled the distance but come out on the losing end again, 1–0, to Tom Hughes and the Boston Braves.

Interestingly, Palmero, a left-hander, compiled a five-season, 41-game career with four big league teams—spaced over *14* years (1915–1928). He won six and lost 15.

1916

MARCH 18. Hiram Bithorn was born in Santurce, Puerto Rico. The offspring of a Danish father and Puerto Rican mother, Bithorn became a superior athlete who mastered skills in basketball and volleyball well enough to participate on representative teams in the 1935 Central American & Caribbean Games. A bronze (basketball) and silver (volleyball) medal winner at the age of 19, Bithorn's most distinguishing accomplishment for himself and his country came seven years after those amateur games, as a pitcher for the Chicago Cubs and the pilgrim Puerto Rican in the major leagues.

APRIL 12. North American baseball's most well-known Hispanic player, Armando Marsans, suited up for the St. Louis Browns as the initial Hispanic player in the franchise's 16-year history.

    Playing for his third team in three years, Marsans was recognized, at this time, nearly as much for his front office defiance as for his field abilities. Debuting as the Browns' Opening Day cleanup hitter, the fleet-footed center fielder was marginally instrumental in the Browns' 6–1 victory over the Cleveland Indians at Dunn Field. He scored one run, without recording a hit, in three at-bats.

MAY 1. Emilio Palmero became the first Latin American pitcher to surrender a major league home run. In his first start of the season, the New York Giants hurler endured a rough outing, losing to the Brooklyn Robins, 8–5, at the Polo Grounds. Permitting all the visitors' runs in four and two-thirds innings of work, Palmero was tagged for a third-inning, three-run home run by Robins right fielder Casey Stengel that sailed into the top tier of seats in the right field grandstand.

Armando Marsans was the major leagues' most recognized Hispanic player in the 1910s. He concluded an eight-year big league career with the New York Yankees in 1918.

1917

JUNE 11. Mike González's primary position was catcher, but a trade to St. Louis in 1915 allowed the backstop to display added defensive versatility. González played first base and the outfield at times in his four-year tenure with the Cardinals. Today, as a first baseman, he was perhaps feeling a bit more spring in his step. González stole home against Philadelphia Phillies starter Joe Oeschger in the bottom of the 15th inning, to give the Cardinals a 5–4 win over the visiting Philadelphians.

The Robison Field victory came after González opened the frame with a double and took third base on a fielder's choice. After Rogers Hornsby was intentionally walked and stole second, González dashed for home when Oeschger utilized a full wind-up to pitch to the next batter, Walton Cruise. Cardinals right-hander Bill Doak threw the toilsome but gratifying complete-game win.

The most significant of González's 12 recorded steals on the season provided the historic sidenote of the first walk-off steal of home plate in the major leagues by a Hispanic player.

1918

MAY 30. Pitcher Oscar Tuero and catcher Mike González were conduits to history as the first Latin American batterymates in the major leagues. In the fifth inning of the first game of a morning-afternoon doubleheader between the Pittsburgh Pirates and St. Louis Cardinals, Havana native Tuero (in his major league debut) relieved ineffective Cardinals starter Gene Packard with one out. Tuero retired the side and finished the game, throwing to catcher and fellow Havana product Mike González. The Pirates, after a five-run binge against Packard, won the game, 8–0.

The Redbirds returned the shutout favor, 4–0, in the second game of the holiday duet at Forbes Field. Catching both games, González went 2-for-6 at the plate, including a triple. He registered four assists in the first contest.

JUNE 21. The Cardinals' Mike González banged out a home run, two doubles, and two singles during a 12–6 Redbirds' victory over the Cincinnati Reds at Robison Field. González became the first Hispanic player to accumulate five hits in a regulation-length, modern era game. The ten total bases will stand as the most recorded by a National League player in one game this season.

JULY 26. Eusebio González took the field for the first-place Boston Red Sox as that franchise's first Latin American player. Subbing late in the game for shortstop Everett Scott, González tripled in his first major league at-bat against White Sox ace Eddie Cicotte. González's teammate, Babe Ruth, playing left field, took an 0-for-4 "collar" in the 7–2 win by Cicotte at Comiskey Park.

González did not receive an opportunity to play in the World Series for the pennant-winning Bosox. Shortly after he manned third base in a game against the Detroit Tigers on August 6, the New England team demoted the infielder to the Toronto Maple Leafs.

After playing in only three games with Boston, and with a 2-for-5 hitting resume to his credit, González would never again appear in the major leagues.

AUGUST 8. In the late fall of 1911, a smallish, 21-year-old right-hander pitched against a New York Giants barnstorming team in Cuba, prior to his own professional debut. Accompanying the Giants during the 12-game exhibition tour was Christy Mathewson. Seven years later, that smallish right-hander, Adolfo Luque, has joined the Cincinnati Reds, managed by Mathewson.

This day, from the mound Mathewson knew oh so well, 28-year-old Adolfo Luque picked up the first major league win by a Latin American pitcher. He defeated John McGraw's New York Giants, 5–2, at the Polo Grounds. Luque, only a few weeks after his purchase from minor league Louisville, allowed four hits, walked three and struck out three. He also secured, during the engagement, the first extra-base hit (a double), stolen base and RBI by a Latin American big league pitcher.

AUGUST 11. A Hispanic pitcher and Hispanic batter faced one another in a major league game for the first time. At Redland Field, St. Louis Cardinals catcher Mike González dug his heels into the batter's box four times against Reds pitcher Adolfo Luque. González reached his Cuban *compay* for hits twice, including a double. Luque surrendered a dozen hits in a 5–3 setback to the Cardinals, the second game of a doubleheader.

The Reds took the first game, 3–2, and González recorded a two-base hit in four at-bats.

SEPTEMBER 2. Hispanic baseball history occurred in a double dose as Armistice Day approached. On the final day of a World War I–abridged season, Adolfo Luque threw a 1–0 shutout against the St. Louis Cardinals at Redland Field—the first shutout entry into major league ledgers by a Latin American pitcher.

The rookie right-hander, who had pitched in four big league games prior to this season, threw his *third* complete game in *six* days. Luque allowed six hits and a walk in the second game of the Labor Day doubleheader; the victory completed a four-game sweep by the third-place Reds over the last-place Redbirds.

Luque's mound opponent and tough-luck loser was Oscar Tuero, a 19-year-old, Cuban-born right-hander. It was the first time Hispanic pitchers opposed one another on a major league mound.

1919

JUNE 6. Relieving in the ninth inning with the tying run on base, Adolfo Luque secured the final three outs of a Cincinnati Reds' 7–6 victory over the Brooklyn Robins at Redland Field. Luque, in his first full big league season, recorded the first save (retroactively) credited to a Latin American pitcher in the major leagues. He preserved starting pitcher Ray Fisher's sixth win on the campaign, inducing three consecutive batters to ground out.

The second-place Reds moved to within four games of the league-leading New York Giants with the win. Managed by Pat Moran, the Reds team sailed past the Giants in the standings over the next months, and captured the pennant by nine games.

OCTOBER 3. In what later developed into the sport's most infamous World Series, on the hill for the Cincinnati Reds, opening the home half of the eighth inning of Game 3 of the World Series against the Chicago White Sox, stood Adolfo Luque. At Comiskey Park, Luque became the first Latin American player to appear in a World Series game and the first to register a strikeout.[6]

The pitcher fanned the first batter he faced, Nemo Leibold, to begin a 1–2–3 inning. The White Sox required no more at-bats as pitcher Dickie Kerr completed his 3–0 shutout in the top of the ninth. Luque made two appearances in the "tainted" Series and pitched five scoreless relief innings for the five-games-to-three champion Reds.

When the best-of-nine-game Series—the first since the 1903 inaugural Series—shifted back to Redland Field, the Havana hurler stepped to the plate in the seventh inning of Game 7 (October 8), as the first Latin American player to bat in a Fall Classic. He fanned against Eddie Cicotte, one of the eight "Black Sox" players implicated in the Series "fix."

1920

JUNE 26. Kill the umpire! Today saw one of Adolfo Luque's first tries at it.

Umpire Bill Klem was assailed by the Cincinnati pitcher after Klem stepped in front of the plate in the eighth inning of a one-run game and hurled an invective at Luque, stationed on the mound. Luque bolted from the hill and landed several ferocious blows on Klem before being pulled away. The incident was part of a riotous second game of a doubleheader at Redland Field, which saw its playing surface strewn with bottles and other discards of displeasure from the crowd.

After a quiet opener in which St. Louis shut out the home team, Klem found himself in the middle of a second-game maelstrom. Two innings before the bout with Luque, he had ruled against the home team on a close and hotly disputed call at the plate, which, along with the ejection of Reds catcher Ivey Wingo for arguing the call too strenuously, precipitated the offensive fan behavior. When the field was cleared and play resumed, the contested run at home plate turned out to be the winner for the Cardinals team, which won, 4–3, and completed its road sweep.

Luque, the first Latin American pitcher ejected from a big league game, would not be castigated by the league (except for a fine), after Klem admitted to verbally provoking the pitcher. Klem also issued a formal, public apology afterward. Hurling over 200 innings for the first time in his career, Luque led the National League in fewest hits allowed per nine innings (7.281) and tied for second in WHIP (1.098) with the Pirates' Wilbur Cooper.

1921

APRIL 13. Adolfo Luque of the Cincinnati Reds became the first Hispanic pitcher to start a major league Opening Day game. Luque went the distance as Cincinnati scored four runs in the eighth inning to reward him with a 5–3, winning effort over the Pittsburgh Pirates at Redland Field.

Despite a losing record (17–19), Luque came into his own in this, his first season as a full-time starter. The right-handed threw 304 innings, second in the National League, and registered 25 complete games, third-most in the loop. His three shutouts, tied with several other pitchers, led the circuit, a category first for a Hispanic major league hurler. Luque's Wins Above Replacement rating of 5.0 was surpassed by only two other pitchers in his league—Burleigh Grimes (8.0) and Grover Cleveland "Pete" Alexander (5.4). WAR measures the number of wins a player adds to his team above what an average or replacement player would add.

As baseball began a runs-scoring renaissance, thanks in large part to the contemporaneous advent of George Herman Ruth and the home run, Luque, along with Eppa Rixey and Pete Donohue, comprised a "Big Three" of starting pitching for Cincinnati that was unrivaled in either league through most of the decade.

1922

APRIL 15. Charles Comiskey obtained his first Hispanic player when he purchased pitcher José Acosta from the Philadelphia Athletics in February. Today, Acosta's Chicago White Sox debut ended inauspiciously. The Cuban pitcher surrendered three runs in one inning of relief against a strong St. Louis Browns team. The visiting Browns, who would finish one game behind the 94-win New York Yankees at the close of the season, humbled the White Sox, 14–0.

Acosta appeared in only five games for the Kid Gleason–managed White Sox, accruing an 0–2 record. In a major league sojourn lasting three seasons, including two campaigns with Washington, Acosta recorded a 10–10 record in 55 games (13 starts).

Incidentally, two seasons earlier with the Senators, Acosta had yielded Babe Ruth's 50th home run (a first in one season). However, it was the only run the 29-year-old Acosta permitted in that September 24, 1920, game, as he recorded a four-hit, complete-game victory over Ruth's Yankees, 3–1.

1923

JUNE 19. Adolfo Luque emerged as the winner of an 11-inning, 1–0 duel against Burleigh Grimes of the Brooklyn Robins at Redland Field. Catcher Bubbles Hargrave's extra-inning sacrifice fly gave the Reds pitcher his second shutout in a row and ownership to the first extra-inning shutout victory by a Hispanic big league pitcher. Luque won his seventh straight start as he approached the tail end of a 29-inning scoreless streak (his second unscored-upon string of more than 20 innings in the two- month-old campaign).

Luque was one of three Cincinnati starting pitchers (Eppa Rixey, Pete Donohue) to win 20 games on the season—a pitching achievement not since repeated on one team in the National League.

JULY 17. "LUQUE IS NO FLUQUE," read a central New York newspaper's sports page headline in its July 15 edition, a reference to Adolfo Luque's 13–2 record and his recent offer to pitch two games of today's doubleheader.

At Braves Field, Luque started—and won—two games, beating Boston, 4–3 and 9–5. The starter went six innings in game one and added a complete-game endeavor in the nightcap. The Reds ace became the first Hispanic pitcher to start and win both games of a major league doubleheader.

Luque, with an ERA mark of 1.93 at season's end, was one of only two starting pitchers in baseball over this entire decade with an ERA under 2.00. Pete Alexander, 1.91 ERA in 1920, was the other.

AUGUST 15. In the middle of a historic pitching season—and the particularly hostile surroundings of 25,000 vengeful fans at the Polo Grounds—Adolfo Luque made a historic mark at the plate, becoming the first Latin American pitcher to hit a home run in the major leagues. He connected against New York's Hugh McQuillan in the first game of a Coogan's Bluff doubleheader. The two-run homer, along with four other runs, helped Luque win his 18th game, 6–3.

It was the first start for Luque since his unruly encounter with Casey Stengel eight days earlier in Cincinnati, which made the pitcher a "marked man" by the Giants and their fans. The fearless battler bearded the lion in his den, and his all-around performance won over the tough, antagonistic crowd and, if not grudgingly, gained the Giants' respect as well.

This game was played without incident, and Luque's Reds also won the afterpiece. As the opening to a near-complete turnaround from last week's humiliating five-game home sweep suffered to New York, the Reds will cop four out of five games in this Polo Grounds rematch series and re-enter the National League pennant race.

AUGUST 24. "A delegation of Cuban fans occupied a box back of the Cincinnati bench and gave Luque plenty of encouragement. As he trotted off the field in the ninth, his admirers leaped on the field to half carry him to the bench."[7] The scene, reported by *the New York Times*, followed the last out at Ebbets Fields, as Adolfo Luque became the first Hispanic pitcher to win 20 games in a major league season.

The 4–0, four-hit shutout of the Brooklyn Robins gave Luque the benchmark victory and earned him his league-best sixth whitewash of the campaign, while keeping the second-place Reds within three games of the also-victorious New York Giants.

Amazingly, Luque was denied *seven* other shutouts this season, complete games in which he did not allow an earned run. Five of the games he won; the other two he lost, 2–1 and 2–0.

SEPTEMBER 29. The greatest major league season recorded by a Hispanic pitcher came to a close. Adolfo Luque, in his easiest conquest of the campaign, recorded his 27th victory (most in the major leagues), 11–1, over the St. Louis Cardinals at Redland Field. With his eight defeats, Luque's winning percentage computed to .771, best in both leagues.

Defeating the same team in the same place where he had won his first game of the season back in April, Luque concluded one of the best pitching seasons ever seen during baseball's offense-vitalized period called the Liveball Era.

Astonishing ancillary statistics for Luque's season included only two home runs allowed in 322 innings pitched (1,301 batters faced!) and an ERA that was 2.06 runs lower than the National League average. Coming out of the bullpen, the star pitcher also finished four games for the Reds, receiving credit for two saves. Luque's Wins Above Replacement player rating of 10.8 was second only to the incomparable Babe Ruth (14.0) in all of baseball.

The season's victory total is still the highest achieved by a Hispanic major league pitcher.

1924

APRIL 2. Roberto Ávila was born in Veracruz, Mexico. Until he became involved with athletics, Ávila's intended career was the law, the path his lawyer father nudged him toward throughout his youth. As it turned out, Roberto Ávila never became an attorney as his father had wanted; instead, he became a barrister of the baseball diamond, exacting jurisprudence on batted balls hit to the right side of major league infields for 11 years.

OCTOBER 14. Kansas City Monarchs player-manager José Méndez had guided his team to the Negro National League pennant with a record of 57–22, chipping in with a 5–2 record on the mound. The Midwestern champion Monarchs faced off against the Eastern Colored League titlist Hilldale Daisies in a first-of-a-kind, best-of-nine-game championship series. Méndez, who earlier had become the first Hispanic player to compete in the Negro League World Series, today became the first Hispanic pitcher to win a NLWS game.

In Game 7 at Muehlebach Field in Kansas City, Méndez, recently operated on and under a physician's order not to participate in the Series, put himself into the game at a crucial juncture. Hilldale had just tied the contest at 3–3 and had the go-ahead run on second base in the top of the ninth inning, with one out. The Cuban pitcher relieved Monarchs starter Bill Drake and retired the next two batters. Méndez hurled three more scoreless innings and received credit for the win when Kansas City scratched across the winning run in the bottom of the 12th.

The Monarchs, with the 4–3 win, evened the series at three games apiece.

OCTOBER 20. The pitching of José Méndez provided the decisive victory for the Kansas City Monarchs over the Hilldale Daisies in the first Negro League World Series, referred to as the Colored World Series.

At Schorling's Park in Chicago, Méndez shut out the Daisies, 5–0, on three hits, to close out the first Series played between the champions of the Negro National League and the Eastern Colored League. Méndez posted a 2–0 mark and a 1.42 ERA in the ten game clash (5–4–1). The right-hander earned the added distinction of becoming the first Hispanic pitcher to start and win a championship-deciding game in North American baseball. As the manager of the Negro National League champions, Méndez also became the first Hispanic manager to win a North American championship series.

The 37-year-old pitcher was described by the *Pittsburgh Courier*'s W. Rollo Wilson as looking "gray, gaunt and grim."[8] Méndez, who had pitched in relief the previous day, took the hill in the starter's role in a decision said to have been influenced by league executive Rube Foster.

1925

MAY 3. Adolfo Luque improved his early-season record to 4–1 with a 5–4 win over the Pittsburgh Pirates at Redland Field. Luque entered the ninth inning with a shutout but apparently tired, giving up four runs and nearly the game.

Fellow right-hander Pete Donohue was summoned from the bullpen to secure the final out of the contest. Luque's near-complete-game exercise earned him his 100th major league win, the first Hispanic major leaguer to reach the century mark in victories.

Despite posting a losing record of 16–18, the hard-luck Luque led the league again in shutouts (four) and ERA (2.63). His 156 ERA+ on the season ranks as the third-best for pitchers with a losing record and at least 250 innings. ERA+ is a measure for comparing pitchers from different eras. It takes into account the pitcher's ballpark and the run-scoring environment of his league. The ERA+ league average is 100, meaning an average pitcher has a ranking of 100.

MAY 25. Thirteen years ago, Mike González became the first Hispanic player in Boston Braves' franchise history. Today, as a pinch-hitter in the seventh inning, González became the first Hispanic player to don a Chicago Cubs uniform. González walked in his lone plate appearance in the game, a 5–3 Cubs loss to the Pittsburgh Pirates at Forbes Field.

JUNE 28. The first professional baseball game in Mexico was played on this date at Parque Franco Inglés in Mexico City. The contest lasted 14 innings before *equipo México* defeated *Nacional de Agraria,* 7–5. The baseball park was owned by one of the league's founding fathers, Ernesto Carmona V, who was also the manager bearing Agraria's initial loss. His victorious opposite number that day was Cuban Jesús Váldez.

The first league championship would be won by 74 Regimiento de San Luis Potosí, one of the other five teams that composed the circuit. Less than three months into the season, the 74 Regimiento team moved from their original base in Puebla to San Luis Potosí.

In a three-game series for the title, the 74 Regimiento team defeated *equipo México,* after both clubs completed their schedule with identical records. Cuban pitcher Oscar Martínez was the winning hurler in a third-game 16–3 rout in favor of the transplanted *poblanos.*

The other original teams that season were Guanajuato and Nacional de Bixler.

NOVEMBER 29. Saturnino Orestes Armas Miñoso was born in Perico, Matanzas, Cuba. "Minnie" Miñoso became an exceptional athlete with a God-given talent to play baseball. It was Miñoso's channeled desire to play baseball at its highest level that eventually hurtled him from an early life as a disadvantaged youth in the sugar cane fields of Cuba to a place as one of the most prominent major league players of the 1950s.

1926

JANUARY 23. Alfonso Carrasquel was born in Caracas, Venezuela. The nephew of major league pitcher Alex, "Chico" Carrasquel, the slick fielding shortstop for the 1950s

Chicago White Sox, elevated the Carrasquel surname to a recognition level as the first family of Venezuelan baseball.

APRIL 29. "It was about the most remarkable thing that has happened to a Cincinnati team in many a moon. A bunch of fans got together after the game and sent a telegram of congratulation to Luque on the way his team scored behind him ... [with] hopes that was just the beginning of a new era or something, in which he may get the breaks like most other good pitchers do in that respect."[9] So wrote Cincinnati sportswriter Tom Swope after the Reds provided the antithesis of their usual low run support and scored 16 times in a game pitched by Adolfo Luque. Facing the Pittsburgh Pirates at Forbes Field, the pitcher himself accounted for a goodly portion of the tally, knocking in four runs—two of them in a ten-run fifth inning.

In the big-inning outburst, Luque singled to center field to drive in a run, then batted again, with two outs, and doubled to plate another. The runs were put to good use, as the hitting and running exertions may have been a factor in tiring out Luque, who was allowed, despite a bumpy ninth inning in which the Pirates scored four times, to complete the 16–9 victory.

One of only three Hispanic pitchers to record 200 hits in their major league careers (Juan Marichal and Liván Hernández are the others), Luque became the first Hispanic big league player to notch two safeties in one inning. Luque hit .346—27-for-78—that season.

Adolfo Luque won 194 games, and saved 28 more, hurling for four National League teams. His greatest fame came with the Cincinnati Reds.

With 31 starts, Luque (13–16) was one of a quartet of Reds pitchers who started 129 of the 157 games Cincinnati played on the campaign, and his 237 career hits set the record for the most hits by a Hispanic major league pitcher.

AUGUST 22. Two days after pitching a complete-game victory over the Boston Braves (5–2), Adolfo Luque was summoned, in relief, into an extra-inning contest versus the same Braves team at Redland Field. Luque hurled three innings and surrendered a go-ahead run to Boston in the top of the 12th frame. In the Reds' turn at-bat, Luque singled and started a two-run, winning rally that gave him and the Reds a 7–6 win.

It was the ninth consecutive game in which the Cincinnati Reds pitcher hit safely. His hitting streak was halted in his next outing, two days later in a complete-game victory against the New York Giants (4–3). With his bat, Luque established the longest hitting streak by a Hispanic major league pitcher.

1927

JULY 13. Rubén Gómez was born in Arroyo, Puerto Rico. Blessed with a "rubber arm," Gómez as a pitcher made an impact in the baseball leagues of several countries, none more so than his own island nation, in which he took the mound for an amazing 29 different seasons.

SEPTEMBER 26. Jesse Haines of the St. Louis Cardinals defeated Adolfo Luque, 3–1, in 13 innings at Redland Field. Haines, a 24-game winner for the Cardinals on the season, permitted no earned runs in masterfully outdueling the Cincinnati Reds' veteran. The 13–12 Luque allowed two runs in the 13th inning, one unearned, in his last start of the campaign for his fifth-place National League club.

The game was one of *22* Luque completed—and lost—in his career, nine innings pitched and three runs or fewer allowed. Of the eight pitchers in major league history who lost more games under the same circumstances, seven are in the Hall of Fame.[10] Luque's 1.68 ERA in the 22 losses is the best among the eight, and he was the only one not to give up a home run (214 innings).

1928

JULY 23. José de la Trinidad Bracho was born in Maracaibo, Venezuela. Bracho evolved into the winningest pitcher in Venezuelan Winter League history with 109, and earned a record-tying six victories for his country in Caribbean Series competition.

NOVEMBER 6. Adolfo Luque's permissible skin tones allowed him to receive mainstream recognition as the first Hispanic star in the major leagues. In a more racially progressive world, that ethnic distinction would have surely belonged to José Méndez. Referred to early on as the "Black Matty," in comparison to Giants legend Christy Mathewson, Méndez was not only shortchanged by the game of baseball but also, regrettably, in the match play of life. The former right-hander, who first made a splash in U.S. newspapers against barnstorming major league teams in Cuba, died of bronchopneumonia in Havana at age 41.

Méndez compiled a .731 winning percentage (76–28) in 15 Cuban Winter League campaigns, ranking as the best all-time in the league.

Shortly after Méndez's death, Negro leagues umpire Bert Gholston offered the following praise for the competitor he had been privy to see perform in his prime: "He was a superman of baseball. As a pitcher, he was skillful, wily, lionhearted, courageous and showed a wonderful change of pace and control. The stage has but one Bert Williams, the ring has seen but one Joe Gans and baseball has but one Jose Mendez."[11]

1929

OCTOBER 8. Catcher Mike González of the Chicago Cubs became the first Hispanic position player to appear in a World Series game. An eighth-inning substitute, González caught the last two innings of Game 1 of the Fall Classic at Wrigley Field. The Cubs were defeated by the Philadelphia Athletics, 3–1.

The following day, in his only World Series at-bat, González pinch-hit without success, as the Cubs lost again, 9–3.

The Series moved east to Philadelphia, where the Athletics dispatched the Cubs in two out of three encounters to capture the ultimate crown.

1930

APRIL 21. The Brooklyn Robins/Dodgers franchise was still 17 years away from becoming baseball's most progressive organization. But today, the franchise took its first step in that reformist direction with the debut of its first Hispanic player. And quite a player at that. Following an off-season trade from Cincinnati, Adolfo Luque made his first appearance for Wilbert Robinson's team.

At Ebbets Field, Luque pitched eight innings, allowed four runs (three earned) and recorded a 15–8 victory over the Boston Braves. Luque was forced to retire in the ninth, with no outs, when he was struck on his pitching hand by a line drive off the bat of pinch-hitter George Sisler. Luque also doubled in two runs as Brooklyn picked up its first win of the young season.

JUNE 25. Humberto Robinson was born in Colon, Panama. Originally signed by the New York Yankees, Robinson made it to the major leagues with the Milwaukee Braves in 1955, ahead of anyone else from his land.

SEPTEMBER 17. One can closely estimate the number of innings that Adolfo Luque's right arm, over the past two decades, has delivered. Fifteen summers as a major leaguer and nearly 3,000 innings of mound work so far, combined with 17 seasons in the Cuban amateur and professional leagues, plus several U.S. minor league campaigns, leaves a total upwards of 5,000 innings.

Age has not withered the veteran National League hurler nor custom staled his infinite pitching fancy. Six weeks after his 40th birthday and seven days after recording the 26th and final shutout of his ground-breaking and illustrious career, Luque (14–8) suffered a 5–3 loss to the St. Louis Cardinals at Ebbets Field. Cardinals pinch-hitter Andy High doubled in two ninth-inning runs to spoil the intrepid right-hander's 200th complete game.

It was Luque's 16th complete game in 24 starts, and his 346th career opening assignment. The majors' unique Hispanic star will finish with 206 complete games in 366 career starts—an astounding 56 percent![12]

1932

MAY 17. Osvaldo Virgil was born in Monte Cristi, Dominican Republic. A graduate of DeWitt Clinton High School in the Bronx, New York, Virgil attained significant ethnic distinctions with the New York Giants and Detroit Tigers.

AUGUST 8, 1932. Esteban Bellán, the first Hispanic major leaguer, died in Havana, Cuba. Born October 1, 1849, Bellán also managed Habana against Almendares in the first game of the Cuban Professional League in 1878.

1933

SEPTEMBER 8. At Fenway Park, outfielder Mel Almada of the Boston Red Sox, represented Mexico as its first native son to enter the major leagues. The 20-year-old started in center field and batted leadoff in both games of a doubleheader debut against the Detroit Tigers.

Purchased from the Pacific Coast League, the left-handed-hitting Almada recorded a 1-for-4 batting output in each game and scored a run in the first game. His first major league hit was struck against Tommy Bridges.

The Sox drop both contests to the Tigers by identical counts of 4–3.

SEPTEMBER 23. Boston's Mel Almada became the first Mexican player to hit a home run in the major leagues. It was a bases-empty clout off Herb Pennock of the New York Yankees. A fifth-inning replacement, Almada homered in the same inning and scored two other runs in a game replete with scoring. Babe Ruth and Lou Gehrig socked home runs as well, leading the Yankees to a 16–12 win at Fenway Park.

The solo homer by Almada was also the first home run hit by a Hispanic player at Fenway Park.

OCTOBER 7. Adolfo Luque struck out Joe Kuhel in the tenth inning at Griffith Stadium, and closed out the World Series title for the New York Giants over the Washington Senators, four games to one. The 43-year-old sovereign of the mound tossed 4⅓ innings of scoreless relief, yielding only two singles and striking out five, to become the first Latin American pitcher to win a World Series game. (Spanish-Irish descendant Lefty Gómez won two games in the 1932 Series.)

Mel Ott's tenth-inning home run, just out of the reach of outfielder Fred Schulte, provided the run that Luque used to snare the 4–3 victory and the championship for the Bill Terry–led Giants. Released by the Brooklyn Dodgers and signed by the Giants in 1932, Luque also singled to center in the ninth inning and became the first Latin American player to hit safely in a World Series game.

DECEMBER 9. In January, the St. Louis Cardinals released 42-year-old Mike González,

Pictured as a member of the New York Giants, catcher Mike González was known more for his connection with the St. Louis Cardinals. With St. Louis in 1924, González led the National League in putouts (413) and games caught (119) (courtesy National Baseball Hall of Fame Library, Cooperstown, New York).

ending the 17-year veteran's big league career. "Mike is one of the smartest men in base-ball," Cardinals Vice President Branch Rickey said at the time. "He can command a place in our organization if he wants it."[13] González spent the 1933 season as player-coach for the Cardinals' Columbus Red Birds minor league team.

Today, Columbus team president George M. Trautman announced that González had been sold to the parent club as "coach and assistant to manager Frankie Frisch."[14] González began the 1934 season as the major leagues' first Hispanic coach. His tenure with the St. Louis team, which included two brief interludes as interim manager, lasted until 1946, when González was suspended by Organized Baseball over his indirect association with the rogue Mexican League.

1934

JANUARY 20. Camilo Pascual was born in Havana, Cuba. Among other distinctions, Pascual became the Caribbean Series' most elite pitcher. In six Caribbean Classic starts, his record was 6–0, with five complete games and an ERA of 1.73.

APRIL 29. Luis Aparicio, Jr. was born in Maracaibo, Venezuela. Aparicio followed in the footsteps of his shortstop-playing father, a renowned figure in Venezuelan baseball in the 1930s and 1940s, and climbed to new heights of achievement with his glove in a long major league career.

AUGUST 18. Roberto Clemente was born in Carolina, Puerto Rico. The fifth child of Luisa Walker and Melchor Clemente, Roberto grew into a world-class athlete and a class-indiscriminate human being. Every bit as lasting as his baseball accomplishments was the acclaim Clemente acquired from the particular humanity he possessed. That humanity displayed itself off the baseball diamond with as much conviction and passion as the physical talents that distinguished him from his ball playing peers on the field.

1935

APRIL 23. Opening Day at the Polo Grounds came with the added attraction of Babe Ruth's return to New York—as member of the Boston Braves. Fighting a cold, the portly Sultan of Swat went hitless in three trips to the plate, with a base on balls. On defense, he misjudged a ball in right field that led to an inside-the-park home run for Giants player-manager Bill Terry. But two innings later, in the fifth, Ruth robbed Terry of another home run bid with a leaping grab at the "yellow frankfurter sign, 410 feet from home plate in deep right-center."[15]

The 40-year-old Ruth was cheered incessantly throughout the game by the 45,000 attendees, and affectionately at his removal in the bottom of the eighth inning with the Braves trailing, 5–3. Ruth, it was noted in various newspapers, departed the field to a confetti shower of torn paper as he exited, walking up the clubhouse steps in center field.

Braves first baseman Buck Jordan tied the contest with a one-out, two-run home run in the ninth inning against Giants reliever Allyn Stout. Forty-four-year-old Adolfo Luque was called into the game and held the Braves scoreless for 2⅔ innings. In the lower half of the 11th, Luque led off with a single, and pinch-runner Kiddo Davis scored the winning run on Mel Ott's two-out hit. Luque, the oldest player in the major leagues, was credited with his first win on the season and the 194th and last of his stupendous career.

The fiscal restraints of the Great Depression obliged major league teams to trim their rosters from 25 to 23 players by May 15. Fighting the numbers game, manager Terry was forced to cut Luque and option infielder Joe Malay to the minors to meet the requirement. As a result, Luque's 20-season big league career concluded on April 26. But a new career, as the first Hispanic pitching coach in the major leagues, subsequently began on Opening Day, 1936, with New York.

Two seasons later, after a falling-out with Terry over salary, Luque didn't report to the club for the 1938 campaign. Absent for three seasons, "the Havana Perfecto" returned as pitching coach under Terry in 1941. He remained at the post under new manager Mel Ott from 1942 through 1945, after which Luque opted to align himself with the rebellious Mexican League.

JULY 27. While playing on a recent touring team of Mexican all-stars in the United States, infielder José Gómez caught the attention of a major league front office.

The Philadelphia Phillies plucked the Mazatlán-born Gómez from the traveling team and signed him to bolster an infield depleted by injuries.

Gómez did not make a significant impact in his first game today, as the Phillies shut out the host Boston Braves, 5–0. Playing second base, Gómez went hitless in three trips, while handling four chances without issue in the field. But his significance as the Philadelphia Phillies' initial Hispanic player became everlasting.

Gómez stuck with the Phillies for the remainder of this season and all of the next before exiting the major league scene. He made a brief return with the Washington Senators in 1942. In three big league seasons, Gómez batted .226 in an even 200 games.

AUGUST 11. After a four-year absence, Martín Dihigo returned to the Negro Leagues this season, along with a host of other black Hispanic players, on a team put together by underworld entrepreneur Alejandro "Alex" Pompez called the New York Cubans. In fan balloting for the third annual Negro League All-Star Game, released today, Dihigo received the second-most votes of any player, behind only Willie Wells. Cubans teammate Luis Tiant, Sr. tallied the most votes for any pitcher, including Satchel Paige. As a late-inning reliever in the game, Tiant earned the distinction of becoming the first Hispanic pitcher in the short history of this star-studded game.

Dihigo and Tiant were integrally linked, albeit in an unfavorable story line, in what developed into the greatest All-Star Game in Negro league history. At Comiskey Park, with a crowd of 25,000 on hand, the thrilling game culminated in an extra-inning home run by George "Mule" Suttles of the West squad against East pitcher Dihigo. The climactic, three-run home run in the bottom of the 11th inning provided the Oscar Charleston–managed West club with an 11–8 victory over the Webster McDonald-guided East team.

With the game tied, 4–4, the visiting East team scored four runs in the top of the tenth inning. But the West answered, loading the bases against Tiant in the bottom of tenth. The multifaceted Dihigo was called in from center field to protect the lead and preserve the victory. Presumably, after only a few warm-up pitches from the mound, the "Cuban Immortal" allowed all the inherited runners, plus a tying run, to dent the plate. In the 11th stanza, after the East failed to muster any offense, Suttles connected for the game-winning blast against Dihigo, who earlier had crashed into the outfield wall while chasing an extra-base hit by Josh Gibson. The contest was delayed ten minutes while Dihigo lay prone on the outfield grass. Suttles, incidentally, had been walked four times previously in the game.

Batting two places ahead of Alejandro Oms in the lineup, Dihigo could take small solace in becoming the first Hispanic player to appear and register a hit (a first-inning single) in the Negro League All-Star Game.

Sug Cornelius was the winning pitcher. East pitcher Slim Jones hit the only other home run in the memorable game.

1936

FEBRARY 27. Major League Baseball arrived for the first time in Puerto Rico. Charlie Dressen's Cincinnati Reds sailed from New York City into San Juan Harbor and took up residence at the Condado Hotel.

Following less than a week of workouts, the team played its first exhibition game today. The Reds, behind three pitchers, downed the Ponce squad, 8–2. Island greats, Francisco "Pancho" Coímbre had two hits and a stolen base and Pedro "Perucho" Cepeda contributed a single. Dominican idol Juan "Tetelo" Vargas also registered one of the six hits allowed by the Reds' hurlers.

MARCH 3. The Cincinnati Reds interrupted their spring training stay and exhibition schedule in San Juan by sending 24 members of their squad across the Mona Passage, via Pan American Airways clipper, to Ciudad Trujillo on Hispañola. The two dozen players comprised the first major league team to play baseball in the Dominican Republic.

The Reds participated in two exhibition games, the first taking place today. Against Escogido, the foreigners had their way, winning 7–1. The Reds also won the next day versus Licey, 4–2.

1937

FEBRUARY 7. Juan Pizarro was born in Santurce, Puerto Rico. Pizarro developed into a left-handed pea-thrower and the best pitcher produced by the eastern Caribbean island.

MAY 8, 1937. Miguel Angel Cuéllar was born in Santa Clara, Las Villas, Cuba. The late-blooming southpaw was not deterred from becoming the 20th century's best Latin American left-handed pitcher.

JULY 21. On June 10, the Red Sox packaged Mel Almada, along with the discontented Wes Ferrell and his brother Rick, in a trade to the Washington Senators. The three-for-two swap delivered Bobo Newsom and Ben Chapman to Beantown. Almada was permanently installed as the Senators' leadoff hitter by manager Bucky Harris.

Today at Comiskey Park, Almada cracked a home run to open the game against

White Sox starter Bill Dietrich. The solo home run (the center fielder's only hit of the contest) was the first of seven runs the Senators scored in their four-run victory over the home team.

The blast was also the first leadoff home run hit by a Hispanic player in the major leagues. Back on May 8, during the Red Sox' first road trip into the Windy City, Almada belted the first home run by a Hispanic player at Comiskey Park—also against Bill Dietrich.

JULY 25. Mel Almada crossed the plate four times for the Washington Senators in the first of two games against the St. Louis Browns at Sportsman's Park. The Mexican outfielder topped himself with five more scoring tallies in the nightcap to set a major league record for runs scored in a doubleheader.

The center fielder, notching six hits and three walks, established the twin bill scoring record during the Senators' dual victories over the Browns, 16–10 and 15–5.

SEPTEMBER 17. Orlando Cepeda was born in Ponce, Puerto Rico. Cepeda, as baseball writer Myron Cope wrote, "was raised at the knee of baseball," a reference to his famous ballplaying father, Perucho Cepeda. "I remember when I was four or five years old," Cepeda told Cope, "my father would bring such men as Satchel Paige and Josh Gibson to our house."[16] Orlando went on to etch his name alongside the hallowed achievements of those same great players.

OCTOBER 20. Juan Marichal was born in Laguna Verde, Dominican Republic. As the major leagues' trailblazing pitcher from his country, Marichal accumulated titanic mound achievements on par with the best moundsman of his era.

1938

APRIL 11. "If I should see Torriente walking up the other side of the street, I would say, 'There walks a ball club.'"[17] This descriptive quote about Cristóbal Torriente, attributed to Negro league pitcher/manager C. I. Taylor, was no doubt recalled today with strains of melancholy by those who remembered the player on the ball field.

Torriente passed away from tuberculosis in New York City at age 44. The Cienfuegos, Cuba, native was said to have been in declining health and suffering from alcoholism.

A power hitter in the mold of the great Babe Ruth, Torriente perennially ranked among league leaders in hitting and slugging in both the North American Negro leagues and the Cuban Winter League of the 1910s and 1920s.

JULY 20. Pedro Oliva was born in Pinar del Rio, Cuba. Using his brother Tony's name Oliva broke into the major leagues with unprecedented hitting distinction in 1964. After he averaged more than five–WAR for his first eight seasons, serious knee injuries dimmed the ascendant star arcing over Oliva as a member of the Minnesota Twins.

JULY 31. The St. Louis Browns acquired Mel Almada from the Washington Senators on June 15, and the outfielder has not stopped hitting since he debuted for St. Louis four days later.

Almada garnered five hits in a doubleheader today against the Boston Braves. The leadoff hitter scored two runs and drove in another in helping lead the Browns to a sweep, 7–6 and 10–3 (in a seven-inning, weather-shortened second game).

The collection of hits gave Almada 50 for the month in 117 at bats. He became the first Hispanic player to record that many hits in one calendar month.

Batting .401 since joining the Browns, the 25-year-old flychaser hit in his 16th and 17th straight games, a streak that stretched out to 29 before being halted. Almada hit safely in a remarkable 47 out of 48 games, and 54 out of 56, culminating on August 19! The pioneer player finished his seven-year big league career in 1939 with the Brooklyn Dodgers.

SEPTEMBER 14. Coach Mike González replaced the fired Frankie Frisch as manager and guided the St. Louis Cardinals to a doubleheader sweep of the Philadelphia Phillies at Shibe Park (12–9, 3–2). One of the first Hispanic players to reach the major leagues, the 47-year-old González became the first Hispanic to manage a team at the same high level.

Though he played under such astute baseball managers as Miller Huggins, Branch Rickey, Joe McCarthy and John McGraw, the fifth-year Cardinals coach was never considered as a permanent replacement by management. González finished with an 8–8 record before being replaced by Ray Blades for the 1939 campaign.

NOVEMBER 13. The Puerto Rican Winter League was born. Initiated under the auspices of the National Semi-Professional Baseball Congress, which included teams from all 48 mainland states, clubs from six cities within the U.S. island territory inaugurated games for what evolved into a long-standing and immensely rich baseball tradition in Puerto Rico.

Mel Almada, Mexico's first big league ballplayer, broke in with the Boston Red Sox and was the first Hispanic player to hit a home run at Fenway Park and Yankee Stadium (courtesy National Baseball Hall of Fame Library, Cooperstown, New York).

The Mayagüez *Indios* traveled to Caguas to play the *Criollos;* Guayama's *Brujos* visited the *Senadores* in San Juan; Humacao's *Grises Orientales* hosted Ponce's *Leones*. Three months later, Guayama defeated San Juan in the island championship series, three games to two, to be crowned first league champion.

1939

APRIL 23. "*Now pitching, number 14, Alex Alexandra … now batting, number 5, Joe DiMaggio.*" So went the conjectured announcement at Griffith Stadium, for the benefit of the more than 20,000 in attendance. The New York Yankees had just chased Washington Senators starter Ken Chase from the game. Having scored three runs to break a 3–3 tie, and with two outs and a man on first base, the Yankees mashers, with the heart of the order coming up, were looking to score some more. Entering the game, at that point in the fourth inning for the Senators, under the imposed alias, was actually Alejandro Carrasquel.

Carrasquel became Venezuela's first major leaguer with his entrance into the game, and he retired Joe DiMaggio on a ground out to prevent further damage. The next two batters the reliever faced, in the following inning, were Lou Gehrig and Bill Dickey; Carrasquel retired both. Carrasquel's first three batters faced in the big leagues were future Hall of Famers, an act few pitchers have ever followed.

The Venezuelan pitcher held the Yankees in check, on five hits and one run, for the remainder of the game. Gehrig, playing in consecutive game 2,126, was the only New York player not to hit safely in the visitors' 7–4 win.

MAY 3. As a reliever, Alex Carrasquel picked up his first win and the first by a South American pitcher in the major leagues. The historic victory occurred over the St. Louis Browns at Sportsman's Park. Carrasquel's Senators rallied from a six-run deficit, scoring seven runs over the final three innings, to pull out an 11–10 road triumph. Hurling a scoreless eighth and ninth innings, Carrasquel secured the special win.

MAY 14. Still pitching under the name Alex Alexandra, Alex Carrasquel of the Washington Senators, in his first major league start, battled Lefty Grove of the Boston Red Sox for 12 innings at Griffith Stadium before succumbing, 5–4, in a complete game effort. Locked in a 2–2 pitching duel through 11 innings, Carrasquel was reached for three runs in the final frame, while Grove surrendered two, as both pitchers finally tired.

The 39-year-old Grove, considered by many to be baseball's greatest left-handed pitcher, received bullpen help in the bottom of the 12th. Before Grove was relieved, he had surrendered nine hits to the Senators, including a single to Carrasquel, the first hit recorded by a Venezuelan player in the major leagues.

MAY 18. The first walkoff home run by a Hispanic player in the major leagues was hardly a leisurely trot around the bases. Trailing by one run in the bottom of the ninth inning, and down to their last out with a man on base, Bobby Estalella stepped to the plate for the Washington Senators. The rookie outfielder drove one deep off the right-center field Griffith Stadium scoreboard and raced completely around the bases, reaching home plate in a head-first slide, ahead of the relayed throw from the outfield. The two-out, two-run, inside-the-park home run turned the Nationals into electrified 3–2 winners over the Detroit Tigers.

Pitching the full nine innings, starter Alex Carrasquel opportunely benefitted from the historic, game-winning hit.

MAY 30. Trying to help his own cause, Washington pitcher Alex Carrasquel homered against the Philadelphia Athletics in the first game of a doubleheader at Griffith Stadium. It was the only run allowed, however, by the A's Nels Potter, who beat Carrasquel, 3–1. But the lost cause for the Senators became a triumphant cause for Venezuela, which could now commemorate its initial major league home run.

More importantly, Carrasquel's exploits were now recognized under his proper surname. Under the archaic reasoning of the times, Carrasquel, since his debut in April, had been pitching under the last name of "Alexandra," to more easily appeal to the ears of North American fans.

But after recent fine performances, Senators owner Clark Griffith stepped in and ended the name charade, announcing to the press, "when a fellow comes that far, I think it's no more than right that he get all the credit that's coming to him under his own name."[18]

JUNE 8. Héctor Espino was born in Chihuahua, Mexico. It was written about the man who would develop into Mexico's most revered slugger that he had "wrists like the barrels of baseball bats and a body like a 5'11" vending machine."[19]

JULY 26. Honoring its long established baseball history, Cuba took a cue from Cooperstown and established its own Hall of Fame in Havana. Ten Deadball and Liveball Era players were selected for inaugural enshrinement, including future National Baseball Hall of Fame inductees José Méndez and Cristóbal Torriente.

AUGUST 31. Ramón Arano was born in Veracruz, Mexico. Immortalized as Mexico's winningest pitcher, Arano's victory totals from the mound rank among the highest recorded by any Latin American hurler.

1940

APRIL 25. Gilberto Torres stepped onto a big league mound for the first time and pitched 1⅓ innings for the Washington Senators against the Philadelphia Athletics at Griffith Stadium. The apparently meager accomplishment engraved the "Torres" surname into major league patrimonial history. His father, Ricardo Torres, had performed as a catcher/first baseman for the same Senators from 1920 to 1922. Gilberto's relief appearance installed the pair as the major leagues' first Hispanic father-son players.

Relieving the Cuban-born Torres from his slab debut in the eighth inning was Alex Carrasquel, who earned a win when the Nationals erupted for six runs in their last at-bat to beat the Athletics, 7–6.

NOVEMBER 23. Luis Tiant, Jr. was born in Havana, Cuba. The only son of a celebrated Cuban Winter League pitcher, Tiant made an indelible mark in the major leagues as both a steadfast and entertaining pitcher.

1941

SEPTEMBER 24. Luis Castro, the 20th century's first Hispanic player, died in New York City. He was 64.

The U.S.-educated Castro was the first Hispanic to manage in North American Organized Baseball. Castro guided the Augusta Tourists of the Class C South Atlantic League in 1909.

1942

MAY 14. Atanasio Pérez was born in Camagüey, Cuba. A consistent run producer over a more than two decade-long major league career, "Tony" Pérez's productivity culminated with induction into the National Baseball Hall of Fame in 2000.

APRIL 15. On March 1, 1936, two weeks shy of his 20th birthday, Hiram Bithorn pitched commendably for the semi-pro Brooklyn Eagles in an exhibition game against the Cincinnati Reds, during the Reds' historic sojourn to San Juan. Bithorn, the Eagles' starter, was not involved in the decision in a 5–4 victory by the Eagles.

Six years removed from that day, in the seventh inning at Sportsman's Park, Bithorn took the mound for the Chicago Cubs, the first Puerto Rican player to appear in the major leagues. The 26-year-old Santurce native tossed two scoreless innings for the Cubs, who bowed to the St. Louis Cardinals, 4–2.

APRIL 16. Guadalajara-born Jesse Flores had the honor of becoming the first pitcher from Mexico to throw a pitch in the major leagues. Flores, a Chicago Cubs hurler, relieved starter Paul Erickson in the third inning at Sportsman's Park. Facing the St. Louis Cardinals, Flores was tagged with the 11–6 Cubs loss, allowing four hits and four runs (two earned) in 1⅓ innings on the mound.

Flores (0–1) appeared in only four games for the Cubs this season, after which they sold the 27-year-old to the Philadelphia Athletics.

JUNE 5. At Wrigley Field, in the second game of a doubleheader, Hiram Bithorn of the Cubs proudly carried his team's and country's colors.

Providing three innings of hitless relief, Bithorn won his first game, 4–3, in ten innings, over the Brooklyn Dodgers. The winning run was set up by Bithorn's first major league hit, a double. The mound victory and hit were the first recorded by a Puerto Rican player in the big leagues.

JULY 18. Last month, after Alex Carrasquel beat the Detroit Tigers, 3–2, in ten innings, Washington sportswriter Shirley Povich wrote, "Alex Carrasquel, tall and dark, did a handsome job of pitching for the Nats…"[20]

This day, Carrasquel's work on the mound could be described as downright beautiful, as he flung a 3–0, five-hitter over the St. Louis Browns at Griffith Stadium. The blanking of the Browns was the third win on the season for the Caracas native, who recorded the first major league shutout by a Venezuelan pitcher.

1943

APRIL 27. The first win by a Mexican pitcher in the major leagues was a doozy! The Philadelphia Athletics' Jesse Flores, in only his second major league start, tossed 15⅔ innings to defeat the Washington Senators, 2–1, at Griffith Stadium. The 28-year-old Flores permitted six hits and walked the same number of batters in the contest that reigned scoreless for 15 innings. Matching zeros with mound opponent Early Wynn through the first 13 frames, the determined pitcher toiled nearly three more innings to obtain the extraordinary decision. Flores' teammates finally broke the ice with two runs in the top of the 16th stanza against Wynn's reliever, Ray Scarborough.

In the bottom of the 16th, Flores allowed a run and required fellow pitcher Roger Wolff to obtain the 48th and final out, to preserve for him the grueling win.

Incredibly, the rookie pitcher again took on marathon mound work later in the season. On September 24, Flores hurled a *16-inning* complete game against the Chicago White Sox at Shibe Park. In that game, Flores shut out the visitors in 14 out of 16 innings, including the last ten. The game, 3–3, was called due to darkness. Among Hispanic pitchers, only Juan Marichal has pitched as long a major league game.

APRIL 28. It will be an enchanting season for the pitcher from the Island of Enchantment. Hiram Bithorn of the Chicago Cubs will win 18 games (fourth-best in the league) for his fifth-place team. Today, Bithorn threw the first of seven whitewashes on the campaign and the initial major league shutout by a Puerto Rican hurler. The 27-year-old right-hander downed the St. Louis Cardinals, 4–0. Bithorn allowed seven hits and struck out three in the Sportsman's Park suppression of the defending world champions. Of added historical note, calling the game was Cuban catcher Salvador "Chico" Hernández. The pair recorded the first big league shutout by a Hispanic battery.

JULY 23. A deft debut for Luis Olmo. The Brooklyn outfielder snared eight fly balls in his first big league start, while earning the distinction as the first Puerto Rican position player to make the major league grade. In total, 18 outfield putouts were recorded by Dodgers flychasers against the Cincinnati Reds at Crosley Field, tying a major league team record in a regulation game. In hurling the 2–0 win, Brooklyn pitcher Whit Wyatt kept the Reds batters in the park and off the scoreboard. Olmo drove home a run in the ninth inning with his second major league hit—a triple.

A note of interest is that Olmo actually first wore the Dodgers uniform almost a week earlier on July 18, in Boston. But the game in which he had his first taste of playing in the major leagues was suspended because of Boston's Sunday curfew, and not completed until September.

Also in the game, Dodgers skipper Leo Durocher employed an unusual starting lineup of all right-handed hitters to combat lefty-throwing mound opponent Johnny Vander Meer. The strategy of benching several left-handed swinging regulars for an equal number of right-handed substitutes worked for "Lippy" Leo, with a big assist from Wyatt's wheeling.

JULY 26. Puerto Rican Power! In his sixth game in the major leagues, Luis Olmo provided a heavy dosage of Puerto Rican pride, hitting the first major league home run by a native player.

The Dodgers outfielder circled the bases for a second-inning, inside-the-park home run off the Pirates' Max Butcher at Forbes Field. The blow accounted for the first of ten runs the Brooks scored to win, 10–6—and also counted as the first home run struck by a Hispanic player at the once-revolutionary steel and concrete Pittsburgh ballpark.

OCTOBER 3. Extending the list of individuals whose careers consisted of only one major league game was one Antonio Ordeñana. In the uniform of the Pittsburgh Pirates, "Tony" experienced the sights and sounds of the major leagues on this day, playing in his only game at baseball's highest organized level.

The Pittsburgh franchise, destined to make headway as one of baseball's most racially forward-thinking teams, took baby steps forward in this area by placing Ordeñana as the starting shortstop in their season finale against the Philadelphia Phillies. As the leadoff hitter, the Cuban player collected two hits and drove in all of the Pirates' runs in their 11–3 defeat, the club's second of the afternoon.

Ordeñana also recorded two putouts and five assists in his role as the franchise's first Hispanic athlete.

1944

MAY 7. Jesús "Chucho" Ramos accredited himself as Venezuela's first big league position player. Playing right field for the Cincinnati Reds, Ramos collected three hits, half of his team's output against St. Louis Cardinals left-hander Max Lanier. At Sportsman's Park, Lanier defeated the Reds, 5–1.

Ramos, who had one putout in the field, played only three more games for the Reds and never played on a major league diamond again. He finished his four-game career hitting 5-for-10, with one double and one run scored.

JULY 2. The first shutout by a Mexican pitcher in the major leagues was spun by Jesse Flores. The Philadelphia Athletics right-hander limited the Detroit Tigers to four hits and three walks, while striking out six, in the second game of a doubleheader.

It took Flores all of one hour and 37 minutes to gain the 2–0 victory and a split at Shibe Park on the day.

SEPTEMBER 16. In the opening game of a doubleheader at Forbes Field, Cincinnati Reds pitcher Tomás de la Cruz defeated the Pittsburgh Pirates, 2–1, while permitting one solitary hit. De la Cruz allowed a first-inning triple to Pirates right fielder Frank Colman, following a walk, and then dispatched the home team without a hit the rest of the way. He allowed three more bases on balls in hurling the route.

A Cuban left-hander, de la Cruz was considered what became known as a "wartime player." He registered a 9–9 record as a one-year major leaguer and recorded the first one-hit game pitched by a Latin American hurler in the big leagues.

OCTOBER 5. Ramón

Jesse Flores is the only Hispanic starting pitcher to pitch into the 16th inning of *two* major league games. The Mexican right-hander finished his seven-year career with the Cleveland Indians.

Bragaña became the first pitcher to accumulate 30 wins in one Latin American league season. Pitching for Azules del Veracruz of the Mexican League, Bragaña recorded his 30th win, defeating the Nuevo Laredo Owls, 6–0, on six hits and six strikeouts. The historic win also clinched the pennant for the Blues, who were under the managerial guidance of their star pitcher during the campaign.

Bragaña's feat was made all the more remarkable by the 89-game schedule played by the 52–37 pennant-winning team. The 35-year-old pitcher appeared in 45 games and tossed four shutouts among his 27 complete games; he threw a stunning 325⅓ innings and compiled an ERA of 3.29. He was defeated eight times.

The Cuban right-hander later became the first pitcher in the league to win 200 games in a career.

1945

MAY 6. "*The Phillies use Lifebuoy,*" read an advertising sign covering a portion of Shibe Park's outfield wall. "*And they still stink!*" loudly rebutted their National League rivals (and some of the Phillies' own cynical fans).

The Phils' pestiferous play from yesterday—ten mishandled chances in the field over two games—carried over to another doubleheader today. The Philadelphia team committed seven more miscues for a two-day, four-game total of 17. Aided by the blunders, visiting Brooklyn posted its second twin-bill triumph in two days.

Ripping four hits in each of today's games (8-for-9), hot-hitting Luis Olmo drove in a pair of runs in the opener and racked up six more RBI in the nightcap. The run production went a long way in helping the Dodgers rake in the set of games, 7–5 and 10–7.

No Hispanic player prior to Olmo had collected as many hits in a single day or driven home as many runs in one big league game.

MAY 18. Luis Olmo of the Dodgers homered and tripled with the bases loaded during Brooklyn's slugfest 15–12 victory over the Chicago Cubs. Olmo, who had a 13-game hitting streak stopped the previous day, became the first Latin American player to hit a grand slam home run in the major leagues.[21] Olmo also became the first major leaguer of the 20th century to accomplish the rare two-hit, seven–RBI feat.

The Ebbets Field win was the 12th in the last 13 games for the men from Flatbush, in second-place, 2½ games behind the New York Giants.

AUGUST 28. Luis Olmo's 100th RBI of the season was a third-inning sacrifice fly for third-place Brooklyn in a 7–1 decision over the Philadelphia Phillies at Ebbets Field. The triple-digit runs-batted-in mark had not been broached by a Hispanic major league player until today.

Olmo compiled a terrific season, his second as a Dodgers regular. The 26-year-old outfielder finished the campaign with 110 RBI (third-best in the league) and hit .313 (sixth-highest in the circuit). His .818 OPS ranked in the top ten among National League hitters. And Olmo's 13 triples led the NL, a category first for a Hispanic big league player.

OCTOBER 1. Rodney Carew was born in Gatun, Canal Zone, Panama. Raised in the segregated section of Gamboa, Carew later emigrated to the United States. As a New

York City teenager, he continued playing the game he had learned in Panama and later developed into one of the premier batsmen in the big leagues.

1946

JANUARY 3. Baseball in Panama can trace its roots as far back as 1905, coinciding with the early construction of the Panama Canal. Amateur baseball thrived for the next three decades, while U.S. professionals played later in the Canal Zone League.

Another league, the Panamanian National League, came into existence with its inaugural game today at Olympic Stadium in Panama City. The Chesterfield Smokers conquered *Cervecería Nacional,* 6–4. Corporate sponsorship also impacted the league's other two clubs, General Electric and *Cadena Panameña de Radiodifusión,* or C.P.R., named after a national radio syndicate.

At the completion of the two-month schedule, the GE squad bested the competition and captured the first league title.

JANUARY 12. The inaugural game of *La Liga Venezolana de Béisbol Profesional* was played in Caracas. *Navegantes del Magallanes,* behind Alex Carrasquel, defeated *Cervecería Caracas,* 5–2. The other clubs in the Venezuela Professional League were Vargas, whose 18–12 record made them the first league champions, and club Venezuela.

Cervecería Caracas, managed by Lefty Gómez, finished second after defeating club Venezuela in a tie-breaking game.

FEBUARY 18. An international contingent of players announced their departures from their major league teams to sign with Jorge Pasquel's refinanced and reinvented Mexican circuit. Luis Olmo and Napoleón Reyes led a group of six Hispanic players who "jumped" at the higher salaries offered below the Rio Grande. Canadians Roland Gladú and Jean-Pierre Roy, and another U.S. player, Danny Gardella, also announced signings of multi-year contractual commitments to Pasquel (though Roy later backed out).

Alex Carrasquel as a member of the Washington Senators, circa 1940. Carrasquel was the second player from South America to reach the major leagues and the first pitcher (courtesy National Baseball Hall of Fame Library, Cooperstown, New York).

Later in the month, Alex Carrasquel added to the brewing fray between Organized Baseball and the renegade league, declaring his intended services to Mexican baseball by signing a three-year, Pasquel-endorsed contract.

Down the road, Gardella sued Major League Baseball over its reserve clause–ownership of players, eventually receiving an out-of-court settlement.

FEBRUARY 21. The major leagues are at full strength this spring, following several years of gradual roster depletions brought about by the Second World War. One of the stars returning to the big league stage was Joe DiMaggio. After a three-year enlistment absence, DiMaggio (1-for-4) played his first game back in Yankees pinstripes in the unlikely setting of Balboa Stadium in Panama.

The New York Yankees had traveled to the Central American country to compete in an 11-game spring exhibition series against all-star teams from the Panamanian National and Canal Zone Leagues. With the trip, the Yankees distinguished themselves as the first major league team to play in Panama. The famous North American club also distinguished itself on the field, emerging victorious 5–4 today, and losing only three games of the remaining ten to the home country clubs.

Panamanian President Enrique Adolfo Jiménez was among a crowd reported to have exceeded 10,000.

MAY 23. The North American press have dubbed Jorge Pasquel a "Mexican Raider." Pasquel's "raids" reached their pillaging peak today, when three prominent members of the St Louis Cardinals—Max Lanier, Lou Klein and Fred Martin—fled for Mexico and the "fabulous sums" offered by the Mexican magnate.

The south of the border circuit, whose ballparks are small, did not draw enough people and generate enough revenues to offset the high salaries of Pasquel's recruits. The following year, the imported players were forced to take pay cuts in an effort to stem the flow of red ink throughout the league.

At a time when the pendulum of player control swung sharply and heavily on the side of the baseball owners, Pasquel's fearless challenge to the monopolistic major leagues imprinted the first small steps of advancement in a labor movement that eventually expanded by giant leaps for future generations of major leaguers.

OCTOBER 26. The first million-dollar baseball stadium in Latin America opened in Havana. With a seating capacity of 35,000, *Gran* Stadium *del Cerro de la Habana* played inaugural host to the Almendares Alacranes and Cienfuegos Elefantes on Opening Day of the Cuban Winter League season. The Scorpions, managed by Adolfo Luque, defeated the Elephants, managed by Martín Dihigo, 9–1.

Expanded to seat over 50,000 people, Gran Stadium was expropriated and renamed Estadio Latinoamericano following the 1959 Cuban Revolution, which systematically wiped away the existence of the long-abiding Cuban Winter League and many of its great players.

1947

MARCH 1. The New York Yankees again set a hemispheric precedent, this time with a visit to South America to promote the game at which they are internationally known to excel.

At Estadio Cervecería Caracas, the Yankees rung in the first game by a major league team on Venezuelan soil. The Bronx Bombers were defeated, 4–3, by club Vargas, which scored twice in the bottom of the ninth inning. Negro leagues pitcher Gentry Jessup was the winner in relief for Vargas.

The Yankees rebounded with victories against Magallanes, 5–4, and a team of Venezuelan All-Stars, 9–2, over the next two days.

The Brooklyn Dodgers arrived in Caracas immediately thereafter and squared off against the Yankees for three games. Following those games, the two big league teams flew to Havana for more exhibition sparring against Cuban teams.

SEPTEMBER 24. In the tenth Negro League World Series, Rafael "Ray" Noble of the New York Cubans hit the first home run by a Hispanic player.

In the Game 4 match between the Negro American League champion Cleveland Buckeyes and the Negro National League pennant-winning Cubans, Noble's circuit clout, which came with bases loaded, broke open a close game and propelled the Cubans to a 9–4 victory. Noble's sixth-inning grand slam was belted against Chet Brewer. Dave Barnhill was the starter and winner for New York.

SEPTEMBER 27. For the season, pitching teammates Patricio "Pat" Scantlebury and Luis Tiant, Sr. of the New York Cubans tied for the third-most victories in the Negro National League. Today, the southpaw hurlers combined to defeat the Cleveland Buckeyes, 6–5, in the sixth and deciding game of the Negro League World Series. At League Park, the Panamanian-born Scantlebury picked up the win in relief of the 41-year-old Tiant, who posted an undefeated record of 10–0 on the campaign.

As their team nickname implied, the Cubans, comprised of mostly Hispanic players, defeated Quincy Trouppe's Cleveland squad four games to one in the Series, with one tie. The Cubans were managed by José María Fernández and owned by New York impresario Alex Pompez.

In about a decade, the Negro leagues—where many great Hispanic ballplayers displayed their baseball prowess—will disband, an ironic casualty of the integration of the major leagues.

1948

APRIL 12. Representatives from the winter leagues of Cuba, Panama and Puerto Rico signed an agreement, in Havana, forming *La Confederación de Baseball Profesional del Caribe*. A fourth country, Venezuela, soon joined, and the four nations will lay the groundwork for establishing the Caribbean Series.

The Caribbean Professional Baseball Federation will act independently, as do all of the winter leagues, under the auspices of North American Organized Baseball.

AUGUST 24. The Negro leagues equivalent of major league baseball's All-Star Game became known as the East-West Game. In the 21st game between the elite players of the Negro American League and the Negro National League, Luis "Canena" Márquez became the first Hispanic player to hit a home run in the exhibition classic.

At Yankee Stadium, Márquez, a Homestead Grays outfielder and Puerto Rican native, connected for a two-run poke against Panamanian and Cleveland Buckeyes pitcher Vibert

Clarke, in the bottom of the third inning. Clarke permitted another run and was the losing pitcher in the 6–1 East victory, in front of 17,928 fans.

1949

FEBRUARY 20. A new Latin American baseball championship tournament was realized with the inauguration of the first *Serie del Caribe* held in Havana, Cuba. The double round robin competition featured championship teams from four Caribbean basin winter league countries: Cuba, Panama, Puerto Rico and Venezuela.

Pat Scantlebury recorded the first win in Caribbean Series history, a 13–9 victory over the Mayagüez Indios. The Canal Zone native, pitching for the Spur Cola Colonites, benefited from strong run support in throwing a 16-hit, complete game victory.

On the receiving end of Scantlebury's pitches was catcher Leon Kellman, who was also the team's manager. Playing shortstop was the tournament's other playing manager, Mayagüez skipper Artie Wilson.

In the nightcap of two games played on this date at Gran Stadium, Dalmiro Finol of Cervecería Caracas slugged the initial Caribbean Series home run. The Venezuelan's blast accounted for the only run of the contest for his team, under the managerial tutelage of José Antonio Casanova. The Caracas team was embarrassed, 16–1, by the Cuban representative, Almendares Scorpions. Conrado "Connie" Marrero cruised to the four-hit win.

FEBRUARY 21. José Bracho's arm and bat carried the Cervecería Caracas team to a 4–2 victory on the second day of the Caribbean Series. The 20-year-old right-hander tossed a six-hitter, defeating Panama's Spur Cola club, earning the young pitcher the initial win by a Venezuelan pitcher in the championship tournament. Bracho stroked two hits and drove in two runs in greatly helping his own cause.

FEBRUARY 25. Prior to the games played on this last day of first Caribbean Series, the Almendares Scorpions had already clinched the first tournament championship. Providing some historic icing on the awaiting championship cake, star third baseman Héctor Rodríguez became the first Cuban player to hit a home run in the Games, belting a solo shot against compatriot Leonardo Goicoechea, pitching for Spur Cola. The long ball was one of three hits collected by Rodríguez, as his squad went on to a 5–2 win and an undefeated 6–0 Series record.

Winner of three games (one in relief) during the international tussle, Almendares left-hander Agapito Mayor was awarded the first MVP trophy. The inaugural Caribbean Series winning manager was Almendares field general Fermín Guerra.

APRIL 19. At Sportsman's Park, Saturnino Orestes "Minnie" Miñoso made his major league debut with the Cleveland Indians. Miñoso walked as a pinch-hitter for reliever

Opposite: **The 1947 New York Cubans, owned by Alejandro Pompez, were Negro Leagues champions. Standing left to right: trainer Pedro Ulacia, Homero Ariosa, Pat Scantlebury, Lorenzo Cabrera, Rafael Noble, José María Fernández, manager, Pedro Díaz, Barney Morris, Claro Duany. Middle row: Lou Louden, Minnie Miñoso, Pedro Pagés, Martin Crue, Dave Barnhill, Silvio García. Front row: Lino Dinoso, Horacio Martínez, José "Pantalones" Santiago, Cleveland Clark, James "Pee Wee" Jenkins, Luis Tiant, Sr.**

Mike García (pitching in his second major league game). Miñoso was left stranded as the Indians failed to muster much offense in a 5–1 defeat suffered at the hands of St. Louis Browns pitcher Ned Garver. The great Bob Feller absorbed the Opening Day loss.

Winning three games in three appearances, Agapito Mayor of the Almendares Scorpions was named the first MVP of the Caribbean Series in 1949. The three victories stand as a mound record for one Caribbean Classic.

Cleveland's first Hispanic ballplayer went on, over the course of 17 seasons, to play in five decades in the major leagues, appearing in three games in 1976 and two games in 1980.

Years after his retirement, performance analysis involving new statistics helped peel back the layers of what evolved into a truly excellent career for the Cuban player. Miñoso reaped a lifetime OPS+ of 130, one of only five 20th century Hispanic players to reach the 130 level. OPS+ measures the on-base and slugging percentages of a player relative to the run-scoring environment in which he played. The league average rank is 100, with 130 meaning 30 percent better than an average player.

JULY 17. In June, Luis Olmo returned to Brooklyn following his reinstatement by the commissioner's office, as part of Major League Baseball's sweeping pardon for all players who had left its ranks for more pay to play in the ineffectual Mexican League.

Olmo played 38 games this season for the Dodgers, the most memorable occurring today at Ebbets Field. Olmo led off the bottom of ninth inning of a tie game against the Chicago Cubs, blasting a drive into the lower left-field stands to give the Dodgers a 4–3 win. The first fence-clearing, walkoff home run by a Hispanic player in the major leagues kept Burt Shotton's team 1½ games up in the National League standings on the second-place St. Louis Cardinals.

OCTOBER 7. The "Shot Heard 'Round the Latin American World." Luis Olmo of the Brooklyn Dodgers tagged Joe Page of the New York Yankees for a home run in Game 3 of the Fall Classic at Ebbets Field, becoming the first Hispanic player to sock a home run in a World Series game. With the game's opening pitch, Olmo, playing left field, had become the first Hispanic position player to start a World Series game.

The Yankees and Page, ahead 4–1 at the time, survived Olmo's ninth-inning belt and a solo home run that followed by Roy Campanella, to come out on top, 4–3.

On Christmas Eve, Olmo, 30, will be dealt to Boston for two outfielders and cash. Luis Rodríguez Olmo will play in only 90 more games with Boston over the next two seasons to complete a nationally inspiring six-season major league career.

1950

FEBRUARY 23. The Caribbean Series reconvened as scheduled in San Juan, Puerto Rico. Native pitcher Luis Arroyo had won 11 games and hurled 148 innings for the Ponce Leones in the just-concluded Puerto Rican Winter League campaign. Arroyo was added to the roster of the league champion Caguas Criollos as a supplemental pitcher for the tournament. On this third day of competition, Arroyo became the first Puerto Rican pitcher to win a Caribbean Series game, in most noteworthy fashion. Entering the bottom of the ninth inning, Arroyo was on the short end of 1–0 pitchers' duel against Magallanes Navigators hurler Terris McDuffie. With two outs and a man on base, Wilmer Fields pinch-hit for Arroyo. The Negro League great connected for a game-winning, two-run home run (on a 1–2 pitch) off McDuffie. The blast sent the home crowd at Sixto Escobar Stadium into delirious celebration.

The next day, Fields pitched a complete game, 6–1 triumph over Cuban representative Almendares.

FEBRUARY 27. Led by a roster of mostly North American players, the Carta Vieja Yankees won for Panama its first Caribbean Series championship. The mostly segregated team capped its Panamanian League title with an upset win over the Caguas Criollos, 9–3, in a winner-take-all game held at jam-packed Sixto Escobar Stadium.

The tie-breaking contest was forced by both teams' superior 4–2 records after the final day of play. The Yankees defeated Caguas in all three games they played against each other. Carta Vieja outfielder Joe Tuminelli was named MVP. He smacked two home runs and knocked in seven runs in the seven-day competition. Wayne Blackburn was Carta Vieja's winning manager.

On the Caguas roster, Luis Olmo became the first Hispanic player to participate in both a World Series and Caribbean Series. Al Gionfriddo, an outfielder with Almendares last year, was the first player to take part in both championship classics.

JUNE 25. It was bound to be the Washington Senators, the franchise that had employed the most Hispanic players over the years, who offered two Hispanic teammates a doubleheader starting assignment for the first time in the major leagues. Senators Connie Marrero and Sandalio "Sandy" Consuegra handled a two-tilt engagement against the Indians at Cleveland Stadium.

The Cuban duo earn a split against the Indians. In the lidlifter, Marrero was felled, 7–6. Marrero yielded four home runs, including a grand slam to Al Rosen in the eighth inning. The Indians' Jesse Flores preserved an Early Wynn victory by retiring Mickey Vernon on a foul pop-up with the tying run on third base in the ninth inning.

Consuegra won the second game, 5–3, with ninth-inning help from Mickey Harris.

1951

FEBRUARY 16. An overflow crowd of 16,713 were on hand at Sixto Escobar Stadium to watch the seventh and deciding game of the 1950–1951 Puerto Rican Winter League

Championship Series, between the Santurce Cangrejeros [Crabbers] and Caguas Criollos.

The score was knotted at 2–2, heading into the bottom of the ninth inning. Criollos hurler Mike Clark was on the mound in relief and had retired dangerous hitters Bob Thurman and Willard Brown to open the inning. Then Dominican José "Pepe Lucas" St. Clair stepped to the plate and—to the maddening delight of Santurce fans—deposited an offering from Clark over the left center field wall for a walkoff home run.

The first such walk-off hit to deliver a Latin American winter league championship was christened "*el Pepelucazo*"—derivative of the player's nickname and the Spanish word for long drive (*batazo*). St. Clair had struck out the day before, ending the sixth game of the Series.

Unjustly, the man who thrillingly provided the first island championship for the Santurce franchise was left off the Crabbers' Caribbean Series roster.

FEBRUARY 25. The Santurce Crabbers added Luis Olmo as a roster supplement to their team prior to traveling to Caracas, Venezuela, to play in the third Caribbean Series. Olmo smacked the first home run by a Puerto Rican player in tournament history in Santurce's encounter versus the Habana Leones today.

The solo shot came in a 4–3 defeat against the slings of Lions hurler Adrián Zabala. It was, however, Santurce's only defeat of the Series.

FEBRUARY 26. Santurce's Luis Olmo connected for two home runs and Rubén Gómez pitched seven strong innings against the Spur Cola Colonites, leading the Crabbers to a 12–1 victory (mercy-rule shortened). Aided by two victories from roster add-on José "Pantalones" Santiago, the Crabbers captured their and Puerto Rico's first Caribbean Series championship.

Olmo, the first player to hit two home runs in a Caribbean Series game, was named tournament MVP, the first player from Puerto Rico to receive the award.

APRIL 17. In the first "Opening Night" game in the American League's 50-year history, and for the first time in the same half-century period that Connie Mack was not managing the Philadelphia Athletics, another "Connie"—Marrero—defeated the Mack-less Athletics, 6–1, at Griffith Stadium.

Marrero, a Washington Senators hurler whose age matched the 40-degree game-time temperature, pitched a seven-hitter, losing his shutout in the ninth inning. And while Cornelius McGillicuddy may not have been in the dugout, the 88-year-old magnate was seated in the stands, along with 8,284 other chilly fans. Mack watched as new Athletics skipper Jimmy Dykes suffered his first defeat to the first Hispanic pitcher to start an American League season-opening game.

JUNE 20. Facing five different pitchers, Cleveland's Bobby Ávila cracked three round-trippers, including an inside-the-parker, and lined

Luis Olmo achieved various initial Hispanic slugging deeds as an outfielder for the Brooklyn Dodgers, not the least of which was hitting the first home run by a Hispanic player in the World Series.

two more hits, amassing 15 total bases in Cleveland's 14–8 pasting of the Red Sox at Fenway Park. The Indians second baseman became forever listed as the first Hispanic player to hit three home runs in a major league game. Avila also earned esteemed ethnic recognition as the first player from Mexico to collect five hits in a big league game.

Ávila, who had hit only two home runs previously in his professional career in the U.S., begun in 1948, became only the third player in the four-decade history of Fenway Park to crash three home runs in one game.

JULY 10. The major league exploits of Chico Carrasquel were posted daily on the front pages of various newspapers in Venezuela. This day's proceedings at Briggs Stadium in Detroit, attended by 52,075 fans, merited page one headlines. The Caracas-born Carrasquel gained distinction as the first Latin American player to appear in the major league All-Star Game.

The second-year, Chicago White Sox player started at shortstop for the American League in its losing effort to the National League, 8–3. Carrasquel, dubbed the new "Mr. Shortstop" by *Colliers*, and soon to be featured as "King of the Shortstops" in an upcoming *Look* article, singled to center field in his first at-bat. The national press received by Carrasquel was well deserved. Beginning this season, the White Sox shortstop will lead the league in defensive WAR for three of the next four years.

Carrasquel was pinch-hit for in the sixth inning by Chicago teammate Minnie Miñoso. Earning the consequential side note of becoming the first Cuban player to compete in the Midsummer Classic, Miñoso finished the game playing right field.

AUGUST 22. Bobby Ávila's first hit in this extra-inning game proved rousingly significant. Ávila whacked a home run in the bottom of the 14th inning off Washington Senators hurler Sandy Consuegra to carry the Cleveland Indians to a 6–5 victory. The two-out, solo smash increased the first-place Indians' lead over the New York Yankees to two games and also crowned Ávila, who had been 0-for-5 with an error, as the first Mexican big league player to hit a walk-off four-bagger.

DECEMBER 30. The first major league player from Puerto Rico died in Ciudad Victoria, Mexico, at the young age of 35. Hiram Bithorn was fatally shot in the stomach the prior evening by a policeman in an altercation stemming from an alleged improper automobile registration. The policeman was indicted on January 10 for homicide and later convicted and sentenced to eight years in prison for the fatal shooting.

The former Chicago Cubs pitcher was buried in his homeland. *The Sporting News* reported:

Hiram Bithorn was the first Puerto Rican player to make it to the major leagues. The former San Juan Senadores pitcher's life was tragically cut short at the age of 35.

"During the day, 6,000 persons, according to police estimates, paraded past the bier in Sixto Escobar Stadium. Thousands also attended the interment in a San Juan cemetery."[22]

1952

SEPTEMBER 2. Mike Fornieles of the Washington Senators became the first Hispanic pitcher to toss a one-hitter in his major league debut. The 20-year-old right-hander shut out the Kansas City Athletics, 5–0, in the nightcap of a Griffith Stadium twi-night doubleheader.

Fornieles became only the second American League hurler (Addie Joss, 1902) to accomplish such a feat. Fornieles was reached for a second-inning single by Athletics catcher Joe Astroth. Issuing five walks over the first three innings, the Cuban hurler permitted only one base runner (a walk) over the last six stanzas.

The first game was also won by the Nats, 3–2, in ten innings.

1953

FEBRUARY 20. Rubén Gómez became the first Hispanic pitcher to hit a home run in the Caribbean Series. On the inaugural day of the competition at Havana's Gran Stadium, the Santurce Crabbers right-hander homered and singled as part of a 14-hit attack against the Chesterfield Smokers. Gómez also hurled the complete game victory (called after seven innings due to time limit), 13–6.

Vic Power also went deep for the Crabbers, as Pedrín Zorilla's club made a firm opening day statement in what turned into a dominant six-day showing by the Puerto Rican Winter League champions.

FEBRUARY 22. On the third day of the Caribbean Series, the Santurce Crabbers staged a shocking, two-out, bottom-of-the-ninth-inning comeback to defeat the Habana Lions, 6–5. Down to their last out and trailing by two runs with no one on base, the Crabbers strung together five consecutive hits against two Lions pitchers to plate three runs for the victory. Rubén Gómez, who had entered the game earlier as a pinch-runner and stayed in to play the outfield, capped the stunning rally by delivering the first walk-off hit (single) by a Hispanic player in Caribbean Series history.

The Habana club had won 11 consecutive Caribbean Series contests before this one.

FEBRUARY 24. On the fifth day of the fifth Caribbean Series, outfielder Bobby Prescott of the Chesterfield Smokers became the first Panamanian player to connect for a home run in the international competition.

Prescott's mates supplemented his long-ball hitting with more than adequate fielding and pitching, as the Smokers topped Habana, 5–3. The loss knocked the host Lions out of title consideration and elevated the undefeated Santurce Crabbers to their second Caribbean Series title.

Santurce's Willard Brown, with four home runs and 13 RBI in the six games, was the easy choice to honor with the Most Valuable Player hardware.

MAY 2. In 1949, Carlos Bernier had become the first Puerto Rican to bat in the Caribbean Series. On this day, Bernier, center fielder of the Pittsburgh Pirates, ripped three triples in a 12–4 Bucs flogging of the Cincinnati Reds at Forbes Field. The three-baggers, in successive trips to the plate, were part of a four-hit day for the 26-year-old rookie from Juana Diaz, Puerto Rico, whose residents could now also boast of their lasting connection to the first Hispanic player to record three triples in one major league game.

1954

FEBRUARY 20. Connie Marrero threw the first shutout by a Hispanic pitcher in the Caribbean Series. At Sixto Escobar Stadium in San Juan, the Almendares right-hander subdued the Carta Vieja Yankees on five hits and two walks. His Scorpions teammates pounded Humberto Robinson and three other pitchers for 13 runs on 16 hits.

Almendares and Carta Vieja, with records of 3–3, finished one game behind the Caguas Criollos, whose championship-winning efforts made the host country fans very proud. So did the selection of Criollos outfielder Manuel "Jungle Jim" Rivera as Series MVP.

JULY 13. The first appearance by a Hispanic pitcher in the major league All-Star Game was a forgettable one. As the first pitcher called out of the bullpen by American League manager Casey Stengel, Sandy Consuegra was tagged for five hits and five runs in only one-third of an inning. Though the White Sox pitcher surrendered a four-run American League lead, the Junior Circuit battled back to take an 11–9 decision in front of 69,751 fans at Cleveland Stadium. Indians third baseman Al Rosen cranked two home runs and drove home five runs in the slugfest.

Consuegra was one of four Hispanic players—all from the American League—to appear in the game. Another was second baseman Bobby Ávila, who validated the appointment as Mexico's first big league All-Star with a 3-for-3, two–RBI showing at the plate. Ávila's other Hispanic teammates were Minnie Miñoso and Chico Carrasquel. The trio went 6-for-12 with two RBI and three runs scored.

Today's showing notwithstanding, pitcher Consuegra performed exceptionally for his 94-win White Sox in 1954. The right-hander, working as a starter and reliever, chalked up a 16–3 record with a 2.69 ERA in 39 games for the third-place Chicago club.

JULY 30. Rubén Gómez led the first-place New York Giants to victory over the Cincinnati Reds with his arm and bat. At the Polo Grounds, Gómez pitched a five-hit, 6–1 triumph and slugged a two-run home run. The home run was the first long ball hit by the second-year major league hurler and the first to be socked by a Puerto Rican pitcher at the major league level.

With the victory, the 64–37 Giants grabbed a three-game advantage over archrival Brooklyn in the National League.

AUGUST 27. As did many traveling members of American League ball clubs this season, Minnie Miñoso and several of his Chicago White Sox teammates spent an enjoy-

At Comiskey Park, shortstop Chico Carrasquel (with bat) and second baseman Bobby Ávila strike a friendly pose. In 1956, with the Cleveland Indians, the pair formed the first Hispanic keystone combination in the major leagues.

able Friday evening in Philadelphia. Not at any cultural event or tourist location, but at Connie Mack Stadium against the terrible Philadelphia Athletics. Miñoso lined two triples and drove in four runs in the White Sox' 11–0 drubbing of the home team.

Miñoso led the league in triples (18) for the second time in his career and also paced the circuit in total bases (304)—a first for a Hispanic big league player.

Hitting .320 for the campaign, the outstanding player finished second in the loop in batting, runs scored, doubles, stolen bases, on-base percentage and slugging percentage. Miñoso's 8.2 WAR topped all American League players. WAR includes a player's contributions in batting, base running and fielding, and adjusts for differences in positional difficulty, scoring environment and home ballpark.

SEPTEMBER 26. Earlier in the season, there had been talk about Bobby Ávila of the now–American League champion Cleveland Indians possibly hitting .400. But a jammed finger hampered his swing in May and silenced future dialogue on the subject. The finger injury might have cost the 30-year-old an even more sensational season. But in the season's final game today, Ávila hit a home run in two at-bats and captured the league batting title with a .341 mark—the first Hispanic to win a major league hitting crown. The last player to hit .400, Ted Williams, finished with a .345 mark, but did not qualify for the title because he fell 14 at-bats short of the 400 required, excluding bases on balls.

Cleveland, already with a new American League season record for wins with 111, lost at home in 13 innings, 8–7, to the Detroit Tigers.

OCTOBER 1. Two Hispanic surnames rang out from the public address system as starting pitchers for a World Series game for the first time.

At Cleveland Stadium, the New York Giants' Rubén Gómez defeated Cleveland Indians 19-game winner Mike García, 6–2. Disappointing the majority of the 71,555 Game 3 fans on hand, Gómez hurled 7⅓ innings of four-hit baseball, with Hoyt Wilhelm recording the final five outs. The powerful Indians suffered the third of four consecutive losses, on the way to being humiliatingly swept from the Fall Classic limelight over just a four-day period.

Notching the win, Gómez became the first Latin American pitcher to start a World Series contest and the first pitcher to win both a World Series and Caribbean Series game.

1955

FEBRUARY 10. Three-year-old University Stadium, in Caracas, hosted its first Caribbean Series. Few of the 36,000 jamming the modern facility went home disappointed, after watching Maracaibo native José "Carrao" Bracho shut out the Carta Vieja Yankees, 9–0, in the nightcap of the inaugural day festivities. Pitching for the Magallanes Navigators, Bracho struck out seven and walked no one during his well-supported gem, which was the first shutout hurled by a Venezuelan pitcher in Caribbean Series competition.

Magallanes, with a 4–2 record, gave the Willie Mays–led Santurce Crabbers a run for their money during the tournament, but finished one game behind the 5–1 champion Crabbers.

MARCH 7. Inexhaustible industrialist. Misfiring mogul. Tumultuous tycoon. In life, Don Jorge Pasquel was all of these and then some.

Pasquel rocked the baseball establishment like few before or since. In 1946, his "player plundering" helped pave the way for major league players of the era to reap greater benefits from grudging contract concessions gained from their repressive bosses. In the wake of Pasquel's "border war" and an attempted (but failed) unionization of players during that same summer, MLB agreed to sweeping changes in the standard players' contract. In August of that year, no longer able to ignore the changing labor front, the owners agreed to a $5,000 minimum salary, establishment of a players' pension fund, weekly spring training stipends of $25 per player and an extension of post-season barnstorming exhibitions to 30 days from ten. In Latin American baseball, Pasquel's actions also residually spawned the Caribbean Professional Baseball Federation in 1948, a solidarization between the Latin American Winter Leagues, which birthed the Caribbean Series.

Jorge Pasquel died on this day, at the age of 47, when the private jet that carried him and six others crashed into the mountains of San Luis Potosí, Mexico. There were no survivors.

APRIL 16. Pedro Cepeda was nicknamed "the Bull" in his youth because of his brawny build. But working in unsanitary conditions, as Cepeda did later in life, can cause the strongest of physical constitutions to erode. Cepeda died from complications of

Jorge Pasquel (sunglasses) and brother Bernardo at Parque Delta in Mexico City during the 1940s. The flamboyant Jorge, as head of the Mexican League, challenged major league baseball's reserve clause and traditional player contracts.

malaria on this date, at the age of 50. Cepeda and son Orlando, along with Felipe Alou and offspring Moises, formed the two greatest father-son duos in Latin American baseball history.

APRIL 20. Bases loaded. Bottom of the ninth inning. Tying run at the plate. What a setting for one's initial major league appearance.

Humberto Robinson of the Milwaukee Braves found himself in this spot when he relieved Lew Burdette at Wrigley Field. Making a memorable splash as the first Panamanian to reach the big leagues, Robinson struck out the Cubs' Hank Sauer and preserved a 9–5, early-season Milwaukee victory.

Two months shy of his 25th birthday, Robinson had earned his spot with the Braves by allowing only one hit in 12 shutout innings in spring training with the big club.

APRIL 23. At first glance at the final score, it appeared as if the Chicago White Sox and Kansas City Athletics had played a softball game instead of the scheduled hardball contest. But the 29–6 final outcome at Municipal Stadium was indeed conducted with a regulation William Harridge signature-embossed American League baseball.

Of the 29 hits pelted by the White Sox in the game, five came off the bat of Chico Carrasquel. The White Sox shortstop also scored five runs, while becoming the first player from Venezuela to lash out five hits in a major league game. Minnie Miñoso scored five runs and drove home an equal number with his four hits. White Sox winning pitcher Jack Harshman smacked one of seven home runs hit by the visiting squad.

APRIL 24. Hispanics in the outfield. At Connie Mack Stadium, stationed in left to right fields: Román Mejías of Cuba, Roberto Clemente of Puerto Rico, and Mexico's Felipe Montemayor. In the uniforms of the Pittsburgh Pirates, in the first inning of the second game of a doubleheader, the three men took their positions, the first time in baseball history a major league outfield had been completely defended by Hispanic players.

The trio handled six chances flawlessly. Clemente was the only one to register a hit, and Montemayor swiped a bag. A Pennsylvania Sunday curfew stopped the second game in the eighth inning with the Pirates trailing, 2–0. It was a cold, wet and dreary day in Philadelphia, and the game had been delayed by the inclement weather. Pittsburgh lost, 3–0, when the game was finished on the team's next trip to the Quaker City in June.

The Pirates won the opener, 6–1, as Clemente and Montemayor contributed three hits and three RBI between them.

MAY 12. It took only two at-bats before Héctor López of the Kansas City Athletics showed that he could hold his own in the major leagues. At Fenway Park, López singled in the fourth inning of his initial game and became the first Panamanian native to collect a base hit at baseball's highest level.

Most of the constructive swinging in the game, however, was accomplished by the home team. The Red Sox downed the Athletics, 12–7.

MAY 14. José Dennis Martínez was born in Granada, Nicaragua. Signed as an 18-year-old amateur pitcher in Nicaragua by the Baltimore Orioles, Martínez will rise to lofty major league pitching heights and impressively win more games and toss more innings than any other Hispanic hurler.

MAY 29. Rookie Roberto Clemente slashed five hits, including three doubles, in his first five trips to the plate, in the second game of a Forbes Field doubleheader between the Pittsburgh Pirates and Philadelphia Phillies. Batting leadoff, Clemente was removed from the game after his fifth hit, in the bottom of the seventh inning, with the Pirates ahead, 8–3. One batter later, the enactment of the 7:00 p.m. Sunday curfew in Pittsburgh halted the game.

The suspended game was resumed July 8, and the Pirates buttoned down the victory, 11–3. The team therefore earned a delayed split of the two games, following the 5–2 defeat in the first contest, six weeks earlier, and Clemente officially became the first Puerto Rican player to collect five hits in a major league game.

JUNE 26. A deep, bases-empty blast by Héctor López filled the cup of national pride for Panama. In the second of two games played in Baltimore, the rookie infielder for the Kansas City Athletics deposited a fifth-inning delivery from the Orioles' Don Johnson into the cheap seats to become the first from his country to hit a home run in the big leagues.

The solo home run by López, who broke in six weeks earlier with Kansas City as the major league's first position player from Panama, put the Athletics ahead, 2–0. López enjoyed a 3-for-3 day, with three runs tallied, in Kaycee's 5–2, second-game win.

The Athletics' Alex Kellner shut out the home team in the opener, 1–0, allowing only one hit.

JULY 12. Sophomore first sacker Vic Power was on his way to hitting .319 and slugging .505 on the campaign for the Kansas City Athletics.

Despite inferior hitting statistics, Mickey Vernon was not only chosen to start at first base in the American League All-Star Game over Power, but the Washington first baseman played all 12 innings of the extravagant summer spectacle held today at County Stadium. Power was included on the squad as a reserve, and in the seventh inning, he pinch-hit for pitcher Early Wynn and popped up. The trip to the plate registered Power as the first Puerto Rican player to represent his league in baseball's star-studded, summer pageant.

The National League came out victorious, 6–5, on Stan Musial's home run.

OCTOBER 2. At Ebbets Field, the initial scoring of Game 5 of the World Series was supplied by a two-run home run by Brooklyn Dodgers left fielder Edmundo "Sandy" Amorós. The Dodgers, behind Roger Craig and Clem Labine, defeated the New York Yankees, 5–3. It was the Dodgers' third straight win at home after losing the first two games at Yankee Stadium.

The second-inning blow by Amorós was the first World Series round-tripper hit by a Cuban player.

OCTOBER 4. All of their yesterdays and all of their tomorrows arrived here today in Brooklyn, U.S.A.

Left fielder Sandy Amoros of the Brooklyn Dodgers made one of the most thrilling and crucial catches in World Series history. In the sixth inning of Game 7 of the World Series at Yankees Stadium, Amorós' Dodgers were clinging to a 2–0 lead. New York had runners on first and second with no one out. Yogi Berra sliced a ball toward the sun-drenched left field corner. After a long run and with little room to spare, Amorós reached out for a one-handed snare of the sure extra-base hit. He quickly relayed the ball back to shortstop Pee Wee Reese, who whirled a throw to Gil Hodges at first base to complete a spectacular 7–6–3 double play.

The next batter grounded out, and three innings later, with the score unchanged, the first and only world championship gloriously descended upon the storied Brooklyn franchise. Twenty-three-year-old Johnny Podres pitched the eight-hit, eternal shutout.

OCTOBER 23. Professional baseball in the Dominican Republic made its first appreciable inroads during the 1920s. For more than two decades, with the exception of one memorable year in 1937, the game was then minimized under the oppressive reign of dictator Rafael Trujillo. In the early 1950s, baseball began to flourish again within a reorganized summer league.

Opening Day festivities to commence a new era of professional baseball in the country were held today. It was fitting that the Licey Tigers, founded in 1907 as the Dominican

Sandy Amoros' pivotal Game 7 World Series catch. The victory-preserving snare enabled the Brooklyn Dodgers to attain their only world championship title in 1955.

Republic's first professional baseball team, played the first game of the Dominican Winter League.

At Ciudad Trujillo Stadium in Ciudad Trujillo (Santo Domingo), the Tigers downed Águilas Cibaeñas, 8–7. Federico "Chi-Chi" Olivo was the victor for the team affectionately know as "*El Glorioso*" to their loyal fans.

At the conclusion of the campaign, Licey finished second to the pennant-winning Escogido Leones. Estrellas Orientales, the fourth club in the loop, brought up the rear.

1956

FEBRUARY 11. At 20 years and ten months old, Pedro Ramos became the youngest pitcher to win a Caribbean Series contest. The right-hander for the Cienfuegos Elephants pitched into the ninth inning of his first Caribbean Series start to record a 9–5 win. Facing the Valencia Industrialists, Ramos took an eight-run lead into the final frame, when he apparently tired and had to be relieved.

The win gave the 2–0 Cuban team a leg up on the rest of field after two days of tournament play.

FEBRUARY 15. Jonathan "Clyde" Parris of the Chesterfield Smokers delighted the fans at Olympic Stadium in Panama City by clubbing the first grand slam home run by a Hispanic player in Caribbean Series play. The 33-year-old Panamanian slugged his historic wallop off Valencia starter Jim Pearce in the first inning of the final game of the competition, the beginning of an ignominious day for Pearce and four other Industrialist hurlers, as the Smokers hit four more long balls on the way to an 18–0 shellacking of the Venezuelans.

In the early game, Cienfuegos earned its first Caribbean Series brass ring by defeating the Caguas Criollos, 4–2. Pedro Ramos hurled the complete-game seven-hitter. Batterymate Ray Noble, who caught every inning for his club and hit .400, was named MVP.

APRIL 17. A trade last fall exchanging the Cleveland Indians' Larry Doby for two Chicago White Sox players, outfielder Jim Busby and shortstop Chico Carrasquel, affected the course of major league and Hispanic baseball history, beginning this Opening Day of the 1956 season.

Playing at Comiskey Park, the Indians were defeated by Carrasquel's former team, 2–1, as Carrasquel paired with second baseman Bobby Ávila to comprise the first Hispanic keystone combination in the big leagues. At the plate, Carrasquel and Ávila were a combined 1-for-7, with Carrasquel managing the only hit. The White Sox's Billy Pierce outdueled the Indians' Bob Lemon.

In the second inning, Ávila and Carrasquel helped turned a 4–6–3 double play.

MAY 19. With one swing of the bat, Héctor López put an end to a five-game Kansas City Athletics losing streak and made ethnic history as the first Panamanian player to hit a walkoff home run in the big leagues. At Municipal Stadium, López slammed a 1–0 pitch by Boston Red Sox right-hander Bob Porterfield over the left field fence, with one out and one man on base, to thrillingly propel the Athletics over the visitors, 5–4. "The Athletics came pouring from their dugout," wrote *Kansas City Star* sportswriter Joe

McGuff, "and gave Lopez a hero's welcome as he crossed the plate."[23] An elated Saturday afternoon crowd of 16,055 was rewarded for their diehard loyalty.

JULY 25. Roberto Clemente became the first Hispanic player to hit an inside-the-park, "ultimate grand slam" home run. Clemente drilled the home run with the bases loaded in the bottom of the ninth inning, against pitcher Jim Brosnan, to hoist the Pittsburgh Pirates over the Chicago Cubs, 9–8. The long drive to center field stayed within the expansive and high-walled outfield boundaries of Forbes Field. The second-year right fielder tacked on added flair to the game's most infrequent home run by circling the bases and sliding into home plate to score the winning run.

In what will be referred to, in later times, as a "walkoff" home run, Clemente became only the eighth player in the modern era and first Hispanic to connect for this rare type of bases-load blow (team down by three runs in its final at-bat).

JULY 27. Héctor López continued to build on his Panamanian legacy in the major leagues. The Athletics third baseman cranked out three singles and two doubles, and scored four runs, in an extra-inning slugfest with the New York Yankees at Kansas City's Municipal Stadium. Using six official at-bats, López became the first player from Panama to collect five hits in a big league game.

A pair of Kansas City errors led to the Yankees scoring an unearned run and prevailing in the game in 14 innings, 10–9. Athletics first baseman Vic Power also garnered five hits in seven at-bats.

AUGUST 31. Bobby Ávila became the first Hispanic player to smack 1,000 hits in the major leagues. The memorable hit came as a triple, in the first inning of the opening game of a doubleheader between the Cleveland Indians and Chicago White Sox at Comiskey Park. Ávila's second-place Indians beat the home team, 3–2, before dropping the nightcap, 1–0, in ten innings.

SEPTEMBER 23. The foreign country that will provide more players to major league baseball than any other by the end of the century presented its first.

Osvaldo Virgil took the field at third base for the New York Giants. The 24-year-old Virgil, originally from the Dominican Republic, went hitless in four trips to the plate during a 6–2 Giants home loss to the Philadelphia Phillies. He had two assists, one putout and one error.

SEPTEMBER 30. A week after his debut, Ozzie Virgil collected his first hit and the first big league safety by a Dominican player.

In the opening game of a doubleheader at Connie Mack Stadium, Virgil

Osvaldo Virgil took the field for the New York Giants in 1956 as the majors' first Dominican ballplayer. After being traded away by the team, Virgil eventually landed back with the relocated franchise in the mid–1960s.

singled in his second time up. Virgil had two other hits, scored once, and knocked in a run, as the Giants denied 19-game winner Robin Roberts a bid for his *seventh* straight 20-win campaign. Virgil's three hits were among 15 the visitors blistered off Roberts in the 8–3 conquest.

In the second game, a 5–2 Giants defeat, Virgil punched out two more hits, including a triple. In the season-closing doubleheader, Virgil notched five hits in eight at-bats, with two extra-base hits, two runs scored and driven in, and a stolen base.

DECEMBER 1. In October 1955, the Chicago White Sox traded Chico Carrasquel, who had led the league in fielding three times and assists once, to make room for someone the front office had appraised as being even better equipped for their shortstop position.

That "someone"—Luis Aparicio—today was named American League Rookie of the Year by the Baseball Writers' Association of America, the first such award for any Hispanic major leaguer.

Outpolling runners-up Rocky Colavito and Tito Francona, the 22-year-old Aparicio led his peers in games, innings, putouts, assists, and errors, and paced the league in stolen bases with 21. It was the first of nine consecutive seasons in which Aparicio led the league in steals.

Aparicio owns the highest career defensive WAR (31.6) among Hispanic major leaguers. Pudge Rodríguez (28.7) and Omar Vizquel (28.4) are next best.

1957

FEBRUARY 11. On the third day of competition of the ninth Caribbean Series, Pantalones Santiago of the Mayagüez Indians shut out the Marianao Tigers, 6–0, at Gran Stadium in Havana. The 28-year-old pitcher allowed only three hits, struck out eight and walked one, in handing the Tigers what will be the team's only loss of the tournament. Canena Márquez provided the most support, with a double, triple and home run. The Indians concluded the four-club challenge with a 2–4 record, three games behind the champion Marianao squad, managed by Napoleón Reyes.

After the game, Santiago was presented with a $1,000 bonus from Mayagüez owner Alfonso Márquez for authoring the shutout, which was the first by a Puerto Rican pitcher in the Caribbean Series.

FEBRUARY 14. At Gran Stadium, Winston Brown of Cerveza Balboa defeated the Caracas Lions for the second time in four days, this time hurling a three-hit shutout. Brown, a product of Bocas del Toro, Panama, had previously beaten the Lions, 2–1, in a complete-game, six-hit effort. The 4–0 win earned him not only the top pitching honors of the Caribbean Series, but also the first blanking by a Panamanian pitcher in the tournament. Brown's two victories helped his 3–3 team to a second-place finish.

APRIL 27. Playing for the team from the New York borough that became home to the Dominican diaspora of future decades, Ozzie Virgil claimed for the Dominican Republic its first major league home run. It was slugged against Robin Roberts with one on in the fourth frame at Connie Mack Stadium, where the Giants pummeled the Philadelphia Phillies, 10–2. Rubén Gómez was the complete-game winner for Virgil's team.

MAY 7. Kansas City's Vic Power ended the game today at Municipal Stadium the same exhilarating way he began it—by hitting a home run. Power's second circuit clout, with one out in the bottom of the tenth inning, powered the Athletics to an exciting 3–2 victory over the Baltimore Orioles. Power slugged the first and last pitches thrown by Orioles starter Hal Brown out of the park to extend to four games a Kansas City winning streak, and to become the first Hispanic major league player to hit a leadoff and walkoff home run in the same game.

MAY 10. Pitching for the Milwaukee Braves in his second big league game, Juan Pizarro obtained his first win. Pizarro, a blazing left-hander from Santurce, Puerto Rico, defeated the St. Louis Cardinals, 10–5, at Busch Stadium. Pizarro also achieved his first big league hit—a home run. It came at the expense of Cardinals starter and loser Sam Jones.

With his blast against Jones, Pizarro, at age 20 years and three months, became the youngest Hispanic pitcher to hit a home run in the major leagues.

JULY 3. The king is dead! Long live the king! In Havana, Adolfo Luque, the major leagues' first Hispanic star, succumbed to the effects of a heart attack suffered several weeks earlier.

In an obituary ode to Luque, sportswriter Frank Graham wrote: "He died of a heart attack. Did he? It sounds absurd. Luque's heart failed him in the clutch. It never did before. How many close ball games did he pitch? When he won, it was sometimes on his heart. When he lost, it was never because his heart missed a beat. Some enemy hitter got lucky or some idiot player behind him fumbled a ground ball or dropped a sinking liner."[24]

Luque won over 360 games in the major, minor and winter leagues. His record as a manager in Cuba and Mexico was 1,353–1,152.[25] He was elected to the Cuban Hall of Fame (1958), the Cincinnati Reds Hall of Fame (1967) and the Mexican Hall of Fame (1985). Luque also received enshrinement into the Latino Baseball Hall of Fame in 2011. *Papá Montero* was 66.

OCTOBER 5. At County Stadium, Juan Pizarro of the Milwaukee Braves pitched 1⅔ innings of relief against the New York Yankees in Game 3 of the World Series.

In the first-inning rescue roll for starter Bob Buhl, the 20-year-and-eight-month-old Pizarro entered the World Series fray as the youngest Hispanic pitcher to appear in a Fall Classic game. The hard-throwing Pizarro allowed two runs on three hits. Prior to exiting, he batted (unsuccessfully) and registered himself as the most youthful Hispanic pitcher to bat in a World Series contest.

The Yankees carried the day on the field by a 12–5 count. But the Braves and Pizarro will be heard celebrating the loudest, five days later, following their seven-game World Series triumph over the Bronx Bombers.

NOVEMBER 1. Trying to elevate its caliber of play, several Nicaraguan teams began signing players from other countries to participate in their summer league. Included were deserting players from the Mexican League. Organized Baseball nipped the "player raiding" situation in the bud by admitting the Nicaraguan Professional Baseball League into its ever-expanding orbit of Latin American winter baseball leagues.

On this date, a legitimized brand of professional baseball, under the National Association of Professional Baseball Leagues, began in Nicaragua with four national clubs inaugurating the Nicaraguan Winter League. León's *Melenudos* will capture the first league title, topping the Boer Indians in the championship series, four games to two. The Cinco Estrellas Tigers and the Oriental Sharks, based in Granada, were the other clubs that rounded out the circuit's first season of competition.

1958

FEBRUARY 8. At Sixto Escobar Stadium, Juan Pizarro of the Caguas Criollos struck out 17 Carta Vieja Yankees to earn the adulation of 13,269 spectators. On the first day of the X Caribbean Series, the young left-hander defeated Panama's squad, 8–0, allowing two lone singles. A day after turning 21, Pizarro established the record for most strikeouts by a pitcher in a Caribbean Series game. Starting with this game, in five Caribbean Series, Pizarro accrued the most career strikeouts by a pitcher in the post-season tournament with 62.

The dominant effort was the only victory in the competition for the champion pitcher of the Puerto Rican Winter League. Pizarro's team was edged out for the title by the Marianao Tigers on the last day of play.

APRIL 15. Bleak houses were left behind in Brooklyn and Manhattan as major league baseball enacted its Manifest Destiny. The first major league game played in California was won by the San Francisco Giants' Rubén Gómez, who tossed a six-hit, 8–0 shutout at Seals Stadium in San Francisco. The standing room only crowd of 23,448 witnessed the Giants right-hander defeat their still-rival and co-relocators-from-New York—the Dodgers, now of Los Angeles. Claiming the first win in a major league game played in California and the initial shutout in San Francisco Giants history, Gómez struck out six and walked six.

Orlando Cepeda, in his major league debut, hit a home run, the first Hispanic player to homer in his initial big league game.

MAY 4. Pittsburgh's Roman Mejías socked three home runs against the San Francisco Giants, pacing the Pirates to a 6–2, first-game win at Seals Stadium. Driving in four runs, the outfielder became the first Cuban player to thump three circuit clouts in a major league game.

The Giants came back to win the nightcap, 4–3, in ten innings.

JUNE 6. The Detroit Tigers' first Hispanic player took the field. In his initial game with the Motor City franchise, third baseman Ozzie Virgil stroked a double in five plate appearances, as the Tigers plastered the Senators, 11–2, at Griffith Stadium.

JUNE 17. Obtained in a mid-winter trade from the Giants, Ozzie Virgil rapped out five hits in his first home game for the Detroit Tigers. Virgil's hits ignited the Bengals' 9–2 Briggs Stadium trouncing of the Washington Senators. Pedro Ramos suffered the loss for the visitors.

With the perfect batting effort, Virgil, the first man of color to suit up for the Detroit Tigers, also became the first Dominican player to post five hits in a major league game.

JUNE 26. Hector López became the first Panamanian player to wallop three home runs in a major league game. The Kansas City Athletics' second baseman accomplished the feat today against three Washington Senators pitchers at Municipal Stadium.

The third home run for López came as a dramatic, two-run, game-winning blow in the bottom of the 12th inning, to boost the Athletics to an 8–6 win. Senators hurler Vito Valentinetti delivered the game-deciding pitch to López, who recorded five RBI on the day.

AUGUST 14. In an unpopular trade among Kansas City fans, Vic Power was sent packing to the Cleveland Indians on June 15. Cleveland was expecting to benefit from

Power's first base fielding prowess, but hardly could have been counting on the base running skills exhibited by the flashy first baseman today. Power stole home twice in the same game—the first Hispanic major league player to do so, in a feat not accomplished in the American League since 1924. Scoring the last two runs of the game for the Indians, Power first recorded the brazen deed in the eighth inning with two outs. Then, in the tenth inning, Power swiped home once again—with two outs, the bases loaded and Rocky Colavito at the plate. Power, who came into the game with only one stolen base on the season, took off from third base and beat the delivery of Detroit Tigers pitcher Frank Lary to catcher Charlie Lau.

The electric run provided the Indians with the walk-off margin of victory, 10–9, at Cleveland Stadium and were the only stolen bases for Power in the 93 games he played for the Indians.

1959

JANUARY 9. Orlando Cepeda of the San Francisco Giants was resoundingly recognized as the best new player in the National League for 1958, with today's press announcement that he had been named the league's Rookie of the Year. Cepeda amassed 309 total bases, hitting 25 home runs, 38 doubles and four triples, the first Hispanic player to lead a major league in doubles. He slugged .512 and drove in 96 runs.

Cepeda, who did not turn 21 until late in the season, became the second Rookie of the Year to be unanimously chosen (Frank Robinson, 1956) for the award and first Puerto Rican to receive the highest first-year-player honor.

AUGUST 10. Chicago's Nellie Fox and Luis Aparicio appeared on this week's cover of *Sports Illustrated*. The keystone duo were spotlighted as important cogs of their "Go-Go" White Sox team, which was battling the Cleveland Indians for supremacy in the American League. Fox and Aparicio led the circuit in putouts, assists and fielding percentage, at their respective second base and shortstop positions.

Additionally, Aparicio's loop-topping 56 stolen bases helped emphasize the "small ball" brand of play employed by the White Sox, favoring tight defense and station-to-station, strategic baseball not seen in the league for decades. The throwback style worked for the White Sox as the squad won the American League pennant by five games. Although the Al López–managed team was defeated in the World Series by the Los Angeles Dodgers, Aparicio will forever be recognized as the first Hispanic athlete to grace the cover of the United States' most prestigious sports magazine.

SEPTEMBER 9. Milwaukee Braves manager Fred Haney pinch-hit for second baseman Félix Mantilla in the seventh inning of a game against the St. Louis Cardinals at County Stadium. Bobby Ávila was called upon to play second base the following inning. Ávila's first time up came in the ninth inning, with one out, the bases loaded, and the Braves trailing, 3–1. Ávila crushed an Ernie Broglio offering deep into the left field seats for a walk-off grand slam home run, the first hit by a Hispanic player—of the fence-clearing variety—in the major leagues. The dramatic swing provided Warren Spahn with his 19th victory. It was the 35-year-old Ávila's 80th and final big league home run, in this his 11th and final major league season.

Soaking in the 1957 World Series in New York, are young Milwaukee Braves conscripts Juan Pizarro (#34), Humberto Robinson (#49) and Félix Mantilla.

SEPTEMBER 15. Camilo Pascual tossed his league-leading sixth shutout, 1–0, over the Kansas City Athletics. At Griffith Stadium, the Washington Senators ace permitted three hits, struck out nine and walked none to win his 16th game. Pitching for the 63–91, last-place Senators, Pascual closed his season with a remarkable 17–10 record and the best ERA of any starting pitcher in baseball.

Some side-notes to Pascual's extraordinary season: Early Wynn's league-leading 22 wins for the first-place Chicago White Sox team clearly outweighed Pascual's overall pitching superiority during the campaign. Wynn won the single Cy Young Award, even though Pascual was better than Wynn in every significant pitching category but victories and innings pitched. Pascual led the league in shutouts with six and complete games with 17 (the first Hispanic pitcher to pace a major league in this category). Wynn, with seven more starts than Pascual (37 to 30), could not match his Washington counterpart in complete games, shutouts, or strikeouts (179 to 185), and Wynn had an ERA more than one-half run higher than the Senators' ace (3.17 to 2.64). Wynn, with his advantage in starts, rather insignificantly topped Pascual in innings, 255⅔ to 238⅔.

Employing modern, statistic valuation measures that were not in use at the time, Pascual's pitching WAR rating was 7.8; Wynn's was 2.8. Including hitting and defense, the Cuban ranked highest in WAR in the *entire* American League with an 8.6 rating (8.0 or above is considered MVP-caliber.) The Washington pitcher's ERA+ computed to 149, compared to Wynn's 121. Pascual recorded the top Fielding Independent Pitching in all of baseball, 2.44. Wynn's FIP failed to make the top ten in the American League. FIP measures a pitcher's skill based on events directly within his sphere of influence: strikeouts, walks and home runs.

None of the National League's three 20-game winners this season bettered Pascual's ERA or recorded as many shutouts or strikeouts, though they all tossed more complete games. Neither did any of NL's three charmed circle entrants come close to matching Pascual's FIP or WAR totals.

OCTOBER 6. The Cuban Sugar Kings won the Triple-A International League championship over the Minneapolis Millers, 3–2, in the deciding seventh game. Playing at Gran Stadium in Havana, the Sugar Kings scored a run in the ninth inning on an RBI single by outfielder Daniel Morejón to pull out the thrilling victory.

The Sugar Kings became the first Latin American-based team to win a North American championship. Scoring the winning run, pitcher Raúl Sánchez, in relief of starter Ted Wieand, obtained the win. Millers reliever Billy Muffett suffered the loss. Just under 30,000 fans witnessed the Junior World Series' crowning finale.

1960

FEBRUARY 14. Camilo Pascual tossed the first one-hit shutout by a Hispanic pitcher in the Caribbean Series. The Cienfuegos pitcher threw only 88 pitches (65 strikes) as he humbled the Caguas Criollos, 4–0, at Olympic Stadium in Panama City. Pascual struck out seven and walked one. Third baseman Félix Torres gained the only hit for Caguas, a soft single over second base in the fifth inning.

For Pascual, the complete game was a record fifth in Caribbean Series play. The victory was the right-hander's sixth in only three competitions. Pascual's six wins tied Rubén Gómez and José Bracho for most victories by a Caribbean Series pitcher. The Cuban pitcher was the only undefeated hurler among the three.

FEBRUARY 14. In the second Caribbean Series in 1950, Wilmer Fields of Caguas hit the first walk-off home run—a two-run, ninth-inning game winner, to lift the Criollos over Magallanes, 2–1. Ten years later, a Hispanic player duplicated the galvanizing feat.

In the second game of the day at Olympic Stadium, Elias Osorio of the Marlboro Smokers bludgeoned a pitch from Rapiños hurler Billy Muffett for a stadium-shaking, two-run home run. The Chitré, Panama, native's game-winning blow occurred in the bottom of the 12th inning, after Rapiños had taken a 6–5 lead in the top of the frame. Reliever Robert Waltz picked up the 7–6 win for Marlboro. Muffett hurled the disappointing distance for the Venezuelan club.

FEBRUARY 15. At Olympic Stadium, the last Caribbean Series game played by Cuba and Panama in the 20th century was won by the Cienfuegos Elephants, 10–7, over the Marlboro Smokers.

Elephants pitcher Pedro Ramos, with relief help from Orlando Peña, recorded the victory, which completed an undefeated, six-game junket for Cienfuegos and crowned a Cuban team with a fifth consecutive Caribbean Series title and seventh overall in the 12-year history of the tournament. (Clubs from Puerto Rico won four, and one team from Panama captured the other title.)

The Cuban Revolution's rejection of professionalism in all sport forced the exit of Cuba and left an irreparable vacuum in the Latin American winter championship competition. The immediate result was that the Caribbean Series would not be played again until 1970. In February of that year, the Dominican Republic joined original member nations Puerto Rico and Venezuela to revive the practical means for baseball bragging rights in Latin American. Those bragging rights, however, will remain tarnished for decades without the participation of a team from Cuba.

APRIL 18. "Pascual was pitching as if he didn't trust the Senators' defense, with the exception of [catcher] Battey."[26] So wrote a reporter about Camilo Pascual's 15-strikeout performance—the most ever by a major league pitcher on Opening Day—in earning for Washington a 10–1 victory over the Boston Red Sox at Griffith Stadium.

The 26-year-old Washington pitcher with the knee-buckling curveball who at 16 was the youngest—and greatest bargain—of "Papa Joe" Cambria's stable of signees from Cuba, cruised to the three-hit win. U.S. President Dwight D. Eisenhower, one of the 28,327 fans in attendance, threw out the traditional first ball and stayed to the end.

Ted Williams spoiled the shutout with a second-inning home run; it was the 493rd lifetime circuit clout for the "Splendid Splinter," placing him even with Lou Gehrig on the all-time home run list. "Nobody in this league can compare with that pitcher,"[27] Williams said of Pascual after the game.

JULY 15. At Roosevelt Stadium in Jersey City, New Jersey, 7,155 came out to see the recently transferred Havana franchise play their first game, an 8–3 loss to the Columbus Jets. The former Cuban Sugar Kings, reigning Triple-A champions, became the Jersey City "Jerseys" in a mid-season move forced by the 18-month-old Marxist revolution in Cuba.

The Sugar Kings' Cuban-born manager, Napoleon Reyes, was labeled a traitor by the Cuban government for continuing at the helm of the team. Reyes responded by saying that he was a baseball man, and worked where he was sent.

JULY 19. San Francisco Giants pitcher Juan Marichal informed his catcher during a pre-game chat in the clubhouse, prior to making his big league debut, that he had never seen a big league game, except on television. Shortly thereafter, Marichal stepped out of the dugout as the first pitcher from the Dominican Republic to take a major league mound. The right-hander proceeded to no-hit the Philadelphia Phillies into the eighth inning, settling for a one-hitter. Marichal hurled a masterful 2–0 victory at Candlestick Park (two other runners reached base on an error and a walk). The 22-year-old, who was leading the Pacific Coast League in strikeouts when he was promoted from Tacoma two days earlier, fanned 12 Phillies batters.

Marichal became the first National League pitcher to throw a one-hitter in his initial major league game, and the second Hispanic hurler to have such a sensational opening to a career.

JULY 23. At Griffith Stadium, the Kansas City Athletics tried to mount a third-inning threat against the Senators' Pedro Ramos. Trailing 3–1, Whitey Herzog stepped to the plate after the first two batters of the frame had singled. Herzog lined back to Ramos, who whirled and threw to first baseman Julio Bécquer to double off Jerry Lumpe. Bécquer quickly fired to shortstop José Valdivielso to catch Bill Tuttle off the second base bag. The three Cubans in the field executed the first all–Hispanic triple play in major league history.

Ramos, in an unusually short outing, was relieved an inning later and did not figure in the decision. The Senators were victorious, 8–3.

AUGUST 14. In the first game of a doubleheader, Camilo Pascual of the Washington Senators poked a bases-loaded fly ball off Yankee Stadium's friendly right field foul pole to break a 1–1 tie. The sixth-inning grand slam, the first by a Hispanic major league pitcher, turned into the deciding swing of the game. The Senators and Pascual, with relief help, held on to defeat New York, 5–4.

A 6–3, 15-inning triumph in the nightcap provided the fourth-place Senators with a rare doubleheader triumph over the intimidating home team. Rudy Hernández, in relief, obtained the nightcap victory, doubly dejecting the Sunday crowd of 29,970 in the Bronx. Adding to Yankees fans' misery, Mickey Mantle was pulled from the marathon by manager Casey Stengel for failing to run out a ground ball (resulting in a double play) in the sixth inning.

SEPTEMBER 3. Armando Marsans, who with Rafael Almeida jointly formed the first pair of 20th century Cuban major league players, died in Havana, at age 72.

Marsans was the first Cuban player to record a base hit in the modern major leagues and the first player to participate in both the major leagues and Negro leagues. After stints with several big league ball clubs, including the Federal League's St. Louis Terriers,

Marsans played with the Cuban Stars East of the Eastern Colored League in 1923, owned by Alex Pompez.

SEPTEMBER 30. After appearing in only nine big league games in 1949, Minnie Miñoso was returned to the minor leagues, not to return to the majors—for good—until 1951.

Over the next ten years, Miñoso earned a not always heralded place among baseball's best players. During the 1950s, only Mickey Mantle posted a higher WAR composite in the American League than Miñoso. WAR takes into account baserunning and defense and values number of games played per season.

Today, the Chicago White Sox star's fourth hit of the game—a tenth-inning, leadoff double—put him in position to score the winning run in a 5–4 win over the Cleveland Indians at Comiskey Park.

Miñoso's second four-hit game of the season helped him accumulate the most hits in the circuit with 184 and become the first Hispanic player to lead a major league in hits.

SEPTEMBER 5. Diomedes "Guayubin" Olivo and his brother Federico were well established pitchers in their native Dominican Republic. Guayubin, a left-hander born in 1919, was nine years older than his right-handed-throwing sibling.

The elder Olivo brother, in the uniform of the Pittsburgh Pirates, appeared in his initial big league game today. At Forbes Field, the 41-year-old Diomedes tossed two scoreless innings in relief of roughed-up Pittsburgh starter Harvey Haddix, and became the oldest Hispanic player to make his major league debut.

The Milwaukee Braves, behind Bob Buhl, defeated the home team, 7–1.

OCTOBER 12. *The Sporting News* has always been the game's greatest public relations outlet. The weekly baseball publication showed that it continued to maintain its pulse on the national pastime's changing facets. A first of its kind recognition for top relief pitchers was established by the prestigious periodical this season with the aptly named Fireman of the Year award. (The creation of the award was lobbied for by longtime contributor, Jerome Holtzman.)

The first American League winner was Mike Fornieles. The 28-year-old Boston Red Sox right-hander set a then-record for most relief appearances in one season in the American League with 70 and became the first Hispanic pitcher to top a major league in saves with 14 (tied). He finished the most games on the season with 48.

St. Louis Cardinals bullpen artist Lindy McDaniel took home the inaugural prize in the senior circuit.

NOVEMBER 1. Fernando Valenzuela was born in Navojoa, Sonora, Mexico. During his celebrated destiny two decades hence, the youthful Valenzuela captivated the baseball world with curious delight, while providing exuberant thrills for a broad range of North American fans.

1961

FEBRUARY 8. The second longest continuous baseball league in the world—behind only the National League—played its final game. At Gran Stadium in Havana, the Cienfuegos Elephants defeated the Almendares Scorpions, 8–2. Elephants right-hander Pedro Ramos tossed a seven-hitter, with four strikeouts and two walks. Winning his eye-popping 16th game of the season, Ramos clinched the pennant for his club, which entered the season's finale in a dead heat with 34–31 Almendares.

Ramos led the Cuban Winter League in wins and innings pitched with 216⅔, after hurling 274 innings for the Washington Senators in the 1960 campaign. Counting spring training games, Ramos hurled well over 500 innings in an 11-month span!

FEBRUARY 16. Three countries tried to keep the spirit of the Caribbean Series alive. Panama, Puerto Rico and Venezuela (sending two teams) collided at University Stadium in Caracas in a six-day competition to determine a Latin American baseball champion. The tournament, called the "Inter-American Series," maintained the same double round robin format of the Caribbean Series. An all–Venezuelan final pitted the champions of the Central League (Valencia) and Occidental League (Rapiños), and guaranteed for the host country its first Latin American winter league tournament championship. Extended to a seventh day, today, because of a first-place tie between the 4–2 Valencia Industrialists and Rapiños Redbirds, the Industrialists captured the title in euphoric fashion. Behind a magnificent ten-inning mound effort from native star José Bracho, the Industrialists defeated the Redbirds, 2–1, on a walk-off home run in the bottom of the tenth by Valencia catcher Dick Windle! Wynn Hawkins was the Redbirds' starter and loser.

The event will reconvene again next winter, but will never fully develop as the intended successor to the Caribbean Series. After the fourth competition in February 1964, staged under the name of the "International Series," the match play will disband.

APRIL 11. The "Season of Glory" began inauspiciously for the New York Yankees as they were shut out, 6–0, on three hits, by Pedro Ramos of the Minnesota Twins. At Yankee Stadium, Opening Day of 1961 yielded for Roger Maris and Mickey Mantle no hits in seven combined at-bats. Defeating Whitey Ford, Ramos retired the last 14 batters, spoiling the managerial debut of the Yankees' Ralph Houk.

For the Twins, leadoff batter Zoilo Versalles stepped to the plate as the first player for the former iconic franchise from Washington, which relocated to Minneapolis/St. Paul this season. With the opening effort today, Ramos gained the dual distinction of hurling the final game for the Washington Senators and the initial game for the new Minnesota Twins franchise.

In ceremonial attendance at the first Opening Day shutout tossed by a Hispanic major league pitcher were the "First Ladies" of baseball: Mrs. Babe Ruth, Mrs. Lou Gehrig, and Mrs. John McGraw. A small crowd of 14,607 was held down by the day's cold weather.

APRIL 11. The Los Angeles Angels fashioned a successful American League debut, defeating the Baltimore Orioles, 7–2, at Memorial Stadium. The Angels' Julio Bécquer played the last three innings at first base as a defensive replacement for 36-year-old Ted Kluszewski.

Bécquer did not bat in the game, but made the under-the-radar posting as the first Hispanic player for the expansion California franchise.

APRIL 16. The old Washington Senators' friendly history with Hispanic ballplayers continued after the team's move from the nation's capital to Minnesota. A new Washington Senators team was born this season as part of the American League's expansion. The resurrected District of Columbia franchise counted but one Hispanic player on its Opening

Day roster. That player, Rudy Hernández, pitched one inning out of the bullpen, allowing one hit, in the Senators' 3–2 home loss to the Cleveland Indians today. The hit came in the ninth inning and allowed an inherited runner to score, which proved to be the difference in the game.

The Dominican-born Hernández, who pitched for last season's original Washington Senators team, will see action in only seven games for the tied-for-ninth-place club.

MAY 15. The first pair of Hispanic brothers to homer in the same major league game were the Alous, with two long-ball efforts today. Property of the San Francisco Giants, Felipe Alou and rookie Mateo Alou each connected in the Giants' 4–1 romp over the Chicago Cubs at Candlestick Park. Felipe belted a first-inning grand slam and Matty blasted a solo shot in the eighth inning. In between, Orlando Cedepa clocked two home runs of his own.

JUNE 5. Federico "Chi-Chi" Olivo of the Milwaukee Braves broke into the big leagues with one inning of relief at Crosley Field. Olivo allowed a solo home run to Cincinnati outfielder Jerry Lynch, the first batter he faced. The blast counted as an insurance run, after the home team had reached starter Lew Burdette for two go-ahead runs in the same eighth inning. The Reds prevailed, 5–3.

With the appearance by Chi-Chi, the Olivo family of Monte Criste, Dominican Republic, could, from this day forward, pridefully point to a family tree that delivered the first Hispanic sibling pitching act to the major leagues.

As relief pitchers, both Diomedes and Chi-Chi's big league careers were short. They won a combined 12 games and recorded 19 saves between them.

JULY 4. The convivial Ernie Banks loved baseball, Wrigley Field and the city of Chicago so much—despite playing on mostly second-division teams with the Cubs—that he sustained a temperament and outlook irresistibly upbeat and bright. Banks was fond of saying "Let's play two!" to punctuate his committed feelings.

After the first game of an Independence Day doubleheader at Wrigley today, Orlando Cepeda must have been loudly echoing the sentiments of his shortstop opponent. Cepeda mauled four Cubs pitchers for five hits, including a long home run, that drove in eight runs, while his teammates ran roughshod on Cubbies hurlers for another 17 safeties and 11 runs. Cepeda's San Francisco Giants trounced Chicago, 19–3.

Cepeda followed up his perfect day at the plate in game one with a 2-for-4 showing in the nightcap, won by Chicago, 3–2. The eight runs knocked home by Cepeda in the opener was four short of the all-time single-game record, but became a big league high for a Hispanic player in one game.

Forty years later, Cepeda won the Ernie Banks Positive Image Lifetime Achievement Award, though he, at times, led a checkered off-the-field life.

AUGUST 9. Matty Alou spelled brother Felipe in right field for the San Francisco Giants and came through in a big way in San Francisco's 6–5 win over the Chicago Cubs at Candlestick Park. Substituting for his ailing brother, Matty collected three hits, including the game-winning home run. The 22-year-old outfielder led off the bottom of the ninth inning against the Cubs' Barney Schultz with a bomb to deep right field that ended the game.

Alou became the first Dominican player to send big league fans home in such dramatic style.

SEPTEMBER 9. The New York Yankees scored four runs in the bottom of the ninth inning to pay off Luis Arroyo's three innings of reliable relief work. The resulting 8–7

Yankees victory over the Cleveland Indians provided Arroyo with his 14th win—and 12th in a row—all in relief.

The left-hander lost five days later but grabbed another win three days afterward, his 15th and final campaign victory—earning laurels as the Hispanic relief pitcher with the most victories in one major league season. In all, Arroyo (15–5) was statistically responsible for 44 of the Yankees' 109 wins, including a league-leading 29 saves.

Pacing the circuit in appearances with 65 and games finished with 54, Arroyo will easily win the American League's Fireman of the Year award.

SEPTEMBER 10. First baseman Orlando Cepeda delivered the big blow in the San Francisco Giants' 7–1 victory over the rival Los Angeles Dodgers at Candlestick Park. Cepeda turned around a pitch from Sandy Koufax (in relief) for a three-run home run in the fifth inning, his 40th circuit clout of the campaign.

A week shy of his 24th birthday, Cepeda became the first Hispanic player to hit 40 home runs in a major league season.

SEPTEMBER 22. At Shibe Park, Roberto Clemente singled and scored during a four-run, ninth-inning rally by the second-division Pittsburgh Pirates that carried the team to a 6–3 victory over the last-place Philadelphia Phillies. The ninth-inning hit was Clemente's second of the game and number 200 for the season.

As such, Clemente became the first Hispanic player to accumulate 200 hits in one big league campaign.

SEPTEMBER 26. He was a man on a mission all year. Having felt slighted in 1960 by the baseball writers for a questionably low eighth-place finish in the MVP voting, Roberto Clemente responded this season with resounding purposefulness. The 27-year-old led all National League right fielders in games played (144) and racked up a career-high *27* assists, including one from the center field position.

Clemente played in his final games of the season today, registering an 0-for-6 showing in the Pirates' doubleheader split versus the Los Angeles Dodgers at Forbes Field. Despite that, Clemente became the first Hispanic player to capture the batting crown (.351) in the Senior Circuit and the first to be able to brag about it from his native Puerto Rico.

SEPTEMBER 27. In a San Francisco Giants' 5–3 loss to the Pittsburgh Pirates at Forbes Field, Orlando Cepeda belted his 46th home run and drove in his 142nd run. In the Giants' 150th game of the season, Cepeda reached his full output of home runs and RBI for the campaign.

The slugging Puerto Rican will top the National League with his home run and RBI totals, becoming the first Hispanic player to lead a major league in the two glamorous categories.

SEPTEMBER 29. The first Hispanic pitcher to lead a major league in complete games (17 in 1959) also became the first to top a big league circuit in strikeouts. Fanning Dick McAuliffe of the Detroit Tigers, Camilo Pascual of the Minnesota Twins registered his seventh strikeout of the game and league-best 221st of the campaign. The Twins' curveballer became the first Hispanic pitcher to reach the 200-strikeout plateau.

After the eighth-inning punch-out of McAuliffe, the Tigers scored two runs off Pascual in the ninth inning to tie the game and two more in the tenth to pull out a 6–4 victory, the club's 101st win. The disappointing, season-ending loss at Metropolitan Stadium dropped Pascual's record to 15–16.

Pascual, who also paced the AL in shutouts with eight, tied Christy Mathewson and Rube Waddell for most shutouts recorded in a season while posting a losing record.

OCTOBER 9. Substituting for an injured Mickey Mantle, Héctor López made the most of his opportunity playing on baseball's biggest stage. At Crosley Field, López cracked a triple and home run and drove in five runs, in the New York Yankees' 13–5, clinching Game 5 World Series' win over the National League champion Cincinnati Reds.

López played in four games, hit .333 (3-for-9) and knocked home the most runs in the Series (seven), while belting the first World Series home run by a Panamanian player.

1962

APRIL 10. The National League welcomed two new teams this season to balance the American League expansion of 1961. Román Mejías was plucked off the Pittsburgh Pirates roster by the expansion Houston Colt .45s last fall. Based on his Opening Day performance for the club today at Colt Stadium, he could not be any happier about it. Starting in right field for the Colt .45s, Mejías

Camilo Pascual led the American League in shutouts, complete games and strikeouts, three times each—an unprecedented achievement by a Hispanic big league pitcher. He holds the major league record for most strikeouts by a pitcher on Opening Day.

clubbed two three-run home runs in Houston's 11–2 inaugural game win. Bobby Shantz hurled the distance.

Mejías left a most memorable mark as the infant club's first Hispanic player and the first player to hit a home run at Colt Stadium, with his initial third-inning belt.

APRIL 11. After a painful absence, National League baseball was about to return to New York. A quick stopover in the Midwest was required before the New York Mets could officially be cheered at a home game. The new franchise, adopting the colors of blue and orange from the two previous New York City National League teams, the Dodgers and Giants, played its initial game. The club, managed by 72-year-old Casey Stengel, was soundly beaten, 11–4, by the St. Louis Cardinals at Busch Stadium.

Félix Mantilla, playing shortstop and batting second for the Mets, recorded one hit and scored one of the visiting team's runs. Mantilla recorded much more for posterity as the first Hispanic player in franchise history.

MAY 30. In the opener of a doubleheader, Cleveland Indians pitcher Pedro Ramos was a one-man cyclone against Baltimore. From the mound, he three-hit the Orioles, 7–0. At the plate, he blasted two home runs. One of them, with the bases filled, came after the preceding hitter was walked intentionally.

The first Hispanic pitcher to hit two home runs in one major league game, Ramos accumulated 15 lifetime home runs, most by a Hispanic major league pitcher in the 20th century.

The Birds regrouped and returned the favor against the Tribe in the nightcap, by the same score.

JULY 10. In front of a record crowd of 45,480 that included the President of the United States, John F. Kennedy, the first All-Star Game of 1962 was played in Washington D.C. Each half of the game's fourth inning opened with Hispanic pitchers taking the mound, and both became pitchers of record in the game.

As the Dominican Republic's first representative in the All-Star Game, the Giants' Juan Marichal also became the first Hispanic pitcher to win a Midsummer Classic, hurling two scoreless innings in the National League's 3–1 triumph. Roberto Clemente, one-half of the "C & C" Hispanic reciprocation to the "M & M" Maris and Mantle duo, shined with his bat, stroking three of the National League's eight hits. The other "C"—Orlando Cepeda—went hitless, but drove in a run. Felipe Alou, in his first All-Star Game, replaced Clemente later in the game and drove in the NL's third run with a sacrifice fly.

Camilo Pascal was the losing hurler, by virtue of two runs allowed.

1963

FEBRUARY 8. On the opening night of the Inter-American Series, held at Olympic Stadium in Panama City, Juan Pizarro hurled a no-hit, no-run game against Venezuela's Valencia Industrialists. Conscripted from Santurce as a roster supplement for the tournament by the Puerto Rican Winter League champion Mayagüez Indios, Pizarro walked four and retired the final 16 batters. In the spectacular 5–0 victory, an acrobatic catch by Mayagüez second baseman Ramón Luis Conde, on a line drive hit by Valencia's Angel Scull, helped preserve the first no-hitter thrown by a Hispanic pitcher in a winter league championship tournament.

The home country's Chiriqui-Bocas Farmers (5–2) defeated Nicaragua's Boer Indians (4–3) in a sudden death playoff game six days later to capture the Latin American crown.

JUNE 15. The first no-hitter by a Hispanic pitcher in the major leagues was authored by San Francisco's Juan Marichal. On "Camera Day" at Candlestick Park, the "Dominican Dandy" struck a historic pose for baseball posterity as he completely muzzled the Houston Colt .45s, 1–0, on only 89 pitches. Marichal struck out five and allowed two walks, one in the fifth inning and the other in the seventh. The win nudged the Giants into the top spot in the National League, one-half game over the St. Louis Cardinals.

"I didn't get excited until the last inning. Then I got a feeling I just can't describe,"[28] said Marichal, who was firmly establishing a place among the league's top echelon of pitchers.

JULY 2. This was one for the pitching ages. Two courageous combatants battled one another, through regulation and then inning after extra inning, in an epic mound contest. One of baseball's greatest pitching duels was recorded as Juan Marichal defeated Warren Spahn, 1–0, in 16 innings at Candlestick Park.

Willie Mays blasted a Spahn offering—a "flat screwball," according to Spahn—over the fence with one out in the bottom of the 16th inning, ending the four hour and ten-minute game. "I knew it was gone the moment I creamed it,"[29] emphasized Mays. The Giants' center fielder also threw out a runner at the plate in the fourth inning, preserving Marichal's masterpiece.

Spahn, a 42-year-old living legend who had been unscored upon for 27 innings, including two prior starts, allowed nine hits. Marichal, a legend in the making, rationed one fewer hit. Spahn finished his career as the winningest left-hander in history with 363.

Both hurlers made scheduled starts five days later. Spahn tossed a five-hit, 4–0 shutout at Houston. Marichal lost to Bob Gibson and the St. Louis Cardinals in the second game of a twin bill at Candlestick Park. The final score was 5–0, but Marichal allowed only two runs before being pinch-hit for in the seventh inning.

The game today was entwined with the anniversary of another magnificent pitching performance in Giants history. Thirty years ago to the day, Carl Hubbell engineered a monumental *18-inning*, 1–0, complete game victory over the St. Louis Cardinals at the Polo Grounds.

SEPTEMBER 3. The San Francisco Giants scored seven unearned runs in the second inning on their way to a 16-run outburst. The support was more than enough for Juan Marichal to become the National League's fourth 20-game winner, and the first Dominican pitcher with that many wins in one season. Manager Alvin Dark gave Marichal the last two innings off in the 16–3, home victory over the Chicago Cubs.

SEPTEMBER 10. The three Alou brothers follow each other to bat in the eighth inning of a San Francisco Giants–New York Mets game at the Polo Grounds. Although each made out, it was the first time three brothers have batted successively in the same inning of a major league game. The Dominican siblings step to the plate in reverse order of birth, with Jesús (in his major league debut) and Matty, as pinch-hitters, followed by the leadoff batter, Felipe. The Mets came out on top, 4–2.

SEPTEMBER 12. Juan Marichal repositioned himself on the pitching mound this season, and it paid splendid dividends. The pitcher moved from the right corner (third base side) to the left corner of the slab (first base). The reason for the change was his excessive walk total of 90 in 1962. The repositioning contributed to higher strikeout numbers, as well; a 25-game winner in 1963, Juan racked up a career-high 248 whiffs.

Marichal struck out 13 batters on this day in hurling the last shutout recorded at the Polo Grounds. A new stadium, pending completion in Flushing, Queens, for the New York Mets in 1964, numbered the storied ballpark's days. Marichal defeated the fledgling Metropolitans, 6–0, on four hits, giving a fitting farewell salute to the mound conquered by Mathewson and Hubbell.

Marichal also socked his first career home run in the game—a first for a Dominican pitcher in the major leagues.

SEPTEMBER 15. In 1955, the Connie Mack Stadium outfield welcomed three Hispanic players simultaneously onto its pasture for the first time. Today, three Hispanic brothers make history by roaming the broad green expanse of Forbes Field over the last two innings of a game between the San Francisco Giants and Pittsburgh Pirates. They are the Alou brothers of Haina, Dominican Republic.

In the bottom of the eighth inning, with the Giants holding a 12–3 lead, Matty Alou replaced Willie Mays. An inning earlier, youngest sibling Jesús had entered the game to spell left fielder Willie McCovey. Elder brother Felipe, the only starter, had shifted from his original right field position to left, to allow Jesús to play right field. When Matty entered the game, Felipe moved to center to allow Matty to perform in his accustomed left field slot.

Twenty-one-year-old Jesús, in the major leagues for less than a week, committed one of two ninth-inning errors that Giants starting pitcher Billy O'Dell brushed off in completing a 13–5 win.

Two days after hurling the first no-hit, no-run game by a Hispanic major league pitcher, Juan Marichal compares screwball grips with New York Giants legend Carl Hubbell.

SEPTEMBER 27. Five days earlier, Camilo Pascual became the first Hispanic pitcher to win 20 games in a major league season twice. Today, the Minnesota Twins pitcher, in his final start, defeated the New York Yankees, 4–3, at Yankee Stadium. The 21st win of the campaign for Pascual came via his league-best 18th complete game. Pascual fanned nine Yankees to boost his AL-topping strikeout total to 202.

Over the past five seasons, the genial Cuban right-hander has led the league in complete games, strikeouts and shutouts three times each. Midway into the second decade of the 21st century, that trifecta feat had yet to be matched by another Hispanic pitcher.

SEPTEMBER 28. On the next-to-last day of the season, Juan Marichal closed his campaign with his sixth straight win. Marichal, 25–8, dispatched the Pittsburgh Pirates, 3–2, at Candlestick Park, in one hour and 42 minutes.

With the complete-game win, Marichal pushed his innings pitched total to an NL-topping 321⅓ innings in 40 starts. The first Hispanic pitcher to lead a major league in innings pitched embarked this season on a string of six 20-win campaigns over the next seven years.

OCTOBER 12. The Polo Grounds still breathes with baseball. The Giants moved years ago. The Mets have also permanently vacated after their final game on September 18. But the old, horseshoe-shaped ballpark was resuscitated for one more game of ball-playing by major league players.

Organized by Vic Power, the first, and lamentably only, "Latin American All-Star Game" was played. Participants included the likes of Marichal, Miñoso, Clemente, Cepeda, and Aparicio. The Hispanic National League won, 5–2. Virgin Islander Al McBean, the winning pitcher, tripled to drive in a run and was one of two players to record an extra-base hit. Pedro Ramos took the loss for the Iberian American League squad.

Prior to the festivities, Hispanic luminaries Adolfo Luque, Hiram Bithorn, Perucho

Cepeda and Francisco Coímbre were recognized with awards for their contributions to the game of baseball. Three of the legendary players' awards were posthumously distributed. Only Coímbre was present to accept his.

1964

JULY 4. Kansas City's Manny Jiménez enjoyed a 4-for-4 day, connecting for three home runs in a row, against the Baltimore Orioles at Memorial Stadium. Jiménez homered twice off Orioles starter Robin Roberts and again against reliever Dick Hall,

and drove in five runs. With the Athletics ahead 6–5 after seven and one-half innings, and Jiménez scheduled to lead off the ninth, manager Mel McGaha, in a defensive move, inserted José Tartabull to take Jiménez's left field spot. The Birds scratched home a tying run in the same eighth frame, and an "early" curfew ended the game in a 6–6 tie after nine innings were played.

An Independence Day fireworks display scheduled after the twilight game, which began at 5:30 pm, dictated that no inning was permitted to start after 8:15 pm. The unresolved game was therefore called and had to be replayed in its entirety, with all game statistics recorded. Jiménez, although denied a chance to hit a possible fourth home run, became the Dominican Republic's initial major leaguer to achieve the single-game home run hat-trick.

JULY 10. Rookie outfielder Jesús Alou stroked six hits in six at-bats against six different Cubs pitchers as San Francisco paddled Chicago, 10–3. Alou, the first Hispanic major leaguer to collect six hits in one game, clubbed a home run to go with five singles in the Wrigley Field contest, and Giants teammate Orlando Cepeda logged a perfect 4-for-4 day with the stick.

Juan Marichal enjoyed the run support and picked up his 12th win.

JULY 19. In his first major league game, Luis Tiant of the Cleveland Indians defeated Whitey Ford (who was 12–2 entering the game) and the New York Yankees, 3–0, in front of 30,061 spectators. Tiant allowed four hits and struck out 11 in the second game of a doubleheader, in the famed "house that Ruth built."

Tiant embarked this day on a tremendous 19-year career in which he earned 229 wins and 49 shutouts.

Yankee Stadium was not the only famed ballpark in which Tiant made an indelible first impression during his first two and a half months in the major leagues. The 23-year-old right-hander also tossed shutouts in his first games on the mound at Dodger Stadium (August 11) and Fenway Park (September 30).

JULY 23. The greatest debut in the major leagues by a Hispanic position player was by Bert Campaneris of the Kansas City Athletics. Campaneris became the first Hispanic player to hit a home run in his first major league at-bat, and only the second player since 1900 to slug two home runs in his first big league game. (Bob Nieman of the 1951 St. Louis Browns was the first, in his first two at-bats.)

At Metropolitan Stadium, with the bases empty, the 22-year-old shortstop from Cuba socked his first round-tripper on the first delivery offered to him by Minnesota Twins pitcher Jim Kaat. The second home run came in the seventh inning with a man on base. Dagoberto also recorded a third hit and stole a base. The A's prevailed in 11 innings, 4–3. (Falling just short of Campaneris' spectacular start will be Dominican Starlin Castro, who on May 7, 2010, homered and tripled in five at-bats in his first game in the big leagues for the Chicago Cubs. The 20-year-old Castro, the first player born in the 1990s to reach the majors leagues, collected six RBI with his two long hits, a modern record for a debuting player.)

SEPTEMBER 24. Rafael Palmeiro was born in Havana, Cuba. Playing for three major league teams in a two-decade span, Palmeiro evolved into one of the most prolific Latin American hitters of all time.

OCTOBER 4. As a September call-up in 1962, 24-year-old Tony Oliva received his first taste of major league pitching. In nine at-bats, he collected four hits, a small but clear harbinger of the dynamic things to come. Property of the Minnesota Twins, Oliva, perhaps needlessly, spent another year in the minors before bursting onto the American League scene in 1964.

In his home ballpark, Metropolitan Stadium, Oliva closed out one of the greatest rookie seasons ever recorded. In the season's finale, the Twins' right fielder went 1-for-3 in a rain-shortened game lost by the Twins, 3–0, to the Los Angeles Angels.

Oliva became the first rookie to lead a major league in batting, with a .323 mark.

NOVEMBER 28. Garnering 19 out of 20 sportswriters' votes, Tony Oliva was named winner of the American League Rookie of the Year award. Oliva amassed the most hits (217) and extra base hits (84) in all of baseball, and, with 374 total bases, tied with Hal Trosky for most ever by a first-year player. The batting champ also led the American League in doubles (43) and became the first Hispanic player to lead a major league in runs scored with 109. His 32 home runs helped him finish third in the league in slugging, behind Mickey Mantle and John "Boog" Powell.

The freshman outfielder became the first Cuban player to be so deservedly honored by the major leagues.

1965

APRIL 13. At Crosley Field, 22-year-old Cincinnati Reds rookie Tony Pérez belted his first big league home run—a grand slam off the Milwaukee Braves' Denny Lemaster. Until today, no Hispanic major leaguer could boast of a bases-loaded clout as his first big league home run.

The Reds plated four more runs in gaining an 8–3 win over the Braves.

JULY 13. Starter Juan Marichal earned the first Hispanic All-Star Game MVP Award with three scoreless innings of work. In the lead at the time of Marichal's departure, the National League registered a 6–5 win against its rival circuit at Metropolitan Stadium.

The dominant Dominican pitcher was enjoying an extraordinary season for the Giants. Three days prior to the All-Star break, Marichal had tossed a 7–0 shutout over the Philadelphia Phillies, and four days from today, the right-hander will blank the Houston Astros at San Francisco, 7–0, already his eighth shutout of the season and the fourth in his last five starts.

In his career, Marichal compiled the second-most All-Star Game innings pitched,

18, and the second-lowest lowest ERA, 0.50 (minimum nine innings), for a starting pitcher in the midsummer showcase's history. (Lefty Gómez and Jim Bunning also tossed 18 innings, trailing Don Drysdale's 19⅓ innings. Mel Harder did not permit a run in 13 innings.)

AUGUST 22. The game could not have had a bigger spotlight on it. Pitted against each other were the National League's two top teams, San Francisco and first-place Los Angeles, separated in the standings by 1½ games. Sunday afternoon. A capacity crowd. And the two best pitchers anywhere, Sandy Koufax and Juan Marichal, on the mound.

But a dismaying incident ensued. Marichal, batting in the third inning, suddenly struck John Roseboro over the head with his bat. Apparently incited by the Dodgers catcher's return throw to the mound, which flicked past Marichal's ear, and a verbal insult hurled by Roseboro, Marichal's violent reaction triggered a bench-clearing brawl. Roseboro suffered a concussion and a sizable, bloodletting gash on his head.

In the aftermath, Marichal was ejected and slapped with the biggest fine in National League history ($1,750), along with an eight-game suspension. The Giants, on Willie Mays' three-run homer, won the game, 4–3, and inched closer to first place.

SEPTEMBER 8. At Municipal Stadium, Kansas City shortstop Bert Campaneris proved he was a true "Athletic," as he became the first major leaguer to play all nine positions in one game. Campaneris started the game at his normal position, then took a one-inning turn at the six remaining non-battery positions, through the seventh inning. The 23-year-old scaled the mound for the eighth frame, with the score 2–1 in favor of the opponent California Angels. In the inning, he was nicked for a run by the Angels, on two walks and a hit.

"Campy" finished by catching the ninth inning. As it happened, there was a play at the plate, which resulted in a jarring collision between Campaneris and Ed Kirkpatrick of the Angels. The slightly-built Campaneris, who gave up a good 35 pounds to Kirkpatrick, held on to the ball to record the last out of the inning, but had to leave the game, shaken up from the impact.

The Athletics, trailing 3–1, scored two runs in the bottom of the ninth to tie the contest, but the visiting California club came back to win, 5–3, in 13 innings.

SEPTEMBER 9. In his first Candlestick Park start since the distressing "Roseboro Incident," Juan Marichal hurled his tenth shutout of the season and notched his 21st win, downing the Houston Astros on four hits, 4–0. The early-arriving crowd of 20,076 heartily applauded Marichal when he took the field for his pitching warm-ups, and cheered again at the sight of the pitcher sprinting to the mound to start the game. The whitewash total became the most in one major league campaign by a Hispanic pitcher.

On the season, the 22–13 Marichal compiled a 10.5 WAR rating, one of only four Hispanic pitchers to top 10.0 in one campaign (Adolfo Luque, 10.8 in 1923; José Rijo, 10.2 in 1993; and Pedro Martínez, 11.7 in 2000).

OCTOBER 3. There was no sophomore jinx for the Twins' Tony Oliva. The second-year outfielder captured his second straight batting crown, an unprecedented achievement in the game's history. The crown fit all the more happily for Tony O., whose .321 average provided a key offensive element as the Twins dethroned the New York Yankees, the perennial American League champions.

NOVEMBER 18. Shortstop Zoilo Versalles became the first Hispanic to win the Most Valuable Player Award. One first-place vote shy of a unanimous selection, the 26-year-old was the main catalyst for a strong Minnesota Twins squad that won 102 games.

A major league "Cuban connection." Left to right: Cleveland Indians catcher Joe Azcue, Minnesota Twins outfielder Tony Oliva, Indians pitcher Pedro Ramos, Twins shortstop Zoilo Versalles. Oliva is the only player to win batting titles in his first two big league seasons. Ramos hurled the first major league Opening Day shutout by a Hispanic pitcher. Versalles was the first Hispanic big league MVP.

Versailles attributed the tutelage of coach Billy Martin for exacting the best from him throughout the campaign. "The Kid from Cuba's" teammate and batting champion, Tony Oliva, placed second.

1966

MAY 26. The Phillies' Jim Bunning learned first-hand why Juan Marichal has been unbeatable so far this season, with a record of 9–0. At Candlestick Park, Bunning matched ten scoreless innings with Marichal before being removed for a pinch-hitter. Marichal pitched through the 14th inning, yielding only six hits and striking out ten along the way, before the Giants scored the required tally for the 1–0 victory.

Peaking at ten straight season-opening wins, the pride of the Dominican Republic finished the year with a 25–6 record and an ERA of 2.23, becoming the first Hispanic pitcher to win 25 games twice in the major leagues.

This was one of three games in which Marichal surpassed Bill James' 100-point level of "Game Score."[30] Since 1950, only Nolan Ryan, with four games, reached the century mark more times in this unique rating system for pitchers' individual games. The only other Hispanic pitchers to top 100 "Game Score" points in a single outing were Mike Cuéllar (July 24, 1967) and José DeLeón (August 30, 1989).

JUNE 5. Sunday doubleheaders were still common fare in 1960s baseball, but Leo Cárdenas of the Cincinnati Reds exhibited uncommon power in today's scheduled twin tilt at Crosley Field. The Reds shortstop clubbed a pair of home runs in each game of a series-concluding matchup between the Reds and visiting Chicago Cubs.

In the first contest, Cárdenas powered the way with five RBI in the Reds' 8–5 triumph. In the nightcap, the Cubs scored five times in the ninth inning to spoil Cardenas' second two-homer game and salvage a split of the four-game encampment, 9–5.

The Cuban shortstop, with an 8–4–6–8 cumulative box score batting line, became the first Hispanic player to sock four home runs in a big league doubleheader.

JUNE 10. "Best Right Arm in Baseball," declared *Time* magazine on its cover, featuring Juan Marichal in a sequence of cutout photos illustrating his unique, high-leg-kick pitching delivery. The San Francisco hurler became the first Latin American athlete honored on the cover of North America's most prestigious news weekly. (The first Latin American "sportsman" to grace the cover of *Time* was José Raúl Capablanca. The Cuban chess grandmaster was featured on the December 7, 1925, cover. Lefty Gómez made *Time*'s portal page in the early 1930s.)

SEPTEMBER 2. Roberto Clemente's 2,000th career hit came as a three-run home run, clouted at Forbes Field against future Hall of Famer Ferguson Jenkins. As the chief offensive weapon in Pittsburgh's 7–3 victory, Clemente's 23rd long ball of the season helped the Pirates seize first place, one game ahead of the San Francisco Giants.

Clemente, the first Hispanic player to gather 2,000 major league hits, also topped the 100-RBI mark for the first time in his career with the long-ball belt.

SEPTEMBER 21. The powerful Pittsburgh Pirates lineup reached Juan Marichal for two runs in the top of the ninth inning to snap a three-all tie at Candlestick Park. Marichal's batterymate, Tom Haller, responded with a game-tying, two-run shot in the bottom of the inning, however. One out later, Marichal won his own game with the second home run of the inning allowed by Pirates reliever Roy Face.

As the first Hispanic major league pitcher to clout a walkoff home run, Marichal provided himself with his 23rd win of the season, 6–5.

OCTOBER 2. No one in American League history had led his league in hits in his first three seasons as a player until Tony Oliva. The right fielder, who also earned a Gold Glove Award for his fielding, tallied 191 hits for a .307 average on the campaign. Oliva, 28, became the fifth player in history to pace the circuit in hits for three straight seasons, and only the second in the American League since Ty Cobb.

Playing in a season-ending doubleheader against the American League champion Baltimore Orioles, Oliva was contained to only one hit in eight at-bats. Also limited to one hit in the two games was the player Oliva finished runner-up to (by nine points) in average—AL Triple Crown winner Frank Robinson.

In his injury-abridged, 15-season career, Oliva led the league in hits five times, more than any other Hispanic major leaguer.

OCTOBER 2. The National League pennant would be decided today, the season's final day. The second-place San Francisco Giants played the third-place Pittsburgh Pirates at Forbes Field, while the league-leading Dodgers of Los Angeles were in Philadelphia to play a doubleheader versus the Phillies.

Ozzie Virgil's pinch-hit in the ninth inning at Pittsburgh sustained the hopes of the San Francisco Giants for a miraculous finish. Requiring the Dodgers to lose both games against the Phillies, the Giants could force a make-up game against the Cincinnati Reds to be played. If it came to that and San Francisco won the make-up game, they would tie Los Angeles and force a pennant playoff.

Virgil gave the Giants life as he tied the contest 3–3 with a two-out base hit, forcing extra innings. The Giants came up victorious with four runs in the 11th frame, 7–3. (The clutch hit was the last career hit for the majors' first Dominican player.) The single by Virgil occurred almost simultaneously with receipt of the encouraging news of the Dodgers' 4–3 defeat in the first game at Shibe Park.

In the Giants' victory, outfielder Matty Alou of the Pirates collected four singles, lifting his circuit-topping average to .342. Alou became the first Dominican major league batting champion, easily besting the second-best batter's .327 average—his brother Felipe.

Later, back in Philadelphia, Sandy Koufax demonstrated why miracles were rarely in season when he was on the mound. Pitching on two days' rest, the exquisite Dodgers left-hander defeated the Phillies, 6–3, and clinched the National League pennant by a final margin of 1½ games.

OCTOBER 27. Tragedy struck the opening game of the Nicaraguan Winter League season. Twelve fans, including four children, were killed, and over 100 people were injured, following a rush toward exit doors that were locked.

During Opening Day ceremonies, a group of university students had come onto the field, waving anti–Anastasio Somoza banners. Many were arrested by police, who summoned army and militia soldiers. Fearing reprisals from the army presence surrounding the stadium, many fans panicked when they found the general admission exits locked at the end of the game. Victims were suffocated in the desperate scramble to leave. It was reported that the authorities had locked the doors in an effort to catch, as they filed out, more of the pre-game demonstrators who had escaped them, by blending into that section of the stands.

Before the tragedy, the León Melenudos defeated the Cinco Estrellas Tigers, 3–1. The game scheduled for the following day, between the Boer Indians and Granada Sharks, was postponed in deference to the terrible occurrence at Estadio Somoza.

NOVEMBER 16. Pittsburgh Pirates management had to be hoping that the Roberto Clementes planned on having a big family.

As a newlywed father-to-be in 1965, Roberto Clemente told his wife Vera that he would try to win a batting title for their first-born child. He did, last season, completing the task six weeks after the August birth of Roberto, Jr.

Last winter, Clemente pledged to a newly pregnant Vera his attempt to win the National League MVP Award for the couple's second child, due the following summer. Voting results were announced today (four months after the birth of Luis Roberto Clemente) and, in a close tabulation over Sandy Koufax, Clemente won the league's top award. Clemente became the first Hispanic MVP in the National League and the first Puerto Rican to win the award.

On the season, the All-Star outfielder hit for more power than ever before, clubbing 29 home runs and ripping 11 triples, and he set his career high in RBI with 119. During his career, Clemente accumulated more than 400 doubles, 100 triples and 200 home runs among his 3,000 hits. Through the 2014 season, fewer than 20 players have scaled such combined offensive plateaus.[31]

1967

JANUARY 25. Roberto Clemente became the first Pittsburgh Pirates player to sign a $100,000 contract and the first Hispanic player to reach this elevated salary level.

Coming off his greatest season, the splendid outfielder received validation of his skills with the monetary figure bestowed upon only a small group of players to date.

MARCH 27. After an extended holdout, Juan Marichal came to terms on a new contract with San Francisco Giants owner Horace Stoneham. Marichal signed for $100,000, becoming the highest-paid pitcher in baseball and the first Hispanic hurler to attain a six-figure salary.

APRIL 11. On Opening Day at Baltimore's Memorial Stadium, a Rookie of the Year campaign began for second baseman Rod Carew of the Minnesota Twins In his first big league game, Carew stroked two singles in four at-bats, in a 6–3 Twins loss to the Orioles.

Carew, the first Panamanian Rookie of the Year Award recipient, hit .292 for the season, one of only four times in 19 major league seasons that he did not hit .300 or higher.

APRIL 24. Omar Vizquel was born in Caracas, Venezuela. From the country whose baseball specialty seemed to be producing magnificent shortstops, Vizquel transformed himself into one of the most dexterous and flashiest fielders at his position the major league game has ever known.

MAY 15. Laying claim as baseball's best all-around player, Roberto Clemente pounded Cincinnati Reds pitching for three home runs and a double, and knocked home all of his team's runs; but the Reds prevailed in ten innings, 8–7, at Crosley Field. Tony Pérez doubled in the winning run.

As the first Puerto Rican player to sock three home runs in a major league game, Clemente was off to a blazing start with the lumber, hitting .390 and pacing the circuit in RBI with 24. That season, the 33-year-old outfielder seized his fourth batting title with a .357 mark and racked up his fourth 200-hit campaign. Only two other Hispanic players, Rod Carew and Vladimir Guerrero, have cracked the 200-hit barrier as many times.

JUNE 12. Eight days after squatting through all 19 innings of a loss in Baltimore, Paul Casanova of the Washington Senators caught 22 innings (and 268 pitches) and singled in the winning run in the bottom of the 22nd frame. At D.C. Stadium, the Senators edged the Chicago White Sox, 6–5, in the longest night game in innings and time elapsed (6 hours, 38 minutes), to that point, in major league history.

Setting the major league standard for innings caught in one game by a Hispanic player, Casanova was 0-for-8 until his lone hit ended the long, long night at 2:44 a.m. He was given the day off the following day by manager Gil Hodges.

Remarkably, yet another 20-inning game behind the plate was in store for the Cuban catcher, in August, versus the Minnesota Twins.

JULY 11. Geography nudged the All-Star Game into the nocturnal arena. Held on the West Coast for the first time, the afternoon game lasted 15 innings and extended into near nightfall in the Midwest and East. The game belonged to the pitchers, but a hitter ended up the hero.

The Cincinnati Reds' Tony Pérez walloped a home run that gave the National League a 2–1 victory in Anaheim, California. The game's MVP picked an opportune moment to become the first Hispanic player to homer in the All-Star Game, victimizing Catfish Hunter in the top of the 15th inning. Tom Seaver recorded the save for NL winner Don Drysdale.

The game contained another historical aside, with Rod Carew playing the first six innings at second base for the losing American League squad. The 22-year-old Carew (hitless in three trips) became the first Panamanian player to suit up in a big league All-Star Game.

SEPTEMBER 27. Mike Cuéllar of the Houston Astros outdueled Jim Bunning of the Phillies in the Astrodome, winning 1–0 in 11 innings. Cuéllar struck out 12 and was reached for only six hits. It was his second straight shutout and the first of eight 1–0, complete-game victories Cuéllar will log in his career, the most by any Hispanic big league pitcher.

OCTOBER 4. At Fenway Park, Boston's José Santiago held more than his own against Bob Gibson and the St. Louis Cardinals in Game 1 of the World Series. However, Santiago, who won eight games without a loss after the All-Star break as a starter and reliever, wound up on the short end of the decision to the St. Louis hurler, 2–1.

The Red Sox's winning pitcher in game 161, played five days earlier, Santiago had pitched seven strong innings against the Minnesota Twins, to make possible teammate Jim Lonborg's dramatic, pennant-clinching victory on the season's last day. Today the Puerto Rican right-hander became the first Hispanic player to hit a home run in his initial World Series at-bat. Slugged off Gibson, the third-inning blast accounted for the Red Sox's only run of the game.

OCTOBER 12. The St. Louis Cardinals captured their second world title in four years with a 7–2, Game 7 victory over the Boston Red Sox at Fenway Park. In the top of the sixth inning, Cardinals second baseman Julian Javier cracked a three-run home run, which all but broke the back of the Red Sox and their followers. The circuit clout extended the Cardinals' lead to 7–1. It was also the first home run hit in the Fall Classic by a Dominican player. Javier, incidentally, had been the Cardinals player who spoiled Jim Lonborg's Game 2 no-hit attempt when he stroked an eighth-inning double. It was the only hit allowed in the game by the Red Sox ace.

The individual pitching force behind the St. Louis celebrations came from one of the game's fiercest mound competitors, Bob Gibson. The intimidating right-hander, who had his right shin fractured by a line drive hit by Roberto Clemente earlier in the summer, hurled his third complete-game victory of the Series, allowing just three hits.

NOVEMBER 7. Bob Gibson said the following when asked to look back at the 1967 Cardinals: "Those Cardinals developed a special chemistry, with Cepeda the chief chemist."[32]

First baseman and leading team alchemist Orlando Cepeda captured every first place vote in the sportswriters' MVP Award balloting, announced today. Cepeda became the first unanimous winner in the National League.

The right-handed slugger was obtained by the Redbirds early in the 1966 season from the Giants in a one-sided trade for pitcher Ray Sadeki. Cepeda was the key factor in the Cardinals' rise to the top of the National League.

It was the third straight year a Hispanic player had won a major league Most Valuable Player Award, and for Cepeda, he became the first Hispanic big leaguer to be named Rookie of the Year and MVP.

1968

FEBRUARY 5. Roberto Alomar was born in Ponce, Puerto Rico. Sired by father Sandy Alomar, Sr. into what will become, including older brother Sandy Jr., Latin America's most accomplished baseball family, the 12-time All-Star distinguished himself as a top-rated second baseman for much of his 17-year major league career.

MARCH 19. Rafael Almeida, the first Cuban player of the 20th century, died in Havana at age 80.

APRIL 15. The pitch, on its parabolic trajectory, spun through the 60-foot, six-inch, prescribed corridor between the mound and home plate, then dropped suddenly across the outer border of the strike zone. The batter, the Angels' Chuck Hinton, flinched at the apparent optical illusion, as he simultaneously heard the thwack of the catcher's mitt and the indicting bellow of the umpire.

The 2,000th career strikeout for Camilo Pascual, his second of the young game against visiting California, was appropriately delivered via his most famous pitch, the curveball. The visiting West Coast team was no match for the once-again ace of the Washington Senators' staff, who doled out seven hits in a 7–0 victory. Pascual had been obtained by the Senators from the Twins at the end of the 1966 season.

A small but appreciative crowd of 4,570 was on hand to witness the first Hispanic pitcher to accumulate that many strikeouts in the major leagues.

MAY 17. An attempt by Luis Tiant to equal the American League record for consecutive shutouts did not materialize. However, the longest consecutive scoreless innings streak by a Hispanic major league pitcher was registered. The unscored-upon streak ended at 41 innings, after Tiant surrendered a sixth-inning home run to Boog Powell of the Baltimore Orioles.

At Cleveland Stadium, with a man on first base and one out, a potential double play was not executed by pivot man Chico Salmon, who fumbled the toss at second base, allowing the inning to continue with two men on base. Since a double play cannot be anticipated, two earned runs from the next batter's (Powell) three-run home run were chalked up to Tiant.

Tagged with the 6–2 loss (two relievers allowed the other three runs), Tiant was placidly practical about his second baseman's costly error. "Chico saved my shutout in New York [May 7]," said the pitcher after the game. "So how can I blame him now?"[33]

JULY 3. The scintillating summer of pitching excellence throughout baseball was a trend Luis Tiant continued today. The Indians right-hander fanned 19 batters in ten innings, and walked none, in defeating the Minnesota Twins, 1–0, at Cleveland Stadium. Tiant afterward called the performance, in which he threw 101 strikes, "the best game I've ever thrown in my life."[34] Three standing ovations from the 21,135 in attendance also saluted the effort, which peaked with three consecutive strikeouts in the tenth, stranding runners on the corners.

Having conceded only 18 earned runs in 146⅓ innings, so far, Tiant's ERA tabulated to a minuscule 1.11. In 1968, Tiant recorded the second lowest Fielding Independent Pitching mark in one season by a Hispanic pitcher, 2.04. FIP evaluates pitchers using their strikeouts, walks, home runs and hit-by-pitches on an ERA scale.

JULY 9. The brothers Alou once again made Hispanic baseball bloodline history. At the All-Star Game in the Astrodome, Felipe and Matty became the first Hispanic brothers to participate in the Midsummer Classic. Matty, a member of the Pittsburgh Pirates, entered the game in the sixth inning, replacing starting left fielder Curt Flood. He scratched out an infield hit in his only at-bat. In the ninth inning, Felipe, of the San Francisco Giants, entered the game to replace his younger sibling in left field. He did not bat in the game.

The National League was victorious, 1–0. NL starter Don Drysdale was the winner and AL opener Luis Tiant, surrendering an unearned run (on his own error), was the loser.

AUGUST 1. This season, even more than usual, it seemed that when Juan Marichal took the ball to the mound, no one could make him give it up. Coming off ten-and 11-inning complete-game victories in his two previous starts, the Giants' right-hander out-dueled Don Drysdale, 2–0, at Dodger Stadium, for his *16th* complete game in a row and 22nd in his first 26 starts.

Although baseball was experiencing a season of unusual pitching superiority, it was the usual superior season for Marichal, who won his 20th game (against four losses). Incredibly, Marichal had now gone the distance in 103 of his last 105 wins as a starter!

This season, Marichal completed 30 games and logged 325⅔ innings, high-water marks in both categories in any one campaign by a Hispanic hurler. In his 16-year big league career, the dynamic Dominican completed more games than any other Hispanic pitcher—244.

AUGUST 29. Pedro "Preston" Gomez became the first Hispanic hired to manage a major league team. Gomez, 45, a coach with the Dodgers and former successful minor league manager, was tabbed to guide the expansion franchise in San Diego, beginning next season. Appropriately for both the Spanish-named city and the occasion of Señor Gomez's selection, the team's nickname remained faithful to its long-standing minor league affiliation, the "Padres."

SEPTEMBER 25. The last major league hit (a first-inning single) struck by Mickey Mantle was the only hit allowed by Luis Tiant, who shut out the New York Yankees for the third time on the season at Yankee Stadium. Tiant recorded his 21st win and ninth whitewash with the one-hit, 3–0 victory. Mantle, the game's most idolized player since Babe Ruth, was walked by Tiant in the ninth inning with two outs. It was the nearly 37-year-old Mantle's last Bronx ballyard plate appearance. The Mick was left stranded at first base when the final batter, Roy White, was retired.

The Cleveland pitcher established a major league record for fewest hits allowed per nine innings—5.30—in one season. (The record was bettered by Nolan Ryan in 1972 at 5.26.) Tiant's final start of the campaign increased his strikeout total by 11 to 264 (third-best in the league) and dropped his ERA to 1.60, the lowest seasonal mark ever recorded by a Hispanic big league starter. The ERA was also the second-lowest by a pitcher with 200 or more strikeouts in 58 years. The Cardinals' Bob Gibson's 1.12 ERA and 268 Ks established the all-time mark, in this 1968 season that became historically known as the "Year of the Pitcher." Tiant's 1968 pitching WAR of 8.4 ranked second in all of baseball to Gibson's 11.2, ahead of 31-game winner Denny McLain's 7.4.

1969

APRIL 8. Baseball initiated its broadest expansion year and crossed international borders for the first time. A new National League franchise was awarded to the city of Montréal, Québec, Canada. The Expos, managed by Gene Mauch, played their first game, at Shea Stadium, against the New York Mets and came out victorious, 11–10.

No Canadian players participated in the team's successful debut, but one Hispanic player did—Puerto Rican José "Coco" Laboy. The franchise's first Hispanic representative played third base and slugged a key three-run home run for the winning "Expos."

The rest of the long season turned out much differently for both clubs, with the Expos losing 110 games and the Mets winning 100.

APRIL 8. Four new teams, two in each major circuit, joined the big league fold this season. The second new National League club hailed from San Diego. At San Diego Stadium, the Padres hosted the Houston Astros and sent 23,370 inaugural day fans home happy with a 2–1 win. Dick Selma pitched a five-hitter to give Preston Gómez his first major league managerial win.

Leading off the game for the Padres was shortstop Rafael Robles. The Dominican infielder did not distinguish himself on the field, but secured a perpetual place as the first Hispanic player for the distinctly Spanish-immersed namesake team.

APRIL 8. Broadened expansion by baseball has now spawned realignment, similar to other major sports. Two divisions, East and West, were incorporated within each major league. In the American League West Division, the Kansas City Royals provided a new Midwest fan base with a memorable first game. At Municipal Stadium, the Royals defeated the Minnesota Twins, 4–3, in 12 innings.

Catching the whole game for the Royals, Ellie Rodríguez became the first Latin American player in franchise history. (Florida-born Spanish descendant Lou Piniella led off the game for Kansas City.) Seventh-place hitter Rodríguez, born in Fajardo, Puerto Rico, collected one hit in five trips. He was pinch-hit for in the bottom of the 12th inning by Joe Keough, who delivered the game-winning base hit.

APRIL 8. The second new team to join the American League's West Division was based in Seattle, Washington. The club played its first game at Anaheim Stadium against the California Angels. Marty Pattin started for Seattle and earned the 4–3 victory, hurling five innings and permitting two runs. Diego Seguí pitched the next three innings, with one run allowed, in what would be credited as a "hold" in today's game. Seguí handed off to Jack Aker, who pitched a scoreless ninth.

Seguí became the first Hispanic player in what was destined to become the Seattle Pilots' short history. The team, plagued by poor attendance, moved to Milwaukee and was refashioned as the "Brewers" just prior to the start of the 1970 campaign.

APRIL 8. The "save" has been introduced as an official pitching category this season. The brainchild of long-time Chicago baseball writer Jerome Holtzman, the new statistic was designed to recognize the contributions of bullpen men to their team's late-game successes.

On Opening Day in Baltimore, Juan Pizarro of the Boston Red Sox became the first American League pitcher to record a save. (Eventually all pitchers, past and current, will have their mound ledgers updated to reflect this viable measure of a relief pitcher's worth.) In a perfect example of the save scenario, Pizarro pitched a perfect bottom of the 12th inning to preserve a 5–4 Red Sox win at Memorial Stadium. The Puerto Rican left-hander retired Frank Robinson, Merv Rettenmund and Brooks Robinson to seal the Orioles' season-opening, stumbling fate.

The prior day, Bill Singer of the Los Angeles Dodgers had notched the first "official" big league save.

APRIL 23. Ten years ago, Mike Cuéllar modestly began his career as a reliever with the Cincinnati Reds. The 22-year-old hurler saw very limited action, then was absent for five years from the big league stage before making his way back for good.

An off-season trade from the Houston Astros to the Baltimore Orioles in 1968 found Cuéllar plying his trade in a new league for the first time. At Memorial Stadium, Cuéllar obtained his first American League win, 3–2 over the Detroit Tigers and Denny McLain, in ten innings.

Cuéllar and McLain will be named co–Cy Young Award winners at the completion of the season, making the Cuban left-hander the first Hispanic recipient of pitching's most prized award.

MAY 18. Rod Carew and César Tovar both steal third base and home in the third inning against the Detroit Tigers at Metropolitan Stadium. With Tovar on third and Carew on first, the teammates executed a double steal. On the next pitch, Carew broke for third and arrived successfully. On the very next pitch, Carew dashed for home, to the delight of the home crowd—and made it!—his third stolen base of the inning. The dual steals of home tied a major league record, but accounted for Minnesota's only runs against the temporarily bewildered Detroit battery of Mickey Lolich and Bill Freehan. The Tigers roared back for an 8–2 win.

Carew became the first Hispanic major leaguer to steal three bases in one inning.

JUNE 16. Home is the hardest base to steal, but Rod Carew was apparently uninformed. One-half of Carew's 12 steals this season have been of home plate. The Twins' second sacker nabbed the home dish for the sixth time, part of back-to-back double steals he and teammate Tony Oliva pulled off against the California Angels at Metropolitan Stadium. In the first inning, Carew, the lead runner on second, stole third base and then home, undeterred by the powerful presence of Harmon Killebrew at the plate. The Twins defeated the Angels, 8–2.

Nagged by injury and also absent for a military reserve duty commitment, Carew managed to play in only 123 games on the season. The lost time proved detrimental to the second baseman, who finished the campaign one short of Ty Cobb's major league record of eight steals of home plate in one season (1912).

JUNE 21. In the bottom of the ninth inning of a 3–3 game against the Minnesota Twins, the Oakland A's Bert Campaneris worked a one-out walk. He promptly stole second but was left stranded when Ted Kubiak and Reggie Jackson made outs. The stolen base was the 33rd on the season for Campaneris and, more notably, the 12th game in a row in which the A's shortstop had swiped a bag—a major league record. The streak, which began on June 10 and included two doubleheaders and three games with two stolen bases, will end tomorrow with an 0-for-4 at the plate by Campaneris against the same visiting team. In all, Campaneris registered 15 steals in the span.

The hard-hitting Twins erupted for 11 runs in the top of the tenth inning to gain a 14–4 extra-inning win at the Oakland Coliseum, to put a damper on Campy's base-stealing feat.

JULY 16. Rod Carew swiped home plate for the seventh time on the season, in the second inning of the first game of a Twins twin-bill sweep over the Chicago White Sox at Metropolitan Stadium (9–8, 6–3). The steal of home by the third-year player, his 15th stolen base in 17 attempts, was the lead leg of a triple steal, with trailing baserunners Harmon Killebrew and Charlie Manuel each moving up a station. Carew recorded another stolen base in the eighth inning and scored the eventual winning run.

To combat the brazen Carew, pitchers began pitching from the stretch whenever he reached third base. Although this turned out to be the last larceny of home plate by Carew on the season, the Panamanian is currently tied for 14th on the all-time list for steals of home and tops all Hispanic players with 17.

AUGUST 5. Roberto Clemente has been called the "fabulous invalid" by the questioning press corps, whom Clemente continues to flabbergast with his potent production amid his repeated grousings over physical ailments.

Currently in the top five in the league in hitting, Clemente, with two hits in today's game at Dodger Stadium, maintained his prestigious placement among the NL's best hitters with a .349 average. The second hit was a single to left field in the ninth inning, in which the Pirates batted around and scored seven runs to wrap up an 11–3 victory over the Los Angeles Dodgers. Two innings earlier, Clemente's teammate, Willie Stargell, slugged a tape-measure home run which cleared the right field pavilion at Dodger Stadium, a drive estimated at 480 feet.

The ninth-inning safety was Clemente's 2,500th career hit, previously uncharted territory for a Hispanic major league player.

AUGUST 13. Most players would not think of switching bats after hitting a home run. But Roberto Clemente had long since proven he was not like most players. Clemente assailed three Giants pitchers for three home runs in a row, plus a fourth hit, during a 10–5 Pirates win at San Francisco. The Pirates' right fielder connected for the circuit in the first, third, and sixth innings, then singled and grounded out. In each home run trip to the plate, Clemente brought with him a different size bat. "I used a 38-ounce bat the first time up," stated the star outfielder, "a 37-ounce bat the next time, and a 36-ounce bat the last time. I didn't go to a lighter bat after the third homer."[35]

Five days before his 35th birthday, the first Hispanic player to hit three home runs in a game twice seemed to be improving with age.

Clemente was denied a fifth batting title by Pete Rose (.348 to .345) at season's finish. Nonetheless, he closed the campaign as possessor of the majors' best batting average for the decade (.328).

Over the past five years, Clemente compiled the highest WAR ranking in both leagues. Clemente's half-decade-long WAR totaled 39.8, ahead of Henry Aaron's 38.9 and Carl Yastrzemski's 38.5. Ron Santo's 38.3 and Willie Mays' 33.7 ratings rounded out baseball's top five for the period.

AUGUST 19. Alejandro Carrasquel, the first pitcher from South America to play in the major leagues, died in Caracas, Venezuela. The vanguard hurler was the first Venezuelan to win a game, throw a shutout, hit safely and homer at the big league level.

Carrasquel, who was 57, was inducted into the Venezuelan Sports Hall of Fame in 1971. In 2003, the former pitcher was part of Venezuela's Baseball Hall of Fame's inaugural class.

AUGUST 29. Those bumbling, lovable baseball losers are no more. In second place, 21 games above .500, and shortly destined to overtake the division-leading Chicago Cubs and fulfill a most *amazin'* season, the New York Mets faced a pitcher who was pretty amazin' himself—Juan Antonio Marichal.

Ten days after losing a 14-inning, 1–0 heartbreaker to the Mets at Shea Stadium, Marichal, the 1960s winningest pitcher (191–88), came back to four-hit the New Yorkers, 5–0, in San Francisco. Marichal's lifetime record stood at 22–3 against the Flushing Meadowers, and now with 186 career victories, he had won 100 more games than he had lost— an unscaled region for a Hispanic major leaguer pitcher.

Through the close of 2015, Marichal's career mark of 243–142 will place him in a select fraternity of 20 pitchers who have retired with 100 or more lifetime wins than losses.

SEPTEMBER 5. Three years since obtaining an "old" Frank Robinson from the Cincinnati Reds, the Baltimore Orioles, it appears, have duped another National League team via the trade. Having snatched Mike Cuéllar from Houston over the winter, the portsider has paid immediate and valuable dividends.

Cuéllar was ordained, this day, as the first Latin American left-hander to win 20 games in the major leagues. (Northern Californian Lefty Gómez was a four-time 20-game winner for the Yankees in the 1930s.) The southpaw gained an 8–4, complete-game decision over the Detroit Tigers at Tiger Stadium, which raised his record to 20–10 in his first season with the high-flying Orioles, winners of 109 regular season games.

SEPTEMBER 16. *Blow, winds, and crack your cheeks! rage! blow!* Lear-like indignation was surely felt by visiting National League hitters who regularly had to brave not only Candlestick Park's howling and sometimes gale-force winds from San Francisco Bay, but also the *oak-cleaving thunderbolts* from the right arm of a pitcher named Marichal.

On an all too typical windy Candlestick night, the Giants' supreme hurler held the Atlanta Braves to four meager singles, winning 2–0. Marichal's league-leading eighth shutout and 19th win edged the Giants past the Braves into first-place by one-half game.

A strong finish by Atlanta, however, earned the Georgia team the National League West crown at the conclusion of the season.

Capturing two more victories, Marichal recorded his sixth 20-win campaign (21–11), the most by any Hispanic pitcher. The magnificent pitcher also snared his first ERA title (2.10), and fell a single out shy of indexing his fourth season with 300 innings pitched. His FIP was 2.39, after a 2.36 rating in 1968.[36]

OCTOBER 1. Minnesota's Rod Carew, who was a terror with his swipes of home plate this season, skipped away with the American League's batting championship. Collecting his final hit of the campaign at Metropolitan Stadium, Carew wrapped up his first hitting title with the first of 15 seasons of hitting .300 or better.

Recording a .332 average, Carew, who turned 24 today, became the first Panamanian player to wear a big league batting crown.

OCTOBER 11. Blessed are the meek, for they shall inherit the earth ... but not in a sweep. In a battle of imminent Cy Young Award winners, Baltimore's Mike Cuéllar outpitched New York's Tom Seaver, 4–1, in Game 1 of the World Series. Cuéllar hurled the

Mike Cuéllar of the Baltimore Orioles was a four-time 20-game winner and became the first Hispanic pitcher to win the Cy Young Award in 1969.

distance on a six-hitter and became the first Latin American pitcher to start, win and complete a World Series game.

"Tom Terrific" came back in a Game 4 rematch with a brilliant ten-inning, 2–1 win at Shea Stadium, and *amazingly,* one day later, the long-servile New York Mets won the World Series in five games over the heavily favored Orioles.

NOVEMBER 29. Mariano Rivera was born in Puerto Caimito, Chorrera, Panama. Rivera would sally forth from his Panamanian fishing town to become the greatest major league relief pitcher in history.

1970

FEBRUARY 2. The Caribbean Series has been revived. After the ideologically motivated withdrawal of Cuba that ended the Latin American championship tournament a decade earlier, and a failed attempt with the Inter-American Series to keep the competition alive, three countries have mobilized to restart the popular spectator games. Original member countries Puerto Rico and Venezuela were joined by a new associate from the Dominican Republic. Panamanian baseball, under financial difficulties, was not able to field a representative squad.

In the first Caribbean Series game for the Dominican delegation, catcher Federico "Freddie" Velázquez of the Licey Tigres clubbed a solo home run against Ponce Leones' hurler Wayne Simpson, etching his name into the history books as the first Dominican player to hit a Caribbean Series home run.

Simpson, however, came out on top, hurling a six-hit, 4–2 victory.

FEBRUARY 10. The reconvened Caribbean Series was played at University Stadium in Caracas, with the three participating teams playing each other four times. The Magallanes Navegantes, the home country's team, delighted the faithful by capturing the championship with a 7–1 record—the first Caribbean Series crown for Venezuela. The Navigators, having already won the championship trophy, won their final game today, 3–2, against the Licey Tigers. Carlos Pascual was the proud Magallanes manager, and first baseman Gonzalo Márquez was named MVP. Márquez became the first native of Venezuela to win the Caribbean Series prize for outstanding performance.

MAY 12. At Wrigley Field, Rico Carty lashed out three singles in his 30th straight game with a hit, breaking the Hispanic major league record of 29 set by Mel Almada in 1938. Carty's visiting Atlanta Braves lost, 4–3, to Chicago, with the big news of the day provided by Ernie Banks. "Mr. Cub" socked his 500th career home run. The ball was retrieved in left field by Carty—this year's National League hitting champ with a lofty .366 average—after it caromed off excited "bleacher bum" hands and back onto the field.

Carty hit safely in the Braves' next game, his 31st in a row. But the following day, May 16, the Dominican outfielder was held hitless by the Reds' Jim McGlothlin.

MAY 20. Rod Carew of the Minnesota Twins hit for the cycle, the first Hispanic player to accomplish the ten-bases feat in the major leagues. The keystone sacker, a blazing 22 for his last 37, drove in two runs and scored a pair for the West Division–leading Twins, 10–5 home winners over the Kansas City Royals.

After the game, Carew, hitting .432, disclosed he had become engaged.

MAY 30. At Fenway Park, Vicente Romo provided four innings of scoreless relief for the Boston Red Sox in the team's 7–5 win over the Chicago White Sox. Sparky Lyle relieved Romo with the tying run at the plate in the ninth inning to secure the game's final out. Romo, one of two brothers from Mexico who reached the major leagues, also clubbed a home run in the sixth inning—the go-ahead sixth run of the game.

accomplished the feat in the second game of a doubleheader against Cleveland 6/21. Gutierrez is from Coro, Venezuela.

César Guttierez relaxes outside of his team hotel the day after recording a 7-for-7 hitting bonanza, in an extra-inning game in Cleveland. Playing for the Detroit Tigers, the Venezuelan shortstop stroked six singles and a double on June 21, 1970.

The solo home run was the first hit by a Mexican pitcher in the major leagues.

JUNE 21. Hail César! Detroit's César Gutérrez tied the major league mark for hits in a game without being retired, gathering seven safeties in an extra-inning contest against the Cleveland Indians. At Cleveland Stadium, the Tigers shortstop, who wears uniform number 7, collected six singles and a double over 12 innings, in the second game of a doubleheader won by the Tigers, 9–8.

Batting second in the order, the Venezuelan equaled the 1892 record of seven consecutive hits in one game by the Baltimore Orioles' Wilbert Robinson.

AUGUST 22. Roberto Clemente collected ten hits over two games against the Los Angeles Dodgers, beginning today at Dodger Stadium.

Clemente's second of five hits in the game (5-for-7) knocked in the Pirates' first run in the third inning. After his fifth hit, in the top of the 16th, he promptly stole second and scored the go-ahead tally for Pittsburgh, as the club gained a 2–1, late-night victory in Tinseltown. Next day, the Pittsburgh team exploded for 23 hits—five by Clemente, who became the fourth player of the century and the first Hispanic to reap ten hits (10-for-13) over consecutive games. The Pirates mercilessly dished out an 11–0 drubbing over the home team.

Clemente's two-game totals were eight singles, a double and a home run, five runs, and four RBI. Hitting explosions such as these helped the gifted outfielder accumulate an OPS+ of 130 for his career.

AUGUST 28. At Candlestick Park, Juan Marichal earned his 200th career victory and the honorary sash as the first Hispanic hurler to reach this major league win total. Defeating the Pittsburgh Pirates, 5–1, Marichal evened his record on the season with his ninth win and sixth in a row. He only recently fully recovered from an adverse reaction to penicillin injections prescribed for an ear infection earlier in the spring.

Marichal entered the season with the tenth-best ERA in modern baseball history at 2.65, and became only the eighth pitcher ever to win 200 games in his first 11 seasons.

SEPTEMBER 9. Mike Cuéllar's fourth shutout of the season came against the New York Yankees, a 1–0 seven-hitter at Memorial Stadium. Cuéllar, who led the American League in games started with 40 and complete games with 21, reigned in his 22nd victory. Cuéllar won 24 games for the Baltimore Orioles, tied for most in the major leagues. The victory total established an all-time season high for a Latin American, left-handed pitcher. (Lefty Gómez won 26 games in 1934.)

Cuéllar's 47 wins in consecutive campaigns tied him with Juan Marichal for the most victories in back-to-back seasons by a Hispanic big league pitcher. The 33-year-old hurler also matched Marichal's 1963 ethnic mark for most starts in a season by a Hispanic hurler.

SEPTEMBER 15. Bert Campaneris recued the Oakland A's from imminent defeat when he stroked a two-out, two-run home run in the top of the ninth inning at County Stadium, to boost his club to a 6–5 victory over the Milwaukee Brewers in the nightcap of a doubleheader. The second-place A's gratefully earned a split of the day's encounters after dropping the opener, 1–0. The game-deciding home run was the second of the contest and 20th overall for the A's shortstop. With well over 30 stolen bases to his credit at this point, Campaneris became the first Hispanic player to hit 20 home runs and steal 20 bases in a big league season.

OCTOBER 3. Pitcher Mike Cuéllar slugged the first grand slam home run in League Championship Series play, in Game 1 of the American League Championship Series between the Baltimore Orioles and Minnesota Twins at Metropolitan Stadium. The jackpot wallop was struck against Twins 24-game-winner Jim Perry, as part of a seven-run fourth inning for Baltimore.

Cuéllar, like Perry, did not bring his best stuff to the hill and, despite the early offensive production, did not last the required five innings to pick up a win. The Birds prevailed, 10–6, on their way to a three-game championship series sweep of the Twins for the second year in a row.

OCTOBER 15. One batter away from being removed from the game, Mike Cuéllar settled down after a rocky first inning and retired 23 of the final 26 hitters he faced. Regrouping on the Memorial Stadium mound, Cuéllar produced a six-hit, route-going effort against the Cincinnati Reds in Game 5 of the World Series. The 9–3 win brought baseball's world championship to Baltimore and elevated Cuéllar as the first Latin American starting pitcher to win a clinching World Series game.[37]

The final out in the Series clincher was appropriately provided by Orioles third baseman Brooks Robinson, who threw out the Reds' Pat Corrales at first base. Robinson, nicknamed the "human vacuum cleaner" for his defensive prowess, displayed spectacular fielding throughout the Series and was named the MVP.

1971

FEBRUARY 6. The opening of the Caribbean Series, scheduled for February 5, was delayed a day due to rain. More of the same wet stuff partially delayed today's rescheduled doubleheader, which anticipated a four-team tourney with the inclusion of a new nation invitee, Mexico. The rain did not prevent either contest from being played to completion, however. In the opening game, in front of 14,000 enthusiastic fans at Hiram Bithorn Stadium in San Juan, the Licey Tigers edged Venezuela's La Guaira's Sharks, 5–4. A two-run home run by Freddie Velázquez in the top of the eighth inning delivered the game to Licey. Pedro Borbon, in relief of starter Reggie Cleveland, was the winner and pocketed the first win by a Dominican pitcher in Caribbean Series competition. Don Shaw pitched a scoreless ninth for the save.

FEBRUARY 6. Baseball Commissioner Bowie Kuhn and National Association president Phil Piton were on hand for opening ceremonies of the XIV Caribbean Series, as it returned to its original 24-game, double round robin format with the addition of a fourth team, Mexico's *Naranjeros* of Hermosillo.

With a 2–4 record, the Orange Growers finished well behind the unvanquished champion Licey Tigers. One of the bright spots on the Mexican roster was Celerino Sánchez, who socked three home runs and drove home nine runs, the top power numbers in the Series.

On this day one, Sánchez smacked a dramatic two-run, bottom of the ninth-inning home run to tie the Santurce Crabbers. The New York Yankees' prospect earned the distinction of smashing the tournament's first home run by a Mexican player. Teammate Zoilo Versalles cranked two solo home runs in a losing cause for the team from Mexico. Tony Pérez singled home Sandy Alomar with the eventual winning run in the top of the 11th inning. Santurce held on for the 5–4 win.

FEBRUARY 9. Hermosillo hurler Manuel Lugo provided first-rate, late-inning relief and Celerino Sánchez connected for a decisive two-run double in the top of the ninth, to lead the Orange Growers to a 7–5 victory over the Santurce Crabbers at Hiram Bithorn Stadium. Sergio Robles kept the Crabbers off the board in the bottom half of the frame to register the save. Lugo's victory was the first win for the Mexican aggregation, 0–3 until today, and the first Caribbean Series win recorded by a Mexican pitcher.

FEBRUARY 11. The Licey Tigers won the Dominican Republic's first Caribbean Series championship, with MVP Manny Mota strategically leading the way. Mota was the manager of his club and led all tournament batters with a .579 average (11-for-19), as the Tigers mauled their competition, posting a 6–0 mark. In the sixth win, today, Licey reliever Chi-Chi Olivo recorded the save by striking out Reggie Jackson and Elrod Hendricks in the bottom of the ninth inning, as Santurce mounted an attempted rally. Beating the Crabbers, 6–4, Licey joined Almendares, Habana, Cienfuegos and Santurce as tournament undefeated champions.

Licey brought their own merengue band, which was kept active throughout the Games by the performance of its unbeaten patriots.

APRIL 25. Tony Oliva socked two home runs, drove in three runs and scored as many, in the Minnesota Twins' 8–0 victory over the New York Yankees. Jim Kaat pitched a two-hitter and stroked two of the Twins' 14 hits in the Yankee Stadium contest.

The long balls were two of 22 hit on the season by Oliva. Adding 30 doubles and three triples, the Twins' right fielder compiled a circuit-topping .546 slugging percentage. Prior to this season, no Hispanic major leaguer had paced his loop in slugging.

Batting .337, Oliva also led the league in hitting for the third time.

MAY 20. The mortal coil of Martín Dihigo, one of the most versatile talents ever to grace a baseball field, was laid to rest in Cienfuegos, Cuba.

"*El Maestro*" died of a heart attack, five days before his 65th birthday.

MAY 30. Manuel Ramírez was born in Santo Domingo, Dominican Republic. Plucked as a first round draft pick out of George Washington High School in the highly concentrated Dominican enclave of Manhattan's Washington Heights neighborhood, Ramírez blossomed into an awe-inspiring hitter with a smooth, lightning-fast swing.

JUNE 4. The previously formidable "Big Three" is now a "Killer Quartet." Mike Cuéllar (8–1), one of a foursome of starting pitchers the Baltimore Orioles have used exclusively since Opening Day, shut out the Milwaukee Brewers, 2–0, yielding four hits.

The whitewash was one of 36 the screwballing pitcher hurled in his career—the most recorded by a Hispanic left-hander.

Baltimore's four starters this season were all 20-game winners, matching the 1920 Chicago White Sox's fabulous foursome of Urban Faber, Claude Williams, Eddie Cicotte and Dickie Kerr as the second starting staff in history with four 20-game victors.

The Orioles' frontliners of Cuéllar (20–9), Dave McNally (21–5), Jim Palmer (20–9) and Pat Dobson (20–8) proved as durable as they were effective, winning a staggering 81 of the Orioles' 101 triumphs and completing 70 of 142 starts. Remarkably, not until the second game of a June 22 doubleheader did manager Earl Weaver turn to a fifth starter.

JULY 13. The All-Star Game, held at Tiger Stadium in Detroit, shone with what turned out to be its brightest collection of stars ever. Featuring an incredible 20 future Hall of Fame members, six of those members socked home runs, one a moon shot by Reggie Jackson. The game's last circuit clout came off the bat of Roberto Clemente in the eighth inning and accounted for the final run of the game for the losing National League. Clemente's solo blast brought the NL to within two runs, at 6–4, but the Senior Circuit was shut down after that.

Clemente became the first Puerto Rican player to hit a home run in the All-Star Game.

JULY 25. Pedro Martínez was born in Manoguayabo, Dominican Republic. Straddling the years around the turn of the next century, Martínez emerged as one of his era's greatest and most dominant pitchers.

AUGUST 10. Juan Marichal mesmerized the Montreal Expos, 1–0. The two-hitter at Candlestick Park was the extraordinary pitcher's 50th career whitewash, a new plateau high for a Hispanic major league hurler.

Over the last 14 days of the season, the 33-year-old moundsman was most instrumental in San Francisco attaining its first NL West Division title. Marichal won four games, including a season finale, 5–1 win in San Diego, to clinch the division title for his club by one game over the Los Angeles Dodgers.

AUGUST 24. No Panamanian pitcher had thrown a shutout in the big leagues prior to today. In his initial major league start, Boquete, Panama, native Ed Acosta delivered the initial big league blanking for the Isthmus country.

Pitching for the San Diego Padres, Acosta, with only 2⅔ innings of big league experience, permitted eight hits to the Philadelphia Phillies in shutting them out, 2–0, at Veterans Stadium. The 6'5" right-hander revealed afterward that he was so nervous about his assignment that he was unable to sleep the night before.

Acosta posted a 6–9 lifetime record in three big league seasons, mostly as a reliever.

AUGUST 25. Roberto Clemente lashed out five singles in six at-bats at Atlanta's Fulton County Stadium, part of a 21-hit barrage that Pittsburgh's "lumber company" unleashed on six Braves' pitchers en route to a 13–6 victory. The win helped the Pirates keep a five-game lead in the East Division.

Clemente's eighth career five-hit game landed him a special, elevated place all to himself among Hispanic major league players.

SEPTEMBER 1. The Pittsburgh Pirates were cruising to the division title, en route to greater October glory. At Three Rivers Stadium today, the team presented an all-minority starting line-up on a major league diamond for the first time. Playing for those front-running Pirates, four Hispanic players—Manny Sanguillen (C), Rennie Stennett (2B), Jackie Hernández (SS) and Roberto Clemente (RF)—took the field, along with

African Americans Gene Clines (CF), Willie Stargell (LF), Dave Cash (3B), Al Oliver (1B) and pitcher Dock Ellis, to face the Philadelphia Phillies.

Except for Ellis, the starters played the entire game, attended by 11,278 fans. The Pirates were victorious, 10–7.

Parenthetically, Jackie Hernández recorded the lowest lifetime batting average of any Latin American major league player in the 20th century. His .208 career mark (minimum 1,000 AB) was seven points below the career hitting ineptitude of Mario Mendoza, he of the infamous "Mendoza Line."

SEPTEMBER 2. César Cedeño hit a not-so "grand slam," inside-the-park home run in the bottom of the fifth inning at the Astrodome. Batting against Claude Osteen of the Los Angeles Dodgers, Cedeño lofted a fly to short right field. From opposite directions, second baseman Jim Lefebvre and right fielder Bill Buckner charged after the ball, with neither catching it. Instead they collided, with the ball brushing the tip of Lefevbre's gloved hand and rolling all the way to the outfield wall.

Cedeño raced around the bases before the defense could retrieve the errant ball in time and was credited with the 170-foot grand slam. The "blow" broke the backs of the Dodgers, who lost the game, 9–3.

At age 20 years and seven months, Cedeño became the youngest Hispanic player to homer with the bases full in the major leagues.

OCTOBER 4. The ten 20-game winners in the American League this season tied a decades-old league record.

Two of the charmed circle hurlers, Mike Cuéllar and Catfish Hunter, met today in the second game of the American League Championship Series at Memorial Stadium. Cuéllar, coming off a third straight 20-win season, limited Hunter's Oakland club to six hits in a 5–1, complete-game win—the first victory recorded by a Hispanic pitcher in the League Championship Series.

The Orioles, now with a two-game advantage, set the stage for a three-game series sweep, delivered the next day in Oakland by Jim Palmer.

OCTOBER 17. "*En el día más grande de mi vida, para los nenes, la bendición mia y que mis padres me hechen mi bendición y Puerto Rico.*" ("On the greatest day of my life, to my children, I give my blessing, and to my parents I ask for theirs, and Puerto Rico's.") Roberto Clemente, staying true to his greatest loves, his family and his country, basked in the glory of his accomplishments during his opening statement, made for a U.S. national television audience moments after Steve Blass outpitched Mike Cuéllar, 2–1, in the deciding game of the World Series. Clemente requested the indulgence from interviewer Bob Prince before he proceeded to answer the long-time Pirates broadcaster's questions. Clemente used a superb seven-game performance during the Series to help lead the Pittsburgh Pirates to the world championship.

The Pirates' regal right fielder reached Cuéllar for a home run in the fourth inning for the game's first run, and José Pagán doubled in the game-deciding run in the eighth inning. Cuéllar had retired the first 11 Bucs batters before Clemente launched a pitch over the left center field wall. It was Clemente's 12th and final hit in the Series. Hitting safely in every game (with a .414 Series average), Clemente exerted himself with fierce abandon around the base paths, displayed stellar defense in right, and showcased his superlative arm on several occasions. Having one hit in all seven games of the 1960 World Series, Clemente established a consecutive games hitting mark in the World Series by a Hispanic player with 14. (New York Yankees outfielder Hank Bauer hit in 17 straight

World Series contests, 1956–1958. Lou Gehrig reached base, by hit, walk or HBP, in a record 23 straight Fall Classic games in the 1920s and 1930s.)

Clemente was named MVP of the Series, the first Hispanic player to earn the most celebrated post-season series laurel. He also became the first Hispanic player to win both the World Series MVP and league MVP awards.

NOVEMBER 13. Iván Rodríguez was born in Vega Baja, Puerto Rico. Rodríguez made his major league debut as a 19-year catcher in 1991 and set new hitting and endurance standards at his position.

DECEMBER 30. The Dominican Republic's most outstanding player of the first half of the 20th century died in Guayama, Puerto Rico. Juan "Tetelo" Vargas, winter and Negro leagues standout, was laid to rest in the city of his adopted country.

The 65-year-old Vargas was a lauded hitter and had an unusually graceful type of speed. The Santo Domingo native was known as "the Dominican Deer." In Spanish, his rhymed nickname was "*el Gamo* [Gah-mo] *Dominicano*."

He was later enshrined in the Puerto Rican Hall of Fame and the Latino Baseball Hall of Fame in the Dominican Republic.

1972

FEBRUARY 4. The Dominican Republic hosted its first Caribbean Series. The six-day tournament was played at Estadio Quisqueya in Santo Domingo. The Dominican Winter League champion from Santiago, Águilas Cibaeñas, ended up in a second-place tie with Venezuela's Aragua Tigers (managed by Rod Carew). Both 3–3 clubs finished two games behind the Ponce Lions, the tournament's top team with a 5–1 record.

The best-pitched game of the competition for Águilas was delivered today by the right arm of Secundino Almonte. The Eagles pitcher blanked Mexico's Guasave Cotton Growers (1–5), on five hits, 3–0. Outfielder Adrian Garrett broke up a scoreless game with a sixth-inning, two-run home run.

The 25-year-old Almonte, a career minor leaguer, merited the perpetual prestige of tossing the first shutout by a Dominican pitcher in the Caribbean Series.

SEPTEMBER 4. Luis Tiant became the first pitcher in major league history to throw four consecutive shutouts twice. The Boston Red Sox right-hander five-hit the Milwaukee Brewers at County Stadium, 2–0, with Carl Yastrzemski providing all the Red Sox scoring with a third-inning home run against Brewers pitcher Jim Lonborg. The Brewers joined the Texas Rangers and Chicago White Sox (twice) as the teams whitewashed in Tiant's three previous starts.

Tiant stretched his consecutive scoreless innings streak to 40⅓ in his next start, a 4–2 victory over New York. He earned a second commendation as the only pitcher besides Walter Johnson to record two scoreless streaks of 40 or more innings in his major league career.

With six shutouts on the season, Tiant posted his second season with an ERA below 2.00 (1.91). He and Pedro Martínez are the only Hispanic starting pitchers to boast two seasons with ERAs under 2.00 in the big leagues.

SEPTEMBER 10. The Astros' César Cedeño stole two bases, #49 and 50 on the season. Both came against the Los Angeles Dodgers battery of Don Sutton and Steve Yeager at Dodger Stadium. The base swipes did not help the Astros add to their two-run total on the day, as the team dropped a 3–2 decision. But with 21 home runs on the campaign, Cedeño became the first Hispanic player to record the diverse combination of at least 20 home runs and 50 stolen bases (22/55).

SEPTEMBER 19. At Metropolitan Stadium, César Tovar tripled leading off the game for the Minnesota Twins and later homered in the ninth inning to win it. In between, the Twins' left fielder singled and doubled. Tovar's extra-base hitting powered Minnesota to a 5–3 victory over the Texas Rangers.

The Caracas-born Tovar became, at the time, the second hitter in major league history (after Ken Boyer) to complete the cycle with a walk-off home run. He also gained ethnic eminence as the first Venezuelan to hit for the cycle and smack a walkoff home run.

An extremely versatile competitor, Tovar, along with Bert Campaneris, were the only players in history to play one full inning at every position in a major league game. Additionally, Tovar shares the record with Eddie Milner for most big league no-hitters broken up with five.

SEPTEMBER 20. "I've never seen an ovation like Tiant got tonight in my 17 years of baseball. Everybody was standing and shouting and cheering."[38] Teammate Luis Aparicio thus described the caliber of fan appreciation rendered to Luis Tiant, who defeated the Baltimore Orioles and fellow countryman Mike Cuéllar, 4–0, in the second game of a doubleheader at Fenway Park.

The collective tribute to Tiant was for raising the Red Sox from also-rans to pennant contenders. It began during the twin bill's interlude when Tiant finished warming up. As he walked in from the right field bullpen, the right-hander was accompanied by standing cheers and applause all the way to the dugout.

A second standing O occurred in the bottom of the eighth inning, with crescendoing applause for Tiant as he walked to home plate from the on-deck circle.

As the top of the ninth inning started, all of the 28,777 in attendance rose as one, once more to give thanks to the man who was about to win his ninth victory in ten starts, six of them by shutout. Every pitch by Tiant in the inning was cheered by the standing spectators. Every twisting, turning delivery was infectiously applauded by the exuberant crowd, until the final out. This game best traced the beginning of a deep, sentimental and lasting affection gained by Tiant from the fans of Boston, bestowed upon few New England team athletes.

This New England athlete, with his 15–6 record in 43 games (19 starts), was named American League "Comeback Player of the Year," the first Hispanic major leaguer bestowed with the eight-year-old award.

SEPTEMBER 30. Two years ago, on a special night in his honor at Three Rivers Stadium, Puerto Rico collectively toasted Roberto Clemente. A large scroll with *300,000* individual signatures of support from residents of the Island was presented to Clemente, along with an array of gifts from various Puerto Rican civic and commercial business organizations.

Today at Three Rivers Stadium, all of baseball toasted the Great One, as Clemente lined a fourth-inning double against Jon Matlack of the New York Mets for the 3,000th hit of his brilliant career. The Pittsburgh fans had cheered his every move yesterday in anticipation of the feat, but the star outfielder was stymied by the Mets' Tom Seaver. The same appreciative chants and applause followed Clemente throughout this game.

Second base umpire Doug Harvey gingerly hands Roberto Clemente the just-retrieved 3000th hit of his career, a double that was stroked against Jon Matlack of the New York Mets at Three Rivers Stadium on September 30, 1972. Clemente became the first Hispanic player to record as many hits in the major leagues.

Playing for the Pirates' third straight division-winning team, Clemente became the first Hispanic player to conquer the 3,000 plateau. His personal reflections: "I dedicate the hit to the Pittsburgh fans, and to the people of Puerto Rico, and to one man in particular. The one man who carried me around for weeks looking for a scout to sign me [Roberto Marín]."[39]

Clemente's hit total will stand as the most by a Puerto Rican player in the major leagues in the 20th century.

OCTOBER 7. A base hit by Gonzalo Márquez rallied the Oakland A's to a Game 1 victory in the American League Championship Series over the Detroit Tigers. The A's were down, 2–1, with runners on first and second and one out, when Márquez came through. A pinch-hitter in the bottom of the tenth inning, Márquez singled to right field, scoring the tying run. When Tigers right fielder Al Kaline committed an error on the hit, the winning run scored from first base.

The Venezuelan Márquez became the first Hispanic player to record a walk-off hit in the major league post-season. The A's defeated the Tigers, three games to two, to advance to the World Series.

OCTOBER 7. In Pittsburgh, Pennsylvania, Puerto Rico and Panama provided the major leagues with its first Hispanic post-season battery. Pitcher Ramón Hernández of

Carolina, Puerto Rico, and catcher Manny Sanguillén of Colón, Panama, teamed up in the ninth inning of the first game of the National League Championship Series for the achievement.

In front of 50,476 fans, the Pirates' tandem recorded the final two outs of the game, sealing a 5–1 Bucs win over the Cincinnati Reds.

OCTOBER 11. *I am a small point in the eye of the full moon.* Johnny Bench cranked an opposite-field blast over Roberto Clemente's head and into the seats for a home run to tie the game. *I only need one ray of the sun to warm my face.* Clemente watched from right field as things unfolded to cost the Pirates a pennant in the ninth inning at Riverfront Stadium. *I only need one breeze from the* Alisios *to refresh my soul.* Minutes later, the fifth game of the National League Championship Series ended; the Reds scored the winning run on a Bob Moose wild pitch and advanced to the World Series. Clemente produced a 1-for-3 showing at the plate in what turned out to be his last major league game. *What else can I ask if I know that my sons really love me?*

The four-line poem, entitled *"Quien Soy"?* ("Who Am I?"), was written by Clemente to his children on the occasion of a Pirates' Father's Day celebration a few years earlier.[40]

A generation later, Clemente's greatness will be all the more validated with modern analytical techniques. Clemente's lifetime WAR metric of 94.5 computes to the highest of any Hispanic player in the 20th century.

OCTOBER 19. Angel Mangual hit .246 and drove in 32 runs as a fill-in player for the Oakland A's during the season. As a pinch-hitter in the bottom of the ninth inning of Game 4 of the World Series, Mangual registered his biggest hit and RBI of the campaign. At the Oakland-Alameda County Coliseum, the Puerto Rican utility man singled with runners on the corners and the score tied 2–2, to provide the A's with the victory over the National League champion Cincinnati Reds. The A's rallied from a 2–1 deficit entering the last inning to secure their second walk-off win of the post-season.

The winning hit by the third-year outfielder, which moved the A's to a 3–1 advantage in games, was the first of its game-ending kind struck by a Hispanic player in World Series play. Oakland won the close, hard-fought Series in seven games—all but one decided by one run.

DECEMBER 31. Roberto Clemente was lost to the world off the coast of his beloved Puerto Rico. A cargo plane he was on, carrying relief supplies to earthquake victims in Nicaragua, crashed into the sea almost immediately after takeoff.

The following day, the President of the United States, Richard Nixon, wrote a personal check for $1,000 and sent it to the Nicaraguan ambassador in Washington, saying "The best memorial we can build to his memory is to contribute generously for the relief of those he was trying to help."[41] The President's statement was taken to heart and his action spawned a memorial fund established under the Clemente name to provide assistance to Nicaragua. The Pirates and the Mellon Foundation of Pittsburgh each contributed $100,000.

1973

MARCH 10. The Commissioner of baseball, Bowie Kuhn, was the guest speaker at the dedication ceremony for the newly completed Hall of Fame building in Monterrey, Mexico.

The first class of 22 immortals included these colossal names in Mexican baseball history: Roberto "Bobby" Ávila, José "Chili" Gómez, Baldomero "Mel" Almada, Alberto Romo Chávez, Jesús "Cochihuila" Valenzuela, Alejandro Aguilar Reyes, Jorge Pasquel, Ernesto Carmona IV, and North Americans Roy Campanella, Josh Gibson and Monte Irvin.

"I can remember when, as a 10-year-old boy in Washington D.C., I went out to see my first baseball hero, Mel Almada," Commissioner Kuhn said as part of his remarks. "It is a big thrill for me today to see my boyhood hero enshrined in your Mexican Hall of Fame."[42]

APRIL 5. Continuing a long-standing tradition, the Cincinnati Reds opened the baseball season at home, one day ahead of other clubs and to a huge crowd. During pregame ceremonies, the Reds raised the 1972 National League pennant over Riverfront Stadium. Once the game commenced, however, there was little flag-waving for the 51,579 in attendance.

Juan Marichal and the San Francisco Giants spoiled the Opening Day festivities with a 4–1 victory over the home team. Marichal pitched a seven-hitter, allowed two walks, and struck out two, in registering his sixth Opening Day victory—the most recorded by a Hispanic major league hurler (tied by Félix Hernández in 2015).

After the season, Marichal was sold to the Boston Red Sox, ending his resplendent career with the San Francisco Giants and precipitating his retirement from the game one season later.

APRIL 6. A dignified ceremony honored a man of unceremonious dignity. Roberto Clemente's uniform number 21 was retired at Three Rivers Stadium. The largest crowd in Pittsburgh's sports history, 51,695, witnessed the season-opening observance.

Mrs. Luisa Clemente Walker, Roberto's mother, received a framed uniform of her son, as did Vera Clemente, Roberto's widow, who was present with her three sons, Roberto Jr., Enrique, and Luis, ranging from ages eight to four.

The Puerto Rican and United States national anthems were played to conclude the occasion of the first uniform number of a Hispanic player to be retired by a major league team.

APRIL 6. The Twins' Tony Oliva socked the first home run as a designated hitter. At the Oakland–Alameda County Coliseum, in his first at-bat of the campaign, Oliva connected against the A's Catfish Hunter, with Rod Carew on base. Oliva and his teammates knocked Hunter out of the game after three innings, and Bert Blyleven hurled a complete-game, 8–3 victory. Oliva, whose stellar career had come to a near halt due to crippling knee injuries, was able to extend his playing career a few more seasons thanks to the American League's new rule.

(Earlier in the day, at Fenway Park, the first designated hitter in baseball history, Ron Blomberg of the New York Yankees, faced Luis Tiant of the Boston Red Sox and drew a first-inning, bases-loaded walk.)

Despite playing on two chronically bad knees over the next four seasons, Oliva remained productive in three of them. He retired after 1976, owning an OPS+ mark of 131—one of five Hispanic players in the century to compile an OPS+ of 130 or better (Miñoso, Clemente, Cepeda and Carew).

JULY 15. On the same Candlestick Park mound that saw him author his first shutout, in a stupendous major league debut 13 years ago, Juan Marichal spun the 52nd and final shutout of his storied career. Marichal allowed four hits and struck out six, cruising to a

12–0 victory over the Pittsburgh Pirates. Willie McCovey slugged home runs #400 and 401 to back his longtime teammate.

The whitewash total endures as the most by a Hispanic big league pitcher.

AUGUST 6. The path cleared by the Board of Directors' waiver of the mandatory five-year waiting period, Roberto Clemente was voted into the Hall of Fame by an overwhelming 93 percent of ballots cast by the Baseball Writers' Association of America, four months after his tragic death.

Today, Clemente became the first Latin American player to be enshrined in Cooperstown. Clemente's widow, Vera, carrying a heavy heart, proudly spoke a few words that resonated as her late husband's own. "This is Roberto's last triumph," she said. "If he were here now, he would dedicate this honor to the people of Puerto Rico, to the people of Pittsburgh, and to the people all over the United States."[43]

It was the second time the waiting period had been waived for a player. The initial occurrence also came under tragic circumstance, allowing induction of a terminally ill Lou Gehrig in 1939.

OCTOBER 9. Bert Campaneris lined a solo home run off Mike Cuéllar, leading off the bottom of the 11th inning, to give the Oakland A's a 2–1 victory over the Baltimore Orioles in the third game of the American League Championship Series. The home run ended one of October baseball's greatest pitching duels, between Cuéllar and Kenny Holtzman of the A's. The circuit clout was Cuéllar's fourth hit allowed, while Holtzman permitted but three safeties to the Orioles in his grand extra-inning effort.

The first post-season, walk-off home run by a Hispanic big leaguer put the A's ahead two games to one in the best-of-five series, which Oakland won in five games.

OCTOBER 9. Cincinnati's Pedro Borbón recorded the first save by a Hispanic pitcher in the post-season. Known for having a "rubber arm," Borbón efficiently set down the three New York Mets batters to face him, in the bottom of the 11th inning of Game 4 of the National League Championship Series. The Borbón-preserved, 2–1 Reds victory at Shea Stadium temporarily staved off elimination for the Big Red Machine. The following day, they lost to Tom Seaver and missed their bid for a second consecutive World Series appearance.

1974

FEBRUARY 1. The XVII Caribbean Series began in Hermosillo, Mexico, with two teams from that country joining representative clubs from Puerto Rico and the Dominican Republic. (Labor strife between players and management in the Venezuelan Winter League prevented the circuit from sending its annual representative.) Following the Opening Day ceremonies, one of the Mexican squads, Yaquis de Obregón, faced off against the Caguas Criollos in the inaugural contest.

Caguas, behind a battery of future major leaguers Craig Swan and Gary Carter, defeated the Obregon team, 2–1. The only Yaquis run was a solo home run by Héctor Espino. Five-year big league veteran Ramón Hernández picked up the save for Caguas, who won the Series with a 4–2 record.

Although his only home run of the tournament came in this game, Espino led all batters in hitting with a .429 average (9-for-21), and was named the competition's Most Valuable Player. The home run king became the first Mexican player to receive the prestigious tournament honor.

FEBRUARY 6. Eleno Cuen of the Mazatlán Deer helped his team save face in front of the partisan fans who came out to cheer their two home clubs over the six-day Caribbean Series. The Sonora-born pitcher tossed a six-hit whitewash over the Caguas Criollos, 1–0. The 21-year-old Cuen threw the last pitch of the final game of the competition, held in Mexico for the first time. He wrapped up the second win of the tournament for Mazatlán and gained the first shutout by a Mexican pitcher in the Caribbean Classic.

Mazatlán's Pacific League rivals, the Yaquis, lost the earlier game, 3–2, to the Licey Tigers. The defeat dropped the Yaquis record to 3–3 (tied with Licey), and clinched the tournament for Caguas prior to the setback to Cuen.

MAY 29. Perhaps it was the fact that he was on a staff of outstanding pitchers who pushed one another to high levels of accomplishment. Or perhaps it was an innate professionalism that drove him to forge such thorough pitching trails. Or simply, it was because there were nine innings to be pitched as a starter. Whatever the motivation, Mike Cuéllar-starter and Mike Cuéllar-finisher have been very much synonymous for the past five seasons and two months, since his arrival in Baltimore.

In his 200th start since joining the Orioles in 1969, the Cuban port-sider completed his 100th game. It was a 10–3 derailing of the Royals in Kansas City, and for Marvelous Mike, a sixth straight distance-traversing start in the current campaign.

Cuéllar will complete more games, 172, than any other left-handed Latin American pitcher in major league history. (Lefty Gómez posted 173 route-going efforts.)

JUNE 14. Luis Tiant pitched 14⅓ innings in a 15-inning, 4–3 loss to the California Angels at Anaheim.

Mickey Rivers scored from first base on a one-out double by Denny Doyle in the 15th frame to defeat the valiant Tiant. The Boston right-hander had thrown ten scoreless innings since allowing three runs back in the third. Entering the contest, the Red Sox hurler had won six games in row and had thrown eight straight complete games. For the first 13 innings, Tiant dueled Nolan Ryan to a 3–3 tie, after Carl Yastremzski's home run in the ninth inning with a man aboard sent the game into extras.

Catching 19 strikeouts off the "Ryan Express," Angels catcher Ellie Rodríguez tied the American League record with 21 putouts in an extra-inning game. Throwing *235* pitches, Ryan walked ten batters, as the Red Sox stranded 16 runners against the fireballer.

Tossing 25 complete games on the season, including this one, Tiant was a 22-game winner for the third-place Red Sox. With 311⅓ innings pitched, Tiant joined Adolfo Luque and Juan Marichal as the only Hispanic pitchers to surpass the 300 innings-pitched mark in one major league season.

AUGUST 27. Benny Ayala of the New York Mets became the first player from Puerto Rico to hit a home run in his initial at-bat in the major leagues. With one out in the second inning, the 23-year-old Ayala cranked a pitch from Houston Astros hurler Tom Griffin beyond the Shea Stadium outfield wall to open the scoring in the game. Starting in left field, Ayala scored again later as the Mets prevailed, 4–2, behind starter Tug McGraw and a three-inning save from Harry Parker.

1975

FEBRUARY 6. Manager José Pagán earned the distinction of being the first Puerto Rican to guide a team from Puerto Rico to the Caribbean Series victory podium. Losing only once in the tournament (today), the *Vaqueros* de Bayamón captured Puerto Rico's seventh Latin American championship and second in a row. Making it all the more sweeter for Pagán and Bayamón, the Series was held at Hiram Bithorn Stadium in San Juan.

Cowboys first baseman Willie Montañez was named Series MVP.

FEBRUARY 9. Vladimir Guerrero was born in Nizao, Peravia, Dominican Republic. Growing into a 6'3", 235-pound, imposing presence on the diamond, Guerrero developed into the rare five-tool player, racking up hitting laurels as an outfielder with four major league teams.

APRIL 17. Over the past three seasons, Juan Marichal's record was 22–32, helped by a 5–1 record in 11 appearances for the Boston Red Sox last season. This year, after signing with the Los Angeles Dodgers as a free agent, Marichal made a pact with himself. "In spring training I promised myself if I couldn't do the job, I would get out,"[44] he told reporters. After two ineffective starts with his new team, the second of which came yesterday against the Cincinnati Reds, the inimitable pitcher lived up to his promise and retired at 37 years of age.

Marichal earned honors as the all-time leader in wins (243) by a Dominican pitcher in the major leagues. Perhaps more significantly, the right-hander hung up his spikes with six campaigns each of 20 wins and 200 strikeouts, with a lifetime ERA of 2.89. Walter Johnson, with seven, is the only pitcher in history with more 20-win and 200 strikeout seasons.

JULY 30. After eight days in the major leagues, José Sosa of the Houston Astros stepped to the plate for the first time and cracked a home run. The blow came with two men on base in the bottom of the eighth inning in the Astrodome. A relief pitcher, Sosa had been called upon in the top of the inning to put down a threat by the visiting San Diego Padres, which the Santo Domingo native did.

The three-run home run by the 23-year-old Sosa, the first by a Hispanic pitcher and Dominican player in his initial at-bat in the major leagues, provided a comfortable cushion for the pitcher to record his first big league save. The final score was 8–4.

SEPTEMBER 16. The Pirates' Rennie Stennett became the first player in the modern era to rap out seven consecutive hits in a nine-inning game. The Panamanian second baseman twice gathered two hits in one inning (the fourth big league player and first Hispanic with this achievement). Stennett rapped four singles, two doubles and a triple, scored five runs and drove in two with the hitting spree that tied Wilbert Robinson's 83-year-old record for most hits in a regulation-length game. The Bucs humiliated the Cubs at Wrigley Field, 22–0, in the most lopsided shutout yet seen in National League history.

Lashing out three more hits against the Phillies at Veterans Stadium the next day, the 24-year-old Pirates infielder became the fifth person in the 20th century rake ten hits over two consecutive games.

SEPTEMBER 28. Another baseball season. Another batting title for Rodney Cline Carew.

The Twins' first baseman gained his fourth title in a row, matching Ty Cobb, Rogers Hornsby and Honus Wagner as the only other major league players with such a string. The new crown—"size .359"—was fitted after a two-hit game in today's season finale. The Twins lost, 6–4, in ten innings to the Chicago White Sox at the Met.

Soon to turn 30, Carew became the first player since Joe DiMaggio to hit .350 or higher for three consecutive campaigns.

OCTOBER 11. Beantown braced for the Big Red Machine. The 108-win Cincinnati Reds rolled into Boston and a rendezvous with baseball history. In Game 1 of what will become one of baseball's most memorable and important World Series, the scoring is started by the hometown pitcher.

Luis Tiant tallied the game's first run (part of a six-run seventh inning), but more significantly he did not allow any to the powerhouse Reds. Tiant pitched a masterful five-hit, 6–0 shutout at "the Fens," in front of 35,205 fanatics, including Tiant's own parents, who had arrived from Cuba a few months earlier.

The first Hispanic pitcher to throw a World Series shutout, Tiant stretched to 36 innings (including playoffs) a streak of not allowing an earned run at Fenway Park.

OCTOBER 14. Part of the Cincinnati Reds' on-field success could be traced to their exceptional up-the-middle defense. All of those premium position defenders not only contributed in their usual, steady way with the glove today, but also with the bat. At Riverfront Stadium, in Game 3 of the World Series, catcher Johnny Bench, shortstop Dave Concepción and center fielder César Geronimo all hit home runs.

The home run by Concepción was the first hit by a Venezuelan player in World Series competition.

Second baseman Joe Morgan's tenth-inning single knocked home the winning run for the Reds in the 6–5 victory over the Boston Red Sox.

OCTOBER 15. Displaying sheer guts, determination, and a courageous heart overflowing with a sole purpose, Luis Tiant's unbending will to win shepherded a sometimes uncertain outcome to victory for the Boston Red Sox. Tossing an indefatigable, 163-pitch complete game, Tiant defeated the Cincinnati Reds, 5–4, in Game 4 of the World Series at Riverfront Stadium. The game and Tiant's pitching bravado endowed this Fall Classic as one of the greatest of all time.

Tiant also scored the game's decisive run after singling in the fourth inning. Center fielder Fred Lynn pitched in with a game-saving, running catch in the ninth inning, with one out and two runners on base. Retiring the next Cincinnati batter, Joe Morgan, the veteran Red Sox hurler became the first Latin American pitcher to record three straight post-season, complete-game victories and to notch two wins by complete game in one World Series.

Even at two games apiece, the hard-fought, 72nd World Series continued to recapture the attention of a wavering generation of fans by reminding all what a matchlessly great game baseball can be.

OCTOBER 16. Reds first baseman Tony Pérez broke out of his World Series slump in style, belting two home runs and driving home four runs in Cincinnati's 6–2, Game 5 win at Riverfront Stadium. The first Hispanic player to hit two home runs in a World Series game provided the offensive cushion the Reds needed to take a three games-to-two lead in the Series and set up a dramatic Game 6 in Boston a few nights later.

1976

FEBRUARY 9. The Caribbean Series was celebrated for the second time in the Dominican Republic with games played in Santo Domingo and Santiago, the home base of the Dominican representative, Águilas Cibañeas. The Hermosillo Orange Growers, however, spoiled any championship designs by the host country and the other participating clubs.

A 6–1 victory over the Aragua Tigers today sealed the deal for 5–1 Hermosillo to bring back the first Caribbean Series championship to Mexico.

Superstar slugger Héctor Espino was selected the tournament's MVP, under the direction of Hermosillo manager Benjamin Reyes. Espino became the first player to win two Caribbean Series MVP awards. Both men—Espino as a hitter and Reyes as a manager—were elected to the Mexican Hall of Fame.

MAY 24. Bert Campaneris stole five bases in one game, one short of the modern era record held by Eddie Collins. Campaneris, the starting American League shortstop in the All-Star Game the last three years, scored three runs and drove in two as the main catalyst in the Oakland A's 12–4 victory over the Minnesota Twins at the Oakland-Alameda County Coliseum. The 34-year-old speedster reached base all five times he batted, swiping second base three times and third base twice. He was caught stealing second once.

In subsequent decades, Collins' record was tied by Otis Nixon, Eric Young and Carl Crawford. The Dominican Republic's Willy Taveras matched Campaneris' five-steal ethnic feat in 2008, playing for the Colorado Rockies.

JUNE 20. Thirty-nine-year-old Mike Cuéllar chalked up his last big league shutout and victory. He stymied the Texas Rangers and Gaylord Perry, 2–0, on three hits and six strikeouts at Arlington Stadium.

Cuéllar, with a dwindling number of major league starts remaining in his left arm, retired in less than a year, owning the most major league wins—185—by a left-handed Latin American pitcher. (Lefty Gómez won 189 games.) Cuéllar also authored four one-hitters, tied with Aníbal Sánchez for most by a Hispanic big league pitcher.

JULY 13. In the All-Star Game at Veterans Stadium in Philadelphia, César Cedeño cracked a two-run, eighth-inning home run against the American League's Frank Tanana. The home run, the last scoring in the game, padded the National League's lead to 7–1.

Playing in his fourth All-Star Game in five years, Cedeño became the first Dominican player to hit a home run in the Midsummer Classic.

SEPTEMBER 12. In 1960, Minnie Miñoso became the first Hispanic player to lead a major league in hits. Today, as the Chicago White Sox DH, Miñoso became the oldest major league player to stroke a base hit. The second-inning single came against Sid Monge of the California Angels, in the first game of a doubleheader at Comiskey Park. The 51-year-old Miñoso batted twice more, struck out and flied out, before being removed for a pinch-hitter late in the game. The White Sox won, 2–1, in ten innings. Rich "Goose" Gossage hurled the extra-inning distance for the victory. The home team also won the nightcap, 5–1, as Jorge Orta served as the White Sox DH.

The previous day, Miñoso, a long-enduring Chicago fan favorite, had qualified as a rare four-decade player, after batting (unsuccessfully) against the Angels' Frank Tanana.

With his return to the big leagues, Miñoso became the first player to receive votes for the National Hall of Fame and then play again in the major leagues.

SEPTEMBER 14. Dennis Martínez made his pitching debut in mid-inning relief for the Baltimore Orioles, and became the first Nicaraguan player to reach the major leagues. Martínez struck out the last two batters of the fourth inning and the first batter he faced in the next frame.

The right-hander, with 5⅔ scoreless innings of work, also obtained the first win of his ground-breaking career—after his teammates staged a four-run, seventh-inning comeback to overtake the Detroit Tigers, 9–7, at Memorial Stadium.

1977

FEBRUARY 3. In their last election before incorporating into one Veterans Committee, the Negro Leagues Committee voted John Henry Lloyd and Martín Dihigo into Cooperstown enshrinement. Dihigo will become the second Hispanic player, both posthumously elected, to cross the grand threshold.

FEBRUARY 9. On the final day of the 1977 Caribbean Series, Rico Carty cracked his fifth home run in six games for the Licey Tigers. At University Stadium in Caracas, the Tigers defeated the Magallanes Navigators, 5–1, to complete a six-game sweep of the field.

Pitching for the Montreal Expos in 1991, Dennis Martínez authored the first perfect game by a Hispanic pitcher in the major leagues. The unimpeachable game occurred against the Los Angeles Dodgers at Dodger Stadium.

The sixth-inning solo shot over the center field wall topped Willard Brown's previous record of four round-trippers for one Series and gave Carty his tenth and final RBI of the competition.

FEBRUARY 19. Mike Gónzalez died of a heart attack in Havana, Cuba, at age 86. Gónzalez struck the first home runs by a Latin American player at Ebbets Field (June 4, 1918) and Wrigley Field (June 9, 1925), two of the noteworthy ethnic accomplishments of the former catcher's 17-year major league career.

Like all club owners in the Cuban Winter League, Gónzalez had his signature Habana Lions franchise taken from him and dissolved—without receiving a dime of compensation—following the 1959 Cuban Revolution The franchise was valued at upwards of $500,000 at the time.

APRIL 6. Everyone deserves a second chance, and the city of Seattle received its chance from Major League Baseball today. Inside a new, completely enclosed facility, the Seattle Mariners debuted as one of two new franchises in the American League. A huge crowd of 57,762 jammed baseball's second domed stadium but were disappointed with the results on the field. Frank Tanana of the California Angels shut out the Mariners on nine hits, 7–0.

As the Mariners' starter and loser in the game, Diego Seguí became the first Hispanic player for the Seattle club. Seguí joined Mike González and Armando Marsans as one of the first several Hispanic players of two different major league franchises.

APRIL 7. If today was any indication, baseball will have no qualms over awarding a second expansion team in Canada. At Toronto's Exhibition Stadium, 44,649 braved a pre-game snowstorm, and then sat in near-freezing weather conditions for more than three hours to watch their new Blue Jays team take on the Chicago White Sox. The frosty faithful were rewarded as the Blue Jays lashed out 16 hits in defeating the visiting club, 9–5. First baseman Doug Ault was the hitting star, slugging two home runs.

Scoring on one of the those home runs was Blue Jays shortstop Héctor Torres, whose plate appearance in the first inning designated the Mexican national as the first Hispanic player in Toronto Blue Jays history.

AUGUST 8. "It is ironic," said Jack Lang, opening the Hall of Fame induction ceremony, "that Martin Dihigo should be one of the last men voted into the Hall of Fame by the special Committee on Negro Leagues. Many historians and men who played in the old black leagues considered Dihigo the greatest player of them all."[45] The United States became the third country (Cuba, Mexico) that similarly immortalized Martín Dihigo's marvelous and versatile baseball career.

Among other illustrious men receiving baseball's most glorious honor this day was Al López. Inducted for his managerial accomplishments, López led two different teams to the World Series during the 1950s. In 17 seasons at the helm of the Cleveland Indians and Chicago White Sox, López accrued a .584 winning percentage. The Tampa-born López was also a top-notch catcher in the National League during the 1930s.

OCTOBER 2. Rod Carew matched baseball's highest post–World War II average, stroking three hits on the last day of the season to complete a copious campaign of hitting. The safeties came during a 6–2 Twins win at Milwaukee. Carew's 239 hits for the season were the most registered by a batter since 1930 (Bill Terry, 254) and the most hits by a Hispanic player in one big league season.

Carew's best month came in June. Baseball's premier hitter recorded 54 hits in 111 at-bats—the most hits by a Latin American player in one month in the major leagues. (Alex Rodríguez also had 54 hits, in August 1996, for the Seattle Mariners.) Carew's average of .388 equaled Ted Williams' 1958 seasonal mark, and his 9.7 WAR ranking was the highest in baseball, a first-time achievement for a Hispanic player.

NOVEMBER 16. Rod Carew won the batting

As a member of the California Angels, Rod Carew became the second Hispanic big league to record 3,000 hits. Carew's 3,053 career hits were the most accumulated by a 20th century Hispanic player.

title in the American League like Secretariat won the Belmont a few years earlier—his .388 average was 52 points better than his closest pursuer. The Twins first baseman went hitless in only 20 of the 148 games he started. He recorded three hits or more in 29 games. Baseball's runs scored leader with 128, Carew tied his career-best in home runs, 14, and drove home an even 100 runs, a career high. The so-called "singles hitter" finished second in the league in slugging, behind Jim Rice and ahead of Reggie Jackson. Carew's OPS extended four decimal places, to 1.019, the highest mark in both leagues.

The array of impressive offensive numbers validated Carew as Panama's first major league MVP recipient, announced today.

1978

JUNE 16. A few years ago, minor league coach Ray Miller coaxed Dennis Martínez into using a more overhand delivery instead of his customary sidearm motion. The change resulted in an accelerated fastball, topping 90 miles per hour, and a major league–breaking curve only one-half dozen miles slower. The altered pitching motion paid its first big dividend today.

The first career shutout for Dennis Martínez and the first by a Nicaraguan pitcher in the big leagues was not an overpowering one, but it was effectual. Striking out three, the 23-year-old pride of Granada permitted nine hits and four free passes in the 6–0 win over the Oakland A's at Memorial Stadium.

SEPTEMBER 30. Minnesota fans have not had much to cheer about the past eight seasons as far as team accomplishments, but at least they have had the pleasure of watching Rod Carew hit, day-in and day-out. In this season's All-Star Game, Carew provided a national audience a sample of how he spoiled Twins fans by becoming the first player to hit two triples in one Midsummer Classic.

Carew copped his sixth batting title in seven years, and seventh overall, finishing with a .333 average. Carew stroked a double today, the lone hit in his last game of the campaign. The hit drove in the last two runs in a four-run 11th inning by the Twins, who downed the Royals, 7–3.

Carew's seven career batting titles are easily the most by any Hispanic big league player.

SEPTEMBER 30. The New York team of character and characters, as Russ Newhan of the *Los Angeles Times* called the Yankees, won for the 52nd time in 72 games to keep a one-game hold on first place over the no-quit Boston Red Sox with two games to play. The 7–0 pitching victor today over the Cleveland Indians was Ed Figueroa, 29-year-old right-hander from Cailes, Puerto Rico. His second shutout of the season delivered for Figueroa his 20th win, against eight losses, and prompted team owner George Steinbrenner to send two magnums of champagne with his compliments to Figueroa in the Yankees' clubhouse after the game.

The proud Puerto Rican proclaimed afterward: "This was the biggest thrill of my life. The second biggest will come tomorrow when we win the division."[46] Figueroa was referring to his precedent-setting 20th victory, a numerical first reached by a native of his island country in the major leagues, and to a division title that would be harder earned for his team than he predicted.

1979

MARCH 13. Johan Santana was born in Tovar, Merida, Venezuela. Santana descended from his Andean mountain birthplace onto the major league scene as a hard-throwing left-hander with a devastating change-up. He captured two Cy Young Awards in the first decade of the new millennium.

JUNE 23. At Riverfront Stadium, Cincinnati Reds bullpen man Pedro Borbón struck out three batters on nine pitches in the ninth inning, in a 5–2 defeat to the San Francisco Giants. The workhorse reliever became the first Hispanic pitcher to realize the economical punch-out feat in the major leagues.

JULY 8. Pitching in Yankees pinstripes now, Luis Tiant faced only 28 batters and allowed only one hit in gaining his last major league shutout. Tiant required only 84 pitches to complete the 2–0 victory over the Oakland A's at the Oakland-Alameda County Coliseum. Rookie outfielder Rickey Henderson spanked a fourth-inning, leadoff single against the ageless pitcher.

Tiant's 49 whitewashes rank him in the top 25 on the all-time pitching charts and second only to Juan Marichal's 52 among Hispanic hurlers.

Tiant retired in 1982 with a career pitching WAR of 66.1. Among Hispanic major league pitchers, only Pedro Martínez posted a higher lifetime ranking—86.0. Tiant's 229 career victories will also be the most recorded by a Cuban pitcher in the major leagues.

NOVEMBER 26. The Toronto Blue Jays' Alfredo Griffin and the Minnesota Twins' John Castino tied in the balloting for the American League Rookie of the Year Award. Both players received seven first-place votes.

Griffin, a 22-year-old Dominican shortstop, ethnically stands alone, however, as the first player from his country to receive the league's top freshman award.

1980

JANUARY 18. José Alberto Pujols was born in Santo Domingo, Dominican Republic. A 13th-round draft pick out of Community College in Kansas City, Missouri, Pujols was destined to rewrite several pages of major league record books, playing for the St. Louis Cardinals and Anaheim Angels.

APRIL 22. An April slugfest at Wrigley Field is uncommon. Today was an exception, as 28 runs were plated by the Chicago Cubs and St. Louis Cardinals. Of the 39 combined hits by the two teams, Cubs shortstop Iván DeJesús accounted for a game-high five. DeJesús stroked five safeties in his first five trips to the plate, including the three extra-base hits required for a cycle. The Santurce, Puerto Rico, native became the first major leaguer from his homeland to hit for the cycle.

The only time DeJesús did not hit safely on the day was during his sixth at-bat, in the bottom of the ninth inning. He grounded out—five batters prior to catcher Barry Foote belting a grand slam to win the game, 16–12.

OCTOBER 1. At Shea Stadium, Pittsburgh's Omar Moreno stole second base in the sixth inning, after driving in the Pirates' sixth run of game with a base hit. Moreno was left stranded, and the Pirates carried on to a 10–5 victory over the New York Mets. Moreno's steal was his 96th, an all-time high in one season by a Hispanic major leaguer.

The National League leader in steals the previous two seasons, Moreno did not record another base larceny in the third-place Pirates' remaining three games. The Panamanian outfielder was edged out, 97 to 96, for the National League stolen base crown by Montreal Expos outfielder Ron LeFlore.

OCTOBER 4. Minnie Miñoso led his circuit ten times in being hit by a pitch, a major league record. All those HBPs (192), plus 814 walks and 1,963 hits, in 17 seasons, helped him achieve the inherent aim of all hitters—not to make outs. During the 1950s, Miñoso's on-base percentage was second in the American League trailing only the great Mickey Mantle. In 1951, Miñoso became the first Hispanic player to lead a major league in stolen bases with 31.

Stolen bases may no longer be a viable option for the former "Cuban comet," who played in his fifth major league decade today. In the uniform of his cherished Chicago White Sox—and still crowding the plate—the 50-something Miñoso pinch-hit for Greg Prior in the seventh inning of the penultimate game of the season at Comiskey Park. Facing Frank Tanana of the California Angels, Miñoso popped up to catcher Dave Skaggs. Miñoso, who broke into the big leagues in 1949, joined Nick Altrock as baseball's only five decade players.

The city of Chicago favorite also pinch-hit in the season finale and grounded out.

OCTOBER 5. On the last day of the season, Milwaukee's Ben Oglivie denied Rick Langford's strong bid for his 20th win, when he homered with one out in the bottom of the ninth inning against the Oakland A's right-hander. The solo home run tied the contest 4–4 and sent the game into extra innings. Oglivie eventually scored the winning run in the bottom of the 15th frame, to give the home team a 5–4 victory.

Oglivie's clutch home run was his 41st and tied him with Reggie Jackson for the most in the American League. The Brewers' first baseman became the first Panamanian player to lead a major league in home runs.

1981

APRIL 9. Yesterday, before he knew when he would start for the Dodgers, Fernando Valenzuela pitched batting practice. Today, on the first day of the season, Valenzuela pitched a five-hit shutout in his National League starting debut against the Houston Astros at Dodger Stadium.

One of the youngest hurlers to start a season's opener and the youngest Hispanic pitcher to start an Opening Day game, Valenzuela was called upon after injuries sidelined other Dodgers starters.

Using 106 pitches, the rookie left-hander humbled the visitors, 2–0, in front of a very appreciative crowd of 50,511.

APRIL 22. A week later, innovative marketers in Los Angeles were printing T-shirts declaring, "I live in the San Fernando Valley"—but with a line drawn through the "San." All because of one man.

Fernando Valenzuela dazzled as a Los Angeles Dodgers rookie in 1981. He led the Dodgers to their first World Series victory since 1965.

That man, Fernando Valenzuela, single-handedly defeated the Houston Astros in the Astrodome, 1–0, today. Tossing his third shutout in four starts, the mound sensation drove in the game's only run with a single in the fifth inning. Valenzuela struck out 11 Astros. The young Mexican hurler, without speaking English, has nevertheless been making pronounced statements with his early pitching outings celebrated in U.S. sports pages during the first weeks of the season.

Chalking up 180 whiffs on the campaign, the southpaw became the first Hispanic rookie pitcher to lead a major league in strikeouts.

APRIL 27. It was called "Fernandomania," and it gained national attention because of efforts like today's.

Fernando Valenzuela authored his fourth shutout in five starts—this one, 5–0, against the archrival San Francisco Giants at Dodger Stadium. The first-year pitcher from Navojoa, Mexico, continued to impress in all areas, collecting three hits and raising his batting average to .438. At the end of the season, Fernando became the first rookie pitcher to win the Silver Slugger Award.

Valenzuela was currently ahead of all major league pitchers in strikeouts with 43 in 45 innings, and had posted a barely perceptible ERA of 0.20.

MAY 4. The first pair of Hispanic brothers to hit home runs as opponents in the same major league game were the Cruzes of Puerto Rico. At Wrigley Field, José Cruz kicked off the scoring for the Houston Astros with a three-run home run in the first stanza. In the uniform of the home-team Cubs, younger sibling Héctor connected in the sixth inning with no one on base.

It was all the offense provided by the brothers for their respective teams, as the Astros defeated Chicago, 5–4.

MAY 8. The Fernandomania Show arrived in New York. Overcoming opening-inning jitters, Valenzuela drew rave reviews with a virtuoso mound performance against the New York Mets.

Before the largest Queens borough crowd of the young season, 39,848, the unlikely-looking star was center stage on the Shea Stadium hill, as he summoned forth a 1–0 shutout—his *fifth* whitewash in seven starts. Escaping unscathed from bases-loaded jams in the first two innings, Valenzuela scattered seven singles, fanned 11, and lowered his ERA to a microscopic 0.29, while lowering the curtain on the Mets.

Valenzuela, 7–0, became the first Hispanic major league pitcher to throw five shut-outs in seven starts.

MAY 14. Fernandomania reached its triumphant peak. A frenzied crowd of 53,906, the largest regular season crowd at Dodger Stadium in seven years, witnessed Fernando Valenzuela collect his eighth straight win in dramatic style. A leadoff home run by Pedro Guerrero in the bottom of the ninth inning gave Fernando the Phenom the 3–2 decision.

The win raised the starring southpaw's lifetime mark to 10–0, including two wins as a September call-up in 1980. The undefeated victory total is the most by a Hispanic pitcher to begin a career. (Liván Hernández won his first nine decisions in 1997.)

Valenzuela lost his next start, 4–0, at home to the Philadelphia Phillies and fell two short of the all-time record of 12 wins without a defeat to start a pitching career.

AUGUST 9. Baseball began to pick up the pieces after its longest labor dispute to date, with the playing of its time-honored All-Star Game. After a two-month interruption of the season, costing approximately one-third of the scheduled games for all clubs and much more than that measured in fan rancor, the 52nd Midsummer Classic was held at Cleveland Stadium. Originally scheduled for July 14, the game featured, apart from a galaxy of contemporary diamond stars, the youngest Hispanic player to appear in the annual interleague clash.

Starting the game for the Nationals, 20-year-old Fernando Valenzuela threw one scoreless inning. The biggest Hispanic rookie sensation in big league history allowed two hits but was unscored upon, as the National League decisioned the American League, 5–4, in front of a record-breaking crowd of 72,086.

Prior to the players' walkout on June 11, Valenzuela, who also became the first Mex-ican pitcher to participate in the All-Star Game, had lost four of six starts. Hitters had been laying off his "scroogie" more and more and forcing longer pitch counts in an attempt to obtain better pitches to hit.

The Angelinos' pitcher spent the two-month strike duration, among other things, traveling through Mexico. Valenzuela received the key to Mexico City from its mayor and experienced a lavish welcome to the presidential palace from the country's chief executive, José López Portillo. The celebrity pitcher was also toasted at a White House luncheon hosted by President Ronald Reagan.

SEPTEMBER 4. At Dodger Stadium, in a pinch-hitting role, David Green of the St. Louis Cardinals debuted as the first position player from Nicaragua in the major leagues. The Managua-born Green pinch-hit for Dane Iorg in the seventh inning with the Cardinals ahead, 5–1. Green grounded into a force-out and finished the game playing center field. St. Louis was a 7–2 victor behind pitcher John Martin.

SEPTEMBER 17. The Crisco Kid rides again! Fernando Valenzuela has taken some light-hearted ribbing over his weight, but his results from the mound have been lean and mean on most National League teams. Today, the big-boned phenom tied the major league rookie record for shutouts with eight when he blanked the Atlanta Braves on three hits, 2–0, at Dodger Stadium.

The impressive accomplishment came in a strike-gutted season that garnered Valenzuela only 25 starts. He equaled the 1910 mark of Canadian-born rookie Russ Ford of the New York Highlanders (in 33 starts), tied in 1913 by Chisox freshman Ewell "Reb" Russell (36 starts).

Valenzuela, 13–4, lost his final three starts, one of them 1–0, and missed setting the rookie shutout record.

SEPTEMBER 26. Twenty-year-old David Green obtained his first big league hit today against Pittsburgh Pirates pitcher Luis Tiant. After beginning his career 0-for-15, Green's second-inning single opened the scoring in the game.

The initial major league safety by a Nicaraguan player drove in the initial St. Louis run in the club's 5–3 win over the Pirates at Busch Stadium.

OCTOBER 3. The leading home run and RBI totals of both leagues were stark reminders of the damaging players' walkout this summer. In the American League, four players shared the home title with a total of only 22. One of the them, Tony Armas of the Oakland A's, cracked his 22nd home run in today's next-to-last game of the season against Kansas City Royals pitcher Mike Jones. The two-run belt padded an A's 8–4 road victory over the Royals.

In this disillusioning season for all baseball fans, Armas became the first Venezuelan player to lead a major league in home runs.

OCTOBER 23. "You talk about pitching with heart and a desire and will to win, Fernando certainly exemplified that,"[47] manager Tommy Lasorda commented after Fernando Valenzuela threw a gut-checking 145 pitches, fought early control problems, and braved through a 5–4 route-going decision over the New York Yankees in World Series Game 3.

After allowing four runs over the first three innings, the 20-year-old mound wonder buckled down and permitted the Yankees no runs and three hits over the final six innings. The gallant effort from the youngest Hispanic pitcher to start a World Series game helped immensely in turning the Series tide around in favor of the Chávez Raviners, losers of the first two games played in New York.

The complete game brought Valenzuela's post-season innings log to 40⅔, the most thrown in one post-season by a Hispanic pitcher. The toast of baseball this season, Valenzuela also became the first Mexican pitcher to win a World Series game.

A raucous crowd of 56,236 cheered their chubby Inca chieftain into delirium following the game's final out.

OCTOBER 28. Five times this post-season the Los Angeles Dodgers faced elimination, and five times the team won to stay alive or advance (twice with Fernando Valenzuela on the mound). In a script nearly as dramatic, the Dodgers lost the first two games of the World Series before remarkably coming back to win four games in a row.

Assisting greatly in the culminating effort today, Pedro Guerrero powered the Dodgers to a Game 6, World Series-clinching victory over the New York Yankees at

Yankee Stadium. The Dominican outfielder lashed out three hits, including a home run, and drove in five runs in the one-sided 9–2 victory.

In a World Series first, three players shared the MVP trophy, with Guerrero among the trio. The others were catcher Steve Yeager and third baseman Ron Cey. The San Pedro de Macoris native became the first from his country to win the glamorous post-season award.

NOVEMBER 11. At the top of the National League in five major pitching categories, Fernando Valenzuela became the first freshman pitcher to win the Cy Young Award. Valenzuela, the first rookie in 26 years to lead the league in strikeouts, edged NL wins leader Tom Seaver (14–2) and ERA champion Nolan Ryan (1.69) in the final balloting. Having celebrated his 21st birthday ten days earlier, the left-hander also became the youngest Hispanic hurler to be recognized with the prestigious mound trophy.

DECEMBER 2. Dodgers southpaw Fernando Valenzuela received the Rookie of the Year Award in recognition of an outstanding and captivating first campaign. The recently-turned 21-year-old led the strike-shortened circuit in shutouts (eight), complete games (11), innings (192⅓), and strikeouts (180).

Valenzuela, the youngest Hispanic player and first Mexican to win the award, helped pitch the Los Angeles Dodgers to their first World Series victory in 16 years.

1982

FEBRUARY 9. The 1981 Caribbean Series was not played due to a dispute over the allocation of revenues and meal money stipends. The disaccord, between the players and the member leagues, was settled in time for this year's scheduled tournament. Most gladdened by the settlement of differences was the team representative from South America.

The Caracas Leones captured for Venezuela the country's third Caribbean Series crown and the first under the leadership of a homegrown manager. In the Games held in Hermosillo, Mexico, Chico Carrasquel was the exceedingly jubilant skipper at tournament's end, guiding his team to a 5–1 record.

With a 2–1 victory today over another Lions team—from Ponce—the Caracas squad proved their superiority over the rest of the field by a two-game margin. Caracas catcher Baudilio "Bo" Díaz was named the top player in the competition with the presentation of the MVP trophy.

JULY 13. The first Midsummer Classic played outside of the United States appropriately honored the game's international constituency.

At Olympic Stadium in Montreal, throwing out—en masse—ceremonial "first pitches" were 12 former big league players from 11 different countries. Included were Minnie Miñoso, from Cuba, and Juan Marichal, from the Dominican Republic. Bobby Ávila represented Mexico, and Orlando Cepeda honored Puerto Rico.

The National League's 11th straight All-Star win—and 19th in the last 20 games played—was sparked by a two-run home run by a native of one of the other recognized countries on hand. Venezuelan Dave Concepción's second-inning blast opened the scoring for the NL and laid the foundation for the 4–1 Senior Circuit victory.

The shortstop said he was inspired by the presence of his idol Luis Aparicio, who was on hand for the pre-game festivities. Fittingly, Concepción, the first Venezuelan player to hit a home run in the All-Star Game, also became the first Venezuelan to be able to share, in his heart, the game's MVP trophy with all of his countrymen.

AUGUST 15. Nicaraguan David Green inaugurated his country into the home run hierarchy with his first career four-bagger. In the opening game of a doubleheader, the St. Louis outfielder propelled into the cheap seats a pitch by reliever Randy Niemann of the Pittsburgh Pirates. The ninth-inning round-tripper accounted for the final run in the Cardinals' 12–5 win at Three Rivers Stadium. The Redbirds swept the Bucs, taking a 5–2 decision in the nightcap.

Green, 21, broke in late in 1981 as the first position player and fourth Nicaraguan to play in the major leagues.

SEPTEMBER 19. The thrill of your first major league hit lasts a lifetime for most players. When that initial hit is a home run, it is extra special. And when the first hit comes as a home run with the bases loaded, well, that is almost beyond the stuff of dreams.

Playing in only his third game, and in his fourth big league at-bat, Seattle Mariners catcher Orlando Mercado blasted a home run with the bases loaded and became the first Hispanic player to record a grand slam as his first big league hit. Mercado, an Arecibo, Puerto Rico, native, unloaded for the bases-packed poke against Texas Rangers reliever Steve Comer, in the bottom of the fifth inning at the Kingdome.

Seattle erupted for eight runs in the inning on the way to a 9–7 win.

OCTOBER 15. Cardinals right-hander Joaquín Andujar started Game 3 of the World Series and emerged victorious, 6–2, over the Milwaukee Brewers at County Stadium. Andujar, who started 37 games for St. Louis during the season and tossed five shutouts, kept the heavy-hitting Brewers off the board for 6⅓ innings, until he was forced out of the game, struck on the knee by a batted ball. Ahead 5–0 at that point, the bullpen maintained the lead, while the Redbirds added an insurance run.

The best was yet to come for the first Dominican pitcher to win a World Series game. Five days later, the 29-year-old from San Pedro de Macoris took the hill in Game 7 and pitched seven innings for the title-clinching win, allowing two earned runs in a 6–3 victory by St. Louis.

1983

FEBRUARY 18. Gained under recent player-management labor agreements, salary arbitration has become a valuable salary-escalating tool for major league players. Having reached a contractual impasse, Fernando Valenzuela and the Los Angeles Dodgers turn to this unbiased, third party measure to settle their differences. The agents for Valenzuela convinced arbitrator Tom Roberts to side with them against the pitcher's owners. As a result, Roberts bestowed the highest arbitration award in history to Valenzuela, a salary of $1,000,000. The Dodgers had offered $750,000 to their third-year hurler, who became the second baseball player to earn one million dollars annually (after Nolan Ryan) and the first Hispanic athlete to rake in the magically lofty sum.

APRIL 18. Miguel Cabrera was born in Maracay, Aragua, Venezuela. Discovered and signed by the Florida Marlins as a 16-year-old diamond in the rough, Cabrera developed a consistent hitting excellence, beginning in the mid–2000s, that remained unrivaled in the major leagues for at least a decade.

MAY 6. Through his first 96 at-bats, Rod Carew of the California Angels registered an amazing .500 batting average. The three safeties gathered today by Carew—who was obtained by the Angels in a trade from Minnesota four years ago—came against the Detroit Tigers, in the Angels' 4–2 win at Tiger Stadium. The trio of hits gave the superlative batter 48 for the season.

The 17-year veteran ended the year hitting .339, his 15th straight season over .300, a feat surpassed by only three players in baseball history (Ty Cobb, Tony Gwynn, Stan Musial and Ted Williams).

JULY 31. The great Juan Marichal was one of four players inducted into the National Baseball Hall of Fame. The Dominican pitcher became the first living Hispanic player duly elected and enshrined in Cooperstown. Marichal was part of a class of inductees that included Brooks Robinson, George Kell and Walter Alston.

The pitcher's 123 ERA+ was the best of any Hispanic pitcher in the 20th century.

AUGUST 24. Bert Campaneris of the New York Yankees stole the 649th and final base of his career. In the eighth inning of a game against the Seattle Mariners, Campaneris swiped second base. Putting himself in scoring position, he tallied an insurance run when the next batter singled. The Yankees came away with a 6–3 home win.

The career steal total by Campaneris was the all-time high by a Hispanic player in the 20th century.

OCTOBER 12. Another bastion is breached. At Memorial Stadium, the Phillies' Guillermo "Willie" Hernández took the sign from Bo Díaz with one out in the fifth inning of Game 2 of the World Series, between the Philadelphia Phillies and Baltimore Orioles. As the Fall Classic's first Hispanic battery, the pair recorded but two outs, with Hernández pinch-hit for in the top of the sixth inning.

The Phillies came up on the short end of a 4–1 score. But there was dignified joy in Aguada, Puerto Rico, and Cúa, Venezuela, for two special sons' joint accomplishments.

1984

JANUARY 10. The biggest Hall of Fame class in 12 years included Luis Aparicio, the first Venezuelan so honored by Cooperstown. Harmon Killebrew, Don Drysdale, Rick Ferrell and Pee Wee Reese rounded out a shining handful of electees, with the Maracaibo-born Aparicio the top vote getter with 341.

An 18-year major leaguer, Aparicio played with three clubs, most notably the Chicago White Sox. At the completion of his career in 1973, Aparicio owned the record for most games played at shortstop, most chances, most assists and most times leading the league in fielding percentage. The smooth fielding shortstop won nine Gold Glove Awards, led the league in steals nine times, and retired with 506 stolen bases.

Aparicio tied with Roberto Clemente with the most seasons of at least 100 hits (18) among 20th century Hispanic players.

APRIL 5. Under existing international rules, the New York Yankees were able to sign José Rijo as a 15-year-old prospect from the Dominican Republic in August 1980. Rijo, a hard-throwing right-hander, made his major league debut on this day, at 18 years and 328 days old.

In Kansas City, the youngest Hispanic pitcher in major league history threw the last 5⅓ innings for the Yankees, summoned with his team down, 14–0. Allowing one run, Rijo was the only bright spot for the New York club in its embarrassing 15–4 road defeat.

MAY 10. Today, three days shy of his 19th birthday, José Rijo became the youngest Hispanic hurler to earn a major league win.

At Yankee Stadium, Rijo tossed the last four frames of a 16-inning game against the Cleveland Indians. After the Indians pushed across an unearned run in the top of the final inning, the Yankees scored two runs in the bottom of the 16th to pull out the victory and provide Rijo with his special win, 7–6. (Three weeks earlier, on April 18, Rijo had become the youngest Hispanic pitcher to reap a big league save with a three-inning scoreless effort against the same Indians.)

JUNE 1. A few days prior to his 45th birthday, "Mexico's Babe Ruth" hit the final home run of his Mexican League career. At *Parque Famosa* in Monterrey, Héctor Espino connected off Veracruz Eagles pitcher David Franco, the 453rd time Espino cleared the fences in his 24-year playing career.

The legendary Monterrey Sultans slugger retired with 453 Mexican League home runs, second only to Nelson Barrera's 455. But Espino's 484 lifetime home runs ranked as the most slugged by a minor league player.[48]

SEPTEMBER 7. At Candlestick Park, pitcher Pascual Pérez and outfielder Milt Thompson of the Atlanta Braves executed a double steal of home and second base. The two-out, fifth-inning swipes helped the Braves increase their lead to 3–1. In the eighth inning, reliever Gene Garber failed to protect a 4–3 lead and cost Pérez a potential win. As a consolation, with his baserunning effort, the Dominican pitcher became the first Hispanic pitcher to steal home in the major leagues. It would be Pérez's only stolen base in an 11-year career.

SEPTEMBER 28. Tony Armas put the finishing touches on a special slugging season. Already the home run champion of the league by a comfortable margin, the Boston Red Sox center fielder clubbed a fifth-inning, three-run home run against Bill Swaggerty of the Baltimore Orioles at Fenway Park. It was Armas' 43rd home run and the game's pivotal blow in providing the Red Sox with a 5–4 victory.

The home run also helped Armas wrest away from teammate Jim Rice the American League RBI title, 123 to 122. The timely blast crowned Armas as the first Venezuelan player to lead a major league in runs batted in.

OCTOBER 12. Permitting only one hit in 2⅓ innings of work, Detroit Tigers relief specialist Willie Hernández shut the door on the San Diego Padres in Game 3 of the World Series. Hernández preserved a 5–2 Tigers win and notched the first save by a Latin American pitcher in World Series play. (Colorado-born Tippy Martínez saved two games of the 1983 World Series.)

Three days later, Hernández took the mound again, in last-out fashion, to wrap up the world championship for the wire-to-wire Tigers, who defeated San Diego in five games.

OCTOBER 30. The advent of specialized relievers, which had developed in earnest over the previous dozen years, was clearly reflected with the one-two American League voting placement of Willie Hernández and Dan Quisenberry for pitching's highest award.

Hernandez secured the honor by 17 points over colleague Quisenberry, becoming the fifth fireman to win the Cy Young Award and the first Puerto Rican.

Hernández won nine games, saved 32 more, and posted a 1.92 ERA out of the bullpen for the world champion Detroit Tigers.

NOVEMBER 6. Willie Hernández became the third relief pitcher to win the MVP Award in the major leagues. Endowed with 16 of 28 first-place votes, the Tigers' left-hander comfortably outpointed his closest competitor, everyday player Kent Hrbek (306 to 247). The Aguada, Puerto Rico, product joined Rollie Fingers and Jim Konstanty as baseball's only other bullpen specialists to be awarded MVP honors. Oakland's Dennis Eckersley will join the select group in 1992.

Hernández also became the first Hispanic pitcher to receive both the Cy Young and MVP Awards from his league.

1985

APRIL 28. Fernando Valenzuela concluded the 1983 season with 752 career innings—one of only 20 pitchers in major league history with 750 innings thrown by the age of 23. He had also hurled 16 shutouts. This season, Valenzuela, with two shutouts to his credit, did not allow an earned run in his first four starts.

Facing the San Diego Padres at Dodger Stadium, Valenzuela had the Padres shut out until the ninth inning of start number five. He surrendered a solo home run to the Padres' Tony Gwynn and lost the game, 1–0. But in the process, Valenzuela established a record-setting number of innings thrown—41⅓—to open a major league season without allowing an earned run.

MAY 11. "This Ramon Bragana is just about as great a pitcher as I ever saw. He has speed, a wonderful assortment of curves and perfect control,"[49] said future Hall of Famer Bill Terry after facing Bragaña in exhibition games during a 1937 spring training trip his New York Giants took to Cuba. Today, on his 76th birthday, Bragaña passed away in Veracruz, Mexico. In a career that spanned nearly three decades, Bragaña won over 200 games in the Mexican League and well over 100 more in the Negro and Latin American leagues.

JUNE 14. The first Nicaraguan player to homer in the major leagues became the first from his country to hit a walk-off round-tripper. At Candlestick Park, David Green, a San Francisco Giant following an off-season trade, took Luis DeLeon deep in the bottom of the 11th inning, to elevate the Giants to a 5–4 win over the visiting San Diego Padres. Green hit 31 home runs in his six-year career, with, safe to say, none as loudly cheered as today's solo shot.

AUGUST 4. "It's something I thought I'd never accomplish, but I've been around for 19 years, and if you stay around long enough, good things happen to you,"[50] said a modest Rod Carew hours after he had singled to left field against Minnesota Twins pitcher Frank Viola for his 3,000th career hit.

Carew became the 16th overall player and the second Hispanic to reach the historic hit plateau. The milestone hit for the 39-year-old first baseman came in the third inning at Anaheim Stadium; California won the game, 6–5.

A plentiful base stealer over the first half of his career, Carew became the first Hispanic player to record 3,000 hits and 300 steals, finishing with 3,053 and 353. The Panamanian's hit total reigns as the most accumulated by Hispanic player in the 20th century.

Carew also registered a career 280 three-hit games, the most by a Hispanic big league player.

OCTOBER 5. The eyes of Arlington, Texas, are upon Rod Carew, playing in his last game. Carew went 0-for 2, but he scored the game's initial run in the top of the first inning after walking. In the next-to-last game of the season, Carew's Angels won, 3–1, over the Rangers. Battling down to the wire for a division crown, the Angels were elbowed out of the post-season by a Kansas City Royals win in their game against the Oakland A's.

Twenty days later, the Angels announced they would not be tendering another contract to the seven-time batting champion. The California club later retired Carew's number 29, as did the Minnesota Twins, a dual honor accorded to only a handful of players in history and none, prior to Carew, to a Hispanic player.

OCTOBER 6. Shades of Ted Williams, sort of. Rufino Linares homered for the California Angels in what turned out to be his final major league at-bat, the first Hispanic player to exit the game on such a high note.

The fourth-year Dominican outfielder, in the DH role today, smacked a three-run, eighth-inning homer against Rick Surhoff of the Texas Rangers, which supplied the victory margin for the Halos at Arlington Stadium, 6–5.

Linares reached the major leagues as a 30-year-old rookie in 1981 with the Atlanta Braves.

1986

APRIL 8. Félix Hernández was born in Valencia, Carabobo, Venezuela. A durable hurler with a corresponding 6'3", 230-pound build, Hernández ranks as one of baseball's best pitchers in the late 2000s and 2010s.

JULY 15. Fernando Valenzuela, a.k.a. "Carl Hubbellito," as his manager, Tommy Lasorda, has called him, equaled "King" Carl's All-Star Game record of five consecutive strikeouts.

In the fourth and fifth innings of the Midsummer Classic held in the Astrodome, Valenzuela struck out four of the American League's elite players: Don Mattingly, Cal Ripken, Jr., Jesse Barfield, and Lou Whitaker. Then Valenzuela fanned the pitcher, Teddy Higuera, who had never batted in the major leagues prior to this game. Valenzuela retired the fifth inning's third batter, Kirby Puckett, on a ground out to shortstop.

The National League lost to the American League, 3–2. Valenzuela was not involved in the decision.

SEPTEMBER 22. This season, Fernando Valenzuela and Milwaukee's Teddy Higuera vied to become the first Mexican pitcher to win 20 games in the major leagues.

Both hurlers reached the benchmark, but today, three days ahead of Higuera, Valenzuela became the first to strike up the mariachi band, winning his 20th game of the campaign. Allowing only two hits and one earned run, Valenzuela beat the Houston Astros in the Astrodome 9–2.

Rising above the poor season his team experienced (73–89), Valenzuela fashioned a 21–11 record, including a hefty 20 complete games.

The Sinaloan Higuera recorded a 20–11 record and the highest WAR ranking—9.4—of any player in baseball. The analytical achievement was a first for a Hispanic pitcher.

1987

APRIL 15. Juan Nieves threw the first no-hit game in Milwaukee Brewers history, and the first by a Puerto Rican pitcher in the major leagues. In just his second start of the season, Nieves walked five and struck out seven, facing 31 Baltimore Orioles batters, in the 7–0 win at Memorial Stadium. Embarrassing the home team, Nieves benefitted from several fine defensive plays behind him, the last of which was a dramatic diving catch in center field by Robin Yount for the final out of the game.

The 22-year-old Santurce native maintained the Brewers' perfect start to the season after nine games, while recording his second win.

JULY 8. Tela, Honduras, is a Caribbean coastal town that has a major league connection, effective this date. The Central American birthplace of Gerald Anthony Young established a permanent ethnic tie with the big leagues by sending its country's first native son to perform at baseball's highest level. Young debuted in center field for the Houston Astros against the Montreal Expos.

Young, who went on to an eight-year career with three National League teams, was 0-for-4 in his first game. The Astros were shut out, 1–0, on a one-hitter by Expos pitcher Floyd Youmans. Nolan Ryan took the hard-luck loss in the Astrodome.

JULY 9. After placing center fielder Billy Hatcher on the disabled list, the Houston Astros had purchased the contract of Gerald Young from Tucson in the Pacific Coast League to take his place. In his second game, Young, a speedy outfielder, collected his first major league base hit and the first by a Honduran player in the major leagues. The fifth-inning single by Young, against New York Mets pitcher Jim Mitchell, led to a Houston score. In the ninth inning, the Astros came away with a 4–3, walk-off win on second baseman Bill Doran's home run.

SEPTEMBER 16. Two days after slashing out four hits and stealing four bases in a game, Houston's Gerald Young cracked his first major league home run. At Candlestick Park, Young reached San Francisco Giants pitcher Dave Dravecky for a sixth-inning, bases-empty, four-base wallop. Dravecky pitched a four-hitter, however, muffling Young's Astros, 7–1. The pitching effort far from muted the baseball followers in Young's Central American homeland, who, from this day forward, singled out Young with pride as the first Honduran to hit a home run in the major leagues.

SEPTEMBER 26. Benito Santiago stroked an 0–2 pitch into left field in his second time up today to set the major league rookie record for hitting in consecutive games. The single, in the top of the fifth inning, came against the Dodgers' Bob Welch, and gave Santiago a hit in 28 straight games, eclipsing a rookie record that dated to just before the turn of the century.

The Ponce, Puerto Rico, product scored the only run for the San Diego Padres in the team's 3–1 loss to Los Angeles at Dodger Stadium.

Santiago's streak reached a stunning 34 games, establishing a record for Hispanic players in the 20th century.

NOVEMBER 17. George "Taco" Bell of the Toronto Blue Jays became the 11-year old franchise's inaugural Most Valuable Player Award winner, and the first Dominican player to be so honored. The 28-year-old Bell smashed 47 home runs and knocked home 134 runs on the season, with a .308 batting average to further substantiate his selection.

Bell also became the first Dominican player to pace his league in RBI.

1988

APRIL 4. Appearing to pick up right where he left off last season, Blue Jays DH George Bell blasted three home runs against Bret Saberhagen of the Kansas City Royals at Royals Stadium. The reigning 1987 AL MVP, Bell became the first major league player to smash three balls out of the park on Opening Day.

Bell knocked in four of Toronto's five runs in the 5–3 victory.

AUGUST 6. Fidel Castro's insidious revolution had denied the major leagues an infusion of Cuban baseball talent for nearly a quarter century, but was not able to cut off Cuba's legacy completely at the game's ultimate level. Some young sons of the families that fled the country's social and political repression during the 1960s matured into base-ball stars in this and the following decade.

One such budding star was José Canseco. Playing in his third full season with the Oakland A's, Canseco, with 31 home runs already, swiped his 30th bag (second base) in the ninth inning at Oakland tonight. Canseco advanced to third base on an error and scored the winning run on a sacrifice fly, giving the first-place A's a 5–4 win over the Seattle Mariners.

Canseco became the 11th player, and the first Hispanic, in major league history to hit 30 home runs and steal 30 bases in one season.

AUGUST 13. Mel Almada, the first Mexican to play in the major leagues and the first Hispanic player to score 100 runs in a single big league season (101, in 1938), died in Hermosillo, Mexico, at age 73.

Almada was the first Latin American player to hit a home run at Fenway Park (September 23, 1933) and at Yankee Stadium (June 2, 1935). He also left the same ethnic, long-ball mark for posterity by hitting for the circuit at Navin Field/Tiger Stadium (August 21, 1935) and Comiskey Park (May 8, 1937).

SEPTEMBER 23. José Canseco achieved what had not been achieved before—40 stolen bases to complement 40 home runs in the same major league season. The dual milestone was reached in his game tonight. The slugger pilfered his 40th base (and second of the contest) in the fifth inning of an eventual 14-inning, 9–8 A's victory over the Mil-waukee Brewers at County Stadium. The 24-year-old Oakland A's right fielder also clubbed his 41st home run of the season.

Canseco's campaign-ending 42 home runs and 124 RBI led the American League, as did his .569 slugging percentage. Canseco became the first Cuban player to lead a major league in home runs and RBI.

OCTOBER 15. Oakland A's players have taken to banging forearms lightly in a manner of congratulatory salute. José Canseco exchanged forearm "bashes" with three team-mates standing at home plate following his bases-loaded home run, in the second inning of Game 1 of the World Series at Dodger Stadium. Canseco's grand slam had him poised to be the hero of the Fall Classic's opening game between the Oakland A's and Los Angeles Dodgers.

But ... a dramatic, bottom of the ninth inning, two-out, two-run, pinch-hit blast into the right field seats by injury-hobbled Kirk Gibson thrillingly ended one of the most unforgettable games in World Series history, 5–4, and sent the first World Series grand slam home run hit by a Hispanic player into obscurity.

1989

APRIL 3. Three weeks away from his 22nd birthday, Omar Vizquel debuted in the major leagues for the Seattle Mariners. At the Oakland-Alameda County Coliseum, Vizquel, perhaps dealing with butterflies, committed an error in the field and went hitless in three trips to the plate. The A's picked up the 3–2 Opening Day win, behind Dave Stewart and several relievers, including Dennis Eckersley.

The error will be an aberration for Vizquel, who not only developed into one the best fielding shortstops in baseball history, but also played in more major league games (2,968) and more seasons (24) than any other Latin American player.

AUGUST 18. Tossing one inning and allowing two runs, Willie Hernández finished a Tigers' 7–3 win over the New York Yankees at Tiger Stadium. Hernández allowed a two-run home run to catcher Bob Geren. In the non-save situation, the relief ace was testing a sore elbow, which had twice landed him on the disabled list. The elbow swelled "like a balloon" after the contest, forcing the left-hander back on the DL.

Hernández underwent elbow surgery within a month. The attempt to correct liga-ment damage and torn muscle around the elbow was not successful. As a result, the 34-year-old pitcher never returned to the big league mound. His 13-year-career abruptly ended with the ethnic mound laurel of most games pitched by a Latin American left-hander in the major leagues, 744. All but 11 came in relief.

NOVEMBER 4. The man Satchel Paige called the best hitter he ever faced, Pancho Coímbre, perished at the age of 80, in a tragic fire that consumed his home in Ponce, Puerto Rico.

When his 13-year canonizing career began in Puerto Rico, with the inception of the indigenous winter league in 1938, Coimbre was already a well-known player in Latin America. A two-time .400 hitter in the PRWL, the Coamo native led the Ponce Lions, the only team for which he played, to four successive winter titles and five in six years during the 1940s.

A sensational contact hitter, Coimbre did not strike out *once* during the course of three PRWL seasons, 1939–1940 to 1941–1942—a total of 550 at-bats! Coimbre retired after the 1950–1951 season at the age of 42; his .337 career average placed him second only to Willard Brown in league history.

Coimbre became the most idolized player in Puerto Rico during the early years of professional baseball, and his appeal among the populace continued long after his playing days ended. Called "*El Pundonoroso*"—"The Honorable One"—because of a righteous demeanor, Coimbre remained active in the game, after hanging up his spikes, as a coach and manager. He worked as coach and scout for the Pittsburgh Pirates for 25 years.

1990

JUNE 4. Ramón Martínez whiffed 18 Atlanta Braves batters, tying a Los Angeles Dodgers club record.

At Dodger Stadium, Martínez struck out 14 of the first 19 hitters he faced in shutting out the Braves, 2–0, on three hits. The speed-balling right-hander equaled Sandy Koufax's team-high total, but failed to record a single strikeout in the ninth inning. Martínez's strikeout total remains the most recorded by a Hispanic major league pitcher in a nine inning game.

JUNE 27. Jose Canseco became baseball's first $5 million man when he signed a five-year, $23.5 million dollar contract with the Oakland A's. A $3.5 million signing bonus added to his 1990 arbitration-elevated $2 million salary raised the outfielder to the lofty payroll status. The controversial player's new contract surpassed the previous most lucrative baseball contract—the Yankees' Don Mattingly's five-year, $19.6 million deal.

JUNE 29. Fernando Valenzuela and several teammates watched on ESPN from the Dodgers clubhouse as Oakland's Dave Stewart completed a no-hitter against the Toronto Blue Jays. "You've seen one on TV," said Valenzuela to those present. "Now come and watch one live."[51]

The starter in that night's game against the St. Louis Cardinals, Valenzuela pitched the second no-hitter of the major league day. Valenzuela set down the side in order in five of the first six innings. (An error by left fielder Kirk Gibson in the first inning temporarily interrupted the carousel of unproductive hitters.) A pair of one-out walks in the seventh forced the left-hander to bear down and retire Terry Pendleton, on a fly out, and José Oquendo on a groundout to keep the surfacing gem virtually unscuffed.

Admittedly, Valenzuela was only "kidding" in his pre-game prediction; nevertheless, the always poised pitcher obtained six more outs over the next two innings without permitting a hit, and defeated St. Louis, 6–0. It was only the second time in baseball history that two no-hitters were thrown on the same day, and the first time one in each league was pitched.

Fernando's no-no was the first by a Mexican pitcher in the major leagues.

JULY 10. In the All-Star Game at Wrigley Field, Dennis Martínez of the Montreal Expos tossed a perfect third inning against his circuit's American League foes. The brief effort by Martínez, whose career had been resurrected with the Expos, earned him the appreciation of National League fans and engendered a special pride from Nicaraguans everywhere as the first athlete from their Central American country to perform in the major league All-Star Game.

The game also marked a most prideful occasion for one particular baseball father. Sandy Alomar, Sr. watched with a swelled chest as his sons, Sandy Jr. and Roberto, suited up for the American and National League squads, respectively. Sandy Jr., a rookie, started behind the plate for the Americans and had two hits. Roberto was a late-inning substitute at second base for starter Ryne Sandberg. Sandy, Sr., himself an All-Star in 1970, could now boast of being the first All-Star father to sire two All-Star offspring, and of combining to form the first Hispanic All-Star father-son tandem.

The American League came out on top in the game, 2–0, on MVP Julio Franco's two-run, pinch-hit double.

OCTOBER 1. In his 33rd and final start of the season, Ramón Martínez hurled his league-leading 12th complete game and gained his 20th victory (against only six losses). Facing the San Diego Padres at Dodger Stadium, Martínez scattered five hits and allowed one run in downing the visitors, 2–1.

The effort provided the 22-year-old Dominican pitcher gladful claim as the major leagues' youngest Hispanic 20-game winner.

OCTOBER 20. In a short series, the strongest of lineups will buckle against outstanding pitching. José Rijo led a staff of Cincinnati Reds pitchers on top of their collective game to pull off a World Series upset over the heavily favored Oakland A's. Pitching on three days' rest, Rijo won his second game of the Series, holding the mighty A's to one run in 8⅓ innings of two-hit work. Randy Myers scooped up two easy outs for the save. At the Oakland-Alameda County Coliseum, Lou Piniella's Reds downed the A's, 2–1, and finished off a humiliating four-game sweep of Tony LaRussa's three-time American League champions.

Tossing 15⅓ innings over two starts, Rijo permitted one run and nine hits, and struck out 14. The performance gained for Rijo the first World Series MVP trophy awarded to a Hispanic pitcher.

1991

JULY 5. Chito Martínez spent six years in the minor leagues and played more than 750 games. Today, the Baltimore Orioles outfielder culminated an ethnically unique journey begun with his birth 25 years ago in Belize City, Belize. Martínez became the first major league player from Belize, formerly known as British Honduras. Playing right field in Yankee Stadium, Martínez collected an infield hit in the ninth inning as the Orioles defeated New York, 7–4.

JULY 10. International pitching star René Arocha abandoned his Cuban National team during a stopover at Miami International Airport, to seek political asylum. The desertion, prior to the commencement of the Pan American Games, became the first by a baseball-reared player under Cuba's Communist regime, in which all athletes were considered government employees.

The 25-year-old pitcher eventually reached the major leagues and had an injury-shortened four-year career with the St. Louis Cardinals and San Francisco Giants. His bold action paved the way for many more defections by Cuban players in the decades to come.

JULY 11. In Oakland, in the first game back from the All-Star break, Chito Martínez clubbed a pinch-hit home run against Oakland A's reliever Gene Nelson. The eighth inning home run accounted for the only run of the contest for the visiting Baltimore Orioles, 8–1 losers. Called up from Rochester less than a week ago, Martínez became the first player from the Central American country of Belize to hit a home run in the major leagues.

In a 158-game career spanning three years, the U.S.-raised Martínez hit 18 career home runs, all with the Orioles.

JULY 21. The first Panamanian was enshrined in baseball's Hall of Fame. Rod Carew, with his 15 .300-average seasons, took his deserved place in Cooperstown.

Several Panamanian flags fluttered in the crowd during his induction speech, as Carew offered the advice that helped him the most: "Don't let anyone distract you from what you are trying to do."[52]

Carew's career Extra Bases Taken percentage of 58 percent was the highest among his contemporary Hall of Fame peers. For comparison purposes, speedster Rickey Henderson's XBT was 55 percent and Lou Brock's was 53 percent. Extra Bases Taken measures the success rate of a runner advancing around the bases on a base hit. Examples: From first base to third on single, from second base to home on a single, and from first base to home on a double.

Cooperstown's newest member accrued a career OPS+ of 131, tying him with Tony Oliva for second-highest among Hispanic players who played exclusively in the 20th century.

JULY 28. Nicaragua is a country known for its widely-read poets and authors. One of its athletic sons, Dennis Martínez, elevated throwing a baseball into an eternal art form befitting his nation's literary prowess. Like the powerful rhyme that outlives marble and the gilded monuments of princes, Martínez's performance today will outlive the concrete arenas in which baseball is played and the bronze sculptures erected in star ballplayers' images.

On a picturesque Sunday afternoon, a Chávez Ravine crowd of 45,560 beheld the pinnacle of pitching in a masterful performance by the 36-year-old Granada, Nicaragua, native. Martínez and perfection were synonymous as Martínez retired, in order, every Los Angeles Dodgers batter he faced, to become the 13th major league pitcher—and the first Hispanic—to record a perfect game.

"It was like I was dreaming. It was like it was someone else down there instead of me,"[53] Martínez said, describing his "out-of-body" recollections to the press immediately afterward.

The right-hander wept from emotion shortly after the last out was recorded. The Expos 2, Martínez 27-for-27.

AUGUST 11. Two years earlier, in his major league debut, 19-year-old Wilson Alvarez of the Texas Rangers failed to record an out. After the first five batters in the game's opening inning reached base against him, Alvarez was relieved. Charged with three runs, Alvarez was pinned with a 6–3 loss to the Toronto Blue Jays and an ERA of "infinity." The young southpaw was promptly returned to the minor leagues after the game.

Acquired by the Chicago White Sox in a trade with the Rangers a few weeks earlier, Wilson Alvarez made his second major league appearance today—and threw a no-hit, no-run game!

At Memorial Stadium, the pitcher from Maracaibo, Venezuela, reversed his fortune from his first big league start in an extraordinary manner, defeating the Baltimore Orioles, 5–0. The 21-year-old pitcher allowed five walks and struck out seven in becoming the first Venezuelan and the youngest Hispanic pitcher to author the rhapsodic mound gem.

OCTOBER 20. The Puerto Rican Baseball Hall of Fame was inaugurated in San

Juan. A group of ten all-time greats made up the unparalleled first class. They included natives Perucho Cepeda, Orlando Cepeda, Roberto Clemente, Pancho Coimbre, Rubén Gómez, Canena Marquez, Juan Pizarro and Vic Power, along with North American stand-outs Willard Brown and Bob Thurman.

1992

MAY 22. After a 17–20 start through 37 games, Montreal Expos manager Tom Runnells was dismissed and bench coach Felipe Alou was named to the post as his replacement. With the appointment, Alou became the first Dominican to manage at the major league level.

Alou started a 14-year managerial career that encompassed ten seasons with the Expos and four with the San Francisco Giants. Dennis Martínez made Alou's first game at the helm an easy one, pitching a 7–1, two-hit victory over the visiting Atlanta Braves.

The 57-year-old Alou turned the underachieving Expos club around and guided the team to 70–55 record the rest of the way and a second-place finish in the National League East, nine games in back of the top-of-the-heap Pittsburgh Pirates.

Alou managed more major league games than any other Latin American; his record in 2,046 games was 1,032–1,013.

JUNE 7. Juan González's nickname of "Igor" was derived from a boyhood affinity with professional wrestler "Igor the Magnificent." The Texas Rangers' center fielder provided a slugging feat at the plate today, much more magnificent than any performance put on by his entertainment idol. González became the youngest Hispanic major leaguer to hit three home runs in one game. The 22-years-and–231-day-old outfielder delivered three deep, fence-clearing drives that chased home four runs, propelling the Rangers to a 5–4 home win over the Minnesota Twins.

JULY 14. It was easy to see, with one look at Iván Rodríguez, how fitting his nickname of "Pudge" was. The young Texas Rangers catcher carried visible remnants of what could be playfully described as baby fat over his boyishly round cheeks.

At the All-Star Game in San Diego tonight, Rodríguez, age 20 years and eight months, stepped up with the grandest of major league big boys and became the youngest Hispanic position player to play in the Midsummer Classic. The second-year Rangers backstop substituted for American League starter Sandy Alomar, Jr. in the sixth inning, with the game well in his league's favor at 10–0.

Rodríguez finished out the game, going 0-for-2 with four putouts, as the American League cruised to a 13–6 victory at Jack Murphy Stadium.

SEPTEMBER 24. Pedro Martínez threw his first pitch in the major leagues, hurling two innings of scoreless relief for the Los Angeles Dodgers against the Cincinnati Reds at Dodger Stadium. Tim Costo, the fourth batter Martínez faced, became the first strikeout victim for the pitcher who would become the all-time Hispanic strikeout king with 3,154. Six days later, Martínez made his first major league start against the same Reds at Riverfront Stadium. He lost, 3–1, throwing six innings and allowing two runs.

OCTOBER 4. Juan "Igor" González homered in the season's last game to edge out Mark McGwire for the American League home run crown, 43 to 42. The home run was slammed at Anaheim Stadium against Bert Blyleven of the California Angels, in a 9–5 Rangers win.

In his second full season with Texas and 16 days shy of his 23rd birthday, the Arecibo, Puerto Rico, native became the sixth-youngest player to lead a major league in home runs and the youngest Hispanic.

1993

APRIL 5. Hispanicfest at Riverfront. Two Hispanic starters met on Opening Day for the first time as Dennis Martínez of the Montreal Expos and José Rijo of the Cincinnati Reds opposed one another at Riverfront Stadium. Rijo, with eight innings of five-hit, shutout work, defeated the veteran Martínez, who allowed two runs in seven innings.

The pitchers' respective managers also formed part of a historic Hispanic occasion as the first pair of opposing Latin American managers in a major league game. Facing one another were Felipe Alou and Tony Pérez. Alou's Expos came out on the short end of the 2–1 score against Pérez's Reds, in front of a crowd of 55,456.

Rijo, with a 14–9 record and 2.48 ERA this season, became one of only four Hispanic pitchers to accumulate a composite WAR metric over 10.0. Rijo ranked 9.3 in pitching WAR, but exceptionally good hitting and defense boosted the pitcher's composite to 10.2 at season's end. Greg Maddux' pitching WAR of 5.8 placed a distant second.

APRIL 5. Florida has been spring training host to major league baseball for many decades. Today, the state took its first big league stride with its own franchise, situated in North Miami. Christened the Florida Marlins, the new team defeated the Los Angeles Dodgers, 6–3, at Joe Robbie Stadium. Joe DiMaggio threw out the first pitch and knuckleballer Charlie Hough pitched six innings for the inaugural win.

Batting third in the lineup, Marlins right fielder Junior Félix became the first Hispanic player for the South Florida team, brought together on the financial strength of waste management businessman H. Wayne Huizenga.

APRIL 5. The National League matched its rival circuit with its 14th team, newly established and located in Denver, Colorado. The new team, dubbed the "Rockies," played its first game today at Shea Stadium in New York. Exploiting the expansion club, Mets pitcher Doc Gooden tossed a 3–0, four-hit shutout in front of more than 53,000 cheering fans.

Collecting two of the hits, Colorado first baseman and cleanup hitter Andrés Galarraga inscribed his name as the Rocky Mountain franchise's first Hispanic player.

APRIL 8. Carlos Baerga of the Cleveland Indians became the first major league player to homer from both sides of the plate in the same inning. The switch-hitting second baseman made history at Cleveland Stadium, first clouting a two-run bomb against New York Yankees southpaw Steve Howe, batting right-handed. Then, hitting left-handed, he connected for a solo shot against right-hander Steve Farr. Baerga also became the first Hispanic player to connect for two four-baggers in one inning. The home runs by the Puerto Rican infielder highlighted a nine-run, seventh-inning scoring binge by the Indians, who thrashed New York, 15–5.

MAY 5. Rookie Pedro Martínez earned his first major league win. At Dodger Stadium, the 21-year-old Martínez pitched two middle innings of scoreless relief versus the New York Mets. The Dodgers tallied two eighth-inning runs to make Martínez the 6–5 winner. The game was started by Pedro's older brother Ramón. The Los Angeles Dodgers announced following the game that it was the first time two brothers had pitched in the same game for their franchise.

Little did the Dodgers suspect that the win would be one of 219 Pedro Martínez would accumulate in his career, to go along with 135 wins by Ramón. The combined victory total made them the sixth-winningest pair of pitching brothers in major leagues history and the most victorious Hispanic mound siblings.

SEPTEMBER 28. It took three weeks and four starts but Dennis Martínez finally garnered his 14th win of the campaign and his 100th in the National League. The keepsake win turned out to be pleasingly worth the wait for the 38-year-old right-hander, who defeated the Florida Marlins, 3–2, at Joe Robbie Stadium. Reliever John Wetteland secured a four-out save for the victory, which came in front of a troop of 300 Nicaraguan fans who had flown to Miami in anticipation of the special occasion, as well as an added contingent of home-spun support.

Martínez, who made his off-season home in Miami, became the first Hispanic pitcher to win 100 games in both leagues.

OCTOBER 3. On the last day of the season, an 0-for-4 at the plate diminished only slightly the elevated batting mark of Andrés Galarraga of the Colorado Rockies. The Rockies' first baseman still closed out the campaign with a stellar .370 mark. It was the highest average recorded by a right-handed hitter since Joe DiMaggio hit .381 in 1939. The visiting Colorado team was defeated, 5–3, at Fulton County Stadium.

A free agent signing by the expansion Rockies, Galarraga was one of the few bright spots on the club, which finished sixth in the seven-team National League West. He also emerged as a shining example for his Venezuelan compatriots, as the first big league batting champion from that Andean country.

OCTOBER 3. Puerto Ricans Angel Miranda, Jaime Navarro, and Ricky Bones, along with Mexican Teddy Higuera, comprised four-fifths of the starting pitching rotation for the Milwaukee Brewers at this season's tail end. Miranda joined regular starters Navarro and Bones in the rotation in June, and Higuera latched on in mid–August. It was the first time four Hispanic hurlers represented a major league team's starting pitching rotation.

OCTOBER 19. Roberto Alomar of the Toronto Blue Jays became the first Hispanic player to collect four hits in a World Series game. Alomar drove in two runs with the safeties and scored twice. The second baseman, along with teammate Paul Molitor, who homered and garnered three hits, lead the Blue Jays to an easy 10–3 win against the Philadelphia Phillies in Game 3 at Veterans Stadium.

The win put the Blue Jays ahead in the Series, two games to one.

OCTOBER 20. The highest runs-scoring output in a World Series game provided unexpected thrills for fans of both pennant-winning squads. At Veterans Stadium, the Toronto Blue Jays erupted for six runs in the top of the eighth inning to take a 15–14 lead over the Philadelphia Phillies. There was no further scoring in the Game 4 slugfest. Surprisingly, only three home runs were hit—all by the Phillies, including two by Lenny Dykstra.

With 2⅓ innings of two-run middle relief work, Tony Castillo was the winning pitcher for Toronto. Castillo thus picked up the first World Series win by a Venezuelan pitcher.

OCTOBER 23. The Philadelphia Phillies were in the unenviable position of trying to stave off World Series elimination, in order to force a seventh game on the road.

In Game 6 at Skydome, the Blue Jays Roberto Alomar collected a double and two singles to lift his hit total to 12 in six games (12-for-25) of the World Series, the most hits by a Hispanic player in one World Series in the 20th century.

The offensive contributions by Alomar in Game 6, which included an RBI and run scored, were part of a five-run offensive tally by Toronto, entering the ninth-inning. The home team found itself trailing the Philadelphia Phillies, 6–5.

In the team's last at-bat, outfielder Joe Carter struck one of the most exhilarating World Series hits ever, connecting for a three-run, line drive home run to left field. The walk-off blow was struck against Phillies reliever Mitch Williams and catapulted the Blue Jays to an 8–6 triumph and a second consecutive World Series title.

1994

AUGUST 11. Following the conclusion of all games played today, the Players Association made good on its promise to keep its players away from major league baseball fields, over unresolved collective bargaining issues. The ensuing strike wiped out the remainder of the season and the World Series.

At the time of the players' strike, the Montreal Expos were comfortably leading their league's East Division with a 74–40 mark, also the best record in baseball. Guiding the team, Felipe Alou, was named National League Manager of the Year, the first Hispanic to achieve this managerial distinction from a major league.

1995

FEBRUARY 7. The San Juan Senators fielded a Hispanic "Dream Team" for the 1995 Caribbean Series. With Major League Baseball embroiled in its worst labor strife in history, the Puerto Rican squad boasted a major leaguer at every position, many of them stars. The starting lineup was composed of: Roberto Alomar, Edgar Martínez, Carlos Baerga, Carlos Delgado, Juan González, Rubén Sierra, Bernie Williams, Rey Sánchez and Carmelo Martínez.

Not surprisingly, San Juan sailed through the Series unbeaten, outscoring the competition, 49 to 15.

After stroking five hits in yesterday's Senators' win, leadoff hitter Alomar lashed out two more hits in his first two trips to the plate today, becoming the first player to record seven straight hits in the Caribbean Series. Leading all hitters with a .560 average and ten RBI, the second baseman was named MVP of the Series. Bernie Williams topped all hitters with three home runs, and Rickey Bones won two games from the mound for the powerhouse Puerto Ricans.

Appropriately enough, the Series was played at Hiram Bithorn Stadium in San Juan, to an ecstatic fandom.

JUNE 3. Tonight, in San Diego, greatness was signaled in spades by Montreal's Pedro Martínez. Only once before in baseball history had a pitcher taken a perfect game past nine innings. Martínez, after retiring 27 successive batters at Jack Murphy Stadium, became the second.

Dueling the Padres' Joey Hamilton in a scoreless tie, Martínez threw nine perfect innings. In the tenth inning, Martínez allowed a double to the first batter, Bip Roberts. Mel Rojas relieved Martínez after the hit (the Expos having scored a run in the top of the tenth). Rojas obtained three outs and preserved the 1–0 victory in the monumental pitching masterpiece by the Montreal starter.

JUNE 9. Zoilo Versalles, the first Hispanic MVP Award recipient, died in Bloomington, Minnesota, at age 55. In his MVP season, Versalles, a shortstop, led the Minnesota Twins to the 1965 World Series, topping the American League in runs, doubles and triples.

JUNE 25. At Jack Murphy Stadium, Andrés Galarraga socked three home runs and knocked home seven of the Colorado Rockies' 11 runs, in the club's eight-run victory over the San Diego Padres. The Rockies first baseman homered in the 6th, 7th and 8th innings, becoming the first Hispanic player to accomplish the consecutive innings longball feat. Galarraga also became the first player from Venezuela to record a three-homer game in the big leagues.

JULY 11. By virtue of guiding his team to the best record in his league at the time of the 1994 players' strike, Felipe Alou was appointed National League manager for the 1995 All-Star Game, played today. Alou became the first Latin American manager in the Midsummer Classic's history. (Spanish extracts Al López and Lou Piniella had skippered elite teams in previous years.)

A former National League All-Star himself, the 60-year-old Alou guided his star-studded club to a 3–2 win at the Ballpark in Arlington. Florida Marlin Jeff Conine's solo home run supplied the difference.

OCTOBER 6. Bernie Williams became the first player to hit home runs from both sides of the plate in one post-season game. In Game 3 of the American League Division Series between the New York Yankees and Seattle Mariners, Williams slugged solo home runs in the fourth and eighth innings. The first dinger came batting right-handed against the Mariners' Randy Johnson. Switching sides of the plate, Williams victimized right-hander Bill Risley later on.

The Yankees' center fielder enjoyed a perfect 3-for-3 day at the dish. His blows, however, accounted for half of the Yankees' scoring in the team's 7–4 loss to the Mariners at the Kingdome.

OCTOBER 22. The journey is now complete. A rising percentage of Hispanic ballplayers now make their living in the major leagues, while "Martínez" has been the most common surname in the game for the past two years. Tonight, three Hispanic players went relatively unnoticed as one pitched, the other received, and the third batted—for the first time in a World Series game.

Batterymates Dennis Martínez and Tony Peña of the Cleveland Indians worked together to retire Javy López of the Atlanta Braves in the second inning of Game 2 of the Fall Classic at Fulton County Stadium. The defensive pair succeeded. But later in the game, López connected for a game-deciding, two-run home run that provided the Braves with a 4–3 win. The home run pitch was thrown by the 40-year-old Martínez, who, as the Indians' starter, also became the oldest pitcher to start a World Series game since 1928 (Pete Alexander, 41).

That home run pitch notwithstanding, Martínez's career, it seems, kept on getting resurrected. After a rejuvenating seven-and-a-half year stint with Montreal, the veteran Nicaraguan pitcher found new life once again, back in the American League with the Cleveland Indians. The right-hander posted a 23–11 record over the past two seasons with powerhouse Cleveland.

1996

AUGUST 16. Major League Baseball traveled south of the border to Monterrey, Mexico, where the New York Mets and San Diego Padres played the first official game outside United States and Canadian borders. The Padres outlasted the Mets, 15–10, in the first of a three-game set, drawing 2,000 fewer fans than Monterrey Stadium's 25,644 capacity.

Pitching in a meaningful game for the first time as a major leaguer on his native soil, an emotion-filled Fernando Valenzuela was the starter and winner for the Padres.

AUGUST 29. It was brother against brother for only the sixth time in baseball history. Big brother Ramon Martínez of the Los Angeles Dodgers defeated the Montreal Expos and younger sibling Pedro, 2–1, at Olympic Stadium in Montreal. Ramon, 28, offset the four-year-younger Pedro's 12-strikeout, complete-game effort by retiring 13 batters in row at one point and permitting only three hits in eight most effective innings.

Post-game statements from the initial pair of Hispanic pitching brothers to start against each other in a major league game were filled with reciprocal good wishes and pride in each other.

Pedro Martínez, left, and older brother Ramón, as teammates with the Los Angeles Dodgers in spring training, 1992. The brothers won more big league games than any other pair of Hispanic pitching siblings.

1997

MAY 23. Pitching 5⅔ innings of scoreless baseball, Fernando Valenzuela earned his 173rd and final major league victory. Starting for the San Diego Padres, Valenzuela held the Florida Marlins to five hits as he combined with four relievers for a 6–3 win at Qualcomm Park.

That July, Valenzuela was released by the St Louis Cardinals and never threw another pitch from a big league mound.

The win total, along with 31 shutouts, 113 complete games and 2,930 innings pitched by Valenzuela, in 17 seasons, stands as the most recorded by a Mexican pitcher in the major leagues. His 424 career starts and innings pitched total also rank as the most by a Hispanic left-handed pitcher.

JUNE 12. Stan Javier of the San Francisco Giants made history as the first player to hit a home run in an interleague game. At the Ballpark in Arlington, the Dominican Republic native connected against Texas Rangers left-hander Darren Oliver in the third inning of the inaugural circuit-mingling game. The right fielder also doubled home San Francisco's fourth run in the seventh inning, which held up for a 4–3 victory, disappointing the packed house of 46,507.

The game featured the first time a National League team utilized the designated hitter (Glenallen Hill) in the regular season.

JULY 8. Sandy Alomar of the Cleveland Indians hit a two-run home run in the bottom of the seventh inning to power the American League to a 3–1 win over the Nationals in the All-Star Game at Jacobs Field.

Alomar was named the star of the game and became the first player to raise the MVP trophy in his home ballpark. The Puerto Rican also became the first from his island country to win the noteworthy prize.

Mariano Rivera nailed down the win for the Junior Circuit with a perfect ninth inning. Rivera, in his first year as a closer with the New York Yankees, became the first Hispanic hurler to record a save in the All-Star Game and the first Panamanian pitcher to compete in one.

JULY 12. The Pittsburgh Pirates' Francisco Cordova (nine innings) and Ricardo Rincón (one inning) pitched the first combined extra-inning no-hitter in history, stifling the Houston Astros over ten innings, 3–0, on three walks and 11 strikeouts.

Pirates pinch-hitter Mark Smith's three-run home run provided the historic conclusion for the Mexican duo, which came in front of a jammed house of 44,119 at Three Rivers Stadium.

SEPTEMBER 7. Mexico's most revered player, Héctor Espinso, died from a heart attack in Monterrey, at age 58.

The national hero's uniform number 21 has since been retired by all teams of the Mexican League and Mexican Pacific Coast League.

SEPTEMBER 25. In the fourth inning at Olympic Stadium, Pedro Martínez of the Expos fanned Kurt Abbott of the Florida Marlins and became the 14th pitcher of the century to pile up 300 strikeouts in a season. The first Hispanic pitcher to register 300 whiffs in one season did not figure in the decision, as he was removed after seven innings with the score tied 1–1.

Montreal, scratching across two late-inning runs, defeated the Florida Marlins, 3–2.

OCTOBER 12. In January of 1996, a record $4.5 million deal was structured between the Florida Marlins and Cuban amateur player Liván Hernández. The 20-year-old pitcher, who had abandoned his national team nearly four months earlier while it was in Monterrey, Mexico, signed a four-year contract that included the largest signing bonus ($2.5 million) ever given to a non-professional athlete.

Less than two years later, Liván Hernández, starting for a flu-ridden Kevin Brown, struck out 15 Atlanta Braves in a complete-game, 2–1 victory at Pro Player Stadium. The three-hit, 143-pitch effort put the Florida Marlins ahead three games to two in the National League Championship Series. The young right-hander, whose nine regular season wins in 17 starts provided the Marlins with a much-needed shot in the arm during their playoff pursuit, cured all ills today. He won for the second time in the post-season, with the game's final pitch, to the Braves' Fred McGriff, a called strike three. The 15 strikeouts tied an LCS record set the previous day by Baltimore's Mike Mussina.

The game that set the record for most strikeouts in one post-season game by a Hispanic pitcher will carry a footnote pertaining to home plate umpire Eric Gregg's extremely generous strike zone. Not to be forgotten, Gregg was as consistent with opposing pitcher Greg Maddux in his balls and strikes calling.

OCTOBER 26. All season, Édgar Rentería had produced in the clutch. Four times during the campaign and once in the playoffs, the shortstop made instant winners of the Florida Marlins with a game-ending hit.

Tonight, 67,204 Pro Player Stadium fans entered into a state of rapturous delirium as the "Barranquilla Baby" singled home the World Series-winning run in Game 7 in the bottom of the 11th inning against Cleveland Indians pitcher Charles Nagy. The arcing single by Rentería, over the mound and into center field, lifted the Marlins to a 3–2 victory and ended the second-longest Game 7 in history. The safety also made the "Fighting Fish" the first wild card team to win the World Series.

The 21-year-old shortstop became the first Hispanic player to stroke a World Series–deciding, walk-off hit.

With two victories to his credit, Liván Hernández was named the Series' MVP. The right-hander won Games 1 and 5, backed by strong run support in both outings. The effective, though far from dominant, pitching earned for Hernández the first World Series MVP trophy for a Cuban player.

NOVEMBER 11. Pedro Martínez of the Montreal Expos won 17 games and struck out 305 batters in 1997. He led the National League in complete games with 13 and ERA with a 1.90 mark. With an ERA+ of 219, he became the second Hispanic major league pitcher to post an ERA+ over 200 (Adolfo Luque, 201, in 1923). The dominant pitching numbers earned for Martínez his first Cy Young Award, announced today.

The 26-year-old Dominican, the first from his country to win the prestigious pitching award, will shortly make good on his earlier promise, if he won, to gift the award to six-time, 20-game winner Juan Marichal. Displaying not only a magnanimous nature but also a historic awareness often lost among modern ballplayers, Martínez presented the award to Marichal, who never won one during his illustrious career, at the annual Boston Baseball Writers Awards banquet.

1998

MARCH 31. The Tampa Bay, Florida, region appeared to have lured the Chicago White Sox away from the Windy City a few years back. Officials even built a domed stadium to make the relocation prospect more desirable for the big league club. After the deal fell through, Bay area officials turned in another direction. The original objective was reached today, in the inaugural game for the Tampa Bay Devil Rays. At domed Tropicana Field, the Devil Rays—an American League expansion team—were defeated, 11–6, by the Detroit Tigers.

Wilson Alvarez, signed by the Devil Rays to a big free agent contract, was the hard-hit starter and loser. Alvarez became the first Hispanic player for the western Florida franchise (and also one of the worst free agent signings in history).

MARCH 31. Baseball's "Expansion Era" came to an end with its tenth new franchise in 30 years and 14th since 1961. A new state-of-the-art facility, under the purchased naming rights of Bank One Ballpark, in Phoenix, Arizona, welcomed the Arizona Diamondbacks. The visiting Colorado Rockies spoiled the Diamondbacks' inaugural game by a one-sided score of 9–2.

Diamondbacks outfielder Karim García, the desert club's first Hispanic player, accounted for one of the runs with a home run.

JUNE 2. On June 18, 1997, on the fourth anniversary of his 200th career win and a month after being released by the Seattle Mariners, Dennis Martínez retired, through a MLBPA press release.[54] With no teams prospecting for 43-year-old pitchers, his 241 career wins seemed to have fallen just shy of Juan Marichal's record of 243 wins among Hispanic pitchers.

Martínez later had second thoughts about his retirement. After putting out "feelers" for a big league return, a winter tryout with the Florida Marlins was unsuccessful. But Martínez remained hopeful and active in Puerto Rico, and gained attention from one major league club.

Today, at County Stadium, Martínez rewarded the Atlanta Braves' faith in signing him prior to spring training by throwing a 12-hit shutout, beating the Milwaukee Brewers, 9–0. It was the 44-year-old Martínez's last career shutout, number 30, and more significantly it was the Nicaraguan right-hander's 243rd win, tying Marichal.

JUNE 20. Never before had the game been witness to a greater home run demonstration than the one over the past 30 days by Samuel Peralta Sosa. The Chicago Cubs' right fielder, who missed three games during the interval due to a sprained thumb, hit his 21st home run since May 21, the most ever in a 30-day span. (The previous record for circuit clouting in clusters was 20 in 30 days, accomplished by Ralph Kiner in 1947 and by Roger Maris in 1961.)

Sosa smashed two long balls for the second game in a row against the Philadelphia Phillies. One of his blasts cleared Wrigley Field's bleachers and landed on the roof of a building across the street. In all, with his 28th and 29th home runs on the season, the enthusiastic Dominican drove in five runs in the team's 9–4 triumph over the Phillies.

JUNE 25. Sammy Sosa set the major league record for home runs in one calendar month, dialing long distance for the 19th time against right-hander Brian Moehler of the Detroit Tigers. The big fly came in a 6–4 Cubs interleague loss at Tiger Stadium; it was

Sammy Sosa, left, and Mark McGwire captivated world audiences with their awe-inspiring (but now tainted) home run exploits of 1998.

the dinger-delirious Sosa's 12th home run in 13 games and 19th in his last 23 contests. Five days later, Sosa extended his own record, connecting against Arizona Diamondbacks reliever Alan Embree.

    An unprecedented display of home run power over the past six weeks has catapulted

Sosa into the long-ball limelight with Mark McGwire. Sosa accumulated a staggering 20 home runs and 40 RBI during June.

JULY 5. Juan González cracked the 100-RBI mark (101) prior to the All-Star Game. González clubbed two two-run home runs against Seattle Mariners pitcher Randy Johnson, in the Rangers' 87th and last game before the mid-season break. The homers provided the cushion for an 8–4 Rangers victory in Arlington. In the seventh inning, after hitting the second homer, González was rendered a standing ovation by the appreciative home crowd of 38,053.

The 28-year-old became only the second player in history to reach this amazing run-production level at this stage of the season. In 1935, Hank Greenberg of the Detroit Tigers produced 103 RBI in only 76 games—and was not even selected to the All-Star team.

JULY 7. The Marlins' Édgar Rentería substituted for the Braves' Walt Weiss at shortstop for the National League and played the final three innings of the All-Star Game. Making the first appearance by a Colombian player in the Midsummer Classic, Rentería scored the final run of the game for the Senior Circuit, which suffered a 13–8 defeat at Coors Field.

Incidentally, Ugueth Urtaín Urbina of the Montreal Expos, by way of Caracas, Venezuela, allowed three runs to the American League and was tagged with the loss. Urbina, 47 years after Venezuela produced the first Latin American player to appear in the All-Star Game, became its country's first mound representative at baseball's midsummer gala.

The Indians' Bartolo Colón, allowing one run in one inning of work, was credited with the AL victory.

AUGUST 9. A most efficient inning in relief recorded by Dennis Martínez of the Braves was all it took to win the 244th game of his career, the most by a Hispanic major league pitcher. The three orderly, eighth-inning outs were achieved by Martínez at Candlestick Park, ironically where the previous winningest Hispanic pitcher, Juan Marichal, won so many of his games. Atlanta scored twice in the top of the ninth inning, and Kerry Ligtenberg retired the Giants without scoring to give Martínez the milestone win, 7–5.

Martínez gained one more victory, also in relief, near season's end to finish off a laudatory career as the all-time winningest (245) Hispanic pitcher, having started more games (562) and thrown more major league innings (3,999⅔) than any other Hispanic hurler.

Martínez retired for good in February of 1999, ending a splendid 23-season career.

AUGUST 10. The assault on Roger Maris' 37-year-old home run mark came from two challengers. That was made resoundingly clear by Sammy Sosa's two home runs at Candlestick Park this day. His 45th and 46th big flies of the season tied Mark McGwire—for the first of seven times in the next six weeks—and led the Cubs to an 8–5 triumph over the San Francisco Giants. Sosa hit nine homers in his last 15 games.

This season, Sosa tied a major league record for most multi-home run games with 11 (Hank Greenberg, 1937).

AUGUST 23. Two home runs for Sammy Sosa against José Lima in a 13–3 Cubs home thrashing of the Houston Astros, and one home run for Mark McGwire in his game, left Sosa two behind, 51 to 53, in the "Maris Home Run Chase."

This chase, unlike the great 1961 home run pursuit between Roger Maris and Mickey Mantle, did not have media and fan bias surrounding it. Both Sosa and McGwire were fan favorites. McGwire, taking a cue from the carefree Sosa, evolved into a media-friendly player as the two embarked on a summer-long, "feel-good" home run extravaganza with few detrimental diversions.

Sosa became the first Hispanic player to hit 50 home runs in one season.

SEPTEMBER 12. The man who had never hit more than 40 home runs in a season became the fourth player in history to wallop 60. Sammy Sosa victimized Valerio de los Santos of the Milwaukee Brewers in the seventh inning at Wrigley Field, sparking a come-from-behind, 15–12 Cubs win.

The Maris Home Run Chase was triumphantly over for one player, but not for Sammy Sosa, one of the driving forces behind a truly magical major league season which saw the most time-honored baseball record eclipsed by a man-mountain of a man named McGwire. A gracious, spirited man of humble origins named Sosa stayed on McGwire's heels throughout the home run sojourn—coaxing, without contention, the competitive best from Big Mac, for the reveling benefit of the baseball world.

SEPTEMBER 18. Vinny Castilla's home run against Scott Sanders, leading of the ninth inning at Qualcomm Park, earned for the Colorado Rockies third baseman a place in the history books. The round-tripper was Castilla's second of the game and 45th of the season. But more significantly, the hit counted as his 200th of the campaign. Castilla became the 19th big league player—and the first Hispanic—to record 40 home runs and 200 hits (46/206) in one season.

Enjoying a career year, Castilla played in every game on the schedule for the fourth-place Rockies, who defeated the San Diego Padres, 4–1.

SEPTEMBER 25. In the season's final weekend, Sammy Sosa took the lead in home runs from Mark McGwire, if only briefly. The 66th and last home run for Sosa in this momentous campaign came against the Houston Astros' José Lima; Houston won, 6–2, at the Astrodome.

Forty-five minutes after Sosa connected, McGwire evened the score in his game. McGwire hit four more home runs in his next two games to attain an unprecedented 70 home runs.

NOVEMBER 18. The RBI king of the American League with 157, Juan González took home the circuit's big award for the second time in three years. The Texas Rangers' slugger received three-quarters of the first-place votes, surpassing runner-up Nomar Garciaparra by a wide margin.

The outfielder became the first Hispanic player to win two league MVP Awards. With his 45 home runs and 50 doubles, González also became the first Hispanic big lea-guer to record 40 home runs and 50 doubles in one season.

NOVEMBER 19. If the MVP Award had been a race like the home run challenge, Sammy Sosa would have nearly lapped Mark McGwire. Sosa took league honors with 30 out of 32 first-place votes to outdistance runner-up McGwire, 438 points to 272.

Sosa's honor complemented Juan González's selection a day earlier; the pair were the first Hispanic tandem to win major Most Valuable Player Awards in the same season.

1999

MARCH 28. Organized Baseball was forced to leave Cuba 38 years ago when it relo-cated their Havana-based minor league Sugar Kings team to Jersey City, New Jersey. OB returned today to Havana with a major league squad, the Baltimore Orioles, to play a

Cuban national team in front of an invitation-only, capacity-filled Estadio Latinoamericano.

The Orioles eked out a 3–2 decision in 11 innings. Future defector and major league standout José Contreras pitched for the Cuban team, hurling eight scoreless innings of relief with ten strikeouts. After Contreras was removed, a single by Harold Baines drove in Will Clark with the go-ahead run.

The Cuban national team did not field its best possible lineup as several highly rated players were still competing in the country's championship National Series. The Commissioner of Baseball, Allan H. "Bud" Selig, sat in a field box seat next to Cuban dictator Fidel Castro throughout the entire contest.

APRIL 4. Major League Baseball opened a season for the first time outside of the United States or Canada. The site was Estadio Monterrey in Monterrey, Mexico, where 27,104 viewed the defending National League champion San Diego Padres lose to the Colorado Rockies, 8–2.

Mexican-born Vinny Castilla collected four hits for Colorado, as did Dante Bichette, who added four RBI.

APRIL 6. At Dodger Stadium, on the day before his 20th birthday, Los Angeles third baseman Adrián Beltre crunched his first home run of the two-day-old season. The second-inning, two-run blast was all the scoring for the Dodgers until the bottom of the tenth inning, when Gary Sheffield delivered a walk-off moon shot, giving the home team and the 33,139 attendees an exciting 3–2 victory over the Arizona Diamondbacks.

Beltre had played 77 games in 1998 for the Dodgers and hit seven home runs. The raw talent had been tied with Dominican compatriot César Cedeno for most home runs collected by a teenage Hispanic big league player—until he established the new mark with less than two hours to spare in the night game.

APRIL 13. Iván "Pudge" Rodriguez knocked in nine runs with his first career grand slam, a three-run homer, and two other hits, as his Texas Rangers spanked the home-team Mariners, 15–6, at the Kingdome.

The Puerto Rican backstop set a new standard for RBI by a Hispanic player in a single major league game.

APRIL 14. Jose Canseco, DH for the Tampa Bay Devil Rays, smacked his 400th career home run, served up by Toronto Blue Jays pitcher Kelvim Escobar. The home run, a solo liner to left, came in the third inning of the squad's 7–6 road loss.

Canseco became the 28th big league batter to reach this prolific power plateau, and the first Hispanic.

On July 4, hitting his 30th home run of the campaign, the slugger became the first player to hit 30 home runs for four teams (Oakland, Texas and Toronto).

APRIL 23. St. Louis Cardinals third baseman Fernando Tatis recorded the game of his life—in one inning. Tatis belted two grand slam home runs in the top of the third inning at Dodger Stadium, the first hitter in baseball history to accomplish this feat. Tatis, from San Pedro de Macoris, also set the record for RBI in one inning with eight.

Both "salamis" were surrendered by Chan Ho Park of the Dodgers, the first pitcher to allow two grand slams in one inning to the same batter in the modern era. The Cardinals coasted to victory, 12–5, on the strength of the 11 runs the club scored in the historic third frame. The home runs were Tatis' only hits on the evening.

MAY 3. The return to Cuba by MLB in March, which was spearheaded by Orioles owner Peter Angelos, was scheduled as a home and home two-game series. In the return match, played today in Baltimore, the hitters fared considerably better than in the first encounter. The Cubans, with a full complement of talent available following the conclusion of their National Series, outslugged the Orioles, 12–6.

In a similar circumstance to the game at Estadio Latinoamericano, Cuban reliever Norge Vera shut down the Birds for seven innings without a hit before he was solved for three hits and three runs in the ninth. Omar Linares, a revered name and superstar in post-revolutionary Cuban baseball, went 4-for-4 as his club lashed out 18 hits. Designated hitter Andy Morales[55] capped the Cubans' scoring with a ninth-inning, three-run homer.

The game at Camden Yards was briefly interrupted in the fifth inning by an anti–Castro, flag-waving protester, who was wrestled to the ground by a Cuban umpire.

MAY 7. Five years after the Chicago White Sox discovered him as an 18-year-old prospect in Panama, Carlos Lee made his major league debut and produced a home run the first time he stepped into the batter's box. Standing in against Oakland A's pitcher Tom Candiotti, Lee socked a second-inning solo home run at Comiskey Park to increase the White Sox' early lead in the game to 3–0.

The big fly by Lee, one of three on the day by the home team, earned historical inscription for Lee as the first player from Panama to hit a home run in his first major league at-bat. A 7–1 win by Chicago no doubt added to Lee's special day.

JULY 25. With the governor of Puerto Rico and the Clemente family present, amid shouts of "Viva Cepeda!" and several Puerto Rican flag-waving contingents in the crowd, Orlando Cepeda was inducted into the National Baseball Hall of Fame.

The star first baseman, who retired with the highest OPS+ (133) of any 20th century Hispanic major leaguer, was elected earlier in the year by the Veterans Committee, the fifth Latin American player and second Puerto Rican to be honored.

Five years earlier, Cepeda, a lifetime .297 hitter with 1,365 RBI, had missed election by a scant seven votes in his last year of BBWAA eligibility.

AUGUST 14. Pudge Rodriguez swiped his 20th base of the season and, with two dozen home runs on the campaign, became the first catcher to clout 20 homers and 20 steals in a big league season. The historic, third-inning theft came against the Chicago White Sox battery of Jim Parque and Brook Fordyce.

In the same game, won by the White Sox at Comiskey Park, 8–7, Rodriguez's Texas Rangers teammate Rafael Palmeiro hit his 30th home run of the season, giving him five straight 30-HR, 100-RBI seasons.

AUGUST 30. The New York Mets' Edgardo Alfonzo produced a 6-for-6 day at the plate, including three home runs. The second baseman drove in five runs while amassing 16 total bases—the most by a Hispanic player in one major league game. The Mets' second baseman also scored six runs, tying a modern era single-game record.

All the crooked numbers were registered during a New York clobbering of the Houston Astros, 17–1, in Houston.

SEPTEMBER 18. Sammy Sosa became the first player in history to hit 60 home runs twice. Sosa slugged the historic four-bagger—a solo shot against Jason Bere of Milwaukee—in the sixth inning of a 7–4, 14-inning Cubs home loss to the Brewers.

The blast gave Sosa more home runs than his last-place Cubs had wins (59).

SEPTEMBER 21. Marilyn. Elvis. Liz. The highest praise offered to mega-stardom is single-name recognition. In the current era of sports, where endearing nicknames once as vivid as the athletes they described have grown out of vogue, the trend leans now more toward the same mono-identities of cinema and pop culture stars of past years: Michael. Cal. Tiger.

In Boston, "Pedro" is the name that requires no surname. Since making his Beantown debut with the Red Sox with a 12-strikeout, 5–0 shutout of the Seattle Mariners in April 1998, Martínez has become familiarly known as "Pedro" to New Englanders, and *"Pedro"* to the rest of the league—with opposite sentiments.

Today, Pedro Martínez threw the only shutout of a truly authoritative campaign. The pitcher, who signed a $75 million contract following his trade to Boston in 1998, three-hit the Toronto Blue Jays at Fenway Park, 3–0. Martínez, whose American League-leading ERA of 2.07 in 1999 was an amazing 2.79 runs lower than the league average, fanned 12 in gaining his 22nd victory. The Jays' Carlos Delgado was his 12th strikeout victim and number 300 for the year.

Martínez became the second pitcher in baseball history, after Randy Johnson (also this season), to whiff 300 batters in both leagues. With 13.20 strikeouts per nine innings (313 total), the Red Sox hurler established a major league record for a starter's strikeout efficiency. The record will be topped by Randy Johnson in 2001 at 13.41.

SEPTEMBER 26. For the first time in six decades, a player reached 160 RBI in one season, and that player was outfielder Manny Ramírez. A first-inning sacrifice fly plated the run that matched a production plateau last scaled by Jimmie Foxx (175 in 1938). Scoring four runs in the top of the ninth inning at Skydome, Ramírez's visiting Cleveland Indians beat the Toronto Blue Jays, 11–7.

Over the last week of the season, Ramírez's ascent to superstardom was completed, as the outfielder pushed home five more runs. The 165 runs batted in became an all-time, single-season high for a Hispanic big leaguer.

SEPTEMBER 27. At Fenway Park, a recurring sign in Spanish read, *"Los Ponchados de Pedro"*—"Pedro's Strikeouts." Tabbing the mountainous strikeout counts Pedro Martínez amassed provided boisterous levels of entertainment for Red Sox fans, no matter their preferred language.

Allowing one earned run in eight innings, Martínez recorded his 23rd and final victory of this acclaimed season, 5–3, over the Baltimore Orioles. Martínez whiffed a dozen Orioles hitters, his eighth consecutive start, dating back to August 19, with at least ten strikeouts—a major league record (tied by Chris Sale in 2015).

On the season, Martínez recorded a truly incredible FIP of 1.40, the best of any modern era pitcher! FIP analogs a pitcher's effectiveness, eliminating the defense's role. It calculates the preventative skills of a pitcher with respect to home runs, HBP and walks, along with strikeouts, the handful of "true outcomes" a pitcher can control from the mound. Martínez's 2.91 career FIP was the best of any Hispanic major league starting pitcher.

OCTOBER 2. With one inning of scoreless relief, Pedro Martínez wrapped up his stupendous season. After notching his 23rd victory five days earlier, Martínez relinquished his final start of the season, against the Baltimore Orioles, to brother Ramón. Pedro relieved his older sibling in the seventh inning and struck out Albert Belle for his 313th strikeout on the campaign. The wild card-winning Red Sox were 8–0 winners at Camden Yards.

Topping the league in wins, strikeouts and ERA (2.07), the fabulous Dominican hurler secured the first Triple Crown from the mound by a Latin American pitcher in the major leagues. (Lefty Gómez topped all three categories in 1934 and 1937.)

OCTOBER 2. Having broken into the major leagues in 1995 and staying on an eventual nine years, outfielder Marvin Benard became the longest tenured big league position player from Nicaragua of the 20th century. Today, playing for the San Francisco Giants, his only club in that span, Benard collected five of the Giants' 18 hits and scored three runs in San Francisco's 16–7 stomping of the Colorado Rockies at Coors Field.

The first five-hit game in the big leagues by a Nicaraguan player strengthened Benard's ultimate standing as the most productive batsman his country has produced to date. His 714 lifetime hits and 54 home runs remain high-water marks for a Nicaraguan major leaguer.

OCTOBER 26. Winners of the first two games of the World Series on the road in Atlanta, the New York Yankees returned to New York in the driver's seat. Although the starting pitching in today's Game 3 for the Yankees was not as good as in the prior two contests, the New York bullpen made up for the deficiency.

Three relievers held the Atlanta Braves scoreless for six and one-third innings, the last two pitched by closer Mariano Rivera. The Yankees chipped away at the Braves' initial lead and tied the game 5–5 in the bottom of the eighth inning. In the home tenth, left fielder Chad Curtis homered and provided New York with a 6–5 victory.

By virtue of the dramatic home run, Rivera became the first Panamanian hurler to win a World Series game.

OCTOBER 27. At Yankee Stadium, Mariano Rivera cemented World Series MVP honors with his second save, to go along with a win, in Game 4 of the Fall Classic between the New York Yankees and Atlanta Braves. Rivera retired all four men he faced after entering the 4–1 game with two outs in the top of the eighth inning. The four-game sweep gave New York their 25th World Series title.

Rivera, Panama's first World Series MVP recipient, was a key component to New York's last two World Series victories, accumulating two wins and 12 saves in the 1998 and 1999 post-seasons.

NOVEMBER 16. It was a sensationally surreal season for Pedro Martínez. He won 23 games in only 29 starts. He struck out 313 batters (more than 100 more than the next closest pitcher). His WHIP was 0.92. His 23–4 record produced an .852 winning percentage. All chart-topping numbers in the league.

The fourth unanimous Cy Young Award in American League history was deservedly his, as was the distinction of becoming the third pitcher, to date, to win the supreme pitching award in both leagues (Gaylord Perry, Randy Johnson).

In the MVP balloting, announced two days later, Martínez was edged out by the Rangers' Pudge Rodríguez with a point total of 252 to 239. The Boston pitcher nipped Rodriguez in first-place votes, eight to seven, but Martínez was left off two writers' ballots completely, because of sentiments that pitchers should not be eligible for this prize.

Hispanic players, incidentally, occupied the first five AL ballot spots.

2000

JANUARY 10. Tony Pérez finally received the call from Cooperstown. Pérez became the first Cuban voted in by the BBWAA. The National Baseball Hall of Fame would beckon entrance on July 23 to Perez, who drove in 90 or more runs 11 straight years, and whose 1,652 lifetime RBI were the most by a Hispanic player in the 20th century. The clutch hitter's eight career pinch-hit home runs are the most by a Latin American player, as are his 11 walk-off blasts, tied with David Ortiz and Albert Pujols. (St. Croix–born and pinch-hitter extraordinaire José Morales socked a dozen pinch-hit homers. Matt Stairs hit the most home runs as an emergency hitter with 23.)

APRIL 23. Bernie Williams and Jorge Posada each pounded home runs from both sides of the plate, driving in eight runs between them, in a 10–7 New York Yankees win over the Toronto Blue Jays at Skydome.

It was the first time in baseball history that switch-hitting teammates struck home runs from both sides of the plate in the same game.

APRIL 25. José Canseco of the Tampa Bay Devil Rays and Antonio Alfonseca of the Florida Marlins were among Cuban and Dominican players who sat out their games to protest the United States government's immigration measures in the case involving Elián González, a Cuban rafter boy. The depleted Marlins fielded 19 players for its game against the San Francisco Giants and lost in 11 innings, 6–4.

Rafael Palmeiro of the Texas Rangers elected to play in his team's game.

JULY 23. It was another one of those special "Pedro Days" in Boston. For the fourth time in his career, Pedro Martínez struck out 15 batters in a game—without walking anyone. Martínez allowed six hits and struck out the side twice in defeating the Chicago White Sox, 1–0, at Fenway Park. The shutout was the third of the campaign for the Red Sox right-hander and his second with 15 Ks and no bases on balls.

During his career, Martínez attained the best strikeout-to-walk ratio of any Hispanic pitcher in big league history, 3,154 strikeouts to 760 bases on balls, a sensational 4.15 ratio.[56]

Including his 2.17 FIP this season, Martínez also cataloged the most seasons by a Hispanic pitcher—five—with a Fielding Independent Pitching analytic under 2.50. Only Juan Marichal and Mike Cuéllar had as many as two such seasons.

JULY 29. In 1998, Jolbert Cabrera joined his brother Orlando in reaching the big leagues, if only for one game. In doing so, the Cabreras became the first siblings from Colombia to make the major league grade. Today, older brother Jolbert sprayed five hits in five at-bats at Camden Yards. Playing center field for the Cleveland Indians, Cabrera scored a run and knocked in one, as the Indians trounced the Baltimore Orioles, 14–3, in the first game of a doubleheader. The 27-year-old Cartagena native achieved the first five-hit game by a Colombian player in the major leagues.

SEPTEMBER 16. Sammy Sosa matched Mark McGwire as the only players with three straight 50-home-run seasons. Sosa's 50th was a two-run, game-tying blast in the sixth inning at Busch Stadium in St. Louis. The last-place Cubs were defeated, 7–6, by the hometown Cardinals.

Ironically, after two 60-home run campaigns, Sosa won his first home run crown this season with the more modest total of 50. The outfielder became the first Dominican player to lead a major league in home runs.

OCTOBER 13. Since allowing a fateful home run to Sandy Alomar in the 1997 ALDS, Mariano Rivera had not permitted a post-season run—a span of 22 appearances and 31⅔ innings—entering today. Rivera was called upon with one out in the eighth inning and the Yankees holding a 4–2 lead over the Seattle Mariners at Safeco Field. The Yankees tacked on to their lead for an 8–2 win and a leg up in the American League Championship Series, two games to one.

The final out came on a grounder by the Mariners' Mark McLemore and boosted Rivera's post-season scoreless innings streak to 33⅓, topping the previous record of 33, held by Whitey Ford (all as a World Series starter).

Fittingly, it was McLemore, four days later in the same ALCS, who ended Rivera's new mark at 34⅓ innings, stroking a two-run double against Rivera in a non-save situation.

NOVEMBER 13. No pitcher in the American League's 100-year history had won back-to-back Cy Young Awards unanimously. But then again, Pedro Martínez had only been pitching in the league for three years.

Martínez (18–6) won his third Cy Young Award in four years, dominating hitters this season like no pitcher ever has. He led the circuit in shutouts (four), strikeouts (284), fewest hits (5.31) and home runs (0.71) allowed per nine innings, while posting a brilliant 1.74 ERA—nearly two full runs lower than the runner-up Roger Clemens (3.70), an unprecedented differential. The 29-year-old hurler's opponents' batting average of .167 broke by one point the previous low mark held by Luis Tiant in 1968. Martínez's WHIP was an unbelievable 0.74—a historic low for a major league starting pitcher. His ERA+ computed to an astonishing 291, the best of any modern era pitcher.

Martínez registered an 11.7 pitching WAR metric, the highest by a Hispanic pitcher in one season. The intricate pitching measurement not only calculates how well a pitcher does at not allowing runs, but also factors in the quality of opposing lineups, team defense and the league scoring environment.

The 86.0 WAR composite Martínez accrued in his career ranks as the highest of any big league Hispanic pitcher.

DECEMBER 13. Manny Ramírez became baseball's second $20 million man. Two days after Alex Rodriguez's jaw-dropping ten-year, $250 million contract with the Texas Rangers was announced, the Boston Red Sox agreed to compensate the free agent right fielder for his exclusive services for $160 million over eight years. Albeit in only 118 games, Ramírez was coming off a season in which he led the league in slugging percentage at .697 and posted an OPS of 1.154.

Ramírez, during a 12-year period from 1995 through 2006, compiled an OPS of .900 or higher every year. Only Jimmie Foxx, Lou Gehrig, Willie Mays and Stan Musial, all with 13, established longer such consecutive seasonal streaks.

2001

JUNE 17. Montreal's Orlando Cabrera earned his first Gold Glove Award this season, but today the Expos' shortstop shined with his bat, clubbing a game-ending home run in the bottom of the ninth inning at Olympic Stadium. The three-run circuit blast, surrendered by Toronto's Paul Quantrill, raised the Expos to a 4–1 interleague win.

The first walk-off home run by a Colombian player in the major leagues was presumably witnessed by nearly all of the 8,440 happy fans in attendance.

AUGUST 11. Pitcher Liván Hernández of the San Francisco Giants hit a home run and went 4-for-4 at the plate, giving him eight straight hits and 12 in his last 13 at-bats. From the mound, he was nearly as stellar, tossing eight innings, with one earned run allowed, in a 9–4 win over the Chicago Cubs at Wrigley Field. Hernández, one of the few

Hispanic pitchers to record 200 hits in their big league careers, became the first Hispanic pitcher to stroke eight straight hits. But a San Francisco teammate took the spotlight away from Hernández by hitting his 50th home run of the season.

Barry Bonds, carving his place as the best player of his generation, became the earliest as well as the oldest player to reach the half-century mark in home runs. The 37-year-old left fielder, who remained ahead of Mark McGwire's record 70-home run pace of 1998, cranked a three-run home run. Bonds arrived at 50 big flies in his team's 117th game, besting Sammy Sosa's previous best mark of 121 games in 1999.

AUGUST 17. Colorado Rockies rookie José Ortiz smashed three long balls out of Coors Field against the Florida Marlins. The circuit blows and four RBI helped spark a Colorado comeback and a one-sided win, 12–5.

The Dominican second baseman became the first Hispanic rookie to hit three home runs in a major league game.

AUGUST 26. After two 60-home-run seasons, Sammy Sosa won his first home run crown in 2000 with the grand total of 50.

Today, the sensational Sosa hit two out of the park, giving him 51, as the Chicago Cubs defeated the St. Louis Cardinals, 6–1, at Wrigley Field. Sosa became the first Hispanic player to hit 50 home runs in four consecutive seasons. Only Babe Ruth and Mark McGwire have achieved similar haughty home run heights (although Ruth's four 50-home-run campaigns were not in consecutive seasons).

Sosa joined Ruth and Jimmie Foxx as the only players with two 50-home run and 150-RBI campaigns.

SEPTEMBER 23. The accolades are never-ending for Sammy Sosa, in this, perhaps his best season ever. The Sensational One made history once again by blasting three big flies against the Houston Astros at Enron Field, becoming the first major league player to hit three home runs in a game three times in one season.

Sosa, his average well above .300 for a second straight campaign, trekked toward an OPS mark of 1.174, the highest accumulated by a Hispanic player in a major league season. Despite Sosa's trio of homers, numbers 56, 57 and 58, the Cubs fell, 7–6, and so do just about all of the team's playoff hopes for this year.

OCTOBER 3. Jose Canseco hit the last home run of his career, a second-inning solo shot on a pitch served up by the Yankees' Mike Mussina. It was the only run for the White Sox in their 2–1 loss in the Bronx. The home run was also the 462nd of the slugger's often stellar, often tumultuous, often bombastic career. After this season, no American League team was willing to take a chance on the Hispanic player with the most home runs (431) hit in the 20th century, and he was signed the following spring by the Major League Baseball-owned Montreal Expos.

Canseco had been healthy for the past two seasons, but rather ironically, the 37-year-old was cut before the 2002 camp broke, after refusing to take a minor league assignment, thus bringing the end to his big league career.

OCTOBER 7. So, so very special was Mr. Sammy Sosa. The superlative slugger crowned his most extraordinary season with several milestone achievements. His 64th home run, hit today, was his 450th lifetime. His 160th RBI was the most achieved in the National League in 71 years. His 425 total bases set a new Cubs' team record and an all-time high for a Hispanic big league player. The slugger's total bases tally of 1,619 over the last four seasons established a new National League mark, besting the 1,617 of Chuck Klein from 1929 to 1932.

Capping the greatest offensive season by a Hispanic hitter, Sosa homered in his final time up on the campaign, accounting for Chicago's last run in its 4–3 loss at Wrigley Field. The Cubs right fielder led the major leagues in runs (146) and RBI (160), and became the first Hispanic player to gather 100 extra-base hits (103), and the first to slug over .700 (.737). The extra-base hits are tied for the most (Hank Greenberg, 1937, and Albert Belle, 1995) by a right-handed batter in a major league season.

Sosa ended up second in the tater title to Barry Bonds' unbelievable total of 73.

OCTOBER 7. Albert Pujols started ripping the cover off the ball in spring training and never stopped. With today's 1-for-4 showing on the season's concluding day, the St. Louis wunderkind established first-year Hispanic records for home runs with 37 and RBI with 130. The 21-year-old Santo Domingo native also set National League rookie records with 88 extra-base hits and 360 total bases.

Pujols' lone hit in today's game was an insignificant single in the face of a 9–2 defeat by the Central Division-winning Houston Astros. Hitting .329, Pujols put the finishing touch on the greatest offensive season by a Hispanic rookie player, as he joined Hal Trosky and Ted Williams as the only freshmen to collect 30 doubles, 30 home runs and 100 RBI.

OCTOBER 14. New York Yankees pitcher Orlando "El Duque" Hernández defeated the Oakland A's in the fourth game of the ALDS. Although not particularly sharp, Hernández had enough to keep the A's at bay for 5⅔ innings, allowing two runs on eight hits. The 9–2 win improved Hernández's post-season record to 9–1.

The best player of the 2000s, Albert Pujols was a three-time National League MVP with the St. Louis Cardinals.

It was the final post-season victory for the Cuban defector. The nine victories were the most earned by a Hispanic pitcher.

2002

FEBRUARY 12. In unprecedented administrative action, Major League Baseball simultaneously acquired the Montreal Expos and approved the sale of the Florida Marlins to the Expos' current owner, Jeffrey Loria. All other 29 teams take equal ownership in the Expos as a result of the move. Omar Minaya and Tony Tavares were hand picked by Commissioner Bud Selig to run the financially struggling Canadian team. Minaya was tabbed as general manager and Tavares was named president. With the appointment, the Dominican-born, Queens, New York–reared Minaya became the first Hispanic general manager of a major league team.

The Expos were sold two years later and relocated to an ownership group based in Washington, D.C.

JUNE 15. A fifth-inning double at Minute Maid Park, stroked by Texas Rangers first baseman Rafael Palmeiro, registered as the 1,000th extra-base hit of his career. The two-base hit was one of only three hits surrendered by Houston Astros starter Wade Miller and two relievers, in an impressive humbling of a powerful Rangers' lineup that listed Iván Rodríguez, Alex Rodríguez and Juan González batting ahead of Palmeiro.

In the 4–0 interleague loss to the rival Astros, the Rangers' first sacker became the 25th major league player and the first Hispanic to reach this significant slugging plateau.

JUNE 22. The Florida Marlins had won four games in a row entering tonight's contest. That was nothing compared to the roll their second baseman was on. Luis Castillo had hit safely in 35 consecutive games, the 11th-longest hitting streak in major league history, entering play tonight against the Detroit Tigers.

At Pro Player Stadium, the Marlins rallied for four runs in the bottom of the ninth inning to keep their winning ways intact, but Castillo, with a hitless showing in four trips to the dish, was unable to prolong his grand streak. The longest consecutive game hitting streak by a Hispanic major league player was stopped with Castillo waiting in the on-deck circle, when the Marlins scored the winning run with one out. The final score was 5–4.

AUGUST 17. At Safeco Field, Bernie Williams singled in his first at-bat, recording his 11th consecutive base hit, one short of the all-time record held by Walt Dropo and Pinky Higgins. The Yankees' center fielder was retired in his next at-bat. Before his third-inning ground out, Williams had not been retired in 13 successive plate appearances, spanning four games and including two walks. Another Williams—Theodore Samuel— holds the all-time mark of reaching base in 16 straight plate appearances.

The Yankees, behind Mike Mussina, defeated the Seattle Mariners, 8–3, in front of a crowd of 46,174.

2003

APRIL 4. The man who as a boy shined shoes to help support his fatherless family now walks in the footsteps of the all-time greats. In baseball's newest ballpark and against baseball's oldest franchise, Sammy Sosa, 34, made history as the third-youngest player, and the first Hispanic, to hit 500 home runs.

Entering the season one swing away from the long-ball milestone, Sosa, in his tenth at-bat of the season, slammed a 1–2 offering from Reds reliever Scott Sullivan into the right field bleachers at Great American Ball Park. The solo blast, by the man who has hit more home runs in the past five seasons than any player in a similar stretch, came 29 years to the day that Henry Aaron tied Babe Ruth with 714 home runs in the same city of Cincinnati.

The Reds won a slugfest, 10–9, to pick up their first win of the young campaign.

JUNE 20. At age 20 years and two months, Miguel Cabrera played his first game in the major leagues. Playing left field for the Florida Marlins, Cabrera was hitless in his first four trips to the plate. But a well-pitched 1–1 game between the Marlins and the visiting Tampa Bay Devil Rays permitted the youngster another opportunity to bat. In the bottom of the 12th inning, with fellow Venezuelan Alex González on base, the Maracay-bred player blasted a home run off Tampa reliever Al Levine to win the game, 3–1.

Cabrera became the third player in the modern era, and the first Hispanic, to clout a walk-off home run in his debut game (the others: Bill Parker and Josh Bard). The future superstar also became the sixth-youngest player to homer in his initial big league game and the most youthful Hispanic representative to accomplish the feat.

JULY 3. A group of 11 players, one owner, one sportswriter and one umpire were enshrined in Andean baseball immortality. Luis Aparicio, Jr., José Bracho, Alex Carrasquel, Chico Carrasquel, José Antonio Casanova, Davey Concepción, Vic Davalillo, Luis García, Vidal López, Diego Seguí and César Tovar were the first players elected to the Venezuelan Baseball Hall of Fame in Valencia. Also part of the honored class were Juan Antonio Yanes, one of the professional league's founding fathers and owner of club Venezuela, sportswriter Abelardo Raidi and umpire Roberto Olivo.

AUGUST 28. Twenty-year-old José Reyes became the youngest player to homer from both sides of the plate, connecting twice at Turner Field. Reyes first stroked a solo home run against Atlanta Braves left-hander Tom Glavine in the fifth inning, and knocked a two-run shot over the wall from a Trey Hodges' right-handed delivery in the ninth. The rookie shortstop accounted for all the Mets runs in the team's 3–1 win over the Braves.

SEPTEMBER 22. Alfonso Soriano has given Yankee fans enthralling reason not to miss the first pitch of ball games this season. At U.S. Cellular Field, the Yankees' second baseman clubbed his 35th home run of the campaign and 13th as leadoff hitter. The home run was the first of two Soriano hit against Chicago White Sox starter Bartolo Colón in the contest. The first big fly by Soriano established a new record for leadoff home runs in a season.

The Dominican INF/OF/DH accumulated 54 home runs out of the leadoff slot in his 16-year career. Only Rickey Henderson, with 81, socked more.

Pitching six innings, Colón was not involved in the 6–3 White Sox win, courtesy of a three-run, tenth-inning home run by Magglio Ordoñez.

SEPTEMBER 25. Fighting a cold and relying on antibiotics to help prepare himself to play in the game this evening at Skydome, Carlos Delgado put on a long-ball performance for all time and like no other Hispanic slugger.

In a monumental power display, the Toronto Blue Jays first baseman cracked home runs in all *four* of his trips to the plate against the Tampa Bay Devil Rays. Delgado homered against three Devil Rays pitchers and drove home six runs. His fourth deep blast, leading off the eighth inning, tied the game 8–8. The Blue Jays scored twice more in the frame to pull out a 10–8 win.

"I was pretty fired up," said Delgado after the game, about his coming to the plate for the fourth time. "I was on Cloud Nine out there and enjoying it."[57] The Puerto Rican, who holds the record for most doubles by a Hispanic major leaguer in one season with

57 (2000), became the 15th player with four home runs in one game and the sixth to accomplish the feat in consecutive at-bats.

Delgado homered in the first inning with two men on base, giving Toronto a three-run advantage. He belted another out of the park leading off the fourth stanza. Another inning-opening home run by Delgado in the sixth tied the game, and he duplicated that feat in the eighth. In all, he victimized Tampa Bay starter Jorge Sosa twice and subsequent relievers Joe Kennedy and Lance Carter. The first-inning four-bagger against Sosa was also Delgado's 300th lifetime home run.

Amassing 16 total bases, Delgado tied Edgardo Alfonzo's Hispanic record for most in one game.

SEPTEMBER 26. Rafael Palmeiro, baseball's quiet superstar, loudly trumpeted his undeniable place among the greatest sluggers in history. As DH for the Texas Rangers, Palmeiro clubbed his 38th home run of the season against Anaheim Angels pitcher Aaron Sele. Palmeiro, who earlier in the year had socked his 500th career home run, became the first player in major league history to hit at least 38 home runs in nine consecutive seasons.

The milestone big fly accounted for Palmeiro's 107th RBI, the tenth season in which the 39-year-old veteran hit at least 35 homers and drove home 100 runs—the most by any Latin American major leaguer. (Alex Rodríguez accomplished the exceptional feat 12 times through 2015.)

SEPTEMBER 28. It is hard to believe Albert Pujols was so good when he was still so young. At 23 years and 255 days, the left fielder/first baseman led the National League in runs (137), hits (212) and doubles (51). He also tallied a league-leading .359 batting mark, becoming the youngest Latin American player to win a batting title.[58] Pujols edged Todd Helton of the Colorado Rockies by .00022, in the closest batting title race in NL history (.359 to .358).

On top of all of this, Pujols slugged 43 home runs and drove home 124 runs. The St. Louis Cardinals' emerging superstar also hit in 30 straight games. He could not carry the entire load, however, as his third-place Cardinals failed to land a post-season berth.

OCTOBER 21. At Pro Player Stadium, a ninth-inning, three-run home run by Bernie Williams of the New Yankees all but put in the bag Game 3 of the 2003 World Series. The blow increased the Yankees' lead in the game to 6–1 over the Florida Marlins, with Mariano Rivera ready to take on a second inning of work in the lower half of the frame. The Marlins were retired without much fuss by Rivera as the Yankees, making their fifth Fall Classic appearance in six years, took a two games to one lead on their National League opponents.

For Williams, it was his second home run in three games and fifth career World Series long ball, a total unequaled by any Hispanic player. The multi-dimensional Puerto Rican, who emerged as a talented jazz guitarist after retirement, collected 80 post-season RBI, the most by a Hispanic player. Additionally, the Yankees' center fielder gleaned the most post-season hits by a Hispanic player with 128 in 121 games.

OCTOBER 22. At the close of play on May 22, the 19–29 Florida Marlins were in last place in their division, 13½ games out of first place. Following an early-season change in managers to Jack McKeon, the young team came together and rebounded mightily to win the National League wild card position. After that, McKeon's boys fashioned a scintillating NLCS comeback series win over the Chicago Cubs to advance to the Big October Dance. Not since the 1914 "Miracle Braves" had a basement team bounced back from such sunken depths to reach the World Series.

Alex González loudly pumps a victory fist as he rounds first base, following his game-ending home run in Game 4 of the 2003 World Series against the New York Yankees. The Florida Marlins' short-stop became the first Hispanic player to hit a walk-off home run in the Fall Classic.

In Game 4 of the 99th Fall Classic, in front of a crowd of 65, 934 at Pro Player Stadium, Miguel Cabrera of the ever-surprising Marlins became the youngest Hispanic player to hit a home run in a World Series game, and teammate Alex Gonzá_ez became the first Hispanic player to hit a walk-off home run.

As the second youngest player (to Andruw Jones) to connect for a World Series circuit clout, the 20-year-old Cabrera's opposite-field home run was clubbed against New York Yankees starter Roger Clemens—after being knocked down by Clemens on the previous pitch. Cabrera's bleacher bomb, with a man on base, was part of a three-run first inning by the Marlins.

The home team did not score again until the bottom of 12th inning, when shortstop González lined a 3–2 pitch from Yankees right-hander Jeff Weaver down the left field line for the 13th walk-off home run in World Series history. The Marlins evened the Series at two games a piece with the 4–3 victory.

After roaring back from a three games-to-one NLCS deficit against the Cubs, the 11-year-old South Florida franchise celebrated its second world championship title with a 2–0 shutout win in Game 6 in New York. The Series upset provided the 72-year-old McKeon a boastful blue ribbon unto himself as the oldest manager to win a World Series.

2004

APRIL 5. Former Rookie of the Year Ozzie Guillén managed his first game in the major leagues and simultaneously became Venezuela's first big league field general. Guillén, at the helm of the Chicago White Sox, suffered a stomach-turning 9–7 Opening Day defeat to the Kansas City Royals at Kauffman Stadium. Kansas City scored six runs in the bottom of the ninth inning, capped by a two-run home run by outfielder Carlos Beltrán.

Guillén managed eight years in Chicago and piloted the Florida Marlins for another season in 2012. He developed into a crassly outspoken personality.

JUNE 3. Forty-five-year-old Julio Franco's first-inning, grand slam home run powered the Atlanta Braves to an 8–4 victory over the Philadelphia Phillies at Turner Field. With the fence-topping drive, Franco became the oldest big leaguer to club a home run with the bases loaded.

Signed by the Braves in January, Franco appeared in 125 games that season, playing first base in the majority of them, and hit an impressive .309 in 320 at-bats.

JULY 26. Rubén Gómez died in San Juan, Puerto Rico. Gómez became an enduring hero to Puerto Rican baseball fans for his dedication to the game as a pitcher. The longtime Santurce Crabber and winner of nearly 350 major, minor and international league games was 77 years old.

OCTOBER 2. At Minute Maid Park, the Rockies' Vinny Castilla socked a second-inning home run against Houston Astros pitcher Roy Oswalt. With relief help, Oswalt won the game, 9–3. Although both teams were playing out the string in their respective divisions, the bases-empty poke by Castilla accounted for his 131st RBI, the top mark in the National League this season and the first major league RBI crown by a Mexican player.

OCTOBER 26. Mexico's first post–World War II baseball idol and initial All-Star representative, Bobby Ávila, died from diabetic and respiratory complications in Veracruz, Mexico. The majors' first Hispanic batting champion in 1954, and later a political public servant for decades in Mexico, was 80.

NOVEMBER 11. After leading the circuit in strikeouts (265) and ERA (2.61), and finishing second in wins (20), Johan Santana of the Minnesota Twins was unanimously chosen as the American League's Cy Young Award winner. The left-hander became the first Venezuelan to win the premier pitching award. A product of the town of Tovar in the western state of Merida, Santana also became the first pitcher from his nation to win 20 games in the major leagues.

"What I was most proud of," said Santana, "was that everybody forgot about all the political unrest in my country. For two months, they forget about everything and talked nothing but baseball. That was the best feeling."[59]

Santana's career ERA± of 136 ranks second all-time to Lefty Grove's G 148, among left-handed starting pitchers.

2005

FEBRUARY 14. Former player José Canseco's biography was released, titled *Juiced: Wild Times, Rampant 'Roids, Smash Hits and How Baseball Got Big.* The book upended baseball with allegations of widespread steroid abuse within its playing ranks. Canseco admitted to using steroids (after denying it while a player) and implicated former teammates, by name, trampling over the long-established player code of ethics inside the locker room.

The disclosures, coupled with those in another book called *Game of Shadows,* soon to be released, resulted in an onslaught of media attention which forced major league baseball and its powerful players' union to address what had been a blindly tolerated or brushed aside issue for years.

On March 17, a congressional committee convened on Capital Hill to investigate the abuse of steroids in professional baseball and the impact of the drugs on younger athletes in lower levels of all public sports. The hearing was attended by former and current superstar players, including Canseco.

A positive end result, in the years to come, will be a stronger labor agreement between management and players for more transparent drug testing and a more cooperative movement by the players themselves to rid the game of performance enhancing substances.

The game will be bequeathed a two-decade period of skewed offensive numbers that will be dubiously referred to as the "Steroids Era." Many of baseball's most outstanding players during this time will be subjected to perpetual suspicions over perceived artificially inflated numbers that will negatively affect their Hall of Fame support, beginning with voting in the 2010s.

APRIL 26. Johan Santana closed his 2004 Cy Young Award campaign undefeated in his last 15 starts, winning 13 of them. This season, the flame-throwing left-hander has picked up right where he left off, capturing four wins in as many decisions, including today's 2–1 triumph over the Kansas City Royals at Kauffman Stadium.

Santana hurled eight innings of five-hit, one-run ball to capture his 17th consecutive victory, the most by any Hispanic pitcher. The Twins pitcher was defeated by Bartolo Colón and the Oakland Athletics in his next start, 2–1, ending the successful ratchet.

The unblemished mark was equaled by José Contreras in 2006.

MAY 26. Chico Carrasquel, the first golden shortstop mined from the rich vein of Venezuelan shortstops, died in Caracas of cardiac arrest at age 77. Carrasquel was the first Hispanic player to lead a major league in assists and fielding percentage (1951).

"Venezuela lost one of its heroes today," said Ozzie Guillén. "As the first great Venezuelan shortstop, Chico helped put our country on the baseball map."[60]

On Opening Day 2004, Carrasquel appeared with Luis Aparicio, Dave Concepción and Ozzie Guillén during pre-game ceremonies at U.S. Cellular Field, honoring Venezuela's legacy of outstanding major league shortstops.

JULY 15. The 500-home-run-and-3,000-hit fraternity is undoubtedly baseball's most elite. The exclusive three-member club welcomed its first Hispanic player today.

At Safeco Field, Rafael Palmeiro of the Baltimore Orioles sliced a double to left field in the fifth inning against the Mariners' Joel Piñeiro, for his 3,000th big league hit. Palmeiro entered the season with 551 home runs and joined Hank Aaron, Willie Mays and Eddie Murray as the only players to achieve such enormous hitting aptitude. Following his two-base hit, Palmeiro scored. He later drove in a run, contributing to the Orioles' 6–3 win.

Stunningly, two weeks later, Palmeiro, the third Hispanic player to attain 3,000 career hits, was suspended for ten days for testing positive for an anabolic steroid in his system. The news was especially jolting for the 20-year veteran player and his many fans, coming less than five months after Palmeiro's appearance before a congressional committee in Washington, investigating the use of performance enhancing drugs within the national pastime. The prolific hitter had adamantly denied using any banned substance, under oath, to the Committee.

AUGUST 16. Rafael Palmeiro, the most productive player in the history of free agency, had his last productive day at the plate. Palmeiro, who registered more walks than strikeouts in his career (1,353–1,348), doubled and singled in four at-bats, with a run scored. The batting efforts contributed to his Orioles' 4–3 victory over the Oakland A's at McAfee Coliseum.

The single turned out to be the 41-year-old Palmeiro's final major league hit, and the 3,020th of his two decade-long major league career. The hit total, as well as his 551 home runs, was the most garnered by a Cuban big league player.

AUGUST 30. Nineteen days after being reinstated from a ten-game suspension for testing positive for an anabolic steroid, Rafael Palmeiro played in his last major league game. At the Rogers Centre in Toronto, Palmeiro went hitless in four trips to the plate as the Baltimore Orioles' DH. The Orioles were defeated by the Blue Jays, 7–2.

The Cuban slugger ignominiously left the major league scene with the most runs (1,663), doubles (585), RBI (1,835) and extra-base hits (1,192) accumulated by a Latin American hitter. And his 2,831 games played were the most by a player who did not participate in a World Series.

In his fourth year of Hall of Fame eligibility in 2014, Palmeiro, who ranked in the top 25 in career hits (25th), total bases (11th), doubles (17th), home runs (12th), RBI (16th), extra-base hits (7th), and runs created (18th), failed to receive a 5 percent share of writers' votes and fell off the BBWAA ballot for future Cooperstown consideration.

OCTOBER 26. Venezuela projected itself grandly on baseball's biggest stage. Caracas native Freddy Garcia hurled seven scoreless innings in Game 4 of the World Series to lead the Chicago White Sox to 1–0 road victory and a four-game sweep over the National League champion Houston Astros. Outfielder Germaine Dye drove in the decisive run with an eighth-inning single.

Watching the proceedings intently on the bench, in only his second season as White Sox manager, Ozzie Guillén became the first Latin American manager to win a World Series.

NOVEMBER 9. No doubt still basking in his World Series triumph, Ozzie Guillén was named the American League's Manager of the Year. Guiding the Central Division–winning Chicago White Sox to 99 regular season wins, and then losing only one game in the post-season, easily earned for Guillén the league's top managerial prize—and ethnic side-note status as the first Venezuelan to pridefully receive the award.

2006

FEBRUARY 4. Yesterday, at José Bernardo Pérez Stadium in Valencia, Venezuela, Edgar González of the Mazatlán Deer collected four hits, including two home runs, in an unblemished day at the plate. The same could not be said for his team, which lost to the Licey Tigers, 10–6, on the second day of the 2006 Caribbean Series. Today in the same park, González recorded four more hits against the Carolina Giants before being put out. The eight consecutive hits were an individual Caribbean Series first, surpassing Robbie Alomar's seven straight hits in 1995.

Mazatlan, the defending Caribbean Series champion, lost all of their tournament games and finished six games in back of the champion Leones del Caracas. The Lions took the crown, February 7, on a bizarre play. Playing the 4–1 Licey Tigers in the Series finale held in Maracay, the 5–0 Caracas club rallied for two ninth-inning runs to pull out a 5–4, Series-winning victory. The deciding run scored on a pop-up to short left field that bounced off the head of minor league shortstop Erick Aybar.

Leones skipper Carlos Subero, at 33, became the youngest manager to guide his team to the title.

MARCH 7. At Cracker Jack Stadium in Orlando, the first game of "Pool D" combatants took place of the inaugural World Baseball Classic. Latin American heavyweight teams from the Dominican Republic and Venezuela faced off, with Team Dominicana defeating Team Venezuela, 11–5. Both clubs sported lineups full of major league stars.

David Ortiz clubbed the international tournament's first home run by a Hispanic player in the second inning against Venezuela starter Johan Santana. It was one of two big flies for Ortiz in the game. Adrián Beltré also cranked two balls out of the park and drove in five runs for his victorious club. Bartolo Colón, with three scoreless opening innings, recorded the initial win for his country in the tournament.

A fifth-inning, two-run home run by team Venezuela first baseman Miguel Cabrera against pitcher Miguel Batista anointed him as the first player from Venezuela to hit a WBC home run.

MARCH 7. Hiram Bithorn Stadium in San Juan was the locale for games of the third bracket, between four of the 16 competing clubs of the World Baseball Classic. Under the lights, Javier Vázquez had the honor of opening Team Puerto Rico's first game. Facing Team Panamá, Vázquez hurled three innings, permitting the only run of the game scored by the Central American team. The home country's squad scored twice to eke out a 2–1 victory in front of 19,043 happy fans.

José Santiago, the third of eight pitchers used in the game by manager José Oquendo, collected the first WBC win for his island country.

MARCH 8. Freddy Garcia and three other Venezuelan pitchers shut out Team Italy,

6–0. Garcia hurled into the fourth inning before being removed in compliance with pitch-count limitations. The effort claimed for Garcia the initial WBC win for a Venezuelan pitcher. Miguel Cabrera hit his second home run in two days.

The Venezuelans and Dominicans will emerge as the winners of their pool. The Bolivarian team, skippered by Luis Sojo, was knocked out in the next round, held in San Juan. The Quisqueyans, managed by Manny Acta, advanced to the semi-finals, where they bowed, 3–1, in an elimination game to Team Cuba.

MARCH 8. At Hiram Bithorn Stadium, Team Panamá battled tooth and nail the representatives from Cuba on the second day of games in the preliminary round of the newly organized and MLB-sponsored World Baseball Classic. Second baseman Yulieski Gourriel hit a two-run home run with two outs in the top of the ninth inning for the Cubans, putting the squad ahead, 6–4. The first home run by a Cuban player in the World Baseball Classic could not have come at a better time, as the Panamanians rallied for two tying runs in the lower half of the inning. The Cubans go on to win, 8–6, in 11 innings. With one inning of scoreless relief, Yadel Martí picked up the initial WBC win for Cuba.

The Panamanian team, managed by Aníbal Reluz, received a big lift earlier with a three-run home run by Rubén Rivera. The former major leaguer's home run, the first struck by a Panamanian player in the WBC, put his team on top, 4–2.

Piloted by Higinio Vélez, Cuba advanced to the inaugural final but lost to a cohesive Japanese squad in the championship game, 10–6. Both clubs finished the tournament with a 5–3 record. South Korea, despite a 6–1 record and two victories over the champion Nippon team, unjustly finished in third place.

MARCH 8. In the second game of the day at Hiram Bithorn Stadium, Team Puerto Rico convincingly defeated the team from the Netherlands, 8–3. One of 14 hits pounded out by the home crowd favorites was a home run by first baseman Javy López. The third-inning solo blast put Puerto Rico ahead, 2–0, and laid claim for López as the first player from Puerto Rico to hit a home run in the World Baseball Classic. Allowing three runs later in the game, Netherlands reliever Jair Jurrjens was pinned with the loss.

The Puerto Rican squad won their bracket with a perfect 3–0 record. But the club failed to advance past the next round, suffering a tense, 4–3, tournament-eliminating defeat to Team Cuba, one week from today on the same Bithorn Stadium turf.

MARCH 8. At Chase Field in Phoenix, Arizona, Team México bounced back from an opening-day 2–0 defeat at the hands of Team USA and defeated the South African national squad, 10–4. Mexican League veteran Francisco Campos registered the first win of the World Baseball Classic for his country. The 33-year-old pitching star of the 2005 Caribbean Series for Mazatlán permitted three runs in four innings of work.

Managed by Mexican baseball legend Francisco "Paquín" Estrada, the South of the Border club was eliminated in the next round of the competition, but knocked Team USA out of the tournament with a 2–1, second-round victory on March 16.

MARCH 9. Mario Valenzuela hit one of two home runs for Team México in its 9–1 triumph over Team Canada in the first round of the World Baseball Classic. Mexico's second victory in "Pool B" assured the club of advancement into the next round of play against the two finalists from Pool "A"—Team Japan and Team South Korea.

A Mexican League player, Valenzuela reached Triple-A in the Chicago White Sox organization in 2004. From this day forward, the outfielder was internationally recognized as the first Mexican national to hit a home run in the World Baseball Classic.

APRIL 29. The baseball world is Albert Pujols' oyster, which he opens with his

Louisville Slugger. Pujols cracked a record 14th home run in April today, leading the St. Louis Cardinals to a 2–1 victory over the Washington Nationals at Busch Stadium. The eighth-inning, solo blast by the star first baseman lifted the Cardinals to their 16th win in 24 games and increased his RBI total to 32.

The mighty Pujols slugged a league-best .671 on the season, while belting 49 home runs and driving in 137 runs—career highs in all three categories. Pujols, as the numbers might indicate, was a key component in the Cardinals' drive throughout the season toward a World Series title.

In 2007, Alex Rodríguez equaled Pujols' mark for most big flies in April.

MAY 14. More than a century after the first Colombian player reached the major leagues, Emiliano Fruto of the Seattle Mariners became that nation's first player to scale a big league mound. Pitching in relief in front of 43,191 disconcerting fans at Angels Stadium, Fruto hurled 3⅔ innings of one-hit ball. The Cartagena native earned a save for his hand in locking up a 9–4 Mariners win.

JULY 4. José Contreras of the Chicago White Sox improved to 9–0 on the season after tossing six and two-thirds scoreless innings against the Baltimore Orioles at U.S. Cellular Field. In the 13–0 White Sox win, the right-hander recorded a victory in his 17th straight decision, dating from last season, when the Cuban defector earned a victory in his last eight starts.

Contreras was defeated in a subsequent opening assignment by the New York Yankees, but only after having tied the record for consecutive big league victories by a Hispanic pitcher, established the prior season by Johan Santana.

JULY 6. Anaheim Angels shortstop Orlando Cabrera slashed two hits in five at-bats against the Oakland A's at McAfee Coliseum. With his first hit, Cabrera succeeded in reaching base for the 63rd consecutive game, on a hit, walk or HBP. In a streak begun on April 24, Cabrera achieved the fourth-longest such streak of the modern era and the longest by a Hispanic player.

The next day, the Colombian player was rendered hitless by the A's Barry Zito, falling a wide 21 games shy of Ted Williams' record of reaching base in 84 games in a row in 1949.

JULY 30. The National Baseball Hall of Fame welcomed its largest class of inductees, as one former major leaguer (Bruce Sutter) and 17 Negro leagues players were beckoned for eternal enshrinement. Among the elected Negro leagues stars were pitcher José Méndez and outfielder Cristóbal Torriente. Both players also starred in their native winter league in Cuba.

A special committee of 12 electors—appointed by the Hall of Fame Board of Directors and chaired by former MLB Commissioner Fay Vincent—cast ballots from a list of 39 pre–Integration Era candidates. Nine votes were required for election (75 percent).

Key West–born Alex Pompez was one of five executives also to receive posthumous placement into Cooperstown's hallowed halls. Pompez, whose parents were Cuban émigrés, owned the New York Cubans. The team won the 1947 Negro League World Series. He later became a successful scout, signing many Hispanic players, including many talented players from the Dominican Republic.

Another venerated front office inductee was Effa Manley, who made history as the first woman to cross the previously all-masculine, grand threshold.

SEPTEMBER 9. Emiliano Fruto gained the first win by a Colombian pitcher in the major leagues, with near-faultless, extra-inning relief work against the Texas Rangers at Safeco Field. Fruto pitched the last 2⅔ innings of a 13-inning, 3–2 Mariners' victory.

Allowing only one hit, the right-hander became a winner when Mariners second baseman José Lopez came through with the winning hit.

SEPTEMBER 28. Vinny Castilla made his last big league appearance a positive one with a pinch-hit single. At Coors Field, he drove home a run and came around to score in the fourth inning of a Rockies' eventual 19–11 loss to the Los Angeles Dodgers.

Once a potent part of the "Blake Street Bombers" lineup that included, among others, Venezuelan Andrés Galarraga, the 39-year-old Castilla bowed out at the completion of the schedule in a few days with 16 major league seasons under his belt. The Oaxaca native possessed the most hits (1,884), home runs (320) and RBI (1,105) by a player from Mexico in the major leagues.

2007

MAY 4. Julio Franco's signing over the winter of 2005 raised more than a few eyebrows. Not for the contract's two-year term or its $2.2 million value, but for the long-in-the-tooth player who agreed to it.

Today, at 48 years and 254 days old, Franco proved he could still get the bat head around and, with one swing, became the oldest major league player to hit a home run.

Starting at first base for the New York Mets, Franco connected for a second-inning, two-run circuit clout against 43-year-old Randy Johnson of the Arizona Diamondbacks. The runs were needed by the Mets in the team's 5–3 victory over the Diamondbacks at Chase Field.

Franco began his long major league tenure with the Philadelphia Phillies in 1982. A multi-purpose infielder throughout his genetics-defying career, Franco was also the oldest player to hit home runs as a pinch-hitter (April 20, 2006; 47 age years, 240 days old) and with the bases loaded (June 3, 2004; 45 years, 285 days old).

He was released by the Mets on July 16 and picked up three days later by the Atlanta Braves, the team for whom he later played the last 15 games of his 23-year big league career. Franco announced his retirement in April of 2008.

JUNE 20. The man who had not hit more than 30 home runs in one season until his eighth major league campaign slugged his 600th home run. Against the Chicago Cubs, a team for which he belted 545 of his home runs, Sammy Sosa connected for the monumental blast against Cubs pitcher Jason Marquis. The solo home run was hit in the uniform of the Texas Rangers, Sosa's second team since his departure from Chicago in 2004. The Rangers defeated the Cubs, 7–3, at the Rangers Ballpark in Arlington.

The 38-year-old Sosa concluded his 18-year big league career this season with the Rangers, with a most productive showing of 92 RBI in only 114 games. He recorded a final total of 609 home runs, the most by a Latin American player.

JUNE 22. Miguel Tejada was not in the starting lineup for the Baltimore Orioles, nor did he play in the game at Chase Field in Arizona. It was the first time, after 1,152 consecutive games, that Tejada was unable to perform for his team. A fractured wrist, suffered two days earlier in San Diego, ended the fifth-longest games-played streak in baseball history and the longest by a Hispanic player.

JULY 10. Alfonso Soriano made sure the National League did not go down without a fight in the All-Star Game played at AT&T Park. Soriano homered with two outs and a man on base in the bottom of the ninth inning to bring the NL stars to within a run of their annual adversaries, 5–4. In a nail-biting finish, the National League loaded the bases before Francisco Rodríguez retired Aaron Rowand for the final out.

Soriano, a big free agent signee by the Chicago Cubs last October, belted his third All-Star home run in six games played, the most hit by a Hispanic player.

SEPTEMBER 3. The 3,000-K club has fewer members than the hallowed societies of 3,000 hits, 300 wins and 500 home runs. Pedro Martínez became the 15th major league pitcher, and the first Hispanic, to strike out 3,000 batters when he whiffed Cincinnati Reds pitcher Aaron Harang. Pitching for the New York Mets, the nearly 36-year-old right-hander struck out Harang to end the second inning at Great American Ballpark.

Pitching for the first time in almost a year because of injury, Martínez hurled five innings, allowing two earned runs, and obtained a 10–4 victory (his first of the season).

The pride of Manoguayabo, Dominican Republic, pitched two more seasons and closed his career with 219 victories and only 100 losses. The winning percentage of .687 is the third-best all-time for modern era starters with at least 1,000 innings pitched (Spud Chandler, .717, and Whitey Ford, .690). At his retirement, Martínez also owned the best career ERA+ mark, at 154, for a starting pitcher. Amazingly, he registered *five* separate seasons with an ERA+ over 200.

SEPTEMBER 26. Baseball has rarely flowed as pre-eminently through generational bloodlines as it has through the Rojas-Alou families. Three sons of José Rojas and Virginia Alou reached and excelled in the major leagues. The eldest of those sons, Felipe, raised one of his boys—Moisés—to be a big leaguer as well. Today, at Shea Stadium, 41-year-old Moisés Alou of the New York Mets hit the 332th and last home run of his major league career.

The solo home run by Alou did nothing to sway the final outcome of the game, which finished 9–6 in favor of the visiting Washington Nationals. But the blow did provide an added marker to the dual crown shared by Felipe and Moisés as the Hispanic father and son to register the most home runs in the major leagues. The 538 big flies hit by the Alous placed them well behind the Bondses (1,094) and Griffeys (782) on baseball's most prolific progenitor-offspring home run list.

Incidentally, a nephew of Felipe, Mel Rojas, also made the big league grade, as did Felipe's cousin, José Sosa.

SEPTEMBER 29. The man who rose from impoverished surroundings to unimaginable heights on the ball field played in his last major league game. Sammy Sosa, the only player with three 60-home-run campaigns (1998, 1999, 2001), singled in four at-bats for the Texas Rangers in the team's 5–1 loss to the Seattle Mariners at Safeco Field.

Sosa, also the right-handed batter with the most strikeouts in history (2,306), became one of several superstar players whose great accomplishments over the past decades were tarnished from proven or suspected involvement with performance enhancing drugs. Among other similarly stigmatized Hispanic star players were Rafael Palmeiro, Manny Ramírez, Alex Rodríguez, Iván Rodríguez and Miguel Tejada.

2008

SEPTEMBER 11. Prior to the 2004 season, at age 24 years and one month, Albert Pujols became the youngest player to sign a $100 million contract. Five seasons later, Pujols continued to live up to the St. Louis Cardinals' record-setting seven-year contract extension. At Busch Stadium, Pujols drove in his 100th run of the season, with a double to left field against Chicago Cubs pitcher Rich Harden. The 28-year-old first baseman became the third major leaguer with 100 RBI in his first eight seasons (Al Simmons, 11, and Ted Williams, 8).

Over the summer, the Cardinals' slugger smacked his 300th lifetime home run, joining Ralph Kiner as the only players with that many circuit clouts in their first eight campaigns. Owner of the best slugging (.653) and OPS (1.114) percentages in both leagues, the Dominican superstar hit .357 and won his second National League MVP Award.

Pujols played in 148 games on the campaign. Excluding one as a defensive replacement in which he did not bat, the outstanding player failed to reach base in only 11 of the games! As if his work on the field was not sufficient, he was also named recipient of MLB's Roberto Clemente Award for his humanitarian diligence away from the ballpark.

SEPTEMBER 24. Francisco Rodríguez of the Anaheim Angels recorded his 62nd save, the most by a relief pitcher in one major league season. Rodríguez pitched a near-perfect ninth inning to preserve a 6–5 Angels win over the Seattle Mariners at Safeco Field. Rodriguez had broken the single-season saves mark of 57 (Bobby Thigpen) on September 13, and this outing was the last rescue opportunity for the Venezuelan right-hander.

K-Rod saved 62 out of 69 attempts for the American League West–champion Angels.

2009

MARCH 8. At Foro Sol Stadium in Mexico City, Team Mexico suffered a humiliating loss to Team Australia, 17–7 (eight innings, mercy rule), in their opening-round game of the 2009 World Baseball Classic. Suffering on the bench was Mexico manager Vinny Castilla. A participant in the inaugural World Baseball Classic in 2006, Castilla became the first person to play and manage in the MLB-backed international tournament.

MAY 8. Carlos Delgado circled the bases for the 473rd time in a regular-season major league game. At Citi Field, Delgado's three-run, eighth-inning bomb provided the Mets with three insurance runs in the team's 7–3 victory over the Pittsburgh Pirates. Delgado, who had two RBI earlier, finished the game with five, for a total of 23 on the young season and grand total of 1,512 in his 17-year career.

A few days later, the Mets announced that their first baseman needed surgery on his hip to repair a torn labrum. The surgery shelved him for the rest of the season, and more reconstructive surgery the following year, in effect, ended the 38-year-old slugger's career.

Delgado was forced to retire in 2011 without having returned to the field. He finished short of 500 home runs, but stepped away with proud ownership of the highest home run and RBI totals of any Puerto Rican player to step on a major league diamond.

Shamefully, in his first year of Hall of Fame eligibility in 2015, the slugger did not receive a five-percent vote from the baseball writers and was eliminated from future BBWAA Cooperstown consideration. He may have been hurt by a "crowded ballot" consisting of a number of exceptional first-year eligibles and a logjam of other worthy players.

JUNE 17. Iván Rodríguez took his position squatting behind the plate for the 2,227th game—an all-time mark for major league catchers. Receiving the throws of five different Houston Astros pitchers, Rodríguez surpassed the previous record for games caught held by Carlton Fisk. Facing his long-time former team, the Texas Rangers, his night was tempered by a 5–4 Astros defeat. At the plate, Rodríguez went 1-for-5.

Playing two more years, Rodríguez finished his 21-season career with 2,427 games behind the dish. The 13-time Gold Glove Award winner, the most ever by a catcher and most by a Hispanic player, also accumulated the highest hit total by a big league backstop with 2,844 and posted a .296 lifetime average.

JULY 14. As he had done hundreds of times in his brilliant career, Mariano Rivera made a brief but efficient appearance out of the bullpen to preserve a victory for his team. This time, at the All-Star Game, Rivera pitched a perfect ninth inning, retiring three elite National League hitters to secure a 4–3 American League win at Busch Stadium.

The All-Star Game save was the fourth for Rivera, establishing a new mark for a relief pitcher in the Midsummer Classic.

JULY 22. On "Manny Ramírez Bobblehead Night," Manny Ramírez was unable to start the game because of an injured hand. But it did not prevent the Los Angles Dodgers' outfielder from pinch-hitting a dramatic home run into the left field seats at Dodger Stadium, identified as "Mannywood." Adding to the sixth-inning excitement, the home run came with the score tied and the bases loaded, providing the margin of victory for the Dodgers in their 6–2 decision over the Cincinnati Reds.

For the 37-year-old Ramírez, the home run was the 21st and final grand slam of his controversial career, the third-most in history and most by a Latin American player.[61] The gifted slugger had been suspended for 50 games earlier in the season for testing positive for a banned substance.

A second violation of major league baseball's drug policy, prior to the 2011 season, resulted in a 100-game suspension for Ramírez. The release of the news, a few days into the season, initiated a stealthy retirement from the recent free agent signee of the Tampa Bay Rays. As a parting example of "Manny being Manny," the 12-time All-Star suited up for five games for Tampa Bay before leaving the team high and dry after the news.

SEPTEMBER 29. Humberto Robinson, Panama's first major league baseball delegate, died in Brooklyn, New York. Robinson compiled an 8–13 record with a worthy 3.25 ERA, pitching in five big league seasons. The former right-hander was 79.

OCTOBER 15. At Dodger Stadium, Manny Ramírez socked a two-run home run against Cole Hamels of the Philadelphia Phillies in Game 1 of the National League Championship Series. Acquired by the Dodgers from the Boston Red Sox at the trading deadline last season, Ramírez was a productive addition to the West Coast club. The Phillies prevailed in the game, 8–6, and went on to take the Series in five contests.

The big fly was the only offensive output on the evening from Ramírez, and was his 29th and final post-season home run, cementing his status as the major league player with the most post-season home runs. Manny's post-season laurels also extend to sharing the all-time hitting streak of 17 consecutive games, established during a 2003 and 2004 playoffs and World Series run he had with the Boston Red Sox. It is a record shared with Derek Jeter and Hank Bauer. All of Bauer's games were World Series contests.

NOVEMER 1. Mariano Rivera closed out Game 4 of the World Series, pitching an impeccable ninth inning against the Philadelphia Phillies at Citizens Bank Park. On the strength of a three-run, ninth-inning uprising and Rivera's "lights out" hurling, the Yankees defeated the National League Champions, 7–4, and took a commanding three games to one lead in the Series.

The game also marked for Rivera his 23rd World Series appearance, topping Whitey Ford's previous mark of 22 pitching outings in the autumn limelight. In this Fall Classic, the great Rivera also increased by two his World Series saves mark, bringing his record total to 11.

NOVEMBER 24. Albert Pujols has been bestowed with several nicknames, a reflection of his abundant talent: Prince Albert, The Machine, Phat Albert, and the Chris Berman, pun-laced sobriquet of Albert Winnie the Pujols. Today, if you please, refer to Mr. Pujols as MVP of the National League for the third time. He became the 12th player and first Latin American to win the award thrice and to win it in back-to-back seasons. (Alex Rodríguez also won the award three times.)

The St. Louis Cardinals' first baseman, who led the league in runs (124), homers (47), on base percentage (.443) and slugging percentage (.658), received all 32 first-place votes.

Proving his all-around greatness, Pujols also set a record for most assists by a first baseman with 185.

2010

APRIL 2. Mike Cuéllar died in Tampa, Florida, of stomach cancer. The best left-handed, Latin American pitcher to toe the big league rubber was 72.

APRIL 12. Albert Pujols hit his fifth home run of the week-old season and the 371st of a record-accumulating career. Now in his tenth major league season, Pujols has clubbed more home runs than any other player over his first decade. The Cardinals' first baseman finished the year with 42 home runs and 408 lifetime. The latter total was comfortably ahead of Eddie Mathews, the previous ten-season record holder.

Pujols' home run today was a three-run shot against Houston's Wandy Rodríguez and helped the Cardinals to a 5–0 home victory, behind Adam Wainwright and Jason Motte.

MAY 2. Not many players finish their first day in the big leagues with a batting average of .800. Wilson Ramos of the Minnesota Twins can boast not only of that hitting mark, but also of becoming the first Hispanic player to record four hits in his first major league game.

At Progressive Field, Ramos, a catcher, singled in his first three trips to the plate and doubled his fifth time up. The Twins' Venezuelan rookie also scored once in completing his starlight initial game. Minnesota received plenty of offensive support from the rest of its lineup, which banged out 16 other hits in the 8–3 road triumph.

MAY 29. The Latino Baseball Hall of Fame was inaugurated in La Romana, Dominican Republic. Twenty-five former players, broadcasters and executives, representing nine countries, were enshrined in the induction ceremony. The group also included 13 National Hall of Fame members.

The new Hall of Fame joined the Hispanic Heritage Baseball Museum, opened in 1999 in San Francisco, California, the Latin American Baseball Hall of Fame Museum, founded in 2003 in San Juan, and the Caribbean Series Hall of Fame, situated in the Sports Museum in Guaynabo, Puerto Rico, as shrines or venues dedicated to recognizing and honoring baseball's great international players.

JUNE 23. Edwin Rodríguez was named interim manager of the Florida Marlins, becoming the first Puerto Rican to manage in the big leagues. The 49-year-old Ponce native was handed over the permanent reigns of the team six days later.

Knowing the Marlins were not including him in the team's plans for 2012, which involved a move into a new, retractable roof stadium, Rodríguez resigned after June 18, 2011. His overall record was 78–85.

AUGUST 25. Félix Hernández became the fourth-youngest pitcher to strike out 1,000 major league batters. The 24-year-old Seattle Mariners right-hander fanned Red Sox DH David Ortiz for the milestone whiff. It came in the sixth inning of the second game of a day-night doubleheader at Fenway Park.

Only Bob Feller, 22, Bert Blyleven and Dwight Gooden, both 23, achieved the feat at an earlier age.

AUGUST 26. The Cardinals' Albert Pujols slugged his 400th career home run, becoming the first major leaguer to hit as many home runs in his first ten seasons. At Nationals Park, the Cardinals' superstar took Washington pitcher Jordan Zimmerman deep, leading off the fourth inning. The home team prevailed, 11–10, in 13 innings, as Pujols was walked intentionally his last three times up.

The 30-year-old Pujols also became the third-youngest player to reach the long ball milestone, behind Alex Rodríguez (29 years, 316 days) and Ken Griffey, Jr. (30 years, 141 days).

SEPTEMBER 11. The best player of the 2000s began a new calendar decade right in step with the last. Albert Pujols drove in his 100th and 101st runs of the season with a sixth-inning double against Atlanta Braves pitcher Tommy Hanson. Pujols knocked home all the Cardinals runs in the club's 6–3, 12-inning road defeat to Hanson's Braves.

For the tenth consecutive season starting his career, Pujols crossed the 100-RBI threshold, an unprecedented achievement for a Hispanic player. The only player with a longer streak is Philadelphia Athletics great Al Simmons, who began his career with 11 straight campaigns of 100 or more runs batted in (1924–1934).

The Cardinals' extraordinary hitter led the league in RBI with 118 and home runs with 42. Hitting .312, Pujols became the first player in major league history to club 30 home runs, drive in 100 runs and hit .300 or better for ten consecutive seasons.

OCTOBER 15. The most acclaimed closer in baseball history registered his 42nd—

and final—save in the post-season. Mariano Rivera nailed down a 6–5 Yankees win over the Texas Rangers in the opening game of the American League Championship Series at Rangers Ballpark in Arlington. Rivera pitched a scoreless ninth inning, allowing one hit, to give the Yankees an initial advantage in the clash to determine the league's World Series representative. The record for most post-season saves was established by Rivera in 47 opportunities.

Texas defeated New York in six games, with Rivera making two other non-save-situation appearances.

OCTOBER 28. Édgar Rentería's fifth-inning solo home run broke up a scoreless World Series encounter between the Texas Rangers and San Francisco Giants at AT&T Park. The home run, the initial scoring of the second game of the Fall Classic, provided the impetus for abundant plate-denting by the Giants, leading to an easy 9–0 win. Matt Cain pitched into the eighth inning for the win.

Rentería tagged the Rangers' C. J. Wilson and became the first player from Colombia to smash a World Series home run.

NOVEMBER 1. The World Series regularly produces unexpected heroes. Édgar Rentería certainly fit the bill in this year's Fall Classic. The disabled list-plagued shortstop of the National League champion San Francisco Giants participated in only 72 regular season games and hit a paltry three home runs.

As someone who seemed to particularly enjoy the World Series spotlight, Rentería clubbed a game-deciding, three-run home run in the seventh inning against Texas Rangers pitcher Cliff Lee. The blow lifted the Giants to a World Series triumph—the franchise's first since leaving New York in 1957. The 3–1, champagne-popping victory occurred on the Rangers' home field.

Rentería batted .412 (7-for-17), hit two home runs and knocked home six runs in the five-game encounter, and brought back home to Colombia the country's first World Series MVP trophy.

The Baranquilla native played one more season in 2011 and top off his career hit total at 2,327, the most of any major league player from Colombia. His 16-season home run and RBI totals of 140 and 923, respectively, were also the most accrued by a player from his South American country.

2011

JUNE 16. Before Johan Santana and Félix Hernández, José Bracho was the name most synonymous with pitching excellence in Venezuela. Bracho died today in Maracaibo, Venezuela. Prior to his death at age 82, Bracho had been elected to the Venezuelan and Caribbean Series Halls of Fame. Another legacy of the famed right-hander was the renaming of the annual award for best pitcher in the Venezuelan Winter League in his honor.

JULY 24. Roberto Alomar became the third Puerto Rican and the first player with a Toronto Blue Jays cap to be inducted into the National Baseball Hall of Fame. Alomar, whose father and brother also distinguished themselves in the major leagues, was accompanied for induction by pitching great Bert Blyleven and executive Pat Gillick.

The first Hispanic player with 200 home runs, 400 stolen bases, and 2,000 hits (one of fewer than ten players in history), Alomar was also recognized as the best defensive second baseman in the game for more than a decade. In 1999, the Ponce native scored 138 runs for the Cleveland Indians, the most in American League history by a switch-hitter. A ten-time Gold Glove Award winner, "Robbie" was named to 12 All-Star teams during his 17-year career.

"To my family, to my fans, to all the Puerto Rican people, and the game of baseball, you are and always will be my life and my love,"[62] said the humbled Alomar from the podium.

The Toronto Blue Jays retired Alomar's uniform number 12 in an on-field ceremony on July 31.

SEPTEMBER 18. When it comes to home runs slugged by major league brothers, one sibling usually does most of the heavy lifting, or swatting. The Guerrero brothers, Vladimir and Wilton, much like the Aarons and the Ripkens, have reaped abundant home run numbers, thanks in large part to one sibling.

Vladimir knocked his 449th and final ball out of the park as DH for the Baltimore Orioles tonight. The home run against Jered Weaver was only a minor setback for the Anaheim Angels' pitcher, who pitched six innings in recording an 11–2 win at Camden Yards.

The 11 home runs chipped in by older brother Wilton in his eight years in the majors helped the pair claim title to most career home runs by two Hispanic brothers.

Nicknamed "Vlad the Impaler," Guerrero's 16-year career ground to a halt after this season. He retired with a stellar lifetime .318 average and an OPS of .931.

SEPTEMBER 19. New York Yankees relief pitcher extraordinaire, Mariano Rivera, recorded his 602nd save, the most by a closer.

At the new Yankee Stadium, Rivera pitched a perfect ninth inning versus the Minnesota Twins, locking up a 6–4 win for the first-place Yankees. With his 43rd save of the season, Rivera surpassed the previous record held by Trevor Hoffman to become baseball's all-time greatest closer.

SEPTEMBER 27. Javier Vázquez had indicated that this would be his final season. Following six wins in a row, counting today, his employer, the Florida Marlins, hoped that he would have a change of mind.

The 35-year-old Vázquez tossed a 3–2, complete-game victory over the Washington Nationals at Sun Life Stadium, allowing five hits and walking no one. On the next-to-last day of the season, Vázquez won his 13th game of the year and 165th lifetime. The tall right-hander also recorded nine strikeouts for a career aggregate of 2,536.

Vázquez did not have a change of mind about his retirement plans. After hurling 14 seasons, the Ponce product went home to Puerto Rico as that island's wins and strikeouts title-holder in the major leagues.

SEPTEMBER 30. Mariano Rivera fanned Wilson Betemit of the Detroit Tigers for the last out of Game 1 of the American League Division Series at Yankee Stadium. The Yankees were victorious, 9–3, and Rivera recorded his 110th—and final—post-season strikeout, the most by a Hispanic big league pitcher.

Rivera appeared in one more game in the Series—the fifth-game, 3–2 ousting of the Yankees by the Tigers. He hurled a perfect ninth inning in his 96th and final post-season game, a major league record. In those 96 games, Rivera allowed a total of 11 earned runs.

With the two relief appearances, Rivera established the lowest post-season ERA in history: 0.70 in 141 October innings.

OCTOBER 4. The Texas Rangers' Adrián Beltré hit three solo home runs against Tampa Bay's Jeremy Hellickson in the fourth game of the American League Division

Series. The bleacher bombs, hit at Tropicana Field, powered the West Division-winning Texas club to a 4–3 victory and advancement into the AL Championship Series with a three games-to-one Series triumph over the wild card Rays.

The Rangers' third baseman became the fourth player to hit three home runs in a non–World Series post-season game. The others: Bob Robertson, George Brett, and Adam Kennedy.

OCTOBER 22. Albert Pujols tied four World Series single-game records and set another in the St. Louis Cardinals' Game 3 blow-out win over the Texas Rangers, 16–7. The victory provided the Cardinals, the National League's wild card representative, with a two games to one advantage in the Series.

At the Ballpark in Arlington, Pujols slugged three home runs, matching Babe Ruth and Reggie Jackson's spectacular feats, and equaled Bobby Richardson's and Hideki Matsui's marks for most RBI with six. The Cardinals' first sacker collected two other hits, tying Paul Molitor's safety record of five. He also equaled the most runs scored with four, accomplished by multiple players. With two singles, Prince Albert established a new Series total bases record of 14.

Tony LaRussa's Cardinals went on to win one of the most dramatic Fall Classics ever played, in seven games. In Game 6, the resilient Cardinals *twice* overcame *last strike, last at-bat, two-run* deficits to win, in 11 innings, 10–9.

2012

APRIL 7. Pitcher Octavio Dotel made his first appearance for the Detroit Tigers, providing 1⅓ innings of work in a 10–0 Tigers rout of the Boston Red Sox at Comerica Park. The Tigers became the 13th major league club to employ the middle reliever. The well-travelled Dotel earned the status as the player who has performed for the most major league teams.

MAY 5. Mexico's winningest pitcher, Ramón Arano, died in Veracruz. A winner of 334 games in the Mexican League, Arano appeared in six decades (1950s to 2000s). He succumbed to cancer at the age of 72.

MAY 17. Brazil, the largest country in South America, is also one of the continent's handful of non–Spanish-speaking countries. The soccer-delirious nation produced its first major league player when Sao Paulo–born Yan Gomes suited up and played for the Toronto Blue Jays against the New York Yankees at the Rogers Centre. Gomes, one could say, crossed multiple international borders leading up to a successful major league debut. The third baseman was recalled from Las Vegas the previous day and flew all night to reach Toronto. His second time up, Gomes singled against New York pitcher Phil Hughes. Gomes went 2-for-3 as the Blue Jays downed the Yankees, 4–1.

MAY 18. In only his fourth big league at-bat, Yan Gomes of the Toronto Blue Jays socked his first home run and the first by a native Brazilian in the major leagues. Gomes, a 2009 10th-round draft pick, connected against Jonathon Niese of the New York Mets, leading off the second inning at the Rogers Centre. Gomes' teammates rocked Niese and a reliever for four other circuit clouts in the game, which ended handily in Toronto's favor, 14–5.

JUNE 3. At Citizens Bank Ballpark, pitcher Carlos Zambrano of the Florida Marlins smacked a solo home run against the Philadelphia Phillies' Joe Blanton. The first run of the game aided a relief-assisted, 5–1 win for Zambrano.

The home run was the only one of the season for Zambrano and the 24th lifetime for the former Chicago Cubs hurler. The volatile Venezuelan pitcher concluded his 12-year career in 2012 with the most home runs by a Hispanic major league pitcher. His lifetime OPS of .636 was also the highest recorded by a Hispanic pitcher.

JUNE 15. The combination of elevated speed and power has always been a rare commodity in the major leagues. Until today only seven men in history had clubbed 300 home runs and stolen 300 bases.

Carlos Beltrán of the St. Louis Cardinals became the eighth man and the first Latin American included in the brotherhood, when he stole his seventh base of the season and 300th lifetime, against the Kansas City Royals' battery of Vin Mazzaro of and Bryan Peña. The 35-year-old outfielder also became the first switch-hitter to record this slugging and base-stealing feat.

The 15-year veteran had 302 home runs entering the 2012 season and clubbed 32 on the year, in a personal, resurgent power campaign for the defending world champion Cardinals. A free agent pickup, he was signed by St. Louis to help fill the offensive void left by the free agency escape of Albert Pujols.

Although Beltrán had two hits in the game, the Royals defeated their I-70 rivals, 3–2, at Busch Stadium.

JUNE 30. Havana native Yasmani Grandal became the first player to homer from both sides of the plate in the same game for his first two major league hits.

Playing in his second big league game, Grandal, a San Diego Padres catcher, went deep against two Colorado Rockies pitchers and drove in three runs in the Padres' 8–4 victory over the Rockies at Coors Field.

AUGUST 15. The 23rd perfect game in baseball history (and third of the season!) was authored by the Mariners' Félix Hernández. At Safeco Field, in front of 21,889 loyal subjects, King Félix vanquished the Tampa Bay Rays, 1–0. He struck out 12 Rays hitters in recording the second perfect game by a Hispanic pitcher and the first by a Venezuelan against big league competition.

The magnum opus was Hernández's fourth shutout of the season, as many as he had recorded in his previous seven big league campaigns.

AUGUST 27. Félix Hernández became the first pitcher in 36 seasons (since Bert

Félix Hernández acknowledges the crowd at Safeco Field moments after throwing a perfect game against the Tampa Bay Rays on August 15, 2012.

Blyleven) and the first Hispanic to throw four 1–0 shutouts in one season. At Target Field, Hernández stifled the Minnesota Twins on five hits, one walk and five strikeouts. Hernández, 13–5, collected his fifth whitewash of the campaign and third 1–0 victory in August. The right-hander became only the third pitcher in history to record as many such brilliant gems in one calendar month. (Carl Hubbell, July 1933, and Dick Rudolph, August 1916, were the others.)

Named Mariners "Pitcher of the Year" for the fifth time in 2012, Hernández could not match Dean Chance's single-season record of five 1–0 shutout victories in 1964.

OCTOBER 3. For the first time in 45 years, the same man headed the batting average, home run, and RBI categories in one major league. That man, Miguel Cabrera, put a subdued ending to a glorious offensive campaign today in Kansas City. Against the Royals, the Detroit Tigers' third baseman went hitless in two trips to the plate before he was removed from the game. His marvelous claim on baseball's Triple Crown of hitting was already secured prior to his first swings. The Central Division-capturing Tigers were victorious in the meaningless game, played out to a 1–0 final score in favor of the road team.

Cabrera, on the season, hit .330, socked 44 home runs and knocked home 139 runs, in becoming the first Hispanic player to capture baseball's Triple Crown of hitting.

OCTOBER 3. Fernando Rodney set a new earned run average standard for the one-inning relief specialist. The Tampa Bay Rays' closer recorded his 48th save of the season. Inducing a fly out from Jim Thome of the Baltimore Orioles in the top of the ninth inning, Rodney preserved a Rays 4–1 home victory. Rodney sharpened his ERA to 0.60, besting the 1990 0.61 ERA of ace closer Dennis Eckersley, who also registered 48 saves that season.

The right-handed Rodney became the closer with the lowest ERA to record at least 20 saves in one campaign.

OCTOBER 3. Omar Vizquel suited up for his 2,968th and final big league game, the most played by a Latin American player in the major leagues. Playing for the Toronto Blue Jays, the 45-year-old native of Caracas went 1-for-3 and fielded four chances at his familiar shortstop position. The Jays defeated the Minnesota Twins, 2–1, at the Rogers Centre.

The hit by Vizquel, a seventh-inning single in his final plate appearance, was the 2,877th of his career—the most registered by a Venezuelan major leaguer and the most by a Hispanic switch-hitter.

Known for his amazing glove work, Vizquel played more games at shortstop, 2,709, than anyone in history. In 24 seasons, he collected 11 Gold Glove Awards for his dazzling dexterity and retired with the highest career fielding percentage at his position, .985.

OCTOBER 28. It is apparently a special year for Venezuelan major leaguers. Four days after hitting three home runs in Game 1 of the 2012 World Series, San Francisco Giants third baseman Pablo Sandoval was awarded the MVP trophy for his elevated performance in the Fall Classic. Sandoval's Giants completed a four-game sweep over the AL champion Detroit Tigers, at Comerica Park, with a 4–3, ten-inning victory.

In Game 1 on October 24, Sandoval cranked home runs in his first three plate appearances, a feat never accomplished before in Fall Classic history.

A heavy-set but agile player endearingly known as "Kung Fu Panda," Sandoval batted .500 (8-for-16) with the three home runs and four runs batted in. The nickname is one that Sandoval relishes as much, it can be presumed, as he relished delivering to Venezuela its first World Series MVP hardware.

NOVEMBER 15. Miguel Cabrera capped his tremendous season by being named American League MVP by an unexpectedly wide margin. The one-sided point tabulation was 362–281, with 22 of 28 first place votes cast for the Tigers infielder, over Anaheim Angels' rookie sensation Mike Trout. The final voting made it clear that baseball writers were not soon to dismiss the established standards of classic run production for newer, more analytical measures.

Cabrera became the first Venezuelan to win a major league MVP Award trophy.

2013

FEBRUARY 13. Félix Hernández became the highest paid pitcher in baseball and the first Latin American player to earn $25 million in a season.

Shortly after signing the seven-year, $175 million contract with the Seattle Mariners, a new long-term deal for Justin Verlander of the Detroit Tigers surpassed Hernandez's deal on a per annum basis.

MARCH 19. It was Merengue versus Reggaeton at AT&T Park in the World Baseball Classic championship game, and the *merengueros* defeated the *reggaetoneros*, 3–0. Propelled by outstanding pitching throughout the tournament, the Dominican Republic culminated an undefeated 8–0 run with the victory over a surprising Puerto Rican squad. Five Dominican pitchers combined for the shutout, with Samuel Deduno hurling the first five innings for the win.

New York Yankees second baseman Robinson Canó became the first Hispanic tournament MVP, amassing 25 total bases, including two home runs and four doubles, with six RBI. Team *Dominicana* skipper Tony Peña became the first Hispanic manager to hoist the championship trophy.

APRIL 10. In 2011, Albert Pujols missed his 11th consecutive season with 30 home runs and 100 RBI by one scant RBI. After signing a ten-year, $240 million free agent contract with the Anaheim Angels over that winter, Pujols, in 2012, fell short of a 12th straight season with an OPS of .900 or higher. But the cumulative slugging of all those magnificent campaigns reached a historic level today, when the 33-year-old superstar recorded his 1,000th career extra-base hit. He became the 36th player, and the seventh Latin American, to accomplish the feat.[63]

Much more significantly, Pujols reached the extra-base hit plateau faster than all but four other players. Prince Albert, in his 6,944th official at-bat, slipped in behind the celestial company of Babe Ruth (5,818 at-bats), Lou Gehrig (6,567 at-bats), Ted Williams (6,745 at-bats) and Jimmie Foxx (6,929).

Although Pujols registered a 4-for-4 day at the plate, he could not fully savor his historic personal achievement (on a fifth-inning, ground rule double), as the visiting Oakland A's defeated the Angels, 9–5.

Dealing with plantar fasciitis for most of the season, Pujols was shut down after the All-Star break, 325 hits away from compatriot Vladimir Guerrero's record 2,590 hits by a Dominican major leaguer.

At the close of the 2015 season, Adrián Beltre had become the all-time Dominican King of hits with 2,767. Pujols was second with 2,666.

MAY 24. A month after striking out 17 batters in a game, Aníbal Sánchez defeated the Minnesota Twins, 6–0, at Comerica Park, allowing one hit. The spoiler came in the ninth inning, a clean single to center field by the Twins' Joe Mauer. Sánchez became the 18th pitcher with five games of one hit or less in a career and the first Hispanic.

The gemstone win by the Venezuelan right-hander was his fourth one-hitter (in addition to a no-hitter), tied with Mike Cuéllar for the most on any big league Hispanic pitcher's resume.

JUNE 6. After the batter in front of him was passed intentionally to set up a double play opportunity, David Ortiz responded with a three-run home run. The bottom-of-the-ninth-inning bomb by the Red Sox DH lifted Boston to a 6–3 victory over the Texas Rangers. The walk-off home run was the 11th of Ortiz's marvelous career—excluding the post-season, where the popular Dominican dramatically excelled as well, clubbing two more walk-off homers.

Matching Tony Pérez and Albert Pujols as the Latin American players with the most career walkoff home runs, "Big Papi" trailed five Hall of Famers who had 12 game-ending clouts and record-holder Jim Thome with 13.

JUNE 20. Panama's greatest slugger announced his retirement. After a 14-year journey with five different teams, Carlos Lee, with 358 lifetime home runs, called it a career. A native of Aguadulce in west-central Panama, Lee accumulated the most doubles (469) and home runs of any Panamanian major leaguer. Nicknamed "el Caballo," the outfielder/DH never struck out 100 times in any season.

The announcement came on the three-time All-Star's 37th birthday.

JUNE 30. Yasiel Puig concluded a stupendous initial month in the major leagues. The Los Angeles Dodgers rookie stroked four hits in a Dodgers 6–1 win over the Philadelphia Phillies at Dodger Stadium. Puig, a 22-year-old Cuban defector who signed a seven-year, $42 million deal with the Dodgers in the off-season, was called up by last-place Los Angeles on June 3.

Puig recorded 44 hits for the month, the second-most by a player in the month of his major league debut. Only Joe DiMaggio, with 48 in 1936, tallied more safeties in his first month in the big leagues. Puig's .436 average was the highest by any player in his first calendar month of play in the modern era. He went 44-for-101 and became the first modern era player to record 44 hits in his first 100 at-bats.

The outfielder's early offensive prowess and all-around energetic play were major catalysts in spurring on the under-achieving Dodgers to win their division.

JULY 10. The Red Sox's David Ortiz attained the most hits as a designated hitter. Stroking a double, leading off the second inning at Safeco Field, Ortiz accrued his 1,869th hit in the role of the pitcher's hitting substitute. The 37-year-old Dominican passed previous record-holder Harold Baines. Ortiz also homered in the game and drove in three runs as Boston paddled the Seattle Mariners, 11–4.

In 2006, Ortiz had established the record for most home runs by a designated hitter in one season with 47.

JULY 16. The chords of Metallica's *Enter Sandman* had not been heard in Queens since the departure of Billy Wagner from the New York Mets in 2009. Putting all musical rivalry aside, the heavy metal anthem also associated with Mariano Rivera was played at Citi Field, as the Yankees' supreme closer entered the All-Star Game in the eighth inning. In his farewell All-Star appearance, Rivera received a minute-and-a-half-long standing ovation from fans, teammates and opponents as he came into the game. In deference to

Rivera, the American League players, except for catcher Salvador Pérez, did not take their defensive positions while Rivera, a 13-time All-Star selectee, warmed up from the mound. Only Warren Spahn, with 14, was named to more All-Star squads as a pitcher.

The incomparable closer proceeded to retire the National League side in order, maintaining the American League's 3–0 lead. Texas stopper Joe Nathan completed the shutout in the ninth inning, and Rivera was named MVP of the game—the first relief pitcher and first Panamanian to win the All-Star Game's lustrous award.

With the award, Rivera became the first player selected as MVP in the World Series, League Championship Series and All-Star Game.

JULY 30. André Rienzo became the first pitcher from Brazil to reach the major leagues. Starting for the Chicago White Sox, the team that signed him as an 18-year-old, international free agent in 2006, Rienzo tossed seven innings and allowed three runs on six hits in his debut. He struck out six and walked three. Pitching against the Cleveland Indians at Progressive Field, the trailblazing right-hander left with a 4–3 lead, but the Indians rallied in the eighth inning for a 7–4 victory.

The game contained an ethnic subplot, with Rienzo facing countryman Yan Gomes three times in the game. The Indians' catcher went 1-for-2, with a walk and one run batted in, against his fellow paulistano.

AUGUST 5. Twelve major and minor league players—all of them Hispanic—accepted 50-game suspensions from Major League Baseball as a result of PED abuse. A 13th played, Alex Rodríguez, was also incriminated by MLB and received a 211-game suspension. The sanctions were the result of the identified players' association with an anti-aging clinic located in Coral Gables, Florida, and were announced two weeks after Brewers outfielder and former league MVP Ryan Braun received a 65-game suspension for banned substance abuse related to the same clinic.

Rodríguez was the only player to appeal his suspension, the harshest ever handed down to a player. The judgment was later reduced through arbitration to 162 games plus the post-season. Rodríguez subsequently sued both MLB and the MLB Players Association, but eventually dropped both suits.

AUGUST 21. In his fifth big league start, André Rienzo gained his first major league win and the first by a Brazilian pitcher at baseball's highest level. The Sao Paulo native defeated the Kansas City Royals, 5–2, at Kauffman Stadium. Benefitting from a five-run, fourth-inning uprising by his teammates, the White Sox pitcher hurled the first six innings, yielding both runs, before handing it off to the bullpen, which secured the historic win.

SEPTEMBER 12. With 77 lifetime saves against the Baltimore Orioles, Mariano Rivera established the record for most saves by a pitcher against one franchise. It was fitting, therefore, that Rivera recorded his 82nd and final big league win against the Maryland team tonight. At Camden Yards, the Yankees scored a run in the ninth inning, after David Robertson failed to hold a 5–2 lead in the bottom of the eighth. Rivera pitched a scoreless ninth to register the 6–5 win.

The great closer became the Latin American relief pitcher with the most career victories. (Southern Californian Jesse Orosco notched 87 relief wins.)

SEPTEMBER 26. In the 1992 expansion draft, the Colorado Rockies and Florida Marlins selected six players from the Yankees' farm system. A 23-year-old, unprotected Mariano Rivera was not among them. An 88mph fastball and recent elbow surgery were certainly dissuading factors for both clubs. After sidestepping a near-trade early in his

A beaming Mariano Rivera celebrates his 2013 All-Star Game MVP trophy. The Panamanian retired at the end of the season as baseball's all-time best closer.

career, Rivera increased his velocity and developed a devastating, singular pitch that converted him into the most dominant and proficient single-inning relief pitcher that the game has ever known. Over the course of the next two decades, Rivera and his "cutter" racked up an all-time, regular-season saves mark of 652, including 44 in 2013.

In his final appearance on a major league mound today, for the 465th time, Mariano Rivera recorded a perfect relief outing. At Yankee Stadium, the 43-year-old closer retired the four men he faced prior to being removed from the game with a visit to the mound by long-time teammates Derek Jeter and Andy Petitte.

An emotion-racked Rivera was cheered off the field, in the ninth inning, by a sell-out crowd of 48,675. The last man to wear the uniform number 42 and the last active player born in the 1960s, Rivera concluded his 19-year career by appearing in his 1,115th game. He tossed 1,233⅔ relief innings. The games and innings were the most by any Latin American reliever. (Jesse Orosco made 1,248 relief appearances and threw 1,277 innings out of the bullpen in his 24-year career.)

The Yankees, hampered by multiple core-player injuries, did not make the playoffs this season. The Tampa Bay Rays, one of the clubs that denied the Yankees a post-season berth, defeated the home team, 4–0, in Rivera's swan song game.

"It's humbling to myself, being able to finish the way the Lord allowed me to finish," the pitcher said after the game. "It was spectacular."[64]

Rivera tied with Bruce Chen for most major league wins by a Panamanian pitcher with 82.

2014

FEBRUARY 1. Cuba has become the longest-lasting dictatorship in the history of the Western Hemisphere. The cosmetic reforms dictator Raúl Castro has promoted in that country since he took control from his brother Fidel in 2006 have extended into the sports arena. In late 2013, a professional boxing match was held in Havana for the first time in more than half a century, pitting Cuban and Russian boxers. With regards to the baseball diamond, it was announced earlier that Cuba would return to the Caribbean Series and that Cuban ballplayers would have more freedom to play in baseball leagues abroad. That freedom will not encompass the boundaries of the United States, however.

On the related international front, today, the return of Cuba as a participant in the Caribbean Series—after a 54-year absence—was a truly welcomed sight for all baseball lovers. Given U.S. State Department pre-approval to compete in the tournament, the 2012–2013 league champions from provincial Villa Clara represented their island nation in the annual tournament, held this year on the Isle of Margarita, Venezuela. (Because the National Series, which crowns the baseball champion in Cuba, extends into the late spring, the Cuban squad for the 2014 Caribbean Classic was, in effect, last season's top club.)

On the field, at Estadio Nueva Esparta, Cuba's Villa Clara *Naranjas* were defeated by Mexico's *Naranjeros de Hermosillo*, 9–4, in a deflating debut. The Cubans, staggered by a rash of defections over the past years, had not won an international tournament since 2005. The team finished 1–3 in the opening round of competition and was sent packing, failing to qualify for the second round. (The team's elimination was a new wrinkle to a new tournament format instituted last year, where the poorest performing team is dismissed after a "first round of play.") Hermosillo, with a 4–2 record, claimed the tournament's illustrious hardware, defeating Puerto Rico's Mayagüez Indios, 7–1, in the title game on February 8.

MARCH 28. Miguel Cabrera signed an eight-year, $248 million contract extension, making him the first position player to earn $30 million annually in the major leagues. The agreement, added to the two years remaining of the eight-year, $152 million contract Cabrera signed with the Detroit Tigers in 2008, locked up the Tigers' incomparable-hitting first baseman through the 2023 season. Cabrera will be 40 years old at the completion of the deal.

Earlier in the off-season, Los Angeles Dodgers left-hander Clayton Kershaw had inked a seven-year, $215 million extension.

APRIL 16. The fourth Colombian pitcher to reach baseball's most elevated stage tossed the first big league shutout by a hurler from his native land. Cartagena's Julio Teheran of the Atlanta Braves outdueled Philadelphia Phillies left-hander Cliff Lee, 1–0, at Citizens Bank Ballpark. Teheran permitted only three hits, struck out four and did not walk a batter in the masterful, 115-pitch effort. A fourth-inning home run by battery mate Evan Gattis supplied the 23-year-old right-hander with the run needed to register the historic deed.

(On May 7, 2011, Teheren debuted with Atlanta at the young age of 20 and became the first Colombian pitcher to start a major league game. Teheren was defeated by the Phillies, 3–0, in the same Citizens Bank Ballpark.)

APRIL 27. Six Dominican players comprised the starting lineup for the Toronto Blue Jays in the team's home game versus the Boston Red Sox. Melky Cabrera (LF), José Reyes (SS), José Bautista (CF), Juan Encarnación (1B), Moises Sierra (RF) and Juan Francisco (DH) were penciled in as starters by Blue Jays skipper John Gibbons. Four of the players drove in at least one run in the Jays' 7–1 triumph over the visitors. The game was won by Blue Jays hurler R. A. Dickey on, coincidentally, R. A. Dickey Bobblehead Day, which helped fill the Rogers Centre to capacity. Including second baseman and Miami Beach native Jonathan Díaz, seven Hispanic players monopolized the Blue Jays' lineup on the day. And a seventh Dominican, Esmil Rogers, registered the last three outs of the game.

Manager Gibbons quipped afterward that his filling out of the lineup card, which contained the most players of the same ethnic nationality in a major league game, might have assured him a job in winter ball in the off-season.

APRIL 27. At U.S. Cellular Field, José Abreu of the Chicago White Sox drove in four runs with a single and home run to set the rookie record for RBI in April, as the White Sox defeated the Tampa Bay Rays, 9–2. The White Sox's first baseman's home run, clubbed against David Price, was his tenth circuit clout, the most by a first-year player in the first month of the season. Lifting his RBI total to 31, Abreu eclipsed Albert Pujols' previously-established power marks of eight homers and 27 RBI by a rookie in the month of April. He finished the month with ten homers and 32 RBI.

A few days later, Abreu became the second player, after Yasiel Puig, to win the "Player of the Month" award in his first month in the major leagues. The ten big flies also tied Abreu for the most home runs in one month by a Hispanic rookie (José Canseco, May 1986). In an impressive as well as historic season, Abreu joined Normar Garciaparra as the only rookies in history to hit 30 home runs and record a hitting streak of at least 20 games. As the "Player of the Month" in April and again in July, Abreu became the first big league rookie to win the award twice.

Despite a stint on the DL limiting his play to 145 games, the former Cuban League player finished third (tied) in the league in home runs, fourth in RBI, and fifth in batting average (.317/36/107). His .581 slugging mark was the highest in both leagues.

Abreu, 27, was signed by Chicago to a six-year, $68 million contract in October 2013. The Cuban defector established residency in a third country (Haiti) in order to negotiate as a free agent.

JULY 3. Carlos Beltrán of the New York Yankees clocked a three-run home run in the fifth inning against Minnesota Twins right-hander Phil Hughes at Target Field. The home run, an integral part of New York's 7–4 triumph over the Twins, moved Beltrán past Lance Berkman into fourth place on the all-time home run list for switch-hitters. The 17-year veteran's 367th career long ball left him trailing only Chipper Jones (468), Eddie Murray (504) and Mickey Mantle (536) for most homers by players who hit from both sides of the plate.

JULY 10. Texas Rangers third baseman Adrián Beltre collected three hits and six total bases during a Rangers 15–6 home drubbing at the hands of the Anaheim Angels. The 35-year-old Beltre topped Brooks Robinson (4,270) for most career total bases by a third baseman with 4,272.

JULY 11. With a fastball regularly clocked at over 100mph, the strikeout has become not only commonplace for pitcher Aroldis Chapman but, thanks to it, record-setting as well. At Great American Ball Park, the Cincinnati Reds' closer fanned the Pittsburgh Pirates' Jordy Mercer leading off the ninth inning, recording his 40th consecutive relief appearance with at least one strikeout, a modern era record. Striking out the side, Chapman, a 26-year-old defector from Cuba, notched his 20th save (and career save number 100), in preserving a 6–5 Reds win over the Bucs.

Chapman extended his record streak to 49, ending with an appearance the following month versus the Colorado Rockies.

JULY 30. Félix Hernández topped all major league pitchers in history with consistent short-term quality. The Seattle Mariners ace hurled his 14th consecutive start of at least seven innings and two or fewer runs allowed. The latest exceptional effort came at Progressive Field as Hernández tossed seven frames, permitting two runs to the Cleveland Indians. The 2010 Cy Young Award winner was defeated, however, by a masterful performance from Indians starter Corey Kluber, who used only 85 pitches to shut out the Mariners, 2–0.

Hernández, who dropped to 11–3 with a 2.01 ERA, bettered Tom Seaver's mark of 13 straight starts with a minimum of seven innings and two or fewer runs, accomplished in 1971. King Félix stretched the streak to 16 starts (9–2, 1.41 ERA), before exiting after five innings in an outing against the Detroit Tigers on August 16.

Seaver tossed ten complete games during his streak, Hernández none.

AUGUST 28. Pitcher Yusmeiro Petit established a major league record for consecutive batters retired. Facing the Colorado Rockies, the San Francisco Giants' right-hander set down his 46th consecutive batter in the third inning at AT&T Park. A strikeout of the Rockies' Charlie Culberson broke the prior record of 45 before opposing pitcher Jordan Lyles broke up the streak with a two-out double. The 29-year-old Venezuelan generated the unfaltering mark—previously held by Mark Buehrle—over eight appearances, two of them, including today's, as a starter.

Petit, it should be mentioned, had a very historic brush with the record books last season. On September 6, 2013, he came as close as possible to a perfect game without achieving one. In his home park, Petit set down 26 batters in a row. But his perfect game attempt was broken up by pinch-hitter Eric Chávez of the Arizona Diamondbacks. Chávez, the 27th Diamondbacks batter, singled on a 3–2 pitch to agonizingly deny the pitcher a chance at baseball immortality.

NOVEMBER 8. After disinheriting its winter league and its players for most of the past half-century, Cuba announced a refounding of its Baseball Hall of Fame, incorporating its original 68 members and ten new, pre- and post-revolutionary players. In a ceremony held at Salón Adolfo Luque in Estadio Lationoamericano and laden with geopolitical themes, four players and an umpire, from the late 19th century to 1961 period, were recognized for enshrinement. Another five former greats from the current Cuban "amateur" baseball were selected. The ceremony was dedicated to Cuban spies serving prison terms for espionage in the United States.

A Martín Dihigo Award was established, to be awarded annually or biannually, to the person or institution most responsible for promoting baseball on the island. The first Martín Dihigo Award was presented to the man responsible for the rupture of Cuban baseball, Fidel Castro. "It's laughable," said Gilberto Dihigo, Martín's son from Miami. "Fidel Castro is an enemy of everything Martín Dihigo represented, that is professional baseball."[65]

The despot was not present at the function.

2015

JANUARY 6. Three pitching titans and a hitting mighty mite were elected to the National Baseball Hall of Fame. Pedro Martínez joined two other first-year eligibles, Randy Johnson and John Smoltz, as well as Craig Biggio, as Cooperstown's newest immortals.

Pitching during an offense-dominated period and for seven seasons at hitter-friendly Fenway Park, Martínez was an absolutely commanding force on the mound for a good part of his 18 major league campaigns. "I did it clean,"[66] Pedro assured everyone in a national television interview on the day of his election.

A few days later, the eight-time All-Star flew home to the Dominican Republic to a hero's welcome. He was greeted by fans, numbering in the thousands, at the airport and lining a nearly 20-mile portion of the highway route to his final destination.

Dominican President Danilo Medina later formally swore in the 43-year-old Martínez as a goodwill ambassador.

MARCH 1. Extinguished in life, the Cuban Comet ascended into the astral baseball heavens. Minnie Miñoso died in Chicago of a ruptured pulmonary artery. He was at least 90 years old.

Miñoso's popularity with fans, especially in Chicago, transcended the sport through his undying love for the game, much like another contemporary Windy City personality Ernie Banks.

An underrated and underpublicized player for much of his career (he had a career OBP of .389—higher than Mays, Aaron and Clemente), Miñoso had dreamed of making the National Baseball Hall of Fame, but was denied in recent years, on more than one occasion, by the HOF's Golden Era Committee.

The seven-time All-Star had recently been elected to the reanimated Cuban Hall of Fame in Havana, but, like co-inductee Camilo Pascual, was prohibited by the Cuban government from attending. The ceremony was closed to all players living outside the island.

Appendix A:
First Latin American
Major Leaguers, by Franchise

Pre-Expansion

Franchise	Player/Debut
Brooklyn/Los Angeles Dodgers	Adolfo Luque—April 21, 1930
Boston/Milwaukee/Atlanta Braves	Mike González—September 28, 1912
Boston Red Sox	Eusebio González—July 26, 1918
Chicago Cubs	Mike González—May 25, 1925
Chicago White Sox	José Acosta—April 15, 1922
Cincinnati Reds	Rafael Almeida—July 4, 1911
Cleveland Indians	Minnie Miñoso—April 19, 1949
Detroit Tigers	Ozzie Virgil—June 6, 1958
New York/San Francisco Giants	Emilio Palmero—September 21, 1915
New York Yankees	Angel Aragon—August 20, 1914
Philadelphia/Kansas City/Oakland A's	Luis Castro—April 23, 1902
Philadelphia Phillies	José Gómez—July 27, 1935
Pittsburgh Pirates	Tony Ordeñana—October 3, 1943
St. Louis Browns/Baltimore Orioles	Armando Marsans—April 12, 1916
St. Louis Cardinals	Alfredo Cabrera*—May 16, 1913
Washington Senators/Minnesota Twins	Jack Calvo—May 9, 1913
	Cabrera was born in the Canary Islands, Spain.

FEDERAL LEAGUE

Franchise	Player/Debut
St. Louis Terriers	Armando Marsans—June 14, 1914

Expansion

Franchise	Player/Debut
Arizona Diamondbacks	Karim Garcia—March 31, 1998
Colorado Rockies	Andrés Galarraga—April 5, 1993
Florida/Miami Marlins	Junior Félix—April 5, 1993
Houston Colt .45s/Astros	Román Mejías—April 10, 1962
Kansas City Royals	Ellie Rodríguez—April 8, 1969
Los Angeles/California/Anaheim Angels	Julio Bécquer—April 11, 1961
Montreal Expos/Washington Nationals	José Laboy—April 8, 1969

Franchise	Player/Debut
New York Mets	Félix Mantilla—April 11, 1962
San Diego Padres	Rafael Robles—April 8, 1969
Seattle Mariners	Diego Seguí—April 6, 1977
Seattle Pilots/Milwaukee Brewers	Diego Seguí—April 8, 1969
Tampa Bay Devil Rays/Rays	Wilson Alvarez—March 31, 1998
Toronto Blue Jays	Héctor Torres—April 7, 1977
Washington Senators II/Texas Rangers	Rudy Hernández—April 16, 1961

Appendix B:
Latin American
Milestones, by Country

Countries are listed in the order of their entry into organized baseball.

Hitting

CUBA

Date	Historical Significance
May 9, 1871	First Hispanic player to record a hit in a major league.
July 4, 1911	First Hispanic player to record a hit in his first major league at-bat.
August 1, 1912	First Cuban player to hit a home run in the major leagues.
June 16, 1914	First Hispanic player to collect five hits in a modern era major league game.
June 21, 1918	First Hispanic player to collect five hits in a nine-inning, modern era major league game.
August 15, 1923	First Latin American pitcher to hit a home run in the major leagues.
April 29, 1926	First Hispanic major leaguer to record two hits in one inning, most lifetime hits recorded by a Hispanic pitcher in the major leagues.
August 22, 1926	Longest hitting streak by a Hispanic major league pitcher.
October 7, 1933	First Latin American player to hit safely in the World Series.
August 11, 1935	First Hispanic player to record a hit in the Negro Leagues All-Star Game.
May 18, 1939	First Hispanic player to hit a walk-off home run in the major leagues.
September 24, 1947	First Hispanic player to hit a home run in the Negro Leagues World Series.
February 25, 1949	First Cuban player to hit a home run in the Caribbean Series.
August 27, 1954	First Hispanic player to lead a major league in total bases.
October 2, 1955	First Cuban player to hit a home run in the World Series.
May 4, 1958	First Cuban player to hit three home runs in one major league game.
August 14, 1960	First Hispanic pitcher to hit a grand slam home run in the major leagues.
September 30, 1960	First Hispanic player to lead a major league in hits.
May 30, 1962	First Hispanic pitcher to hit two home runs in one major league game.
July 23, 1964	First Hispanic player to hit a home run in his first major league at-bat.
October 4, 1964	First major league rookie to win the batting title.
April 13, 1965	First Hispanic player to hit a grand slam as his first career home run.
October 3, 1965	First player to win batting titles in his first two major league seasons.
June 5, 1966	First Hispanic major leaguer to hit four home runs in a doubleheader.
October 2, 1966	Hispanic player to lead the league in hits most times.
July 11, 1967	First Hispanic player to hit a home run in the major league All-Star Game.
September 15, 1970	First Hispanic player to hit 20 home runs and steal 20 bases in one major league season.

Date	Historical Significance
October 3, 1970	First player to hit a grand slam in the League Championship Series.
April 6, 1973	First major league designated hitter to hit a home run.
October 9, 1973	First Hispanic major league player to hit a post-season, walk-off home run.
October 16, 1975	First Hispanic player to hit two home runs in a World Series game.
August 6, 1988	First Hispanic player to hit 30 home runs and steal 30 bases in one major league season.
September 23, 1988	First player to hit 40 home runs and steal 40 bases in a major league season. First Cuban player to lead a major league in home runs and RBI.
October 15, 1988	First Hispanic player to hit a grand slam in the World Series.
April 14, 1999	First Hispanic major league player to hit 400 home runs in the major leagues.
January 10, 2000	Most career pinch-hit home runs by a major league Hispanic player.
August 11, 2001	First Hispanic major league pitcher to record eight straight hits.
June 15, 2002	First Hispanic major leaguer to record 1,000 career extra-base hits.
September 26, 2003	First major leaguer to record at least 38 home runs in ten consecutive seasons. First Hispanic player with ten seasons of 35 home runs and 100 RBI.
July 15, 2005	First Hispanic major league player to record 500 home runs and 3,000 hits.
August 16, 2005	Cuban player with the most hits and home runs in the major leagues.
August 30, 2005	Hispanic player with the most runs, doubles and RBI in the major leagues.
March 8, 2006	First Cuban player to hit a home run in the World Baseball Classic.
June 30, 2012	First player to hit home runs from both sides of the plate in the same game for his first two major league hits.
June 30, 2013	Hispanic player to record the most hits in the month of his major league debut.
April 27, 2014	Most home runs and RBI by a major league rookie in the month of April.

COLOMBIA

Date	Historical Significance
May 14, 1902	First Hispanic player to record a hit in a modern era major league game.
May 29, 1902	First Hispanic player to collect four hits in a modern era major league game.
May 30, 1902	First Hispanic player to hit a home run in the major leagues.
October 26, 1997	First Hispanic player to record a walk-off, World Series-winning hit.
July 29, 2000	First Colombian player to record five hits in a major league game.
June 17, 2001	First Colombian player to hit a walk-off home run in the major leagues.
July 6, 2006	Most consecutive games reaching base safely by a Hispanic player in the major leagues.
October 28, 2010	First Colombian player to hit a home run in the World Series.
November 1, 2010	Colombian player with the most hits, home runs and RBI in the major leagues.

MEXICO

Date	Historical Significance
September 8, 1933	First Mexican player to record a hit in the major leagues.
September 23, 1933	First Mexican player to hit a home run in the major leagues.
July 21, 1937	First Hispanic player to hit a leadoff home run in the major leagues.
July 31, 1938	First Hispanic major league player to record 50 hits in one month.
June 20, 1951	First Hispanic player to hit three home runs in a major league game. First Mexican player to record five hits in a major league game.
August 22, 1951	First Mexican player to hit a walk-off home run in the major leagues.
September 26, 1954	First Hispanic player to win a major league batting title.
August 31, 1956	First Hispanic major leaguer to record 1,000 hits.
September 9, 1959	First Hispanic major league player to hit a fence-clearing, walk-off, grand slam home run.
May 30, 1970	First Mexican pitcher to hit a home run in the major leagues.

Date	Historical Significance
February 6, 1971	First Mexican player to hit a home run in the Caribbean Series.
June 1, 1984	Minor league player with the most lifetime home runs.
September 18, 1998	First Hispanic player to record 40 home runs and 200 hits in a major league season.
October 2, 2004	First Mexican player to lead a major league in RBI.
February 4, 2006	First player to record eight consecutive hits in the Caribbean Series.
March 9, 2006	First Mexican player to hit a home run in the World Baseball Classic.
September 28, 2006	Mexican player with the most hits, home runs and RBI in the major leagues.

VENEZUELA

Date	Historical Significance
May 14, 1939	First Venezuelan player to record a hit in the major leagues.
May 30, 1939	First Venezuelan player to hit a home run in the major leagues.
February 20, 1949	First player to hit a home run in the Caribbean Series.
July 10, 1951	First Latin American player to record a hit in the All-Star Game.
April 23, 1955	First Venezuelan player to record five hits in a major league game.
June 21, 1970	First Hispanic player to collect seven hits in a major league game.
September 19, 1972	First Hispanic major leaguer to complete the cycle with a walk-off home run. First Venezuelan player to hit for the cycle and a walk-off home run.
October 7, 1972	First Hispanic major leaguer to record a walk-off hit in the post-season.
October 14, 1975	First Venezuelan player to hit a home run in the World Series.
October 3, 1981	First Venezuelan player to lead a major league in home runs.
July 13, 1982	First Venezuelan to hit a home run in the major league All-Star Game.
September 28, 1984	First Venezuelan player to lead a major league in RBI.
October 3, 1993	First Venezuelan player to win a major league batting title.
June 25, 1995	First Hispanic major leaguer to hit home runs in three consecutive innings. First Venezuelan player to hit three home runs in one game.
October 22, 2003	First Hispanic player to hit a walk-off World Series home run.
March 7, 2006	First Venezuelan player to hit a home run in the World Baseball Classic.
May 2, 2010	First Hispanic player to record four hits in his first major league game.
June 3, 2012	Hispanic pitcher to hit the most home runs in the major leagues.
October 3, 2012	First Hispanic major league player to win the Triple Crown of hitting.
October 3, 2012	Hispanic switch-hitter with the most career hits in the major leagues. Venezuelan player with the most career hits in the major leagues.
October 28, 2012	First player to hit home runs in first three World Series plate appearances.

PUERTO RICO

Date	Historical Significance
June 5, 1942	First Puerto Rican player to record a hit in the major leagues.
July 26, 1943	First Puerto Rican player to hit a home run in the major leagues.
May 6, 1945	First Hispanic player to record eight hits in a major league doubleheader. First Hispanic player to drive in six runs in a major league game.
May 18, 1945	First Latin American player to hit a grand slam in the major leagues. First Hispanic player to drive in seven runs in a major league game.
August 28, 1945	First Hispanic player to drive in 100 runs in a major league season. First Hispanic player to lead a major league in triples.
August 24, 1948	First Hispanic player to hit a home run in the Negro Leagues East-West All-Star Game.
July 17, 1949	First Hispanic player to hit a fence-clearing, walk-off home run in the major leagues.
October 7, 1949	First Hispanic player to hit a home run in the World Series.

Date	Historical Significance
February 25, 1951	First Puerto Rican player to hit a home run in the Caribbean Series.
February 26, 1951	First player to hit two home runs in a Caribbean Series game.
February 20, 1953	First Hispanic pitcher to hit a home run in the Caribbean Series.
February 22, 1953	First Hispanic player to record a walk-off hit in the Caribbean Series.
May 2, 1953	First Hispanic player to hit three triples in a major league game.
July 30, 1954	First Puerto Rican pitcher to hit a home run in the major leagues.
May 29, 1955	First Puerto Rican player to record five hits in a major league game.
July 25, 1956	First Hispanic player to hit an inside-the-park, walk-off grand slam in the major leagues.
May 7, 1957	First Hispanic major leaguer to hit a leadoff and walk-off home run in the same game.
April 15, 1958	First Hispanic player to hit a home run in his initial major league game.
July 4, 1961	First Hispanic player to drive in eight runs in a major league game.
September 10, 1961	First Hispanic player to hit 40 home runs in a major league season.
September 22, 1961	First Hispanic player to record 200 hits in a major league season.
September 26, 1961	First Puerto Rican player to win a major league batting title.
September 27, 1961	First Hispanic player to lead a major league in home runs and RBI.
September 2, 1966	First Hispanic major leaguer to record 2,000 hits.
May 15, 1967	First Puerto Rican player to hit three home runs in one major league game.
October 4, 1967	First Hispanic player to hit a home run in his first World Series at-bat.
August 5, 1969	First Hispanic major leaguer to record 2,500 hits.
August 13, 1969	First Hispanic player to hit three home runs in a game twice.
August 22–23, 1970	First Hispanic major leaguer with ten hits in consecutive games.
July 13, 1971	First Puerto Rican player to hit a home run in the major league All-Star Game.
August 25, 1971	First Hispanic major league player to record eight five-hit games.
October 17, 1971	First Hispanic player to record a World Series-deciding, game-winning RBI.
September 30, 1972	First Hispanic major leaguer to record 3,000 hits. Puerto Rican player with the most hits in the major leagues.
October 19, 1972	First Hispanic player to record a walk-off hit in the World Series.
August 27, 1974	First Puerto Rican player to hit a home run in his first major league at-bat.
April 22, 1980	First Puerto Rican major leaguer to hit for the cycle.
May 4, 1981	First Hispanic brothers to hit home runs as opponents in the same major league game.
September 19, 1982	First Hispanic player to hit a grand slam as his first major league hit.
April 8, 1993	First major leaguer to hit home runs from both sides of the plate in one inning. First Hispanic major leaguer to hit two home runs in one inning.
October 19, 1993	First Hispanic player to record four hits in a World Series game.
October 23, 1993	First Hispanic player to record 12 hits in the World Series.
February 7, 1995	First player to record seven consecutive hits in the Caribbean Series.
October 6, 1995.	First player to hit home runs from both sides of the plate in a post-season game.
July 5, 1998	First Hispanic player to record 100 RBI prior to the All-Star Game.
November 18, 1998	First Hispanic player to record 50 doubles and 40 home runs in a major league season.
April 13, 1999	First Hispanic player to drive in nine runs in one major league game.
August 14, 1999	First major league catcher to hit 20 home runs and steal 20 bases in the same season.
April 23, 2000	First major league teammates to hit home runs from both sides of the plate in the same game.
August 17, 2002	Hispanic major leaguer to record the most consecutive base hits.
September 25, 2003	First Hispanic player to hit four home runs in a major league game.
October 21, 2003	Hispanic player to hit the most home runs in the World Series, collect the most post-season hits and drive in the most post-season runs.

Date	Historical Significance
March 8, 2006	First Puerto Rican player to hit a home run in the World Baseball Classic.
May 8, 2009	Puerto Rican player with the most home runs and RBI in the major leagues.
June 17, 2009	Major league catcher to record the most hits.
July 3, 2014	Most home runs hit by a Hispanic switch-hitter in the major leagues.

DOMINICAN REPUBLIC

Date	Historical Significance
February 16, 1951	First Hispanic player to record a championship, walk-off home run in the Latin American Winter Leagues.
September 30, 1956	First Dominican player to record a hit in the major leagues.
April 27, 1957	First Dominican player to hit a home run in the major leagues.
June 17, 1958	First Dominican player to record five hits in a major league game.
May 15, 1961	First Hispanic brothers to hit home runs in the same major league game.
August 9, 1961	First Dominican player to hit a walk-off home run in the major leagues.
September 12, 1963	First Dominican pitcher to hit a home run in the major leagues.
July 4, 1964	First Dominican player to hit three home runs in one major league game.
July 10, 1964	First Hispanic player to collect six hits in one major league game.
September 21, 1966	First Hispanic major league pitcher to hit a walk-off home run.
October 2, 1966	First Dominican player to win a major league batting title.
October 12, 1967	First Dominican player to hit a home run in the World Series.
February 2, 1970	First Dominican player to hit a home run in the Caribbean Series.
May 12 1970	First Hispanic player to hit in 30 consecutive major league games.
August 2, 1972	First Dominican major leaguer to hit for the cycle.
September 10, 1972	First Hispanic player to hit 20 home runs and steal 50 bases in one major league season.
July 30, 1975	First Hispanic pitcher to hit a home run in his first major league at-bat.
July 13, 1976	First Dominican player to hit a home run in the All-Star Game.
February 9, 1977	First player to hit five home runs in one Caribbean Series.
October 6, 1985	First Hispanic player to hit a home run in his final major league at-bat.
April 4, 1988	First major leaguer to hit three home runs on Opening Day.
June 12, 1997	First player to hit an interleague home run in the major leagues.
June 20, 1998	Major league player with the most home runs in a 30-day period.
June 25, 1998	Major league player with the most home runs in a single calendar month.
August 10, 1998	Hispanic player with the most multi-home run games in one major league season.
August 23, 1998	First Hispanic player to hit 50 home runs in a major league season.
September 12, 1998	First Hispanic player to hit 60 home runs in a major league season.
September 25, 1998	Hispanic player with the most home runs in one major league season.
April 6, 1999	Hispanic major leaguer with the most home runs as a teenager.
April 23, 1999	First major league player to hit two grand slam home runs in one inning and most RBI by a player in one inning.
September 18, 1999	First player to hit 60 home runs in a major league season twice.
September 26, 1999	Hispanic player with the most RBI in a major league season.
September 16, 2000	First Dominican player to lead a major league in home runs.
December 13, 2000	Hispanic player with the most consecutive seasons with an OPS of .900.
August 17, 2001	First Hispanic rookie to hit three home runs in a major league game.
August 26, 2001	First Hispanic major leaguer to hit 50 home runs in four consecutive seasons.
September 23, 2001	First major leaguer to hit three home runs in a game three times in one season. Hispanic player to record the highest OPS in one major league season.
October 7, 2001	Hispanic player to hit the most home runs in one major league season. Hispanic player to record the most total bases in one major league season. Hispanic player to score the most runs in one major league season. First Hispanic player to collect 100 extra-base hits and slug .700 in one major league season.

Date	Historical Significance
October 7, 2001	Hispanic rookie with the most home runs and RBI in one major league season.
June 22, 2002	Longest consecutive hitting streak by a Hispanic major leaguer.
April 4, 2003	First Hispanic player to hit 500 home runs in the major leagues.
September 22, 2003	Player with the most leadoff home runs in one major league season. Hispanic player with the most career leadoff home runs.
March 7, 2006	First Hispanic player to hit a home run in the World Baseball Classic.
April 29, 2006	Major league players with the most home runs in the month of April.
June 20, 2007	First Latin American player to hit 600 home runs in the major leagues.
July 10, 2007	Hispanic player with the most home runs in the All-Star Game.
September 26, 2007	Hispanic father-son duo with the most home runs in the major leagues.
September 11, 2008	First Hispanic player to record 300 home runs in his first eight seasons. First Hispanic player to record 100 RBI in each of his first eight seasons.
July 22, 2009	Latin American major leaguer with the most career grand slam home runs.
October 15, 2009	Player with the most post-season home runs in the major leagues. Hispanic player with the longest consecutive post-season hitting streak.
April 12, 2010	Player to hit the most home runs in his first ten major league seasons.
August 26, 2010	First major leaguer to hit 400 home runs in his first ten seasons.
September 11, 2010	First major leaguer to record a .300 average, 30 home runs and 100 RBI in ten consecutive seasons.
September 18, 2011	Hispanic brothers with the most home runs in the major leagues.
October 4, 2011	First Hispanic player to hit three home runs in a post-season game.
October 22, 2011	First Hispanic player to hit three home runs in a World Series game.
April 10, 2013	Dominican player with the most hits in the major leagues.
June 6, 2013	Hispanic major leaguer with the most career walk-off home runs, including post-season.
July 10, 2013	Designated hitter with the most hits in the major leagues.

PANAMA

Date	Historical Significance
February 24, 1953	First Panamanian player to hit a home run in the Caribbean Series.
May 12, 1955	First Panamanian player to record a hit in the major leagues.
June 26, 1955	First Panamanian player to hit a home run in the major leagues.
February 15, 1956	First Hispanic player to hit a grand slam home run in the Caribbean Series.
May 19, 1956	First Panamanian player to hit a walk-off home run in the major leagues.
July 27, 1956	First Panamanian player to record five hits in a major league game.
June 26, 1958	First Panamanian player to hit three home runs in one major league game.
February 14, 1960	First Hispanic player to hit a walk-off home run in the Caribbean Series.
October 9, 1961	First Panamanian player to hit a home run in the World Series.
October 1, 1969	First Panamanian player to win a major league batting title.
May 20, 1970	First Hispanic major leaguer to hit for the cycle.
September 16, 1975	First modern era major leaguer to record seven hits in a nine-inning game. First Hispanic player to record two hits in an inning in the same game twice.
September 28, 1975	First Hispanic major leaguer to record four consecutive batting titles.
October 2, 1977	Hispanic player with the highest single-season batting average in the major leagues. Hispanic player with the most hits in a major league season. Latin American player with the most hits in a single month.
September 30, 1978	Hispanic player with the most major league batting titles.
October 5, 1980	First Panamanian player to lead a major league in home runs.
May 6, 1983	Hispanic player with the most consecutive .300 seasons in the major leagues.
August 4, 1985	First Hispanic major league player to record 3,000 hits and 300 stolen bases. Hispanic major leaguer with the most hits in the 20th century.
May 7, 1999	First Panamanian player to hit a home run in his first major league at-bat.

Date	Historical Significance
March 8, 2006	First Panamanian player to hit a home run in the World Baseball Classic.
June 20, 2013	Panamanian player with the most home runs in the major leagues.

NICARAGUA

Date	Historical Significance
September 26, 1981	First Nicaraguan player to record a hit in the major leagues.
August 15, 1982	First Nicaraguan player to hit a home run in the major leagues.
June 14, 1985	First Nicaraguan player to hit a walk-off home run in the major leagues.
October 2, 1999	First Nicaraguan player to record five hits in a major league game. Nicaraguan player with the most career hits and home runs in the major leagues.

HONDURAS

Date	Historical Significance
July 8, 1987	First Honduran player to appear in the major leagues.
July 9, 1987	First Honduran player to record a hit in the major leagues.
September 16, 1987	First Honduran player to hit a home run in the major leagues.

BELIZE

Date	Historical Significance
July 5, 1991	First Belizean player to appear and record a hit in the major leagues.
July 11, 1991	First Belizean player to hit a home run in the major leagues.

BRAZIL

Date	Historical Significance
May 17, 2012	First Brazilian player to appear and record a hit in the major leagues.
May 18, 2012	First Brazilian player to hit a home run in the major leagues.

Pitching

CUBA

Date	Historical Significance
November 15, 1908	First Hispanic pitcher to shut out a major league team.
November 18, 1909	First Hispanic pitcher to no-hit a major league team.
May 1, 1916	First Hispanic pitcher to surrender a home run in the major leagues.
August 8, 1918	First Hispanic pitcher to win a major league game.
September 2, 1918	First Hispanic pitcher to throw a major league shutout.
April 13, 1921	First Hispanic pitcher to lead a major league in shutouts. First Hispanic pitcher to throw 300 innings in one major league season.
June 19, 1923	First Hispanic pitcher to throw an extra-inning shutout in the major leagues.
July 17, 1923	First Hispanic pitcher to start and win both games of a major league doubleheader.
August 24, 1923	First Hispanic pitcher to win 20 games in a major league season.
September 29, 1923	First Hispanic pitcher to lead a major league in wins and ERA.
October 20, 1924	First Hispanic pitcher to win a North American championship game.
May 3, 1925	First Hispanic pitcher to win 100 major league games.
September 26, 1927	Pitcher to record the best ERA in games lost of nine innings or more with three or fewer runs allowed.
September 17, 1930	First Hispanic pitcher to record 200 complete games in the major leagues.

Date	Historical Significance
October 7, 1933	First Hispanic pitcher to win a World Series game.
September 16, 1944	First Hispanic pitcher to throw a major league one-hit game.
October 5, 1944	First pitcher to win 30 games in a Latin American league season.
February 20, 1949	First Cuban pitcher to win a Caribbean Series game.
April 17, 1951	First Hispanic pitcher to start an American League season-opening game.
September 2, 1952	First Hispanic pitcher to throw a one-hitter in his major league debut.
February 20, 1954	First Hispanic pitcher to throw a shutout in the Caribbean Series.
September 15, 1959	First Hispanic pitcher lead a major league in shutouts and complete games.
February 14, 1960	First Hispanic pitcher to throw a one-hit Caribbean Series game. Pitcher to record the most complete games in the Caribbean Series. Pitchers to record the most victories in the Caribbean Series.
April 18, 1960	Pitcher to record the most strikeouts on Opening Day in the major leagues.
October 12, 1960	First Hispanic pitcher to lead a major league in saves.
April 11, 1961	First Hispanic pitcher to throw an Opening Day shutout in the major leagues.
September 29, 1961	First Hispanic pitcher to lead a major league in strikeouts. First Hispanic pitcher to strike out 200 batters in a major league season.
September 27, 1963	First Hispanic two-time 20-game winner in the major leagues. First Hispanic pitcher to lead a major league in shutouts, strikeouts and complete games three times each.
September 27, 1967	Hispanic pitcher with the most 1–0 complete game victories in the major leagues.
April 15, 1968	First Hispanic major league pitcher to record 2,000 strikeouts.
May 17, 1968	Longest consecutive scoreless innings streak by a Hispanic major league pitcher.
July 3, 1968	Hispanic pitcher with the most strikeouts in a major league game.
September 25, 1968	Hispanic pitcher with the lowest ERA in a major league season. Hispanic pitcher with fewest hits allowed per nine innings in a season. First Hispanic major league pitcher to record an ERA under 2.00 with 200 strikeouts.
September 5, 1969	First Hispanic left-handed pitcher to win 20 games in the major leagues.
October 11, 1969	First Hispanic pitcher to throw a complete-game World Series victory.
September 9, 1970	Latin American left-handed pitcher with the most wins in a major league season. Hispanic pitchers with the most wins in consecutive major league seasons and most starts in a major league season.
October 15, 1970	First Hispanic starting pitcher to win a clinching World Series game.
June 4, 1971	Hispanic left-handed pitcher with the most shutouts in the major leagues.
October 4, 1971	First Hispanic major league pitcher to win a League Championship Series game.
September 4, 1972	First major league pitcher to throw four consecutive shutouts twice.
May 29, 1974	Latin American left-handed pitcher with the most complete games in the major leagues.
October 11, 1975	First Hispanic pitcher to throw a shutout in the World Series.
October 15, 1975	First Hispanic pitcher to win two games in one World Series.
June 20, 1976	Latin American left-handed pitcher to record the most major league wins.
July 8, 1979	Cuban pitcher with the most wins and shutouts in the major leagues.
October 12, 1997	Hispanic major league pitcher with the most strikeouts in one post-season game.
October 14, 2001	Hispanic pitcher with the most major league post-season wins.
March 8, 2006	First Cuban pitcher to record a win in the World Baseball Classic.
July 4, 2006	Hispanic major league pitchers with the most consecutive wins.
July 11, 2014	Pitcher with the most consecutive relief appearances with at least one strikeout.

VENEZUELA

Date	Historical Significance
May 3, 1939	First Venezuelan pitcher to win a major league game.
July 18, 1942	First Venezuelan pitcher to throw a major league shutout.

Date	Historical Significance
February 21, 1949	First Venezuelan pitcher to win a Caribbean Series game.
February 10, 1955	First Venezuelan pitcher to throw a shutout in the Caribbean Series.
February 14, 1960	Pitchers with the most victories in the Caribbean Series.
August 11, 1991	First Venezuelan pitcher to throw a major league no-hit, no-run game.
October 20, 1993	First Venezuelan pitcher to win a World Series game.
November 11, 2004	First Venezuelan pitcher to win 20 games in the major leagues.
April 26, 2005	Hispanic major league pitchers with the most consecutive wins.
March 8, 2006	First Venezuelan pitcher to record a win in the World Baseball Classic.
September 24, 2008	Pitcher with the most saves in a major league season.
August 15, 2012	First Venezuelan pitcher to throw a perfect game in the major leagues.
August 27, 2012	First Hispanic pitcher to win four 1–0 shutouts in one major league season.
May 24, 2013	Hispanic major league pitcher with the most games of one hit or less.
July 30, 2014	Pitcher with the most consecutive starts of at least seven innings and two or fewer runs allowed.
August 28, 2014	Pitcher with the major league record for consecutive batters retired.

PUERTO RICO

Date	Historical Significance
June 5, 1942	First Puerto Rican pitcher to win a major league game.
April 28, 1943	First Puerto Rican pitcher to throw a major league shutout.
February 23, 1950	First Puerto Rican pitcher to win a Caribbean Series game.
October 1, 1954	First Latin American pitcher to start a World Series Game. First pitcher to win a World Series and Caribbean Series game. First Puerto Rican pitcher to win a World Series Game.
February 11, 1957	First Puerto Rican pitcher to throw a shutout in the Caribbean Series.
February 8, 1958	Pitcher with the most strikeouts in a Caribbean Series game. Pitcher with the most career strikeouts in the Caribbean Series.
April 15, 1958	Pitcher with the first win and shutout in a major league game played in California.
February 14, 1960	Pitchers with the most victories in the Caribbean Series.
September 9, 1961	Hispanic relief pitcher with the most wins in one major league season.
February 8, 1963	First Hispanic pitcher to throw a no-hit, no-run game in a winter league championship tournament.
April 8, 1969	First American League pitcher to record a major league save as an official statistic.
September 30, 1978	First Puerto Rican pitcher to win 20 games in the major leagues.
October 12, 1984	First Hispanic pitcher to record a World Series save.
April 15, 1987	First Puerto Rican pitcher to throw a major league no-hit, no-run game.
March 7, 2006	First Puerto Rican pitcher to record a win in the World Baseball Classic.
September 27, 2011	Puerto Rican pitcher with the most wins and strikeouts in the major leagues.

MEXICO

Date	Historical Significance
April 27, 1943	First Mexican pitcher to win a major league game.
July 2, 1944	First Mexican pitcher to throw a major league shutout.
February 9, 1971	First Mexican pitcher to win a Caribbean Series game.
February 6, 1974	First Mexican pitcher to throw a shutout in the Caribbean Series.
May 8, 1981	First Hispanic pitcher to throw five shutouts in seven starts.
May 14, 1981	Hispanic pitcher with the most consecutive wins at the start of a career.
September 17, 1981	Hispanic rookie pitcher with the most major league shutouts in one season.
October 23, 1981	First Mexican pitcher to win a World Series game. Hispanic major league pitcher with the most post-season innings.

Date	Historical Significance
April 28, 1985	Most consecutive innings without an earned run allowed to start a major league season.
July 15, 1986	Hispanic pitcher with the most consecutive strikeouts in the All-Star Game.
September 22, 1986	First Mexican pitcher to win 20 games in a major league season.
June 29, 1990	First Mexican pitcher to throw a major league no-hit, no-run game.
May 23, 1997	Mexican pitcher with the most wins, shutouts, complete games and innings in the major leagues.
July 12, 1997	First combined, extra-inning no-hitter in the major leagues.
March 8, 2006	First Mexican pitcher to record a win in the World Baseball Classic.

PANAMA

Date	Historical Significance
February 20, 1949	First pitcher to win a Caribbean Series game.
May 6, 1955	First Panamanian pitcher to win a major league game.
February 14, 1957	First Panamanian pitcher to throw a shutout in the Caribbean Series.
August 24, 1971	First Panamanian pitcher to throw a shutout in the major leagues.
July 8, 1997	First Hispanic pitcher to record a save in the major league All-Star Game.
October 26, 1999	First Panamanian pitcher to win a World Series game.
October 13, 2000	Major league pitcher with the most consecutive post-season scoreless innings.
July 14, 2009	Pitcher with the most All-Star Game saves.
November 1, 2009	Pitcher with the most World Series saves.
October 15, 2010	Major league pitcher with the most post-season saves.
September 19, 2011	Pitcher with the most career saves in the major leagues.
September 30, 2011	Major league pitcher with the lowest post-season ERA. Hispanic major league pitcher with the most post-season strikeouts.
September 12, 2013	Hispanic relief pitcher to record the most victories in the major leagues.

DOMINICAN REPUBLIC

Date	Historical Significance
July 19, 1960	First Dominican pitcher to win a major league game and throw a shutout.
July 10, 1962	First Hispanic pitcher to record a win in the All-Star Game.
June 15, 1963	First Hispanic major league pitcher to throw a no-hit, no-run game.
July 2, 1963	Hispanic pitcher with the longest extra-inning shutout in the major leagues.
September 3, 1963	First Dominican pitcher to win 20 games in the major leagues.
September 28, 1963	First Hispanic pitcher to lead a major league in innings pitched.
September 9, 1965	Hispanic pitcher with the most shutouts in one major league season.
May 26, 1966	First Hispanic pitcher to win 25 games in a major league season twice.
August 1, 1968	Hispanic pitcher with the most complete games and innings in one major league season. Hispanic pitcher with the most consecutive complete games in one season. Hispanic major league pitcher with the most career complete games.
August 29, 1969	First Hispanic major league pitcher to record 100 more career wins than losses.
September 16, 1969	Hispanic pitcher with the most 20-game-winning seasons.
August 28, 1970	First Hispanic pitcher to win 200 major league games.
September 9, 1970	Hispanic pitchers with the most wins in consecutive major league seasons and most starts in a major league season.
February 6, 1971	First Dominican pitcher to win a Caribbean Series game.
August 10, 1971	First Hispanic pitcher to record 50 shutouts in the major leagues.
February 4, 1972	First Dominican pitcher to throw a shutout in the Caribbean Series.
April 5, 1973	Hispanic pitcher with the most Opening Day wins.
July 15, 1973	Hispanic major league pitcher with the most career shutouts.

Date	Historical Significance
October 9, 1973	First Hispanic major league pitcher to record a post-season save.
April 17, 1975	Hispanic pitcher with the most seasons with 20 wins, 200 strikeouts and an ERA under 3.00. Dominican pitcher with the most wins in the major leagues.
June 23, 1979	First Hispanic pitcher to strike out the side on nine pitches.
October 15, 1982	First Dominican pitcher to win a World Series game.
June 4, 1990	Hispanic major league pitcher with the most strikeouts in a regulation-length game.
September 24, 1992	Hispanic major league pitcher with the most career strikeouts
September 28, 1993	First Hispanic pitcher to win 100 games in both major leagues.
June 3, 1995	First Hispanic pitcher to take a perfect game past nine innings.
September 25, 1997	First Hispanic pitcher to strike out 300 batters in one major league season.
September 21, 1999	First Hispanic pitcher to strike out 300 batters in both major leagues. Hispanic pitcher with the most strikeouts per nine innings in a season.
October 2, 1999	First Latin American major league hurler to win pitching's Triple Crown.
March 7, 2006	First Dominican pitcher to record a win in the World Baseball Classic.
September 3, 2007	First Hispanic major league pitcher to record 3,000 strikeouts
October 3, 2012	Pitcher with the lowest ERA with at least 20 saves in one major league season.

NICARAGUA

Date	Historical Significance
September 14, 1976	First Nicaraguan pitcher to win a major league game.
June 16, 1978	First Nicaraguan pitcher to throw a major league shutout.
July 28, 1991	First Hispanic pitcher to throw a perfect game in the major leagues.
June 2, 1998	Nicaraguan pitcher with the most major league shutouts.
August 9, 1998	Hispanic pitcher with the most wins, starts, and innings in the major leagues.

COLOMBIA

Date	Historical Significance
September 9, 2006	First Colombian pitcher to win a major league game.
April 16, 2014	First Colombian pitcher to throw a major league shutout.

Miscellaneous

CUBA

Date	Historical Significance
May 9, 1871	First Hispanic major league player.
December 27, 1874	First widely recorded game outside of the United States.
December 29, 1878	First professional baseball league outside of the United States.
November 15, 1908	First major league team to play in Cuba.
July 4, 1911	First Cuban player in the major leagues in the 20th century.
September 28, 1912	First Hispanic catcher in the major leagues.
June 5, 1913	Youngest Hispanic major league player. Youngest Hispanic player to hit a home run in the major leagues.
September 6, 1913	Youngest Hispanic player to hit safely in a major league.
May 20, 1914	First Hispanic pitcher to appear in the major leagues.
May 31, 1914	First Hispanic player ejected from a major league game.
June 11, 1917	First Hispanic player to register a walk-off steal of home plate.
May 30, 1918	First Hispanic battery in the major leagues.
August 11, 1918	First Hispanic pitcher and batter to face one another in the major leagues.
September 2, 1918	First Hispanic starting pitchers to oppose one another in the major leagues.

Date	Historical Significance
October 3, 1919	First Hispanic player to appear in the World Series and first Hispanic pitcher to strike out a batter in the World Series.
June 26, 1920	First Hispanic pitcher ejected from a major league game.
April 13, 1921	First Hispanic pitcher to start a major league Opening Day game.
October 14, 1924	First Hispanic manager to win a North American league pennant. First Hispanic player to appear in the Negro Leagues World Series.
October 20, 1924	First Hispanic manager to win a North American championship title.
October 8, 1929	First Hispanic position player to play in the World Series.
December 9, 1933	First Hispanic coach in the major leagues.
April 23, 1935	First Hispanic pitching coach in the major leagues.
August 11, 1935	First Hispanic player in the Negro Leagues All-Star Game. First Hispanic pitcher in the Negro Leagues All Star Game.
September 14, 1938	First Hispanic manager in the major leagues.
April 25, 1940	First Hispanic father-son major league player duo.
April 28, 1943	First shutout recorded in the major leagues by a Hispanic battery.
October 26, 1946	First million-dollar baseball stadium in Latin America.
February 25, 1949	First Caribbean Series champion. First Caribbean Series winning manager. First Caribbean Series MVP.
June 25, 1950	First Hispanic pitchers to start both games of a major league doubleheader.
July 10, 1951	First Cuban player to appear in the All-Star Game.
July 13, 1954	First Hispanic pitcher to appear in the All-Star Game.
April 24, 1955	First all–Hispanic outfield in the major leagues.
October 4, 1955	Sandy Amoros' victory-preserving World Series catch for the Brooklyn Dodgers.
February 11, 1956	Youngest pitcher to win a Caribbean Series game.
October 6, 1959	First Latin American-based team to win a North American league championship title.
February 15, 1960	The last champion of the original Caribbean Series.
July 23, 1960	First all–Hispanic triple play in the major leagues.
February 8, 1961	Last game of the Cuban Winter League.
November 28, 1964	First Cuban player to win the "Rookie of the Year" Award in the major leagues. First Hispanic player to lead a major league in runs scored.
September 8, 1965	First player to play all nine positions in a major league game.
November 18, 1965	First Hispanic player to win the Most Valuable Player Award in the major leagues.
June 12, 1967	Most innings caught by a Hispanic catcher in a major league game.
July 11, 1967	First Cuban player to win the MVP Award in the All-Star Game.
August 29, 1968	First Hispanic hired as a full-time manager in the major leagues.
April 23, 1969	First Hispanic pitcher to win the Cy Young Award.
June 21, 1969	Major league player with the most consecutive games with a stolen base.
September 1, 1971	First all-minority starting lineup in a major league game.
September 20, 1972	First Hispanic player to win "Comeback Player of the Year" Award.
May 24, 1976	Hispanic players with the most stolen bases in a major league game.
September 12, 1976	Oldest major league player to record a hit. First Hispanic major leaguer to play in four decades.
August 8, 1977	First Cuban player inducted into the National Baseball Hall of Fame.
October 4, 1980	First Hispanic player to play in five major league decades. First Hispanic player to lead a major league in stolen bases.
August 24, 1983	Hispanic major leaguer with the most career stolen bases.
June 27, 1990	First major leaguer to earn $5 million in annual salary.
April 5, 1993	First major league game with two Hispanic managers.
October 26, 1997	First Cuban player to win the MVP Award in the World Series.

COLOMBIA

Date	Historical Significance
April 23, 1902	First Hispanic major league player of the 20th century.
September 24, 1941	First Hispanic manager in North American organized baseball.
July 7, 1998	First Colombian player to appear in the major league All-Star Game.
May 14, 2006	First Colombian pitcher to appear in the major leagues.
November 1, 2010	First Colombian player to win the MVP Award in the World Series.

MEXICO

Date	Historical Significance
March 10, 1907	First major league team to play in Latin America.
June 28, 1925	First professional league in Mexico.
September 8, 1933	First Mexican player to appear in the major leagues.
July 25, 1937	Player with the most runs scored in a major league doubleheader.
April 16, 1942	First Mexican pitcher to appear in the major leagues.
February 18, 1946	First signings of major league players in the "player war" with Mexico.
July 13, 1954	First Mexican player to appear in the major league All-Star Game.
April 24, 1955	First all–Hispanic outfield in the major leagues.
April 17, 1956	First Hispanic keystone combination in the major leagues.
February 1, 1974	First Mexican player to be named MVP in the Caribbean Series.
February 9, 1976	First Caribbean Series tournament victory for the country of Mexico. First player to be named Caribbean Series MVP twice.
April 9, 1981	Youngest Hispanic pitcher to start an Opening Day game in the major leagues.
April 27, 1981	First rookie pitcher to win the Silver Slugger Award.
August 9, 1981	Youngest Hispanic player to appear in the major league All-Star Game. First Mexican pitcher to appear in the All-Star Game.
October 23, 1981	Youngest Hispanic pitcher to win a World Series game.
November 11, 1981	First major league rookie and youngest Hispanic pitcher to win the Cy Young Award.
December 2, 1981	First Mexican player and youngest Hispanic player to win the Rookie of the Year Award in the major leagues.
February 18, 1983	First Hispanic player to earn $1,000,000 in annual salary.
September 22, 1986	First Hispanic pitcher to lead the major leagues in WAR.
August 16, 1996	First major league regular season game played outside of the U.S. and Canada.
April 4, 1999	First major league regular season-opening game played outside of the U.S. and Canada.
March 8, 2009	First person to appear in the World Baseball Classic as a player and manager.

PUERTO RICO

Date	Historical Significance
February 27, 1936	First major league team to play in Puerto Rico.
November 13, 1938	First professional winter league in Puerto Rico.
April 15, 1942	First Puerto Rican player to appear in the major leagues.
April 28, 1943	First shutout recorded in the major leagues by a Hispanic battery.
July 23, 1943	First Puerto Rican position player in the major leagues.
October 7, 1949	First Hispanic position player to start a World Series game.
February 27, 1950	First Hispanic player to play in the World Series and the Caribbean Series.
February 26, 1951	First Caribbean Series tournament victory for the country of Puerto Rico. First Puerto Rican player to be named MVP in the Caribbean Series.
April 24, 1955	First all–Hispanic outfield in the major leagues.
July 12, 1955	First Puerto Rican player to appear in the major league All-Star Game.
May 10, 1957	Youngest Hispanic pitcher to hit a home run in the major leagues.

Date	Historical Significance
October 5, 1957	Youngest Hispanic pitcher to appear in the World Series.
August 14, 1958	First Hispanic major leaguer to steal home twice in one game.
January 9, 1959	First Puerto Rican player to win the Rookie of the Year Award in the major leagues.
September 26, 1961	Hispanic player with the most outfield assists in one major league season.
November 16, 1966	First Puerto Rican player to win the Most Valuable Player Award in the major leagues.
January 25, 1967	First Hispanic player to earn $100,000 in annual salary.
November 7, 1967	First Hispanic player to win the Most Valuable Player Award in the major leagues unanimously. First Hispanic player to win Rookie of the Year and MVP Awards.
September 1, 1971	First all-minority starting lineup in a major league game.
October 17, 1971	First Hispanic player to win the MVP Award in the World Series. First Hispanic player to win both World Series MVP and league MVP Awards. Most consecutive games reaching base safely in the World Series by a Hispanic player.
October 7, 1972	First Hispanic post-season battery in the major leagues.
October 11, 1972	Hispanic major league player with the highest career WAR metric of the 20th century.
April 6, 1973	First Hispanic major leaguer to have his uniform number retired.
August 6, 1973	First Latin American player inducted into the National Baseball Hall of Fame.
February 6, 1975	First Puerto Rican manager to win the Caribbean Series.
October 12, 1983	First Hispanic battery in the World Series.
October 30, 1984	First Puerto Rican pitcher to win the Cy Young Award.
November 6, 1984	First Hispanic pitcher to win the Cy Young and MVP Awards.
September 26, 1987	Longest consecutive games hitting streak by a major league rookie.
August 18, 1989	Most career games by a Latin American left-handed pitcher in the major leagues.
July 10, 1990	First All-Star father with two All-Star sons and first Hispanic All-Star father-son combination.
June 7, 1992	Youngest Hispanic player to hit three home runs in one game.
July 14, 1992	Youngest Hispanic position player to appear in the All-Star Game.
October 4, 1992	Youngest Hispanic player to lead a major league in home runs.
October 22, 1995	First Hispanic players pitching, catching, and batting at the same time in a World Series game.
July 8, 1997	First Puerto Rican player to win the MVP Award in the major league All-Star Game.
November 18, 1998	First Hispanic player to win the Most Valuable Player Award in a major league twice.
November 19, 1998	First time Hispanic players win Most Valuable Player Awards in both major leagues in the same season.
June 17, 2009	Most games caught by a major league catcher. Most Gold Glove Awards won by a Hispanic major leaguer.
June 23, 2010	First Puerto Rican manager in the major leagues.
June 15, 2012	First Hispanic player to hit 300 home runs and steal 300 bases in the major leagues.

DOMINICAN REPUBLIC

Date	Historical Significance
March 3, 1936	First major league team to play in the Dominican Republic.
October 23, 1955	First professional winter league in the Dominican Republic.
September 23, 1956	First Dominican player to appear in the major leagues.
July 19, 1960	First Dominican pitcher to appear in the major leagues.
September 5, 1960	Oldest Hispanic player to debut in the major leagues.

Date	Historical Significance
June 5, 1961	First Hispanic brothers to pitch in the major leagues.
July 10, 1962	First Dominican player to appear in the major league All-Star Game.
September 10, 1963	First trio of Hispanic brothers in the major leagues.
September 12, 1963	Last shutout at the Polo Grounds.
September 15, 1963	First trio of Hispanic brothers to play in one major league outfield.
July 13, 1965	First Hispanic player to win the MVP Award in the All-Star Game.
June 10, 1966	First Latin American athlete to appear on the cover of *Time*.
March 27, 1967	First Hispanic pitcher to earn $100,000 in annual salary.
July 9, 1968	First pair of Hispanic brothers to play in the All-Star Game.
February 11, 1971	First Caribbean Series tournament victory for the Dominican Republic. First Dominican player to be named MVP in the Caribbean Series. First Dominican manager to win the Caribbean Series.
September 2, 1971	Youngest Hispanic player to hit a grand slam in the major leagues.
May 24, 1976	Hispanic player with the most stolen bases in a major league game
November 26, 1979	First Dominican player to win the Rookie of the Year Award in the major leagues.
October 28, 1981	First Dominican player to win the MVP Award in the World Series.
April 5, 1984	Youngest Hispanic major league pitcher.
May 10, 1984	Youngest Hispanic pitcher to win a major league game.
September 7, 1984	First Hispanic pitcher to steal home.
November 17, 1987	First Dominican player to win the Most Valuable Player Award in the major leagues.
October 1, 1990	Youngest Hispanic pitcher to win 20 games in a major league season.
October 20, 1990	First Hispanic pitcher to win the World Series MVP Award.
May 22, 1992	First Dominican manager in the major leagues.
April 5, 1993	First Hispanic pitchers to oppose one another on Opening Day in the major leagues.
April 5, 1993	First major league game with two Hispanic managers.
June 5, 1993	Hispanic pitching siblings to win the most major league games.
August 11, 1994	First Hispanic to win the Manager of the Year Award in the major leagues.
July 11, 1995	First Hispanic to manage in the major league All-Star Game.
October 22, 1995	First Hispanic players pitching, catching, and batting at the same time in a World Series game.
August 29, 1996	First Hispanic pitching brothers to start a game against each other in the major leagues.
November 11, 1997	First Dominican pitcher to win the Cy Young Award.
November 19, 1998	First time Hispanic players win Most Valuable Player Awards in both major leagues in the same season.
September 27, 1999	Pitcher with the most consecutive games with ten or more strikeouts. Hispanic pitcher with the best single-season FIP metric and the best career FIP metric.
November 16, 1999	First Hispanic pitcher to win the Cy Young Award in both leagues.
November 13, 2000	Pitcher with the fewest baserunners allowed per nine innings in a major league season. Pitcher with lowest opponents' batting average against in a season. Modern era pitcher with the best ERA+ in one season. Hispanic major league pitcher with the highest WAR metric in one season and career.
December 13, 2000	First Hispanic player to earn $20 million in annual salary.
February 12, 2002	First Hispanic general manager in the major leagues.
August 28, 2003	Youngest major league player to hit home runs from both sides of the plate.
September 28, 2003	Youngest Hispanic player to win a major league batting title.
June 3, 2004	Oldest major league player to hit a grand slam home run.
May 4, 2007	Oldest major league player to hit a home run.
June 22, 2007	Most consecutive games played by a Hispanic major league player.

Date	Historical Significance
November 24, 2009	First Hispanic major league player to win the Most Valuable Player Award three times and the first to win the award in back-to-back seasons.
April 7, 2012	First player to play for 13 major league teams.
March 19, 2013	First Latin American team to win the World Baseball Classic. First Hispanic player to win the MVP Award in the World Baseball Classic. First Hispanic manager to win the World Baseball Classic.
April 27, 2014	Most players of the same ethnic nationality in a major league game.
July 10, 2014	Player with the most career total bases as a third baseman.

VENEZUELA

Date	Historical Significance
April 23, 1939	First Venezuelan player to appear in the major leagues.
May 10, 1944	First Venezuelan position player to appear in the major leagues.
January 12, 1946	First professional winter league in Venezuela.
March 1, 1947	First major league team to play in Venezuela.
July 10, 1951	First Hispanic player to appear in the major league All-Star Game.
April 17, 1956	First Hispanic keystone combination in the major leagues.
December 1, 1956	First Hispanic player to win the Rookie of the Year Award in the major leagues.
August 10, 1959	First Hispanic athlete to appear on the cover of *Sports Illustrated.*
February 16, 1961	First Inter-American Series champion.
February 10, 1970	First Caribbean Series tournament victory for the country of Venezuela. First Venezuelan player to be named MVP of the Caribbean Series.
February 9, 1982	First Venezuelan manager to win the Caribbean Series.
July 13, 1982	First Venezuelan player to win the MVP Award in the All-Star Game.
October 12, 1983	First Hispanic battery in the World Series.
January 10, 1984	First Venezuelan player elected to the National Baseball Hall of Fame.
April 3, 1989	Hispanic player to play in the most major league games. Hispanic player to play in the most major league seasons.
August 11, 1991	Youngest Hispanic pitcher to throw a major league no-hit, no-run game.
July 7, 1998	First Venezuelan pitcher to appear in the All-Star Game.
August 30, 1999	Hispanic player with the most runs in one major league game. Hispanic player with the most total bases in one major league game.
June 20, 2003	Youngest Hispanic player to hit a walk-off home run. Youngest Hispanic player to hit a home run in his first major league game.
October 22, 2003	Youngest Hispanic player to hit a home run in the World Series.
April 5, 2004	First Venezuelan manager in the major leagues.
November 11, 2004	First Venezuelan pitcher to win the Cy Young Award.
October 26, 2005	First Latin American manager to win the World Series.
November 9, 2005	First Venezuelan to win the Manager of the Year Award in the major leagues.
February 4, 2006	Youngest manager to win a Caribbean Series.
August 25, 2010	Youngest Hispanic major league pitcher to record 1,000 strikeouts.
October 28, 2012	First Venezuelan player to win the MVP Award in the World Series.
November 15, 2012	First Venezuelan player to win the Most Valuable Player Award in the major leagues.
February 12, 2013	First Hispanic player to earn $25 million in annual salary.
March 28, 2014	First Hispanic player to earn $30 million in annual salary.

PANAMA

Date	Historical Significance
January 3, 1946	First professional winter league in Panama.
February 21, 1946	First major league team to play in Panama.

Date	Historical Significance
February 27, 1950	First Caribbean Series tournament victory for the country of Panama.
April 20, 1955	First Panamanian player to appear in the major leagues.
April 11, 1967	First Panamanian player to win the Rookie of the Year Award in the major leagues.
July 11, 1967	First Panamanian player to appear in the All-Star Game.
May 18, 1969	First Hispanic player to steal three bases in one major league inning.
June 16, 1969	Hispanic player with the most steals of home plate in a major league season.
July 16, 1969	Hispanic major league player with the most lifetime steals of home plate.
September 1, 1971	First all-minority starting lineup in a major league game.
October 7, 1972	First Hispanic post-season battery in the major leagues.
October 2, 1977	First Hispanic player to lead the major leagues in WAR.
November 16, 1977	First Panamanian player to win the Most Valuable Player Award in the major leagues.
October 1, 1980	Hispanic player with the most stolen bases in a major league season.
October 5, 1985	First Hispanic player to have a uniform number retired by more than one major league club. Hispanic player with the most career three-hit games.
July 21, 1991	First Panamanian player inducted into the National Baseball Hall of Fame.
July 8, 1997	First Panamanian pitcher to appear in the All-Star Game.
October 27, 1999	First Panamanian player to win the MVP Award in the World Series.
November 1, 2009	Pitcher with the most World Series appearances.
September 30, 2011	Major league pitcher to appear in the most post-season games.
July 16, 2013	First Panamanian player to win the MVP Award in the All-Star Game.
September 26, 2013	Latin American pitcher to appear in the most major league games and throw the most in innings in relief.

NICARAGUA

Date	Historical Significance
November 1, 1957	First professional winter league in Nicaragua.
September 14, 1976	First Nicaraguan player to appear in the major leagues.
September 4, 1981	First Nicaraguan position player to appear in the major leagues.
July 10, 1990	First Nicaraguan player to appear in the major league All-Star Game.
April 5, 1993	First Hispanic pitchers to oppose one another on Opening Day in the major leagues.
October 22, 1995	First Hispanic players pitching, catching, and batting at the same time in a World Series game.
June 2, 1998	Oldest Hispanic pitcher to throw a major league shutout.

Combined Chronological History: 1871–2015

Date	Historical Significance
May 9, 1871	First Hispanic major leaguer. First Hispanic player to record a hit in a major league.
December 27, 1874	First widely recorded game outside of the United States.
December 29, 1878	First professional league outside of the United States.
April 23, 1902	First Hispanic major league player of the 20th century.
May 14, 1902	First Hispanic player to record a hit in a modern era major league game.
May 29, 1902	First Hispanic player to collect four hits in a modern era major league game.
May 30, 1902	First Hispanic player to hit a home run in the major leagues.
March 10, 1907	First major league team to play in Latin America.
November 15, 1908	First major league team to play in Cuba. First Hispanic pitcher to shut out a major league team.

Appendix B

Date	Historical Significance
November 18, 1909	First Hispanic pitcher to no-hit a major league team.
July 4, 1911	First Hispanic player to record a hit in his first major league at-bat. First Cuban player in the major leagues in the 20th century.
August 1, 1912	First Cuban player to hit a home run in the major leagues.
September 28, 1912	First Hispanic catcher in the major leagues.
June 5, 1913	Youngest Hispanic major leaguer. Youngest Hispanic player to hit a home run in the major leagues.
September 6, 1913	Youngest Hispanic player to hit safely in a major league.
May 20, 1914	First Hispanic pitcher to appear in the major leagues.
May 31, 1914	First Hispanic player ejected from a major league game.
June 16, 1914	First Hispanic player to collect five hits in a modern era major league game.
May 1, 1916	First Hispanic pitcher to surrender a home run in the major leagues.
June 11, 1917	First Hispanic player to register a walk-off steal of home.
May 30, 1918	First Hispanic battery in the major leagues.
June 21, 1918	First Hispanic player to collect five hits in a nine-inning, modern era major league game.
August 8, 1918	First Hispanic pitcher to win a major league game.
August 11, 1918	First Hispanic pitcher and batter to face one another in the major leagues.
September 2, 1918	First Hispanic pitcher to throw a shutout in the major leagues. First Hispanic starting pitchers to oppose one another in the major leagues.
October 3, 1919	First Hispanic player to appear in the World Series and first to strike out a batter in the World Series.
June 26, 1920	First Hispanic pitcher ejected from a major league game.
April 13, 1921	First Hispanic pitcher to start a major league Opening Day game.
June 19, 1923	First Hispanic pitcher to throw an extra-inning shutout in the major leagues.
July 17, 1923	First Hispanic pitcher to start and win both games of a major league doubleheader.
August 15, 1923	First Hispanic pitcher to hit a home run in the major leagues.
August 24, 1923	First Hispanic pitcher to win 20 games in a major league season.
September 29, 1923	First Hispanic pitcher to lead a major league in wins and ERA.
October 14, 1924	First Hispanic manager to win a North American league pennant. First Hispanic player to appear in the Negro Leagues World Series.
October 20, 1924	First Hispanic pitcher to win a North American championship game. First Hispanic manager to win a North American championship title.
May 3, 1925	First Hispanic pitcher to win 100 major league games.
June 28, 1925	First professional league in Mexico.
April 29, 1926	First Hispanic major leaguer to record two hits in one inning. Most lifetime hits recorded by a Hispanic pitcher in the major leagues.
August 22, 1926	Longest hitting streak by a Hispanic major league pitcher.
September 26, 1927	Pitcher with the best ERA in games lost of nine innings or more with three or fewer runs allowed.
October 8, 1929	First Hispanic position player to play in the World Series.
September 17, 1930	First Hispanic pitcher to record 200 complete games in the major leagues.
September 8, 1933	First Mexican player to appear in the major leagues. First Mexican player to record a hit in the major leagues.
September 23, 1933	First Mexican player to hit a home run in the major leagues.
October 7, 1933	First Hispanic pitcher to win a World Series game. First Hispanic player to hit safely in the World Series.
December 9, 1933	First Hispanic coach in the major leagues.
April 23, 1935	First Hispanic pitching coach in the major leagues.
August 11, 1935	First Hispanic player in the Negro Leagues All-Star Game. First Hispanic player to record a hit in the Negro Leagues All-Star Game. First Hispanic pitcher in the Negro Leagues All-Star Game.

Date	Historical Significance
February 27, 1936	First major league team to play in Puerto Rico.
March 3, 1936	First major league team to play in the Dominican Republic.
July 21, 1937	First Hispanic player to hit a leadoff home run in the major leagues.
July 25, 1937	Player with the most runs scored in a major league doubleheader.
July 31, 1938	First Hispanic major league player to record 50 hits in one month.
September 14, 1938	First Hispanic manager in the major leagues.
November 13, 1938	First professional winter league in Puerto Rico.
April 23, 1939	First Venezuelan player to appear in the major leagues.
May 3, 1939	First Venezuelan pitcher to win a major league game.
May 14, 1939	First Venezuelan player to record a hit in the major leagues.
May 18, 1939	First Hispanic player to hit a walk-off home run in the major leagues.
May 30, 1939	First Venezuelan player to hit a home run in the major leagues.
April 25, 1940	First Hispanic father-son major leaguer duo.
September 24, 1941	First Hispanic manager in North American organized baseball.
April 15, 1942	First Puerto Rican player to appear in the major leagues.
April 16, 1942	First Mexican pitcher to appear in the major leagues.
June 5, 1942	First Puerto Rican pitcher to win a major league game. First Puerto Rican player to record a hit in the major leagues.
July 18, 1942	First Venezuelan pitcher to throw a major league shutout.
April 27, 1943	First Mexican pitcher to win a major league game.
April 28, 1943	First Puerto Rican pitcher to throw a major league shutout. First shutout recorded in the major leagues by a Hispanic battery.
July 23, 1943	First Puerto Rican position player in the major leagues.
July 26, 1943	First Puerto Rican player to hit a home run in the major leagues.
May 10, 1944	First Venezuelan position player to appear in the major leagues.
July 2, 1944	First Mexican pitcher to throw a major league shutout.
September 16, 1944	First Hispanic pitcher to throw a major league one-hit game.
October 5, 1944	First pitcher to win 30 games in a Latin American league season.
May 6, 1945	First Hispanic player to record eight hits in a major league doubleheader. First Hispanic player to drive in six runs in a major league game.
May 18, 1945	First Hispanic player to hit a grand slam home run in the major leagues. First Hispanic player to drive in seven runs in a major league game.
August 28, 1945	First Hispanic player to drive in 100 runs in a major league season. First Hispanic player to lead a major league in triples.
January 3, 1946	First professional winter league in Panama.
January 12, 1946	First professional winter league in Venezuela.
February 18, 1946	First signings of major league players in the "player war" with Mexico.
February 21, 1946	First major league team to play in Panama.
October 26, 1946	First million-dollar baseball stadium in Latin America.
March 1, 1947	First major league team to play in Venezuela.
September 24, 1947	First Hispanic player to hit a home run in the Negro Leagues World Series.
August 24, 1948	First Hispanic player to hit a home run in the Negro Leagues East-West All-Star Game.
February 20, 1949	First pitcher to win a Caribbean Series game. First player to hit a home run in the Caribbean Series. First Cuban pitcher to win a Caribbean Series game.
February 21, 1949	First Venezuelan pitcher to win a Caribbean Series game.
February 25, 1949	First Caribbean Series champion. First Caribbean Series-winning manager. First Caribbean Series MVP. First Cuban player to hit a home run in the Caribbean Series.
July 17, 1949	First Hispanic player to hit a fence-clearing, walk-off home run in the major leagues.
October 7, 1949	First Hispanic player to hit a home run in the World Series. First Hispanic position player to start a World Series game.

Date	Historical Significance
February 23, 1950	First Puerto Rican pitcher to win a Caribbean Series game.
February 27, 1950	First Caribbean Series tournament victory for the country of Panama. First Hispanic player to play in the World Series and the Caribbean Series.
June 25, 1950	First Hispanic pitchers to start both games of a major league doubleheader.
February 16, 1951	First Hispanic player to record a championship-winning, walk-off home run in the Latin American Winter Leagues.
February 25, 1951	First Puerto Rican player to hit a home run in the Caribbean Series.
February 26, 1951	First Caribbean Series tournament victory for the country of Puerto Rico. First player to hit two home runs in a Caribbean Series game. First Puerto Rican player to be named MVP in the Caribbean Series.
April 17, 1951	First Hispanic pitcher to start an American League season-opening game.
June 20, 1951	First Hispanic player to hit three home runs in a major league game. First Mexican player to record five hits in a major league game.
July 10, 1951	First Hispanic player to appear in the major league All-Star Game. First Hispanic player to record a hit in the All-Star Game. First Cuban player to appear in the All-Star Game.
August 22, 1951	First Mexican player to hit a walk-off home run in the major leagues.
September 2, 1952	First Hispanic pitcher to throw a one-hitter in his major league debut.
February 20, 1953	First Hispanic pitcher to hit a home run in the Caribbean Series.
February 22, 1953	First Hispanic player to record a walk-off hit in the Caribbean Series.
February 24, 1953	First Panamanian to hit a home run in the Caribbean Series.
May 2, 1953	First Hispanic player to hit three triples in a major league game.
February 20, 1954	First Hispanic pitcher to throw a shutout in the Caribbean Series.
July 13, 1954	First Hispanic pitcher to appear in the major league All-Star Game. First Mexican player to appear in the major league All-Star Game.
July 30, 1954	First Puerto Rican pitcher to hit a home run in the major leagues.
August 27, 1954	First Hispanic player to lead a major league in total bases.
September 26, 1954	First Hispanic player to win a major league batting title.
October 1, 1954	First Latin American pitcher to start a World Series game. First pitcher to win a World Series and a Caribbean Series game. First Puerto Rican pitcher to win a World Series game.
February 10, 1955	First Venezuelan pitcher to throw a shutout in the Caribbean Series.
April 20, 1955	First Panamanian player to appear in the major leagues.
April 23, 1955	First Venezuelan player to record five hits in a major league game.
April 24, 1955	First all–Hispanic outfield in the major leagues.
May 6, 1955	First Panamanian pitcher to win a major league game.
May 12, 1955	First Panamanian player to record a hit in the major leagues.
May 29, 1955	First Puerto Rican player to record five hits in a major league game.
June 26, 1955	First Panamanian player to hit a home run in the major leagues.
July 12, 1955	First Puerto Rican player to appear in the major league All-Star Game.
October 2, 1955	First Cuban player to hit a home run in the World Series.
October 4, 1955	Sandy Amoros' victory-preserving World Series catch for the Brooklyn Dodgers.
October 23, 1955	First professional winter league in the Dominican Republic.
February 11, 1956	Youngest pitcher to win a Caribbean Series game.
February 15, 1956	First Hispanic player to hit a grand slam home run in the Caribbean Series.
April 17, 1956	First Hispanic keystone combination in the major leagues.
May 19, 1956	First Panamanian player to hit a walk-off home run in the major leagues.
July 25, 1956	First Hispanic player to hit an inside-the-park, walk-off grand slam home run in the major leagues.
July 27, 1956	First Panamanian player to record five hits in a major league game.
August 31, 1956	First Hispanic major leaguer to record 1,000 hits.
September 23, 1956	First Dominican player to appear in the major leagues.

Date	Historical Significance
September 30, 1956	First Dominican player to record a hit in the major leagues.
December 1, 1956	First Hispanic player to win the Rookie of the Year Award in the major leagues.
February 11, 1957	First Puerto Rican pitcher to throw a shutout in the Caribbean Series.
February 14, 1957	First Panamanian pitcher to throw a shutout in the Caribbean Series.
April 27, 1957	First Dominican player to hit a home run in the major leagues.
May 7, 1957	First Hispanic major leaguer to hit a leadoff and walk-off home run in the same game.
May 10, 1957	Youngest Hispanic pitcher to hit a home run in the major leagues.
October 5, 1957	Youngest Hispanic pitcher to appear in the World Series.
November 1, 1957	First professional winter league in Nicaragua.
February 8, 1958	Pitcher with the most strikeouts in a Caribbean Series game. Pitcher with the most career strikeouts in the Caribbean Series.
April 15, 1958	Pitcher with the first win and shutout in a major league game played in California. First Hispanic player to hit a home run in his initial major league game.
May 4, 1958	First Cuban player to hit three home runs in a major league game.
June 17, 1958	First Dominican player to record five hits in a major league game.
June 26, 1958	First Panamanian player to hit three home runs in one game.
August 14, 1958	First Hispanic player to steal home twice in one major league game.
January 9, 1959	First Puerto Rican to win the league Rookie of the Year award in the major leagues.
August 10, 1959	First Hispanic athlete to appear on the cover of *Sports Illustrated*.
September 9, 1959	First Hispanic major leaguer to hit a fence-clearing, walk-off grand slam home run.
September 15, 1959	First Hispanic pitcher to lead a major league in shutouts and complete games.
October 6, 1959	First Latin American-based team to win a North American league championship title.
February 14, 1960	First Hispanic pitcher to throw a one-hit Caribbean Series game. Pitcher with the most complete games in the Caribbean Series. Pitchers with the most victories in the Caribbean Series.
February 14, 1960	First Hispanic player to hit a walk-off home run in the Caribbean Series.
February 15, 1960	The last champion of the original Caribbean Series.
April 18, 1960	Pitcher with the most strikeouts on Opening Day in the major leagues.
July 19, 1960	First Dominican pitcher to appear in the major leagues. First Dominican pitcher to win a major league game and throw a shutout.
July 23, 1960	First all–Hispanic triple play in the major leagues.
August 14, 1960	First Hispanic pitcher to hit a grand slam home run in the major leagues.
September 5, 1960	Oldest Hispanic player to debut in the major leagues.
September 30, 1960	First Hispanic player to lead a major league in hits.
October 12, 1960	First Hispanic pitcher to lead a major league in saves.
February 8, 1961	Last game of the Cuban Winter League.
February 16, 1961	First Inter-American Series champion.
April 11, 1961	First Hispanic pitcher to throw an Opening Day shutout in the major leagues.
May 15, 1961	First Hispanic brothers to hit home runs in the same major league game.
June 5, 1961	First Hispanic brothers to pitch in the major leagues.
July 4, 1961	First Hispanic player to drive in eight runs in a major league game.
August 9, 1961	First Dominican player to hit a walk-off home run in the major leagues.
September 9, 1961	Hispanic relief pitcher with the most wins in a major league season.
September 10, 1961	First Hispanic player to hit 40 home runs in a major league season.
September 22, 1961	First Hispanic player to record 200 hits in a major league season.
September 26, 1961	First Puerto Rican player to win a major league batting title. Hispanic player with the most outfield assists in one major league season.

Date	*Historical Significance*
September 27, 1961	First Hispanic player to lead a major league in home runs and RBI.
September 29, 1961	First Hispanic pitcher to lead a major league in strikeouts. First Hispanic pitcher to strike out 200 batters in a major league season.
October 9, 1961	First Panamanian player to hit a home run in the World Series.
July 10, 1962	First Hispanic pitcher to record a win in the major league All-Star Game. First Dominican player to appear in the All-Star Game.
May 30, 1962	First Hispanic pitcher to hit two home runs in one major league game.
February 8, 1963	First Hispanic pitcher to throw a no-hit, no-run game in a winter league championship tournament.
June 15, 1963	First Hispanic major league pitcher to throw a no-hit, no-run game.
July 2, 1963	Hispanic pitcher to throw the longest extra-inning shutout in the major leagues.
September 3, 1963	First Dominican pitcher to win 20 games in the major leagues.
September 10, 1963	First trio of Hispanic brothers in the major leagues.
September 12, 1963	First Dominican pitcher to hit a home run in the major leagues. Last shutout at the Polo Grounds.
September 15, 1963	First trio of Hispanic brothers to play in one major league outfield.
September 27, 1963	First Hispanic two-time 20-game winner in the major leagues. First Hispanic pitcher to lead a major league in shutouts, strikeouts and complete games three times each.
September 28, 1963	First Hispanic pitcher to lead a major league in innings pitched.
July 4, 1964	First Dominican player to hit three home runs in one major league game.
July 10, 1964	First Hispanic player to collect six hits in a major league game.
July 23, 1964	First Hispanic player to hit a home run in his first major league at-bat.
October 4, 1964	First major league rookie to win the batting title.
November 28, 1964	First Cuban player to win the Rookie of the Year Award in the major leagues. First Hispanic player to lead a major league in runs scored.
April 13, 1965	First Hispanic player to hit a grand slam as his first career home run.
July 13, 1965	First Hispanic player to win the MVP Award in the All-Star Game.
September 8, 1965	First player to play all nine positions in a major league game.
September 9, 1965	Hispanic pitcher with the most shutouts in one major league season.
October 3, 1965	First player to win batting titles in his first two major league seasons.
November 18, 1965	First Hispanic player to win the Most Valuable Player Award in the major leagues.
May 26, 1966	First Hispanic pitcher to win 25 games in a major league season twice.
June 5, 1966	First Hispanic major leaguer to hit four home runs in a doubleheader.
June 10, 1966	First Latin American athlete to appear on the cover of *Time*.
September 2, 1966	First Hispanic major league player to record 2,000 hits.
September 21, 1966	First Hispanic major league pitcher to hit a walk-off home run.
October 2, 1966	Hispanic player to lead the league in hits the most times.
October 2, 1966	First Dominican player to win a major league batting title.
November 16, 1966	First Puerto Rican player to win the Most Valuable Player Award in the major leagues.
January 25, 1967	First Hispanic player to earn $100,000 in annual salary.
March 27, 1967	First Hispanic pitcher to earn $100,000 in annual salary.
April 11, 1967	First Panamanian player to win the Rookie of the Year Award in the major leagues.
May 15, 1967	First Puerto Rican player to hit three home runs in one major league game.
June 12, 1967	Most innings caught by a Hispanic catcher in a major league game.
July 11, 1967	First Hispanic player to hit a home run in the major league All-Star Game. First Cuban player to win the MVP Award in the All-Star Game. First Panamanian player to appear in the All-Star Game.
September 27, 1967	Hispanic pitcher with the most 1–0, complete-game victories in the major leagues.

Date	Historical Significance
October 4, 1967	First Hispanic player to hit a home run in his first World Series at-bat.
October 12, 1967	First Dominican player to hit a home run in the World Series.
November 7, 1967	First Hispanic player to win the Most Valuable Player Award in the major leagues unanimously. First Hispanic player to win the Rookie of the Year and MVP Awards.
April 15, 1968	First Hispanic major league pitcher to record 2,000 strikeouts.
May 17, 1968	Longest consecutive scoreless innings streak by a Hispanic major league pitcher.
July 3, 1968	Hispanic pitcher with the most strikeouts in a major league game.
July 9, 1968	First pair of Hispanic brothers to play in the All-Star Game.
August 1, 1968	Hispanic pitcher with the most complete games and innings in one major league season. Hispanic pitcher with the most consecutive complete games in one season. Hispanic major league pitcher with the most career complete games.
August 29, 1968	First full-time Hispanic manager in the major leagues hired.
September 25, 1968	Hispanic pitcher with the lowest ERA in a major league season. Hispanic pitcher with fewest hits allowed per nine innings in a season. First Hispanic pitcher to record an ERA under 2.00 with 200 strikeouts.
April 8, 1969	First American League pitcher to record a major league save as an official statistic.
April 23, 1969	First Hispanic pitcher to win the Cy Young Award.
May 18, 1969	First Hispanic player to steal three bases in one major league inning.
June 16, 1969	Hispanic player with the most steals of home in a major league season.
June 21, 1969	Major league player with the most consecutive games with a stolen base.
July 16, 1969	Hispanic player with the most lifetime steals of home.
August 5, 1969	First Hispanic major league player to record 2,500 hits.
August 13, 1969	First Hispanic player to hit three home runs in a game twice.
August 29, 1969	First Hispanic major league pitcher to record 100 more career wins than losses.
September 5, 1969	First Hispanic left-handed pitcher to win 20 games in the major leagues.
September 16, 1969	Hispanic pitcher with the most 20-game-winning seasons.
October 1, 1969	First Panamanian player to win a major league batting title.
October 11, 1969	First Hispanic pitcher to throw a complete-game World Series victory.
February 2, 1970	First Dominican player to hit a home run in the Caribbean Series.
February 10, 1970	First Caribbean Series tournament victory for the country of Venezuela. First Venezuelan player to be named MVP of the Caribbean Series.
May 12, 1970	First Hispanic player to hit in 30 consecutive major league games.
May 20, 1970	First Hispanic major leaguer to hit for the cycle.
May 30, 1970	First Mexican pitcher to hit a home run in the major leagues.
June 21, 1970	First Hispanic player to collect seven hits in a major league game.
August 22–23, 1970	First Hispanic major leaguer with ten hits in consecutive games.
August 28, 1970	First Hispanic pitcher to win 200 major league games.
September 9, 1970	Latin American left-handed pitcher to record the most wins in a major league season. Hispanic pitchers to record the most wins in consecutive major league seasons and most starts in one major league season.
September 15, 1970	First Hispanic player to hit 20 home runs and steal 20 bases in one major league season.
October 3, 1970	First player to hit a grand slam home run in the League Championship Series.
October 15, 1970	First Hispanic starting pitcher to win a clinching World Series game.
February 6, 1971	First Mexican player to hit a home run in the Caribbean Series.
February 6, 1971	First Dominican pitcher to win a Caribbean Series game.
February 9, 1971	First Mexican pitcher to win a Caribbean Series game.
February 11, 1971	First Caribbean Series tournament victory for the country of the Dominican Republic. First Dominican player to be named MVP in the Caribbean Series. First Dominican manager to win the Caribbean Series.

Date	Historical Significance
April 25, 1971	First Hispanic player to lead a major league in slugging.
June 4, 1971	Hispanic left-handed pitcher with the most shutouts in the major leagues.
July 13, 1971	First Puerto Rican player to hit a home run in the major league All-Star Game.
August 10, 1971	First Hispanic pitcher to record 50 shutouts in the major leagues.
August 24, 1971	First Panamanian pitcher to throw a shutout in the major leagues.
August 25, 1971	First Hispanic major league player to record eight five-hit games.
September 1, 1971	First all-minority starting lineup in a major league game.
September 2, 1971	Youngest Hispanic player to hit a grand slam home run in the major leagues.
October 4, 1971	First Hispanic major league pitcher to win a League Championship Series game.
October 17, 1971	First Hispanic player to win the MVP Award in the World Series. First Hispanic player to win both World Series MVP and league MVP Awards. Most consecutive games reaching base safely in the World Series by a Hispanic player. First Hispanic player to record a World Series-deciding, game-winning RBI.
February 4, 1972	First Dominican pitcher to throw a shutout in the Caribbean Series.
August 2, 1972	First Dominican major leaguer to hit for the cycle.
September 4, 1972	First major league pitcher to throw four consecutive shutouts twice.
September 10, 1972	First Hispanic player with 20 home runs and 50 steals in one major league season.
September 19, 1972	First Hispanic major leaguer to complete the cycle with a walk-off home run. First Venezuelan player to hit for the cycle with a walk-off home run.
September 20, 1972	First Hispanic player to win the Comeback Player of the Year Award.
September 30, 1972	First Hispanic major leaguer to record 3,000 hits. Puerto Rican player with the most hits in the major leagues.
October 7, 1972	First Hispanic major league player to record a walk-off hit in the post-season.
October 7, 1972	First Hispanic post-season battery in the major leagues.
October 11, 1972	Hispanic major leaguer with the highest career WAR metric of the 20th century.
October 19, 1972	First Hispanic player to record a walk-off hit in the World Series.
April 5, 1973	Hispanic pitcher with the most Opening Day wins.
April 6, 1973	First Hispanic major leaguer to have his uniform number retired.
April 6, 1973	First major league designated hitter to hit a home run.
July 15, 1973	Hispanic major league pitcher with the most career shutouts.
August 6, 1973	First Hispanic player inducted into the National Baseball Hall of Fame.
October 9, 1973	First Hispanic player to hit a post-season, walk-off home run.
October 9, 1973	First Hispanic major league pitcher to record a post-season save.
February 1, 1974	First Mexican player to be named MVP in the Caribbean Series.
February 6, 1974	First Mexican pitcher to throw a shutout in the Caribbean Series.
May 29, 1974	Latin American left-handed pitcher with the most complete games in the major leagues.
August 27, 1974	First Puerto Rican player to hit a home run in his first major league at-bat.
February 6, 1975	First Puerto Rican manager to win the Caribbean Series.
April 17, 1975	Dominican pitcher with the most wins in the major leagues.
July 30, 1975	First Hispanic pitcher to hit a home run in his first major league at-bat.
September 16, 1975	First modern era major leaguer to record seven hits in a nine-inning game. First Hispanic player to record two hits in an inning in the same game twice.
September 28, 1975	First Hispanic major leaguer to record four consecutive batting titles.
October 11, 1975	First Hispanic pitcher to throw a shutout in the World Series.
October 14, 1975	First Venezuelan player to hit a home run in the World Series.
October 15, 1975	First Hispanic pitcher to win two games in one World Series.
October 16, 1975	First Hispanic player to hit two home runs in a World Series game.

Date	Historical Significance
February 9, 1976	First Caribbean Series tournament victory for the country of Mexico. First player to be named Caribbean Series MVP twice.
May 24, 1976	Hispanic players with the most stolen bases in a major league game.
June 20, 1976	Latin American left-handed pitcher with the most major league wins.
July 13, 1976	First Dominican player to hit a home run in the major league All-Star Game.
September 12, 1976	Oldest major league player to record a hit. First Hispanic major leaguer to play in four decades.
September 14, 1976	First Nicaraguan player to appear in the major leagues. First Nicaraguan pitcher to win a major league game.
August 8, 1977	First Cuban player inducted into the National Baseball Hall of Fame.
February 9, 1977	First player to hit five home runs in the Caribbean Series.
October 2, 1977	Hispanic player with the highest single-season batting average in the major leagues. Hispanic player with the most hits in a major league season. Hispanic player with the most hits in a single month. First Hispanic player to lead the major leagues in WAR.
November 16, 1977	First Panamanian player to win the Most Valuable Player Award in the major leagues.
June 16, 1978	First Nicaraguan pitcher to throw a major league shutout.
September 30, 1978	Hispanic player with the most major league batting titles.
September 30, 1978	First Puerto Rican pitcher to win 20 games in a major league season.
June 23, 1979	First Hispanic pitcher to strike out the side on nine pitches.
July 8, 1979	Cuban pitcher with the most wins and shutouts in the major leagues.
November 26, 1979	First Dominican player to win the Rookie of the Year Award in the major leagues.
April 22, 1980	First Puerto Rican major leaguer to hit for the cycle.
October 1, 1980	Hispanic player with the most stolen bases in a major league season.
October 4, 1980	First Hispanic major leaguer to play in five decades. First Hispanic player to lead a major league in stolen bases.
October 5, 1980	First Panamanian player to lead a major league in home runs.
April 9, 1981	Youngest Hispanic pitcher to start an Opening Day game in the major leagues.
April 22, 1981	First Hispanic rookie to lead a major league in strikeouts.
April 27, 1981	First rookie pitcher to win the Silver Slugger Award.
May 4, 1981	First Hispanic brothers to hit home runs as opponents in the same major league game.
May 8, 1981	First Hispanic pitcher to throw five shutouts in seven starts.
May 14, 1981	Hispanic pitcher with the most consecutive wins at the start of a career.
August 9, 1981	Youngest Hispanic player to appear in the major league All-Star Game. First Mexican pitcher to appear in the All-Star Game.
September 4, 1981	First Nicaraguan position player to appear in the major leagues.
September 17, 1981	Hispanic rookie pitcher with the most shutouts in a major league season.
September 26, 1981	First Nicaraguan player to record a hit in the major leagues.
October 3, 1981	First Venezuelan player to lead a major league in home runs.
October 23, 1981	Youngest Hispanic pitcher to win a World Series game. First Mexican pitcher to win a World Series game. Hispanic major league pitcher to record the most post-season innings.
October 28, 1981	First Dominican player to win the World Series MVP Award
November 11, 1981	First major league rookie and youngest Hispanic pitcher to win the Cy Young Award.
December 2, 1981	First Mexican player and youngest Hispanic player to win the Rookie of the Year Award in the major leagues.
February 9, 1982	First Venezuelan manager to win the Caribbean Series.
July 13, 1982	First Venezuelan player to hit a home run in the major league All-Star Game. First Venezuelan player to win the MVP Award in the All-Star Game.

Date	Historical Significance
August 15, 1982	First Nicaraguan player to hit a home run in the major leagues.
September 19, 1982	First Hispanic player to hit a grand slam home run as his first major league hit.
October 15, 1982	First Dominican pitcher to win a World Series game.
February 18, 1983	First Hispanic player to earn $1,000,000 in annual salary.
May 6, 1983	Hispanic player with the most consecutive .300 seasons in the major leagues.
July 31, 1983	First Dominican player inducted into the National Baseball Hall of Fame. Hispanic major league pitcher with the best ERA+ metric of the 20th century.
October 12, 1983	First Hispanic battery in the World Series.
August 24, 1983	Hispanic major leaguer with the most career stolen bases.
January 10, 1984	First Venezuelan player elected to the National Baseball Hall of Fame.
April 5, 1984	Youngest Hispanic major league pitcher.
May 10, 1984	Youngest Hispanic pitcher to win a major league game.
June 1, 1984	Minor leaguer with the most lifetime home runs.
September 7, 1984	First Hispanic pitcher to steal home.
September 28, 1984	First Venezuelan player to lead a major league in RBI.
October 12, 1984	First Hispanic pitcher to record a World Series save.
October 30, 1984	First Puerto Rican pitcher to win the Cy Young Award.
November 6, 1984	First Hispanic pitcher to win the Cy Young and MVP Awards.
April 28, 1985	Most consecutive innings without an earned run allowed to start a major league season.
June 14, 1985	First Nicaraguan player to hit a walk-off home run in the major leagues.
August 4, 1985	First Hispanic major leaguer with 3,000 hits and 300 stolen bases. Hispanic major league player with the most hits in the 20th century.
October 5, 1985	First Hispanic player to have a uniform number retired by more than one major league club. Hispanic player with the most career three-hit games.
October 6, 1985	First Hispanic player to hit a home run in his final major league at-bat.
July 15, 1986	Hispanic pitcher with the most consecutive strikeouts in the All-Star Game.
September 22, 1986	First Mexican pitcher to win 20 games in a major league season. First Hispanic pitcher to lead the major leagues in WAR.
April 15, 1987	First Puerto Rican pitcher to throw a major league no-hit, no-run game.
July 8, 1987	First Honduran player to appear in the major leagues.
July 9, 1987	First Honduran player to record a hit in the major leagues.
September 16, 1987	First Honduran player to hit a home run in the major leagues.
September 26, 1987	Longest consecutive game hitting streak by a major league rookie.
November 17, 1987	First Dominican player to win the Most Valuable Player Award in the major leagues. First Dominican player to lead a major league in RBI.
April 4, 1988	First major leaguer to hit three home runs on Opening Day.
August 6, 1988	First Hispanic major leaguer to hit 30 home runs and steal 30 bases in one season.
September 23, 1988	First player to hit 40 home runs and steal 40 bases in a major league season. First Cuban player to lead a major league in home runs and RBI.
October 15, 1988	First Hispanic player to hit a grand slam home run in the World Series.
April 3, 1989	Hispanic player to play in the most major league games. Hispanic player to play in the most major league seasons.
August 18, 1989	Most career games by a Hispanic left-handed pitcher in the major leagues.
June 4, 1990	Hispanic major league pitcher with the most strikeouts in a nine-inning game.
June 27, 1990	First major leaguer to earn $5 million in annual salary.
June 29, 1990	First Mexican pitcher to throw a major league no-hit, no-run game.
July 10, 1990	First Nicaraguan player to appear in the major league All-Star Game. First All-Star father with two All-Star sons and first Hispanic All-Star father-son combination.
October 1, 1990	Youngest Hispanic pitcher to win 20 games in a major league season.

Date   *Historical Significance*

October 20, 1990   First Hispanic pitcher to win the World Series MVP Award.
July 5, 1991   First Belizean player to appear and record a hit in the major leagues.
July 11, 1991   First Belizean player to hit a home run in the major leagues.
July 21, 1991   First Panamanian player inducted into the National Baseball Hall of Fame.
July 28, 1991   First Hispanic pitcher to throw a perfect game in the major leagues.
August 11, 1991   Youngest Hispanic pitcher to throw a major league no-hit, no-run game. First Venezuelan pitcher to throw a major league no-hit, no-run game.
May 22, 1992   First Dominican manager in the major leagues.
June 7, 1992   Youngest Hispanic major leaguer to hit three home runs in one game.
July 14, 1992   Youngest Hispanic position player to appear in the major league All-Star Game.
September 24, 1992   Hispanic major league pitcher with the most career strikeouts.
October 4, 1992   Youngest Hispanic player to lead a major league in home runs.
April 5, 1993   First Hispanic pitchers to oppose one another on Opening Day in the major leagues. First major league game with two Hispanic managers.
April 8, 1993   First major leaguer to hit home runs from both sides of the plate in one inning. First Hispanic major leaguer to hit two home runs in one inning.
June 5, 1993   Hispanic pitching siblings with the most major league wins.
September 28, 1993   First Hispanic pitcher to win 100 games in both major leagues.
October 3, 1993   First Venezuelan player to win a major league batting title.
October 19, 1993   First Hispanic player to record four hits in a World Series game.
October 20, 1993   First Venezuelan pitcher to win a World Series game.
October 23, 1993   First Hispanic player to record 12 hits in a World Series.
August 11, 1994   First Hispanic to win the Manager of the Year Award in the major leagues.
February 7, 1995   First player to record seven consecutive hits in the Caribbean Series.
June 3, 1995   First Hispanic pitcher to take a perfect game past nine innings.
June 25, 1995   First Hispanic major leaguer to hit home runs in three consecutive innings. First Venezuelan player to hit three home runs in one game.
July 11, 1995   First Latin American to manage in the major league All-Star Game.
October 6, 1995   First player to hit home runs from both sides of the plate in a post-season game.
October 22, 1995   First Hispanic players pitching, catching, and batting at the same time in a World Series game.
August 16, 1996   First major league regular season game played outside of the U.S. and Canada.
August 29, 1996   First Hispanic pitching brothers to start a game against each other in the major leagues.
May 23, 1997   Mexican pitcher with the most wins, shutouts, complete games and innings in the major leagues.
June 12, 1997   First player to hit an interleague home run in the major leagues.
July 8, 1997   First Hispanic pitcher to record a save in the All-Star Game. First Puerto Rican to win the MVP Award in the major league All-Star Game. First Panamanian pitcher to appear in the All-Star Game.
July 12, 1997   First combined extra-inning no-hitter in the major leagues.
September 25, 1997   First Hispanic pitcher to strike out 300 batters in a season.
October 12, 1997   Hispanic major league pitcher with the most strikeouts in one post-season game.
October 26, 1997   First Hispanic player to record a walk-off, World Series-winning hit. First Cuban player to win the MVP Award in the World Series.
November 11, 1997   First Dominican pitcher to win the Cy Young Award.
June 2, 1998   Oldest Hispanic pitcher to throw a major league shutout. Nicaraguan pitcher with the most major league shutouts.
June 20, 1998   Major league player with the most home runs in a 30-day span.
June 25, 1998   Major league player with the most home runs in a single month.
July 5, 1998   First Hispanic player to record 100 RBI prior to the major league All-Star Game.

Date	Historical Significance
July 7, 1998	First Colombian player to appear in the major league All-Star Game. First Venezuelan pitcher to appear in the All-Star Game.
August 9, 1998	Hispanic pitcher with the most wins, starts, and innings in the major leagues.
August 10, 1998	Hispanic player with the most multi-home run games in one major league season.
August 23, 1998	First Hispanic player to hit 50 home runs in a major league season.
September 12, 1998	First Hispanic player to hit 60 home runs in a major league season.
September 18, 1998	First Hispanic player to record 40 home runs and 200 hits in a major league season.
September 25, 1998	Hispanic player with the most home runs in one major league season.
November 18, 1998	First Hispanic player to win a major league Most Valuable Player Award twice. First Hispanic player to record 50 doubles and 40 home runs in a major league season.
November 19, 1998	First time Hispanic players win Most Valuable Player Awards in both major leagues in the same season.
April 4, 1999	First major league regular season-opening game played outside of the U.S. and Canada.
April 6, 1999	Hispanic major leaguer with the most home runs as a teenager.
April 13, 1999	First Hispanic player to drive in nine runs in a major league game.
April 14, 1999	First Hispanic player to hit 400 home runs in the major leagues.
April 23, 1999	First major league player to hit two grand slam home runs in one inning, and most RBI by a player in one inning.
May 7, 1999	First Panamanian player to hit a home run in his first major league at-bat.
August 14, 1999	First major league catcher with 20 home runs and 20 steals in the same season.
August 30, 1999	Hispanic player with the most runs in one major league game. Hispanic player with the most total bases in one major league game.
September 18, 1999	First player to hit 60 home runs in a major league season twice.
September 21, 1999	First Hispanic pitcher to strike out 300 batters in both major leagues. Hispanic pitcher with the most strikeouts per nine innings in a season.
September 26, 1999	Hispanic player with the most RBI in a major league season.
September 27, 1999	Pitcher with the most consecutive games with ten or more strikeouts. Hispanic pitcher with the best single-season FIP metric. Hispanic pitcher with the best career FIP metric.
October 2, 1999	First Latin American major league hurler to win pitching's Triple Crown.
October 2, 1999	First Nicaraguan player to record five hits in a major league game. Nicaraguan player with the most career hits and home runs in the major leagues.
October 26, 1999	First Panamanian pitcher to win a World Series game.
October 27, 1999	First Panamanian player to win the MVP Award in the World Series.
November 16, 1999	First Hispanic pitcher to win the Cy Young Award in both leagues.
January 10, 2000	Most career pinch-hit home runs by a Hispanic major leaguer.
April 23, 2000	First major league teammates to hit home runs from both sides of the plate in the same game.
July 23, 2000	Hispanic major league pitcher with the best career strikeout-to-walk ratio.
July 29, 2000	First Colombian player to record five hits in a major league game.
September 16, 2000	First Dominican player to lead a major league in home runs.
October 13, 2000	Major league pitcher with the most consecutive post-season scoreless innings.
November 13, 2000	Pitcher with the fewest baserunners allowed per nine innings in a major league season. Pitcher with the lowest opponents' batting average against in a season. Modern era pitcher with the best ERA+ in one season. Hispanic major league pitcher with the highest WAR metric in one season and career.
December 13, 2000	Hispanic player with the most consecutive seasons with an OPS of .900. First Hispanic player to earn $20 million in annual salary.

Date	*Historical Significance*
June 17, 2001	First Colombian player to hit a walk-off home run in the major leagues.
August 11, 2001	First Hispanic major league pitcher to record eight straight hits.
August 17, 2001	First Hispanic rookie to hit three home runs in a major league game.
August 26, 2001	First Hispanic major leaguer to hit 50 home runs in four consecutive seasons.
September 23, 2001	First major leaguer to hit three home runs in a game three times in one season. Hispanic player with the highest OPS in one major league season.
October 3, 2001	Hispanic major leaguer with the most home runs in the 20th century.
October 7, 2001	Hispanic player with the most home runs in one major league season. Hispanic player with the most total bases in one major league season. Hispanic player with the most runs in one major league season. First Hispanic player to collect 100 extra-base hits and slug .700 in one major league season.
October 7, 2001	Hispanic rookie player with the most home runs and RBI in one major league season.
October 14, 2001	Hispanic pitcher with the most major league post-season wins.
February 12, 2002	First Hispanic general manager in the major leagues.
June 15, 2002	First Hispanic major leaguer to record 1,000 career extra-base hits.
June 22, 2002	Longest consecutive game hitting streak by a Hispanic major leaguer.
August 17, 2002	Hispanic major leaguer with the most consecutive base hits.
April 4, 2003	First Hispanic player to hit 500 home runs in the major leagues.
June 20, 2003	Youngest Hispanic player to hit a walk-off home run. Youngest Hispanic player to hit a home run in his first major league game.
August 28, 2003	Youngest major leaguer to hit a home run from both sides of the plate.
September 22, 2003	Player with the most leadoff home runs in one major league season. Hispanic player with the most career leadoff home runs.
September 25, 2003	First Hispanic player to hit four home runs in a major league game.
September 26, 2003	First major leaguer to record at least 38 home runs in ten consecutive seasons. First Hispanic player with ten seasons of 35 home runs and 100 RBI.
September 28, 2003	Youngest Hispanic player to win a major league batting title.
October 21, 2003	Hispanic player with the most home runs in the World Series, the most post-season hits, and the most post-season runs batted in.
October 22, 2003	First Hispanic player to hit a walk-off World Series home run. Youngest Hispanic player to hit a home run in the World Series.
April 5, 2004	First Venezuelan manager in the major leagues.
June 3, 2004	Oldest major league player to hit a grand slam home run.
October 2, 2004	First Mexican player to lead a major league in RBI.
November 11, 2004	First Venezuelan pitcher to win the Cy Young Award.
July 15, 2005	First Hispanic major leaguer to record 500 home runs and 3,000 hits.
August 16, 2005	Cuban player with the most hits and home runs in the major leagues.
August 30, 2005	Hispanic player with the most runs, doubles, RBI and extra-base hits in the major leagues.
October 26, 2005	First Hispanic manager to win the World Series.
November 9, 2005	First Venezuelan to win the Manager of the Year Award in the major leagues.
February 4, 2006	First player to record eight consecutive hits in the Caribbean Series. Youngest manager to win a Caribbean Series.
March 7, 2006	First Hispanic player to hit a home run in the World Baseball Classic. First Venezuelan player to hit a home run in the World Baseball Classic. First Dominican pitcher to record a win in the World Baseball Classic. First Puerto Rican pitcher to record a win in the World Baseball Classic.
March 8, 2006	First Cuban player to hit a home run in the World Baseball Classic. First Panamanian player to hit a home run in the World Baseball Classic. First Puerto Rican player to hit a home run in the World Baseball Classic. First Cuban pitcher to record a win in the World Baseball Classic. First Mexican pitcher

Date	Historical Significance
	to record a win in the World Baseball Classic. First Venezuelan pitcher to record a win in the World Baseball Classic.
March 9, 2006	First Mexican player to hit a home run in the World Baseball Classic.
April 29, 2006	Major league players with the most home runs in the month of April.
May 14, 2006	First Colombian pitcher to appear in the major leagues.
July 6, 2006	Most consecutive games reaching base safely by a Hispanic major leaguer.
September 9, 2006	First Colombian pitcher to win a major league game.
September 28, 2006	Mexican player with the most hits, home runs and RBI in the major leagues.
May 4, 2007	Oldest major league player to hit a home run.
June 20, 2007	First Hispanic player to hit 600 home runs in the major leagues.
June 22, 2007	Most consecutive games played by a Hispanic major leaguer.
July 10, 2007	Hispanic player to hit the most home runs in the All-Star Game.
September 3, 2007	First Hispanic major league pitcher to record 3,000 strikeouts. Hispanic major league pitcher with the best career ERA+ metric.
September 26, 2007	Hispanic father-son duo with the most home runs in the major leagues.
September 29, 2007	First major leaguer to hit 60 home runs in three seasons.
September 11, 2008	First Hispanic player to record 300 home runs in his first eight seasons. First Hispanic player to record 100 RBI in each of his first eight seasons.
September 24, 2008	Pitcher with the most saves in a major league season.
March 8, 2009	First person to appear in the World Baseball Classic as a player and manager.
May 8, 2009	Puerto Rican player with the most home runs and RBI in the major leagues.
June 17, 2009	Major league catcher with the most hits. Most games caught by a major league catcher.
July 14, 2009	Pitcher with the most All-Star Game saves.
July 22, 2009	Latin American major league player with the most career grand slam home runs.
October 15, 2009	Player with the most post-season home runs. Hispanic player with the longest post-season hitting streak.
November 1, 2009	Pitcher with the most World Series saves. Pitcher with the most World Series appearances.
November 24, 2009	First Hispanic major leaguer to win the Most Valuable Player Award three times and first to win the award in back-to-back seasons.
April 12, 2010	Player with the most home runs in his first ten major league seasons.
May 2, 2010	First Hispanic player to record four hits in his first major league game.
June 23, 2010	First Puerto Rican manager in the major leagues.
August 25, 2010	Youngest Hispanic pitcher to record 1,000 career strikeouts.
August 26, 2010	First major leaguer to hit 400 home runs in his first ten seasons.
September 11, 2010	First major leaguer to record a .300 average, 30 home runs and 100 RBI in ten consecutive seasons.
October 15, 2010	Major league pitcher with the most post-season saves.
October 28, 2010	First Colombian player to hit a home run in the World Series.
November 1, 2010	First Colombian player to win the MVP Award in the World Series. Colombia player with the most hits, home runs and RBI in the major leagues.
September 18, 2011	Hispanic brothers with the most home runs in the major leagues.
September 19, 2011	Pitcher with the most career saves in the major leagues.
September 27, 2011	Puerto Rican pitcher with the most wins and strikeouts in the major leagues.
September 30, 2011	Major league pitcher with the most post-season appearances. Major league pitcher with the lowest post-season ERA. Hispanic major league pitcher with the most post-season strikeouts.
October 4, 2011	First Hispanic player to hit three home runs in a post-season game.
October 22, 2011	First Hispanic player to hit three home runs in a World Series game.
April 7, 2012	First player to play for 13 major league teams.
May 17, 2012	First Brazilian player to appear and record a hit in the major leagues.
May 18, 2012	First Brazilian player to hit a home run in the major leagues.

Date	Historical Significance
June 3, 2012	Hispanic pitcher with the most home runs in the major leagues.
June 15, 2012	First Hispanic player to hit 300 home runs and steal 300 bases in the major leagues.
June 30, 2012	First player to hit home runs from both sides of the plate in the same game for his first two major league hits.
August 15, 2012	First Venezuelan pitcher to throw a perfect game in the major leagues.
August 27, 2012	First Hispanic pitcher throw four 1–0 shutouts in one major league season.
October 3, 2012	Pitcher with the lowest ERA with at least 20 saves in one major league season.
October 3, 2012	First Hispanic major leaguer to win the Triple Crown of hitting.
October 3, 2012	Hispanic switch-hitter with the most career hits in the major leagues. Venezuelan player with the most career hits in the major leagues.
October 28, 2012	First player to hit home runs in his first three World Series plate appearances. First Venezuelan to win the MVP Award in the World Series.
November 15, 2012	First Venezuelan to win the Most Valuable Player Award in the major leagues.
February 12, 2013	First Hispanic player to earn $25 million in annual salary.
March 19, 2013	First Latin American team to win the World Baseball Classic. First Hispanic player to win the MVP Award in the World Baseball Classic. First Hispanic manager to win the World Baseball Classic
April 10, 2013	Dominican player with the most hits in the major leagues.
May 24, 2013	Hispanic major league pitcher with the most games of one hit or less.
June 6, 2013	Hispanic major leaguer with the most career walk-off home runs, including postseason.
June 20, 2013	Panamanian player with the most home runs in the major leagues.
June 30, 2013	Hispanic player with the most hits in the month of his major league debut.
July 10, 2013	Designated hitter with the most hits in the major leagues.
July 16, 2013	First Panamanian player to win the MVP Award in the All-Star Game.
July 30, 2013	First Brazilian pitcher in the major leagues.
August 21, 2013	First Brazilian pitcher to win a game in the major leagues.
September 12, 2013	Hispanic relief pitcher with the most victories in the major leagues.
September 26, 2013	Hispanic pitcher with the most major league appearances and the most innings in relief.
March 28, 2014	First Hispanic player to earn $30 million in annual salary.
April 16, 2014	First Colombian pitcher to throw a major league shutout.
April 27, 2014	Most players of the same ethnic nationality in a major league game.
April 27, 2014	Most home runs and RBI by a major league rookie in the month of April.
July 3, 2014	Most home runs hit by a Hispanic switch-hitter in the major leagues.
July 10, 2014	Player with the most career total bases as a third baseman.
July 11, 2014	Pitcher with the most consecutive relief appearance with at least one strikeout.
July 30, 2014	Pitcher with the most consecutive starts of at least seven innings and two or fewer runs allowed.
August 28, 2014	Pitcher with the major league record for consecutive batters retired.

Notes

1. Esteban Bellán notched four hits in one game against the New York Mutuals, July 3, 1871.

2. Luis Bello, "Torices Club Sold to Proprietor of Soft Drink Plant," *The Sporting News,* September 7, 1955.

3. More on Calvo and Acosta's historic day from the next day's *Washington Post*: "Calvo made a great impression on the handful of fans. On every occasion the "Cube" met the ball hard. His home run came in the sixth when he shot the ball over second base. [Outfielder] Shotton came running in to get the ball on the first bound, but it hopped over the fielder's shoulder. It carried all the way to the farthest corner of the ball yard, and Calvo made the circuit without even a play being made at the plate. "Acosta, the other Cuban with the local club, was sent in to pinch hit for Altrock in the third inning. He laid down a bunt and was safe when [pitcher] Mitchell juggled the ball [ruled an error]."

4. Alfonso Flores, "Player Raids Only Beginning Says Pasquel," *The Sporting News*, April 4, 1946.

5. On August 3, 1871, Esteban Bellán raked out five hits against the Boston Red Stockings.

6. Nine-year major leaguer and Spanish-American Charley Hall participated in two games of the 1912 World Series as a member of the Boston Red Sox. Hailing from Ventura, California, Hall was christened Carlos Luis Hall, his Hispanic ancestry coming from his mother's family. Hall was the first Hispanic pitcher to throw a shutout (September 9, 1906) and hit a home run (August 4, 1911) in the major leagues. He was also the initial Hispanic big league hurler to toss a one-hitter (August 27, 1910). As a member of the St. Louis Cardinals, Hall, in a relief role, and Mike González formed the first Hispanic battery, April 21, 1916.

7. Untitled. *New York Times*, August 25, 1923.

8. W. Rollo Wilson, "Eastern Snapshots," *Pittsburgh Courier*, October 11, 1924.

9. Tom Swope, "Reds Throw Feast for Adolfo Luque," *The Sporting News,* May 6, 1926.

10. The eight hardest-luck losers were: Ted Lyons, 34 games, 33 CG; Gaylord Perry, 30, 29 CG; Warren Spahn, 28, 26 CG; Bucky Walters, 25, 24 CG; Early Wynn, 24, 24 CG; Nolan Ryan, 24, 23 CG; Bob Gibson, 24, 22 CG; Red Ruffing, 23, 23 CG. Only Walters is not in the Hall of Fame.

11. Phil Dixon with Patrick J. Hannigan, *The Negro Baseball Leagues: A Photographic History* (Mattituck, NY: Amereon House, 1992), 130.

12. Official records incorrectly give Luque 367 starts. Luque also recorded an amazing 88.5 percent decision rate in his career starts.

13. "Place for Gonzales (sic) as Manager Cardinal 'Farm,'" *Lincoln Evening Journal,* January 27, 1933.

14. "Cards Sign Gonzales as an Aide to Frisch," *Sedalia Democrat*, December 10, 1933.

15. Edward J. Neil, "Polo Grounds Greet Ruth with Open Arms but the Mightly One Fails to Hit," *Alton Evening Telegraph*, April 24, 1935

16. Myron Cope, "Closeup of Orlando Cepeda," *Sport,* April 1962.

17. James A. Riley, *The Biographical Encyclopedia of the Negro Leagues* (New York: Carroll & Graf, 1994), 788.

18. Untitled. *The Sporting News,* June 1, 1939.

19. Eric Nusbaum, "The Unknown Slugger," sbnation.com, May 21, 2013.

20. Shirley Povich, "Carrasquel Wins in 10th as Nats Split," *Washington Post*, June 22, 1942.

21. Tampa-born Al López hit a grand slam home run for the Brooklyn Dodgers, on July 2, 1939, against Hugh Mulcahy of the Phillies at Shibe Park.

22. "Mexican Policeman Indicted for Shooting Hi Bithorn," *The Sporting News*, January 23, 1952.

23. McGuff, Joe. "Lopez Sinks the Bosox," *Kansas City Star,* May 20, 1956.

24. Frank Graham, "Adolfo Luque is Dead?" *The Sporting News*, July 17, 1957.

25. Layton Revel and Luis Muñoz, "Adolfo Luque," Center for Negro League Baseball Research, cnlbr.org.

26. Shirley Povich, "K-Man Camilo's 15-Whiff Sendoff Lifts Nats Hopes," *The Sporting News,* April 27, 1960.

27. Ibid.

28. "Marichal Thanks God for No-Hitter," *Washington Post,* June 16, 1963.

29. Curly Grieve, "Willie Knew His Blast Was Homer," *San Francisco Examiner,* July 3, 1963.

30. The individual statistical analysis is determined as follows: (1) Start with 50 points. (2) Add one point for each out recorded. (3) Add two points for each inning completed after the fourth. (4) Add

one point for each strikeout. (5) Subtract two points for each hit allowed. (6) Subtract four points for each earned run allowed. (7) Subtract two points for each unearned run allowed. (8) Subtract one point for each walk.

31. The other prominent players are: Earl Averill, Jim Bottomley, George Brett, Johnny Damon, Steve Finley, Jimmie Foxx, Lou Gehrig, Goose Goslin, Rogers Hornsby, Willie Mays, Joe Medwick, Paul Molitor, Stan Musial, Vada Pinson, Jimmy Rollins, Babe Ruth, Al Simmons and Robin Yount. (Only Damon, Finley, Pinson, and Rollins are not members of the Hall of Fame.) Source: Elias Sports Bureau.

32. Orlando Cepeda & Herb Fagen, *Baby Bull: From Hardball to Hard Time and Back* (Dallas: Taylor Trade, 1998).

33. Russell Schneider, "Shutout Ace Tiant Sees Homer Wreck His Dream," *The Sporting News,* June 1, 1968.

34. Fred Down. "Tiant Fans 19 in Ten Frames," *Anniston Star,* July 4, 1968.

35. Charley Feeney, "Sanguillen Turns Mistake into Profit," *The Sporting News,* August 30, 1969.

36. Marichal, Mike Cuéllar (2.27, 1966; 2.24, 1968) and Pedro Martínez (2.39, 1997; 1.40, 1999; 2.17, 2000; 2.24, 2002; 2.21, 2003) were the only Latin American pitchers to record at least two seasons with a Fielding Independent Pitching level below 2.50. Others with one each: Camilo Pascual 2.44, 1959; Luis Tiant, 2.04, 1968; Aníbal Sánchez, 2.39, 2013; Mario Soto, 2.42, 1982, Fernando Valenzuela, 2.44, 1981.

37. Lefty Gómez won the clinching games of the 1936 and 1937 World Series for the Yankees.

38. "Fans Celebrate; Red Sox Don't—Yet," *Fort Lauderdale News,* September 21, 1972.

39. Charley Deeney, "Roberto Collects 3000th Hit, Dedicates It to Pirates Fans," *The Sporting News,* October 14, 1972.

40. Roberto Clemente poem from 10/11/1972 date history entry is taken from Bruce Markenson's book, *Roberto Clemente The Great One* (Champaign, IL: Sports Publishing, 1998), 302.

41. "Nixon Donation Snowballs Into Memorial Fund," *The Sporting News,* January 20, 1973.

42. Ray Gillespie, "Mexico Honors 22 Immortals at Shrine Dedication." *The Sporting News,* March 24, 1973. This was the third class of Mexican Hall of Fame inductees. A Mexican Hall of Fame had first been established in 1958 with a Parque Delta dedication in Mexico City. The inaugural members were Lucas Juárez, Julio Molina, Fernando Barradas, Antonio Delfín and Leonardo Alanis, as voted in by Mexican sportswriters. A second class of players was elected in 1964: Angel Castro, Lázaro Salazar, Epitacio Torres, Martín Dihigo, Genaro Casas and Ramón Bragaña.

43. "Baseball Inducts Six, One with Sorrow," *New York Times,* August 7, 1973. Lefty Gómez was elected into the National Hall of Fame in 1972.

44. "Marichal Retires from Baseball," *New York Times,* April 18, 1975.

45. Jack Lang, "Dihigo and Lloyd Voted into Shrine," *The Sporting News,* February 19, 1977.

46. "NY's Figueroa Toasts Victory No. 20," *Santa Cruz Sentinel,* October 1, 1978.

47. Mike Davis. "It Was a Good Ending for a Bad Night," *San Bernardino County Sun,* October 24, 1981.

48. Hector Espino biographical information from Baseball-reference.com.

49. Peter Williams, *When the Giants Were Giants: Bill Terry And The Golden Age of New York Baseball* (Chapel Hill, NC: Algonquin Books, 1994), 225.

50. Ross Newhan, "Carew Collects 3,000 Hit in Angel Win," *Los Angeles Times,* August 5, 1985. Since the beginning of Division Era in 1969, Carew's career number of three-hit games were the fifth most in baseball. Tony Gwynn (297), Paul Molitor (290), Wade Boggs (286) and Derek Jeter (285) had more.

51. "3 No-Hitters, Two Celebrations," *The Sporting News,* July 9, 1990.

52. Ira Berkow, "A Rumble in Valhalla," *New York Times,* July 22, 1991.

53. James Buckley, Jr., *Perfect: The Inside Story of Baseball's Sixteen Perfect Games* (Chicago: Triumph Books, 2002).

54. "Longtime Oriole Martínez Retires," *New York Times,* June 19, 1997.

55. Morales later deserted his team and his island country. In a first attempt to reach the United States, Morales fell short of arriving on American shores, and was repatriated. Undeterred, Morales clandestinely left Cuba in another freedom-seeking foray and made it, successfully reaching U.S. soil in the second undertaking. The courageous player eventually signed with the New York Yankees but washed out in a bid to play with that team.

56. Martínez is second all-time to Curt Schilling's 4.38 ratio (minimum 2,000 strikeouts and 2,000 innings).

57. "Jays' Delgado Smacks Four Homers," *South Florida Sun Sentinel,* September 26, 2003.

58. Alex Rodríguez won the batting title in 1996 at the age of 21.

59. Bob Nightengale, "Venezuela's Favorite Son Returns Favor," *USA Today,* February 23–March 1, 2005.

60. "Chico Carrasquel, First Latino to Start in a Major League All-Star Game," *Los Angeles Times,* May 27, 2005.

61. Alex Rodríguez holds the record for most career grand slams with 24 through the 2014 season.

62. "Roberto Alomar Enters the Hall of Fame," mlb.com, July 25, 2011.

63. The other Latin American players to collect more than 1,000 extra base hits: R. Palmeiro, M. Ramírez, S. Sosa, D. Ortiz, A. Beltre, C. Beltrán.

64. Ronald Blum, "Iconic Reliever Closes out Hall of Fame Career," *Miami Herald,* September 29, 2013.

65. *Ahora Con Óscar Haza* (television program), November 10, 2014.

66. "Pedro Martínez Elected to the Hall of Fame," *Boston Herald,* January 6, 2015.

Bibliography

Antero Nuñez, José. *Series del Caribe*. Caracas, Venezuela: Impresos Urbina, 1987.

Buckley, James, Jr. *Perfect: The Inside Story of Baseball's Sixteen Perfect Games*. Chicago: Triumph, 2002.

Crescioni Benítez, José A. *El Béisbol Profesional Boricua*. San Juan: First Book Publishing of Puerto Rico, 1997.

Dixon, Phil, with Patrick J. Hannigan. *The Negro Baseball Leagues: A Photographic History*. Mattituck, NY: Amereon House, 1992.

Figueredo, Jorge, S. *Beisbol Cubano: A un Paso de las Grandes Ligas, 1878–1961*. Jefferson, NC: McFarland, 2005.

_____. *Cuban Baseball: A Statistical History, 1878–1961*. Jefferson, NC: McFarland, 2003.

_____. *Who's Who in Cuban Baseball, 1878–1961*. Jefferson, NC: McFarland, 2003.

González Echevarría, Roberto. *The Pride of Havana: A History of Cuban Baseball*. New York: Oxford University Press, 1999.

Holway, John. *The Complete Book of Baseball's Negro Leagues: The Other Half of Baseball History*. Fern Park, FL: Hastings House, 2001.

Lester, Larry. *Black Baseball's National Showcase: The East-West All-Star Game, 1933–1953*. Lincoln: University of Nebraska Press, 2001.

Paur, Jeff, and David Walton, eds. *The Sporting News Baseball Register*. 2001 edition. St. Louis: The Sporting News, 2001.

_____. *The Sporting News Baseball Register*. 2002 edition. St. Louis: The Sporting News, 2002.

Revel, Layton, and Luis Muñoz. *Forgotten Heroes: Pedro Anibal "Perucho" Cepeda*. Booklet. Carrollton, TX: Center for Negro League Baseball Research, 2009.

Riley, James E. *The Biographical Encyclopedia of The Negro Leagues*. New York: Carroll & Graf, 1994.

Roberts, Brendan, ed. *The Official Major League Baseball Fact Book*. 2000 edition. St. Louis: The Sporting News, 2000.

Roberts, Brendan, and David Walton, eds. *The Sporting News Baseball Register*. St. Louis: The Sporting News, 2000, 2001, 2002.

Siwoff, Seymour, ed. *The Elias Book of Baseball Records*. 2013 edition. New York: Elias Sports Bureau, 2013.

Spatz, Lyle, ed. *The SABR Baseball List and Record Book*. New York: Scribner, 2007.

Treto Cisneros, Pedro. *Enciclopedia del Béisbol Mexicano*. Segunda edicion. Mexico City: Revistas Deportivas, S.A., 1994.

Van Hyning, Thomas E. *Puerto Rico's Winter League: A History of Major League Baseball's Launching Pad*. Jefferson, NC: McFarland, 1995.

Virtue, John. *South of the Color Barrier: How Jorge Pasquel and the Mexican League Pushed Baseball Toward Racial Integration*. Jefferson, NC: McFarland, 2008.

Williams, Peter. *When the Giants Were Giants: Bill Terry and the Golden Age of New York Baseball*. Chapel Hill, NC: Algonquin, 1994.

Articles

Armour, Mark. "Felipe Alou." SABR Baseball Biography Project. http://sabr.org/bioproj/person/b79ab182.

"Chicago's José Abreu Now 2nd Rookie in Last 65 Years with Two 18-Game Hit Streaks." Bleacher Report, August 1, 2014. www.bleacherreport.com.

Blum, Ronald. "Iconic Reliever Closes out Hall of Fame Career." *Miami Herald,* September 29, 2013.

Corcoran, Cliff. "42 Things You Need to Know About Mariano Rivera." *Sports Illustrated*, September 20, 2013. http://www.si.com/strike-zone/2013/09/20/mariano-revera-42-things-to-know.

Costello, Rory, and José Ramírez. "Paul Casanova." SABR Baseball Biography Project. http://sabr.org/bioproj/person/a96308de.

DeNicola, Christina. "Marlins Newcomer Andre Rienzo Paving Way as Brazilian-born Big Leaguer." Foxsports.com, February 28, 2015.

Eisenberg, John. "Chino Martinez: Winning Package of Contradictions." *Baltimore Sun*, August 16, 1991.

"Falleció El Carrao Bracho." *El Universal*, June 17, 2006. http://www.eluniversal.com/2011/06/16/fallecio-el-carrao-bracho.

Fleming, Dave. "Raffy and the Big Hurt." Bill James Online, December 17, 2013. http://www.billjamesonline.com/raffy_and_the_big_hurt/.

García, Manuel. "A Class Above the Rest." Website of the Dominican Republic Sports and Education Academy, June 29, 2010. http://www.drsea.org.

Gerard, Joseph. "Juan 'Tetelo' Vargas." SABR Baseball Biography Project. http://sabr.org/bioproj/person/bd033c14.

González, Alden. "Nearing 500 Homers, Pujols a Wonder All These Years Later." Website of Major League Baseball, April 17, 2014. http://m.mlb.com/news/article/72408854/nearing-500-homers-albert-pujols-a-wonder-all-these-years.

"Gomes First Brazilian-Born Big Leaguer." Fox Sports online, May 28, 2012. http://www.foxsports.com.

Hageman, Peter. "Award Context: Tony Oliva's 1964 Rookie of the Year." Going 9 Baseball website, April 23, 2009. http://www.going9baseball.com/2009/04/23/award-context-tony-oliva/.

Hill, Justice B. "Negro League Honors Long Time Coming." Website of Major League Baseball, July 30, 2006. http://m.mlb.com/news/article/1584543/.

Leach, Matthew. "Albert Pujols Belts 400th Career Home Run." ESPN website, August 27, 2010. http://www.espn.go.com.

Linderbergh, Ben. "Does Bill James' Game Score Still Work?" Overthinking It (column), Baseball Prospectus, June 25, 2014. http://www.baseballprospectus.com/article.php?articleid=23991.

Malinowski, Erik. "The Short Flight of 'El Parajo,' the Cuban Legend Who Played His Only Game in the Major Leagues 100 Years Ago Today." Buzzfeed, May 16, 2013. http://www.buzzfeed.com/erikmalinowski/the-short-flight-of-el-pajaro#.cn7nmmYDY.

McKenna, Brian. "Lou Castro." SABR Baseball Biography Project. http://sabr.org/bioproj/person/f212f545.

Nowlin, Bill. "Eusebio González." SABR Baseball Biography Project. http://sabr.org/bioproj/person/57ab7340.

Nusbaum, Eric. "The Unknown Slugger: Hector Espino Is One of the Greatest Hitters in Baseball History, Yet Most Americans Know Nothing About Him." SBNation, May 21, 2013. http://www.sbnation.com/longform/2013/5/21/4348250/hector-espino-mexico-baseball-home-run-king-profile#3965459.

"The Oldest Players to Make Their Debut in the Major Leagues: Satchel Paige and the Rest." *The J.G. Preston Experience* (blog), September 15, 2013. https://prestonjg.wordpress.com/2013/09/15/the-oldest-players-to-make-their-debut-in-the-major-leagues-satchel-paige-and-the-rest/.

Posnanski, Joe. "A Whole Lot About 1–0 Games." *JoeBlog* (blog), September 6, 2011. www.joeposnanski.blogspot.com.

———. "The Wonder of Minnie." NBC Sports online, March 2, 2015. http://sportsworld.nbcsports.com/remembering-minnie-minoso/.

Revel, Layton, and Luis Muñoz. *Forgotten Heroes: Pedro Anibal "Perucho" Cepeda.* Booklet. Carrollton, TX: Center for Negro League Baseball Research, 2009. Downloaded from http://www.cnlbr.org/Portals/0/Hero/Pedro-Anibal-Perucho-Cepeda.pdf.

Stahl, John, and Rebecca Glidewell-Hall. "Charley Hall." SABR Baseball Biography Project. http://sabr.org/bioproj/person/f442d879.

Toot, Peter. "Breaking the Latino Barrier." *Elysian Fields Quarterly* 18, no. 4 (Fall 2001).

Trotta, Daniel. "Cuba Back in Caribbean Series After 54 Year Absence." Reuters, January 31, 2014. http://www.reuters.com/article/2014/01/31/us-cuba-baseball-idUSBREA0U16J20140131.

"Twelve Players Suspended for PED," Fox Sports, August 5, 2013. Last modified May 28, 2014. http://www.foxsports.com/mlb/story/major-league-baseball-alex-rodriguez-ped-use-080513.

Villa, Beto. "Las Series del Caribe." Latino Baseball, posting date unknown. http://www.latinobaseball.
    com/index.php?option=com_content&view=article&id=4085&Itemid=6 baseballlatino.com.
Wilson, Duff, and Michael S. Schmidt. "Missing From Mitchell Report, Sosa is Included in Grimsley
    Affidavit." *New York Times* online, December 21, 2007. http://www.nytimes.com/2007/12/21/sports/
    baseball/21mitchell.html?pagewanted=print&_r=0.

Web References

attheplate.com
baseball-almanac.com
baseballhalloffame.org
baseballlibrary.com
baseballpastandpresent.com
baseball-reference.com
baseball-reference.com/bullpen
cubanball.com
cubanbaseball.blogsot.com
espn.com
latinobaseball.com
mlb.com
paperofrecord.com
retrosheet.org
sabr.org
seamheads.com
wikipedia.org

Index

Numbers in **_bold italics_** refer to pages with photographs.